E*d*

...d Employment

Volume 1: Educated Labour – the Changing Basis of Industrial Demand

This reader is one part of an Open University integrated teaching system and the selection is therefore related to other material available to students. It is designed to evoke the critical understanding of students. Opinions expressed in it are not necessarily those of the course team or of the University

Education, Training and Employment

Volume 1: Educated Labour – the Changing Basis of Industrial Demand

A Reader edited by Geoff Esland
at the Open University

Addison-Wesley Publishing Company

Wokingham, England • Reading, Massachusetts • Menlo Park, California
New York • Don Mills, Ontario • Amsterdam • Bonn • Sydney
Singapore • Tokyo • Madrid • San Juan

in association with

The Open
University

Cover designed by Chris Eley
and printed by The Riverside Printing Co. (Reading) Ltd.
Typeset by Columns Design and Production Services Limited, Reading.
Printed in Great Britain by Mackays of Chatham PLC, Kent.

First printed 1990.

British Library Cataloguing in Publication Data
Education, training and employment.
  Vol. 1, Educated labour : the changing basis of industrial
  demand : a reader.
  1. Great Britain. Vocational education
  I. Esland, Geoff   II. Open University
  370.1130941

  ISBN 0–201–54424–5

Preface

This is the first of two volumes of readings entitled *Education, Training and Employment*. Volume 1 is organized around the theme *educated labour – the changing basis of industrial demand*, and Volume 2 focuses upon *the educational response*.

Both volumes – which are designed to be complementary – form part of the Open University MA Module *Education, Training and Employment* (E817), but they are also intended to appeal to a wider audience with an interest in policy development in employment-related education and training.

For much of the past two decades vocational education and training (VET) have remained high on the political agenda as the economic crises of the 1970s led to rising inflation, and the recession, industrial collapse and high levels of unemployment of the early 1980s. Crisis management characterized much of the state's response to these events giving rise to schemes and initiatives designed to limit the social damage which followed widespread de-industrialization. A major consequence of this policy has been the piecemeal and often partisan nature of public debate about the causes and effects of industrial decline and a tendency to lose sight of the wider picture. From the mid-to-late 1970s, the institutions responsible for education and training were particularly singled out for criticism as employers and government attacked what they saw as the source of an anti-industrial (and anti-capitalist) culture. Arnold Weinstock's 1976 *Times Educational Supplement* article 'I blame the teachers' (23–1–76) epitomized the antipathy of employers to education at the time.

The displacement of responsibility for economic failure and decline from the political and economic arenas to the educational and training institutions (and the individuals within them) has had the effect of distorting public policy debate about the relationship between economic change, education and employment. The concentration on changing the content of education and the attitudes of teachers and learners has led to the neglect of the part played by political and economic factors (such as the nature of Britain's industrial policy) in determining the shape and quality of the national workforce. It has also provided legitimation for the imposition of a market forces model on the education provided by schools and colleges.

One of the main objectives in compiling these readings has been to bring together analysis and research which consider employment-related education and training in a broader political–economic context than has been customary in much of the official discourse on the subject, and which provide a critical examination of the VET policies of the 1980s. The aims of these readers, as of the course itself, can be summarized as setting out:

1. to introduce a number of approaches to the analysis and understanding of education and training policies, with particular reference to their political and economic implications;
2. to consider the changes taking place in the UK economy and their implications for the nature of education, training and employment;
3. to examine recent developments in vocational education and training in schools and the further education sector.

For students on the Open University course the two Readers are accompanied by a study guide, a number of set books, and an audio cassette.

■ Outline of contents

□ **Volume 1: *Education, Training and Employment: educated labour – the changing basis of industrial demand***

Much is heard of the British economy's need for a more highly educated and trained workforce. Higher level skills are believed to be necessary in order for Britain to compete with the knowledge-based, high-technology, high quality service economies of the advanced industrial world. The reality, however, is somewhat different, as the UK has the lowest post-16 participation rate in education and training of any of the major industrial economies.

The collection begins with an analysis of the reasons for Britain's manufacturing decline and de-industrialization and moves to a consideration of the changes in work organization required by the introduction of the methods of 'flexible specialization'. Although there is support for the view that flexible specialization leads to job enhancement for certain groups of workers, there is also evidence that other workers face increasing marginalization and de-skilling.

Discussion of these issues is followed by a group of studies which examine the importance of labour markets in the determination of employment opportunities for young people, and the factors which lead to inequalities of access. As a number of commentators have pointed out, a central feature of the political analysis of youth unemployment has been its emphasis on the so-called lack of employment skills among school leavers. In rejecting explanations which 'blame the victim', these readings underline the importance of social and geographical factors in the distribution of unemployment – particularly those pertaining to gender and ethnicity.

These are followed by two chapters which explore the history of training policy in the UK and particularly its failure to promote a shift from the 'low skill–low quality equilibrium' characteristic of British industry. Finally, we include three chapters – two of them from employers – which focus on the criteria used by companies in job recruitment. Concluding the collection is a comparative study of training in the retail industries of Britain and France.

☐ Volume 2: *Education, Training and Employment: the educational response*

A major feature of industrial demand for reform has been the call for supply-side changes in the preparation of the workforce. The readings in Volume 2 look at a range of policy initiatives designed to make schools and colleges more aware of the 'needs of business and industry'. As a number of them make clear, this policy has met with a good deal of scepticism and criticism from educationalists.

Volume 2 begins with two chapters which discuss the relevance of economic goals to education, and the influence of 'human capital' theories on educational investment. These are followed by two studies – one of which draws comparisons between France, Britain and Germany – which examine the rise of employer demands for greater emphasis in schools on the preparation for work.

These are followed by two chapters which offer a critical examination of attempts to impose the principles of economic utility on education. The first puts forward a philosophical analysis of the differences between education and training, and the second argues that the priority given by some state education systems to the demands of their industrial lobbies raises serious questions about the nature of power and democracy in those societies.

Each of the following seven chapters focuses on a different element of the 'new vocationalism', including TVEI, the education–industry movement, enterprise, and the role of the Training and Enterprise Councils. In considering the dominant ideology underlying the vocational curriculum many of them reflect on the growing gulf between the political vision it is promoting and the principles of general education.

The following three chapters consider the operation of youth training in the UK, raising the issue as to the degree to which YTS has been an unemployment scheme rather than a source of training. The final chapter consists of a review of recent developments in EC vocational training policy.

In addition to the Open University audience for which they are intended, it is hoped that these two volumes will be of interest to many students and professionals with an interest in education and training and more general concerns of social, industrial and economic policy.

Acknowledgements

I would particularly like to thank the members of the E817 Module Team on whose behalf this Reader has been compiled and who participated in the selection of readings: Heather Cathcart, Roger Dale, Peter Raggatt and Lorna Unwin. I am also grateful for the assistance of Frank Coffield and Marten Shipman who advised the Module Team on several aspects of the development of the teaching materials. The contributions of Alison Robinson, Megan Ball and John Taylor to the preparation of this Reader have also been much appreciated.

Geoff Esland
September 1990

Introduction

Although the political contexts are very different, the issues surrounding education, training and economic performance at the beginning of the 1990s are little changed from those which dominated the debates of a decade and a half ago when James Callaghan made his Ruskin College speech. Then, as now, the relationship between education and training, the biases towards under-achievement built into school assessment, the continuing low staying-on rates of young people after 16, the reluctance of companies to invest adequately in training and retraining, the low quality of some of the training programmes on offer, the existence of skills shortages alongside pools of unemployment – all continue to shape the policy discussions of the present time. It is also evident that in spite of the numerous initiatives designed to change the institutional structures of education and training in the UK, the problems which have beset British economic performance for much of the post-war period have proved to be more intractable than might be inferred from the remedies on offer, and continue to pose major questions about the future preparation of the workforce.

If the economic considerations concerning education and training are no less pressing than they were in the mid-1970s, there are indications that the political strategies implemented since that time – the vocationalizing of the curriculum, the increased emphasis on stratified education and training, the promotion of an 'enterprise' culture – are now increasingly seen as having failed to address the essential elements of the problem, and indeed in some senses to have made it worse. As several of the readings in these two volumes testify, the tendency for some of the vocational education and training (VET) initiatives to trivialize economic realities, as well as the new forms of curricula and work experience on offer, has tended to undermine their credibility – particularly among school leavers. It is also believed by many commentators that the fundamental problems of transforming what Finegold and Soskice have called the low skills–low quality equilibrium characteristic of British industry have not been addressed by the policies of the 1980s. Indeed, in the year in which the last remaining British computer manufacturing firms have been sold off to Japanese companies – ICL to Fujitsu and Apricot to Mitsubishi – the prognosis for a reversal of this trend is not good.

One of the predominant characteristics of public policy towards education and training in the UK has been its essentially fragmented approach, allied to a superficial analysis of the underlying economic problems. This tendency has often given rise to the preference for mono-causal explanations characteristic of much of the public debate, in which a single element of the national polity or culture is abstracted from the system as a whole and made to bear responsibility for a process which is much more complex. This has been particularly true of the part attributed to the education system in explanations of national decline where there has emerged a veritable industry built upon the quest for the origins of the 'British malaise'.

Central to this preference for mono-causal explanations is an attachment to those which give priority to aspects of *national culture* in the process of national decline (DI 1977; Wiener 1981) and which look to the changing of 'attitudes' as the basis of reform. Although the political concern to reform education and training has ostensibly been focused around Britain's industrial decline, very few, if any, of the policy initiatives have adequately addressed the basis of this decline. Some of the responsibility for this neglect must rest with the Ruskin College speech and the subsequent Great Debate which, in its diagnosis of Britain's economic problems, focused almost entirely on the alleged shortcomings of the education system – and, in particular, the supposed anti-industrial attitudes of teachers. The agenda established by this prime ministerial venture into educational policy led to a series of initiatives designed to change the prevailing *culture* of education in which the raising of economic awareness and the promotion of positive attitudes towards industry among teachers and pupils were seen as one of the keys to economic recovery.

Although the educational legislation of the 1980s has been concerned to change the basis of the management, organization and control of educational institutions, the reliance on 'attitude changes' among teachers and educationalists still remains a feature of many current initiatives.

Similarly, in relation to the rapidly rising levels of unemployment among school leavers, the development of policy has been largely predicated on the view that the source of the problem has been the lack of appropriate work skills and disciplines among young people, the remedy for which is thought to lie in training programmes which inculcate basic rather than higher skills.

The individualizing of responsibility for the nation's economic ills which has featured repeatedly in official reports has, as Stronach points out in Volume 2 (Chapter 9), remained largely unaffected by the substantial body of research which highlights the underlying structural changes in industrial production and the diversity of factors affecting local labour markets. One of the consequences of this individualization of complex social and political forces has been to restrict the debate on the relationship between education and the economy and to exclude some of the major structural factors outside of education which continue to sustain conditions inimical to Britain's economic interests. If the national economy is to break out of the prevailing low skills–low quality equilibrium and become the knowledge-based, high-technology, highly skilled, high value added economy purveyed in the political rhetoric it is essential that those factors which are continuing to sustain the low skills equilibrium are addressed.

In compiling this collection of readings we have been concerned to situate the development of education and training policy within a broader political and economic framework which addresses the consequences of de-industrialization and decline and considers the implications for employment of the new service economy era. In any assessment of education and training policy it is important to ask what kind of economy is developing in Britain. How probable is it that the high quality service occupations much talked of by politicians will replace the manufacturing capacity now extinct? What is the evidence that companies will generate a rising demand for higher level skills rather than follow the well-established routes of rationalization, casualization and de-skilling? How deeply will the much-heralded techniques of 'flexible specialization' reach into the organization of industrial production? If they do, what is to prevent them from inducing the economic marginalization of large sectors of the workforce particularly among women and ethnic minority groups? In a period marked by the massive restructuring of economic forces in Europe we also need to consider the ways in which employment opportunities in Britain will be shaped by the policies of the EC and those foreign-owned companies already established in the UK. These and similar questions form the basis of the module study guide which is designed to accompany these readers.

Volume 1 is broadly concerned with the economic and political contexts of education and training policy, while Volume 2 focuses on the various vocational initiatives in schools and colleges.

Volume 1 begins with the chapter by Judge and Dickson, 'The British State, Governments and Manufacturing Decline'. In their analysis of the main factors in Britain's economic decline, Judge and Dickson draw out the long-standing tensions between the needs of British industry and the institutions of finance capital which, they argue, are invariably given priority by the British state. According to Judge and Dickson, the determination of British governments for much of this century to maintain the value of sterling as a reserve currency, in conjunction with their adherence to free trade and reluctance to operate policies of industrial planning have combined to ensure that in each downward cycle of the economy manufacturing industry became increasingly debilitated and unable to prepare adequately for the next upswing. They also discuss additional factors such as the high concentrations of research and development expenditure on defence in Britain and the culture of 'free collective bargaining' among trade unions. The outcome of the Thatcherite strategy, which Judge and Dickson claim is as much a consequence as a cause of industrial decline, has been a lop-sided restructuring of Britain's industries in which de-industrialization has been accompanied by the expansion of those multinational companies capable of performing in global markets.

Chapter 2 by Rowthorn, 'De-industrialization in Britain', compares the contraction of manufacturing industry in Britain with the experiences of a number of other economies and considers three explanations for this decline: the *maturity thesis*, the *trade specialization thesis* and the *failure thesis*. While accepting many of the criteria of weakness and failure in British manufacturing industry, Rowthorn argues that because of other structural features it would have declined anyway. The questions arising from this analysis concern the displacement of labour from manufacturing industry and its absorption into other sectors of the economy. What are the political choices available for stimulating employment both in new forms of manufacturing and also in alternative sectors of the economy?

In Chapters 3, 4 and 5 the focus shifts to the debates about the development of 'flexible specialization' (FS) which has been hailed as the consumer-oriented successor to mass production. In Chapter 3, 'Fordism and Post-Fordism', Murray (1985) develops the arguments originally put forward in his article 'Benetton Britain' and explores the characteristics of Fordism and Post-Fordism as both *cultural* and *economic* forms.

An important element of the current debates on the operation of flexible specialization concerns the extent to which it is used ideologically to promote more efficient management practices in the deployment of labour. The influential NEDO study, *Changing Working Patterns*, by Atkinson and Meager (an extract from which appears as Chapter 4), established the existence of four types of 'flexibility' in the management of work: *numerical, functional*, and *pay flexibility* and *distancing strategies*. It also extended the analysis of a dual labour market consisting of *core* and *peripheral* workers. Although the authors were careful to state that in most of the 72 large firms they investigated there were few signs of significant change in company culture, their findings have been criticized as promoting the very strategies that were under investigation (Pollert, 1988).

Murray's emphasis on the importance of recognizing the opportunities which FS presents for work enhancement is addressed by Phillimore in Chapter 5, 'Flexible specialization, work organization and skills'. Here Phillimore considers the operation of flexible specialization from the point of view of *optimists, pessimists*, and *sceptics*, and cautiously concludes that while there is evidence that certain sectors of *core* workers will experience opportunities for acquiring new skills, it is undoubtedly the case that FS offers management a ready means to further divide and control workers – particularly those who are not unionized. The requirement for *numerical flexibility* experienced by many firms, to enable them to adjust to changing consumer demand, 'implies a ready supply of low skill, low security labour'.

Chapters 6–8 focus upon labour market structures and their influence on employment opportunities for young people. As youth unemployment began its steep rise from the mid–1970s, the view commonly expressed by employers and politicians was that a prime cause of young people's unemployment was their own 'unemployability' arising from inadequate basic skills and a lack of appropriate work disciplines. The populist belief that young people (and their teachers) were largely to blame for their unemployment has inflected much of the public debate on VET policy and, in spite of the strong rebuttals from many of the researchers in this field, its influence still persists – particularly in relation to the curriculum.

One of the strongest challenges to the unemployability orthodoxy has come from the work of Roberts and his colleagues (Roberts 1986; 1989) which has consistently maintained the primacy of labour market variations in the determination of employment opportunities. In Chapter 6, 'Mass Unemployment Returns', extracted from his book *School Leavers and their Prospects*, Roberts summarizes the arguments as to why young people have been disproportionately represented among the ranks of the unemployed during the past two decades, and underlines the salience of ethnic and gender attributes in creating further inequalities of access to work.

The issue of structural inequality in relation to employment is central to much of the research on labour markets and constitutes a powerful reminder of the inadequacy of those explanations of unemployment which 'blame the victim'. Chapters 7 and 8, taken from Gallie's collection of papers, *Employment in Britain*, provide extensive commentaries on the literature and research dealing with class, gender and ethnicity in respect of employment opportunities. Purcell, in Chapter 7, examines issues of gender in relation to employment – both in terms of access to jobs and the culture of the workplace through which the 'gendering of jobs' occurs. Jenkins, in Chapter 8, looks at ethnic discrimination in relation both to black and white workers in Great Britain and to Catholic and Protestant workers in Northern Ireland. Jenkins argues that as job opportunities are reduced, definitions of 'skill' in the recruitment practices of employers are changed as part of a tightening of the criteria of suitability and acceptability.

Chapters 9 and 10 move on to an assessment of national training policy itself. In Chapter 9, Keep and Mayhew outline the fractured history of vocational education and training in the UK, drawing attention to the lack of consistency and coherence in the state policy towards industrial training. Alternating between intervention and *laissez-faire*, successive governments have failed to establish an effective national system of training. Acknowledging the complexity of this deep-seated failure, Keep and Mayhew argue that it is necessary to explore the mutually reinforcing pressures militating against industrial support for training rather than isolate apparent weaknesses in the institutions which provide VET.

A similar systemic view is taken by Finegold and Soskice in their paper 'The Failure of Training in Britain' (Chapter 10), where the argument is put forward that Britain's failure to educate and train its workforce is both a cause and an effect of its poor economic performance. In depicting Britain as trapped in a low skills–low quality equilibrium, Finegold and Soskice argue that changing education and training policy alone is unlikely to improve economic performance significantly. After analysing what they describe as the Conservative Government's 'scattershot' approach to education and training policy, they conclude with a range of recommendations for future policy.

Chapters 11 and 12 provide an employer perspective on the education and training problems of the UK. Both pieces, which appeared in the Social Affairs Unit publication, *Trespassing? Businessmen's Views on the Education System* exhibit a good deal of the 'we blame the schools and teachers' line of argument, and represent a number of the ideas which have been influential in employer commentary on education and training. Corfield in 'The Education–Industry Mismatch' argues that one of the main problems for industry is the existence of skills shortages, and takes the view that it is the task of the education service to provide industry with the number and quality of skilled workers that it needs. He is critical of the divisions between education and training in which the able enter an over-specialized higher education system, while the least able 'wallow amidst a plethora of schemes which give limited experience, maximum hope and little opportunity'.

In Chapter 12, Walter Goldsmith, former Director-General of the Institute of Directors, is rather more trenchant in his criticisms of the education service, which he characterizes as having been subject to mismanagement and 'the plummeting of standards in pursuit of the chimera of "equality"'. In 'The Business of Education' he highlights the need for a number of policies espoused by the political Right, some of which had their legislative expression in the 1988 Education Reform Act.

Moore's paper 'Education, Employment and Recruitment' (Chapter 13) provides something of a rejoinder to the arguments advanced by Corfield and Goldsmith. It points out that the alleged failure of teachers for the low quality of young workers 'is a main feature of the rhetoric which legitimizes the changes which are being imposed' on education, and argues that educational qualifications are of only limited relevance in employer recruitment practices. In rebutting the 'ill-informed' nature of employer views on educational courses and qualifications, Moore argues that labour market structures are much more salient in determining the acceptability of young workers to employers.

The final chapter by Jarvis and Prais, 'Two Nations of Shop-keepers', provides one of the few detailed cross-national comparisons of education and training in relation to a specific industrial sector – that of retailing in Britain and France. The study highlights the substantial differences in training priorities and resourcing between the two countries, but does so in the context of the organizational changes affecting substantial parts of the retailing sector. The changes in skill requirements brought about by the introduction of electronic pricing and the move towards out-of-town shopping complexes raises important questions about appropriate levels of training and resource.

References

Department of Industry (1977) *Industry, Education and Management: a discussion paper*. London: Department of Industry.

Murray, R. (1985) 'Benetton Britain'. *Marxism Today*, November.

Pollert, A. (1988) 'The "Flexible Firm": fixation or fact', in *Work, Employment and Society*, **2**(3), September.

Roberts, K., Dench, S. and Richardson, D. (1986) *The Changing Structure of Youth Labour Markets*. London: Department of Employment (Research Paper No. 59).

Roberts, K., Parsell, G., and Connolly, M. (1989) *Britain's Economic Recovery, the new demographic trend and young people's transition into the labour market*. ESRC 16–19 Initiative, Occasional Paper No. 8. London: The City University.

Wiener, M.J. (1981) *English Culture and the Decline of the Industrial Spirit, 1850–1980*. Cambridge: Cambridge University Press.

Contents

Chapter 1

The British State, Governments and Manufacturing Decline

D. Judge and T. Dickson

The collapse of manufacturing in Britain since 1979 is the culmination of a more protracted decline. Most sectors of the economy have been hit by the post-1979 recession, but it is manufacturing industry which has been most severely affected. Indeed, the process of 'de-industrialization' is peculiarly, some would say almost uniquely, a British problem (see Smith, 1984, p. 34). No other advanced industrialized nation has experienced the contraction in manufacturing employment and the falls in output that have afflicted the United Kingdom. Whilst most OECD countries have suffered a setback in industrial production in the 1980s, they have, none the less, maintained production levels well above those of the UK.

So, why has manufacturing industry in Britain fared so badly? If the question is simple, the answer is complex. In fact, various competing answers abound. These range from economic explanations – the failure of investment policies (Pollard, 1984), the inability to maintain world trading shares in manufactures (Singh, 1977), the erosion of the industrial base through the expansion of the public sector (Bacon and Eltis, 1978), the dominance of finance capital (Longstreth, 1979); through social causes – an inappropriate educational system (Musgrave, 1967), an anti-entre-preneurial, anti-business culture (Nairn, 1982), the nature of British trade-unionism (Kilpatrick and Lawson, 1980); to political factors, such as the absence of coherent and lasting industrial policies (Smith, 1984), or the vagaries of adversarial politics (Chandler, 1984). In themselves, such

Source: D. Judge and T. Dickson (1987) 'The British state, governments and manufacturing decline', in *The Politics of Industrial Closure*, T. Dickson and D. Judge (eds), Macmillan, London and Basingstoke, pp. 1–42.

1

monocausal explanations have proved to be incapable of adequately answering our initial question. A satisfactory answer can only be found through a comprehensive examination of the political, economic and social factors contributing to manufacturing decline in Britain. This chapter seeks to provide just such an examination and to use the state as the focusing point around which this analysis can be conducted; for the intermediation of the state in the relationships between the various fractions of capital, and between capital and labour, serves to define and explain the relative position of manufacturing in the British economy and its cumulative weakness.

The striking feature of the development of the British state since the 17th century has been its subordination to 'an independent sphere of private interests and private exchange' (Gamble, 1985, p. 72). As Stuart Hall (1984, p. 10) points out, 'the organizational principles which enabled commerce and trade to expand – free trade, the laws of the market and contract – were also the principles on which the new relationships between state and individual were modelled'. In the operationalization of these principles, the economic interests of the propertied classes became conjoined with the political structure of the liberal state. This conjunction has subsequently been modified, but never fundamentally altered. Hence, the existing state structure proved flexible enough to accommodate the rise of manufacturing and the irrevocable changes wrought to the class system in the 19th century. The nature of the state, and its overarching concern with the preservation of the system of free exchange, certainly facilitated this accommodation, but so, too, did the nature of the dominant class. For the commercialized aristocracy in Britain had mutual interests with the emergent bourgeoisie – in profit, property, contract and trade; and these interests served to fuse a bourgeois–aristocratic alliance in England that was to be crucial to the development of the economy and the state in industrialized Britain.

The significance of this alliance for some Marxists, such as Nairn (1982) and Anderson (1964), is that an old-style mercantilism, a limited and old-bourgeois form of capitalism, underpinned British industrialization in the 19th century. In this sense, the seeds of Britain's long-term economic decline were endemic within its initial industrial success. The emphasis of this old-style capitalism was upon short-term profit maximization, small enterprises, trade, and finance-oriented investment. In turn, this emphasis reflected the values of the established commercial and financial classes; and according to this interpretation, industrialism was unable to challenge the hegemony of the aristocratic classes. The essence of the Nairn–Anderson thesis, therefore, is that traditional values, an aristocratic ethos which was anti-industrial, prevailed throughout the 19th century and subverted the establishment of a separate identity on the part of the emergent industrial bourgeoisie. This value system simultaneously denigrated the worth of entrepreneurial endeavour and industrialism whilst emphasizing the importance of financial and commercial endeavour in the world market. Hence, the very nature of the dominant class alliance as it developed in the 18th century, an alliance which germinated the industrial revolution and propagated the liberal state, ultimately served to frustrate a second industrial revolution required to maintain Britain's economic pre-eminence in the late 19th century.

The Nairn–Anderson thesis of unbroken aristocratic hegemony has not gone unchallenged. Most recently, Paul Warwick (1985) has demonstrated the discontinuities in this aristocratic cultural ascendancy. He argues that by the early 19th century the values of entrepreneurial endeavour and material enrichment outweighed aristocratic pretensions. However, the very success of 'bourgeois ideological production', and the propagation of the values of egalitarian openness, meritocracy and social mobility inherent within liberalism, came to pose its own threat to the newly ascendant class. Consequently, the very class which had gained from the openness of 18th century aristocratic society sought to restrict working class access to economic, social and political power. Social exclusiveness came rigidly to demarcate the upper levels of the social hierarchy. Thus, although members of the working class gained selective admission to the franchise in return for their quiescence and 'responsibility', they were simultaneously excluded from key social and state positions. The invention by the Victorian bourgeoisie of the role of the naturally privileged and superior 'gentleman' played a vital role in this strategy of exclusion. As part of this invention, an educational system was 'deliberately constructed to create class barriers and inhibit mobility across them' (Warwick, 1985, p. 123), a civil service was developed whose upper ranks constituted a 'sort of (bourgeois) freemasonry' (see Leys, 1983, p. 234), and a military system was established wherein the commanding officers were recruited almost exclusively from public schools. In this process, the relatively fluid structure of late 18th century society was transformed into a static and class-divided society by the beginning of the 20th century. The significance of this cultural inversion for our analysis is that: 'if the price for creating this new society was the loss of technological and industrial leadership . . . it was, apparently, a price influential Victorians thought worth paying' (Warwick, 1985, p. 123).

This cultural revolution was, however, only the most apparent manifestation of the complex economic, social and political changes taking place in late 19th-century Britain. The acquisition of an imperialist mentality by the British ruling class was another, and a natural response to the expansion of industrial capitalism on a world scale in the last decades of the 19th century. The manner in which British capitalists chose to respond to the industrial competition of Germany and the United States in this period set the pattern for manufacturing for most of the following century. Indeed, the imperial legacy helps to explain the industrial decline of Britain almost a century later.

■ Free trade imperialism: the fracturing of capital's interests

The decades at the end of the 19th century and the beginning of the 20th century were crucial in the development of the British economy and the British state. In this period, British pre-eminence in the world economy continued; with British supremacy contingent upon the internationalism of the world economy. Not surprisingly, therefore, the state sought to promote, and even enforce, this internationalism through free trade and imperial preference policies. Both industrial and finance capital in Britain derived benefits from the pursuit of free trade imperialism. On the one hand, industrial capital could still secure manufacturing growth and increased output through exports to an informal and formal empire. By retreating into empire markets, significant sectors of British industry therefore escaped the need to compete against the new industrial powers of Germany and the United States in the developed markets. Moreover, exports to the undeveloped world secured high levels of employment in the staple industries in Britain.

Finance capital, on the other hand, had a more universal interest in internationalism. British investments overseas were seen to be one of the most powerful means of integrating the international economy. Simply, British investments fuelled world trade. Increasingly, as all the major financial networks came to be routed via the City of London, so an integrated monetary system came to be centred on the British Central Bank. Whilst the Bank of England was nominally a private company, it acted, nevertheless, to promote national financial interests. It did this through maintaining the stability of the pound, ensuring the operation of the Gold Standard, and by using the bank rate to influence the international flow of capital in Britain's favour. In these circumstances, free trade and the international role of sterling were believed to be the preconditions of Britain's economic pre-eminence and prosperity. Britain's financial interests came to be treated synonymously with Britain's national interest. State policies came to reflect the 'universal' interests of finance capital. Indeed, the 'City's dominance has been so complete that its position has often been taken as the quintessence of responsible financial policy' (Longstreth, 1979, pp. 161–2).

That the parameters of economic policy have been largely set by finance capital since the late 19th century has arisen in large part because industrial capital has been unwilling, or unable, to assert its requirements as *national* requirements for the well-being of the whole economy. For long periods in the 19th century, industrial capital was not required to assert its requirements given the compatibility of its interests with those of finance capital over the freedom of international trade, the need for a strong currency and the availability of short-term loans. What British industrialists never systematically sought, nor gained, was state recognition of their interests as being synonymous with the wider national economic interest. This contrasted sharply with the position in the newly industrialized states. In Germany and Japan, for instance, the state and industrial capital combined resources not only to protect and subsidize domestic industry but also to foster close links between the banks and heavy industry; to provide and manage a basic infrastructure; to encourage cartels; and to mobilize strong nationalist ideologies. In Britain, however, industrialists were unable or unwilling to influence the state to protect the national economy via tariffs, or to intervene, institutionally, to promote industrial development. Paradoxically, therefore, the commitment of industrialists in the first industrial nation to the icons of *laissez-faire* principles and the market inhibited their ability to utilize the state to further their interests long after changing international conditions required such intervention to compete effectively with their main rivals in the USA and Germany. The hegemony of finance capital thus served to insulate state policies from such pressure as was occasionally exerted by industrial capital.

The dominance of finance capital over state policy is most clearly visible at those times of rapid change and increased competition in the international economy. At such times the respective interests of the two fractions of capital tend to segment and become differentiated. This was apparent at the turn of the 19th century over the issues of protection and foreign investment. On the question of Tariff Reform:

> 'When … Joseph Chamberlain tried to rally the manufacturing interest in the Conservative Party behind the cause of protection for domestic industry, in the hope of launching a manufacturing revival, he was bitterly opposed by the financial interests. He and the manufacturers were decisively defeated.'
> (Eatwell, 1982, pp. 65–6)

Similarly, on the issue of investment overseas, the interests of finance capital and domestic industry were fractured by the end of the 19th century. In the second half of the 19th century foreign investment multiplied rapidly; to the extent that by 1875 the cumulative net total of British assets abroad passed £1 billion, doubled to over £2 billion in 1900 and doubled again to £4 billion by 1914 (Crouzet, 1982, p. 365). A case can be made, however, that the export of capital neither directly nor detrimentally affected domestic investment in British manufacturing, as the latter was traditionally based upon reinvestment of profit by individual firms, or by short-term bank loans, which were readily available, or by raising finance within an entrepreneur's family. However, as foreign competition increased at the end of the century, and as the need to invest in new plant and technologies became necessary to enter the second phase of industrialization – as, in other words, investment needed to be long-term and extensive – so investment overseas restricted the opportunities for growth and structural change in domestic industry. At this stage the interests of finance and industrial capital diverged. This divergence was reinforced institutionally in the divorce between the banking system and industry. Unlike the German banking system, which not only provided long-term finance, but also actively participated in industrial decision-making, the English banks played a passive and restrictive role. They did not conceive of an active industrial role – to encourage technological development, to stimulate industrial concentration or to promote effective organization of the productive process. Generally, banks were reluctant to provide risk capital or long-term loans to British industry. The safety of capital investment, the defence of the free movement of capital, and the maintenance of the value of sterling were the basic preoccupations of the financial institutions. These preoccupations, which had tied industrial capital to the financial sector for much of the 19th century, now separated the two sectors by the end of the century. And this separation has underpinned the decline of manufacturing industry throughout the 20th century.

Not only was the policy of free trade imperialism crucial in the development of the relationships within British capital at the end of the 19th century, but it was also of significance in determining the relations between labour and industrial capital. In fact, by the last quarter of the 19th century, the state in Britain, partly in response to increasing democratization and to a growing working class electorate, had legalized the status of trade unions and acknowledged some of the collective rights of workers. In this context, new unions of unskilled workers developed alongside the older craft unions and for the most part the new organizations adopted craft union practices and sought to defend past gains and acquired customs (see Clarke, 1977, p. 12). Significantly, the customs and norms defended were those which pre-dated mass production techniques. Thus a peculiarly British dimension to the organization of labour in manufacturing was propagated – one which combined a defensive orientation with decentralized and uncoordinated union structures. The impact of this dimension was considerable, for, although reorganization of production was a continuous process in the 19th century, the strength of the trade unions and their willingness to resist changes on the grounds of past practice meant that concessions on work practices by British manufacturers were more common than in the newly industrialized countries. Indeed, as Kilpatrick and Lawson (1980, p. 90) argue, 'frequently these concessions provided the basis for further resistance so that one way or another industrial change proceeded more slowly than it would have done in the absence of resistance, and proceeded much more slowly than in other countries'. One consequence of such resistance was that British industrialists tended to avoid confrontations over the restructuring of production processes when other alternatives existed. British entrepreneurs, therefore, largely sidestepped conflict over the introduction of those new production techniques required to compete with German and

US industries by directing their attention to the markets of the empire and the undeveloped world. Industrial capital and labour alike thus had a vested interest in imperialism and in insulating themselves from the effects of increased competition in the European markets.

■ Industrial development between the wars

The striking thing about economic development in Britain in the inter-war years is how the legacies of 19th-century economic pre-eminence continued to bind policy-makers to attitudes unsuited to the vastly different conditions pertaining in the new international economy and political order. Economic policy continued to be guided by the City's conception of 'sound financial principles'. Generally, the internationalist perspective of finance capital was undiminished, as the return to the Gold Standard in 1925 demonstrated. This move was seen 'as an expression of London's rightful place in the world financial system, as the only basis for the revival of British capitalism and for the imposition of a world monetary order' (Longstreth, 1979, p. 166). Few industrialists were willing to question such assertions. And only the most percipient industrialists sought assurances that the re-establishment of the Gold Standard would not curtail domestic credit. Only with hindsight did industry see the cost of this financial policy to be a depressed domestic market, increased unemployment and further damage to its international competitiveness through an over-valued exchange rate.

The irony of the international orientation of British finance capital was that its external aspirations for free trade and sterling were finally checked by the operations of the international financial markets themselves. The Wall Street Crash of 1929 and the general turmoil of banking and financial transactions led to pressure on sterling and the eventual decision to float the pound in 1931. Even in taking this decision the Bank of England's stated priority was to 'conserve the international utility of the London money market' (W. A. Brown, quoted in Pollard, 1983, p. 145). Nonetheless, the ending of the Gold Standard marked a significant retreat by finance capital, a position compounded by the introduction of imperial tariff policy in 1932. Yet this retreat was enforced by external pressures. Within Britain, finance capital still maintained its hegemony over the state's policy-makers. This was demonstrated in the commitment of successive governments to balanced budgets and their refusal to intervene in the capital market through national investment banks or industrial development corporations.

When the state did intervene in the inter-war years it was not part of a coherent or developed industrial policy. A series of *ad hoc* interventions facilitated company mergers and the extension of monopolies, but invariably for defensive or protectionist reasons rather than on strategic grounds. By 1939, therefore, the British state was more interventionist and more protectionist than at any stage in its previous industrial history. Yet the state lacked, because its policy-makers did not conceive, nor were required by industry to conceive of, coherent industrial policy. Successive governments presided over a complex mixture of advances and retreats in industry. Advances were made in the modernization and expansion of 'second phase' industries – in chemicals and motor manufactures, for example. At the same time, however, the old staple industries continued to decline, with the subsequent loss of employment. More generally, the retreat from free competition effectively meant in Hobsbawm's (1968, p. 183) graphic phrase that 'Britain became a non-competing country at home as well as abroad'. The changes made in the inter-war period thus did not constitute a fundamental restructuring of the relations between the state and industry in Britain. The legacy of the 19th century was still to fix governments' attention upon external policy, even though the ending of free trade and the liberal world economy redirected their activities towards domestic policy. But in the arena of internal economic policy, British governments were ill at ease and ill-prepared to take action. Only with the recovery of an international role for sterling and the revitalization of City financial institutions after the Second World War was the mismatch resolved between governments' external orientations and their immediate policy concerns.

■   1945 and after: the resilience of finance capital

The end of the Second World War heralded a phase of reconstruction in the major economies ravaged by war. In comparison with the crippled economies of Germany and Japan, British industry was better placed to recapture its export markets. This was despite its inheritance of under-investment, labour-intensive production processes and inefficiencies. In fact, within a year pre-war production levels had been achieved, and increased by 30 per cent up to 1950. Correspondingly, exports reached their pre-war levels in 1946 and rose a further 70 per cent in the next four years (Smith, 1984, p. 76). Britain thus made a head start on its competitors. However, once more British industry was to be rapidly overtaken as its historical legacies came to prevail over the short-term innovations of the war period.

The resilience of financial capital and the gradual reassertion of its political strength was one major legacy. After the war Britain was allowed to act as a junior partner in the new open international order imposed by the US. Sterling retained its position as a major international currency, both because it was the unit of exchange for the sterling area and also because of its role in international trade (see Pollard, 1983, pp. 362–4; Coakley and Harris, 1983, pp. 33–5). The City's provision of financial services for the world and its traditional pattern of trading thus locked Britain more firmly into the new economic order than most of its major competitors; and the defence of sterling in this order was a major priority. As a result, British governments had little option but to maintain the sterling area, and, given the City's pre-eminence, to adopt policies favourable to the free flow of capital for portfolio and industrial investment overseas. For most of the first quarter of a century after the war, therefore, British governments were preoccupied with the 'problem of the sterling balances'. Successive administrations either sought to force overseas holders of sterling to hang on to the currency or, after 1958 and the convertibility of these balances, to persuade them to continue holding sterling. Maintaining confidence in sterling was of paramount importance for British governments.

Confidence in sterling was directly correlated with the British balance of payments. It is no coincidence, therefore, that the 'balance of payments was the focus of the one really determined effort of planning in which the [1945–51] Labour government engaged' (Cairncross, 1985, p. 503). Nor was it by chance that the stabilization policy of successive Chancellors for over twenty years was determined by the external balance. A preoccupation with the balance of payments has been the continuous thread of British post-war economic policy (Gamble and Walkland, 1984, pp. 88–9). Throughout, British economic policy-makers looked at the world with 'traders' and bankers' eyes' (Pollard, 1984, p. 35) with their gaze firmly fixed on the fluctuations and uncertainties of the international financial and currency markets.

It was, and is, this international focus of British policy-makers which has proved to be so detrimental to industrial regeneration in Britain. Yet, the influence of internationally-oriented finance capital upon manufacturing decline is not direct. There is no simple correlation between the outflow of capital and the level of investment in domestic industry. Instead, there is a complex of forces leading to investment failure. It cannot be assumed that financial investment overseas could, or would, have been invested in British industry. Rather, it can be argued that

> 'the policies intended to maintain the position of sterling discouraged and distorted industrial investment through high interest rates to attract foreign funds and prevent the flight of "hot money", ... and recurrent bouts of deflation to restrain home demand and "free" resources for export production' (Jessop, 1980, p. 32).

In other words, the needs of the domestic economy tended to be subordinated to the maintenance of Britain's international financial networks. This subordination was apparent in the 'stop–go' cycle of the

1950s and 1960s when what was effectively stopped was domestic investment and the 'will to invest' (Pollard, 1984, p. 49). After every crisis, the ability of British industry to 'go' for growth was impaired by the restriction of investment. The problem was simply that 'whenever something went wrong with the balance of payments, domestic investment was hit on the head' (Eatwell, 1982, p. 129). But in taking a smack at investment in this manner manufacturing productivity was undermined, and this in turn contributed to a progressive deterioration in the balance of payments to which governments then had to react. Government reaction invariably aimed at sustaining foreign confidence in sterling and the integrity of British financial institutions.

It should not be assumed, however, that there is always a direct and explicit contradiction between the interests and requirements of finance capital and industrial capital. Such conflict is dependent upon both fractions acting consistently as homogeneous and discrete entities. This, however, is not the case. Within the industrial sector, for instance, there are significant differences between small and large firms, between multinational and national conglomerates and between export- and domestic-oriented manufacturers. Indeed, the growth of the monopoly sector, particularly after 1960, has witnessed the largest British manufacturing firms increasingly engaged in transnational operations. In the twenty-year period 1950–70 the proportion of British firms operating six or more foreign subsidiaries increased from one-fifth to one-half, and by 1970 all of the top 100 manufacturing companies had become multinational (Gamble, 1985, p. 110). Britain is now second only to the US in the number of multinational corporations. The importance of this fact is that multinational corporations' investment decisions are based on long-term plans and a global outlook. The domestic manufacturing base and market is thus not the single, nor even the major, consideration for these companies. Their dependence upon the viability of production within the UK is much reduced. In consequence, something resembling an 'overseas alliance' between the internationally-oriented manufacturing and financial sectors has operated for much of the post-war period. This has left nationally-based industrial capital in the same political position it had occupied all century, 'namely that of junior partner to financial interests that were not directly geared to national economic reconstruction' (Coates, 1985, p. 48).

If the term 'overseas alliance' is therefore to have any meaning, it must also encompass the role of the state alongside the international perspectives of British finance and multinational capital. The success of internationally-oriented capital in defining the economic interests of the state as its own was noted earlier. But not only has Britain's economic policy been imbued with an external perspective, British defence and foreign policies have also, as a corollary, been conceived on a global scale.

The consequences of British governments' fixation with international status have been profound for manufacturing industry. Successive governments have been ensnared in an imperialist mentality, directly expressed through the maintenance of the empire in the immediate post-war period and cruelly exposed in the Suez debacle; or indirectly observed in support of US imperialist excursions. Moreover, British fears of militarist expansion by the Soviet Union, and the consequences of this for its alliance with the US, served to sustain a world military role long after Britain's industrial performance warranted, or could afford, such a role. The very cost of the military budget itself impeded the competitive growth of British industry. Investment in key sections of British manufacturing was effectively crippled, and the momentum of the export drive was slowed, by the British rearmament programme at the crucial time of reconstruction in the early 1950s (see Cairncross, 1985, p. 231; Aaronovitch, 1981, p. 70). Thereafter, the level of defence expenditure has detrimentally affected the balance of payments (Calvocoressi, 1979, p. 217), skewed the research and development effort in Britain (see below, p. 14) and has been maintained at higher levels than for any other OECD country apart from the US.

■ The state, manufacturing and the working class

A further legacy contributing to Britain's industrial malaise has been the particular operation of the defensive power of organized labour. The inheritance of British trade unions was a resistance to change and decentralized structures. Unlike their major European and Japanese counterparts, they had neither been destroyed by the state in the 1930s nor fragmented by internal divisions. If anything, the British trade union movement emerged from the Second World War intact and strengthened. Indeed, the tentative incorporationist strategy pursued by the state in the decade before the outbreak of war culminated in the effective working partnership between the government and the General Council of the Trades Union Congress (TUC) in the 1940s. The major achievement of labour in this period was to secure the commitment that governments had 'as one of their primary responsibilities the maintenance of a high and stable level of employment' (Cmnd 6527, 1944). This commitment shaped the direction of state policy for a whole generation after 1945.

Full employment effectively undermined the disciplinary sanction of industrialists against labour, so strengthening the bargaining power of trade unions. Simultaneously, the decentralized system of collective bargaining was enhanced, with shop-floor institutions increasingly replacing the formal, national union machinery. These informal institutions, of shop-steward and joint shop-steward committees, established close control over many key aspects of the production process – not least the terms on which reorganization would, or would not, occur. Workplace collective bargaining in the context of full employment, therefore, served to slow the pace of the technological restructuring of British industry. Throughout the post-war period this defensive power of workers was demonstrated in 'restrictive practices concerning demarcation, apprenticeships, manning levels, work rates, overtime, etc., and in shop-floor resistance to re-organization of the labour process' (Jessop, 1980, p. 35). In turn, this resistance reinforced the reluctance of significant sectors of industry to re-equip or restructure their British plants. In particular, British multination-als looked overseas to areas where labour was cheap, unorganized and compliant, and where the rate of exploitation was higher than in Britain.

In contradistinction to the international perspective of multinational industrial capital, finance capital and successive economic policy-makers, the primary focus of labour in Britain has been domestic, introspective and limited. The horizons of labour interests have been drawn at plant, or at best company, level. The defence of working conditions, customs and wages within these horizons has been the paramount objective of trade unions. The ramifications of this posture beyond these horizons have not preoccupied the participants in the decentralized bargaining process. Even if a 'national' interest has been articulated (and successive governments have attempted just this in their various incomes policies), the very decentralization of the bargaining process in industry has militated against consistent action in pursuit of this interest. Paradoxically, the very activities and policies of governments in promoting the 'national' interest have merely reinforced the defensive and parochial orientation of British trade unions. Equally paradoxically, the very strength of trade union defensiveness designed to maintain employment stability has inherent within it the prospect of long-term destabilization of employment. It has been argued, for example, that in major recessions the inflexibilities in work organization may contribute to higher unemployment by ensuring that significant readjustments to labour take place through the closure of plants (Bowers, Deaton and Turk, 1982, p. 146).

■ Industrial policy: 1945–79

Post-war Britain has not had a settled industrial policy. At best there has been a series of policies or overlapping approaches each having its 'own period of prominence, [and] each relying less than it might have on what went before' (Morris and Stout, 1985, p. 862). In part this discontinuity stems from the free-market legacy of the 19th century, with industrial firms retaining a predilection to keep government at 'arm's length' from their own operations. Equally significantly, governments have been unable to develop a consensual base upon which coherent industrial policies could be founded. The inability of the industrial sector to assert its interest as a hegemonic interest has itself frustrated the development of the foundations of an extensive state policy towards industry. As noted above, governments have largely attempted to influence industry through macro-economic policy. However, by the 1950s the unsophisticated techniques of macro-economic management convinced policy-makers of the need to supplement demand management with micro-economic, supply-side policies to regulate manufacturing output. But, if governments could not fail to appreciate the linkage of macro- and micro-economic policies, they, nevertheless, remained unclear as to how they were linked and related to each other. This confusion was only increased by the divergent pressures arising from industry, and by the atomized and subordinate status of manufacturing within the state itself. As a consequence, industrial policy has remained unstable, incoherent and basically reactive. Policies have ebbed and flowed with the return of successive governments, leaving only the thinnest sedimentary strata of consistent policy upon which industry has been able to build.

The basic sediment of industrial policy has formed around regional policy. With its origins in the Special Area legislation of the 1930s, post-war regional policy up to 1979 was designed to alleviate regional unemployment problems. Its initial focus after 1945 was to safeguard and create new jobs in the assisted areas. Later in this period, however, priority was afforded in practice, if not in principle, to modernization, rationalization and the fostering of investment in industry *irrespective* of the employment consequences (Martin and Hodge, 1983, p. 136).

A second sedimentary stratum washed over by successive government policies is selective support for ailing industries. Labour and Conservative governments alike have committed vast sums of public money to supporting declining industries. Amongst the most celebrated recipients of such aid have been Rolls-Royce, Upper Clyde Shipbuilders, British Leyland, Chrysler (UK), and International Computers Limited. A large part of this *ad hoc* approach to government aid to such industries was, of course, itself a legacy of the previous bargain on full employment implicitly struck between post-war governments and unions. A fear of the electoral consequences of being seen to depart from this bargain thus conditioned the actions of successive governments. None the less, whilst governmental assistance matched labour's defensive approach to jobs, industrial capital remained ambivalent to such aid – pragmatically accepting *ad hoc* interventions on the one hand, yet, on the other, proclaiming a general ideological antipathy to such 'encroachments'.

A third stratum of industrial policy, more continuous and strategic than the first two, can be categorized as 'innovative policy'. Its main component has been the stimulation of new products and processes through research and development (R & D). As early as 1916 the state recognized the importance of R & D by encouraging industry to develop its own research associations and by directly financing research in universities through the Department of Scientific and Industrial Research. In 1948 the National Research Development Corporation (NRDC) was established to stimulate inventions deemed to be in the national interest. more recently, the Labour government in 1977 introduced the Product and Process Development Scheme (PPDS), and the Microprocessor Application Project (MAP) in 1978. Both schemes were designed in part to finance and stimulate innovation.

There has thus been no shortage of agencies and finance for R & D. Britain in fact devotes around the same proportion of its industrial output to R & D as other major industrialized nations. But, significantly, Britain's governments have chosen to direct state R & D expenditure in different directions to those of her European and Japanese competitors. Over 50 per cent of British R & D resources has been devoted to military projects – primarily aviation and military electronics. This is yet more evidence of the legacy of Britain's imperial past and the fixation of the state's policy-makers with military and defence matters. The consequence of this R & D strategy has been that relatively few resources have been devoted to the dynamic civil industrial growth sectors of the economy. As Smith (1984, p. 93) concludes, the result of this 'research and development disaster was that British industry was progressively outstripped in technological terms by rival producers'.

A fourth, and intermittent, stratum of post-war policy has developed around the concepts of 'industrial strategy' and 'indicative planning'. Although this is not the place to dwell upon the details of planning since 1945, it is worth noting the reasons why a fully fledged industrial strategy has never developed. The success of 'planning' overseas in industrially innovative countries such as Japan and France – particularly France – attracted the attention of both major political parties in Britain. At various stages, up to 1979, all governments acknowledged the need for a forum within which consensus around these strategies could be built. Equally, since the late 1950s and the experience of 'stop–go', all governments have recognized that macro- and micro-economic policies are mutually depend-ent and that the specific problems of manufacturing industry could not be dealt with by macro-economic policies alone. In addition, the Labour party, in its more radical phases, has been attracted to the idea of planning, to facilitate a transition to 'democratic socialism', or more generally out of a recognition that market forces alone have signally failed to regenerate British industry.

This commitment to planning on the part of the Labour party has undoubtedly cooled the enthusiasm of the Conservative party for such policies. Nonetheless, both parties in office have utilized a range of 'planning' structures – though admittedly with different levels of en-thusiasm and official commitment. Thus the Attlee government engaged in a limited attempt to initiate an industrial strategy through the introduction of Development Councils; the Macmillan government dabbled with indicative planning in the early 1960s with the establishment of the National Economic Development Council (NEDC) and its 'assessment of possibilities' for economic growth; the Wilson government after 1964 devised not only a coherent, ambitious, but flawed National Plan, but also the corresponding institutional arrangement of the Department of Economic Affairs (DEA). Even the Heath administration, after its initial flirtation with neo-liberalism, was, by 1972 and the Industry Act of that year, back within the fold of administrative planning for aid to industry and an interventionist strategy. Indeed, it was within the framework of the 1972 Act that much of the 1974–79 Labour government's industrial strategy was implemented (see Grant, 1982, p. 50). But this government more strongly and explicitly espoused a long-term industrial strategy and sought to develop an institutional framework, around the Sector Working Parties of the NEDC and the newly established National Enterprise Board (NEB), within which the strategy could be effected. Yet, for all that successive governments have accepted the need for some form of planning, the results have been modest. Either the institutional structures have been stunted, as in the case of the NEDC, or short-lived, as in the case of the Development Councils (1947–53), the DEA (1965–69), the Industrial Reorganization Corporation (1966–70), and the NEB (1975–81).

One reason for the discontinuities in 'planning' in Britain has been the antipathy of industrial capital both to the concept itself and to its associated institutional structures. This opposition has reached its peak in periods of Labour governments and 'socialist' planning; but even Conservative flirtations with indicative planning in the early 1960s, or in Heath's industrial 'strategy' after 1972, were respectively greeted with little, or no, enthusiasm. The most powerful explanation, however, circles back to a constant theme of this chapter, namely, the preoccupation of all British governments with the balance of payments and the exchange rate. Put at its simplest: the micro-economic policies of successive governments have been undermined by their preoccupation with macro-economic policies. It is significant, for example, that the distinction between macro- and micro-economic policies was reinforced in the 1960s in the institutional separation of the Treasury from the DEA. The Treasury's overriding concern with the value of sterling ultimately buried the National Plan. Similarly, the industrial strategy of the Labour government between 1974 and 1979 was neutralized, and on the question of unemployment significantly reversed, through its subordination to the economic imperatives of macro-economic policies. When confronted by the speculative movements of foreign currency and the unwillingness of foreign holders of sterling to leave short-term funds in London (particularly after the Treasury-inspired fall in the value of the pound in March 1976), the Labour government accorded priority to restoring international confidence in sterling. In this process its industrial strategy was effectively sacrificed. Planning was thus undermined by the very inability of government to control the macro-economic universe in which domestic industry had to operate.

In the absence of consistent, coherent and continuous industrial policies, or even a consensual basis for the development of such policies, post-war governments have sought remedies to British industry's competitive weakness primarily by attempting to increase the rate of exploitation of labour – through wage cuts, incomes policies, industrial relations legislation, etc. Yet for these remedies to work, it required the compliance, or at least the acquiescence, of organized labour. British trade unions had to be either co-opted or coerced into renouncing their voluntarist predilections. Each successive post-war government consequently has sought to restrain incomes and increase labour productivity through a variety of statutory and 'voluntary' programmes. In doing so, they have confronted a series of paradoxes. The first of these is simply that the state employs, directly or indirectly, a significant proportion of the workforce, and so has considerable potential control over labour. Although governmental control of incomes may, in principle, be easier to impose in the public sector, governments face in return the prospect of more overt political resistance from their workforce, since responsibility for wage levels cannot be ascribed to the market or some other outside 'impersonal' force or agency. A second paradox, more generally, is that incomes policies depend upon the cooperation of the workforce, yet the implementation of these policies generates disillusionment with the very political and institutional framework within which such incomes restraint is enacted. The history of post-war incomes policies has been characterized, therefore, by the transient nature of these policies and their propensity to generate industrial militancy (see Crouch, 1977; Panitch, 1976). A third paradox is that there has been a mismatch between the requirements for a centralized structure for tripartite and state control of wages and the decentralized structure and outlook of most British trade unions. In this sense, the resistance of industrial capital to state intervention, on the grounds of an attachment to the need to allow 'the market' to operate, has been echoed by the determination of organized labour not to depart from the principle of 'free collective bargaining'. The strength of this outlook has been reflected in the way that the power of shop-floor work-groups has normally counteracted the bargains which have been struck at the national level – as the 'winter of discontent' of 1978–79 so vividly demonstrated.

In response, governments have attempted to undermine the strength of organized labour from two directions. On one side, a direct, statutory challenge has been launched through industrial relations legislation. The 1969 White Paper, *In Place of Strife*, has been attributed to the Labour government's failure to continue a tough incomes policy and its need to 'restrict the power of labour in order to placate overseas holders of sterling' (Crouch, 1979, p. 70). This intention was translated into the 1971 Industrial Relations Act. In attempting to curb unofficial strikes and prescribe a pattern of 'legitimate' industrial action, the Conservative government clearly sought to alter the balance of power decisively in favour of employers. In the face of massive union opposition, the provisions of the 1971 Act increasingly became inoperable and the Heath government was forced to attempt, unsuccessfully, the containment of trade unions through tripartite agreements. Ultimately, and disastrously for the Conservative government, a comprehensive statutory wages policy was introduced.

By 1974 and their return to power, the leadership of the Labour party had been persuaded, by the failure of industrial relations legislation and statutory wage policies, to reconstruct controls on trade unions within the wider framework of the Social Contract and 'socialist planning'. Thus, for all that the original Labour Party–TUC Liaison Committee agreement did not explicitly feature an incomes policy, by July 1975 such a policy had become the centrepiece of the Social Contract. The Labour leadership secured the self-denial and diminution of real living standards of workers through maintaining the form, if not the substance, of the Social Contract. Whatever short-term industrial gains were secured under the Contract were secured at the expense of the greater exploitation of labour and the avoidance of radical restructuring of the economy. The economic crisis inherited by Labour did not prove to be 'the occasion for fundamental change and not the excuse for postponing it', as predicted by Tony Benn (Labour Party, 1973, p. 187). Rather, as Leo Panitch (1979, p. 61) observes, 'the crisis became the basis for maintaining the existing balance of wealth and power in British society by increasing the exploitation of the working class'.

■ Thatcherism: lessons from the past

Incoming governments are confronted with the inheritance of the past. The novelty of Mrs Thatcher's 1979 administration is that upon securing office it dismissed most of the post-war orthodoxies of economic and industrial policy. Preceding Labour and Conservative governments alike (with the exception of Mr Heath's limited neo-liberal experiment) were seen, through their perversion of the market order under Keynesian orthodoxies, to have contributed directly to economic decline and the erosion of Britain's industrial base. In Mrs Thatcher's eyes, her predecessors had intervened too much and conceded too much to labour. The results of the social democratic consensus were manifest: on the one side, a bloated, bureaucratic state supervised a large, 'unproductive', public sector and required a massive debt to fund its services. This state structure had been actively promoted and supported by an aggressive and self-interested labour movement. On the other side was an over-burdened private sector, with industry sapped of efficiency and enterprise, and with a diminished reputation on the world stage. If the problem was obvious then so, too, for Mrs Thatcher and her acolytes, were the solutions. These were based as much upon the petty-bourgeois experience of the Conservative leader, upon her prejudices and 'feelings', as upon their intellectual sugar-coating by the works of Hayek and Friedman. Moreover, the solutions were simple – to do what her post-war predecessors had not done, and not to do what most had in fact done.

At the heart of the Thatcherite strategy has been the re-alignment between internal and external policy (Gamble, 1985, pp. 142–5). Whilst external policy had remained essentially liberal, free trade and market-oriented since the 19th century, domestic policy was geared to matching British industry to the requirements of international capitalist competition. These requirements were couched in an internationalist perspective derived from finance capital and its dominance of, and competitiveness in, world markets. Thus, for Thatcherism, the international market provided not only the context within which British industry had to operate, but also its salvation. Through the operation of the market, the rigidities and inefficiencies of domestic industry would be shaken out, so leaving a more competitive corporate sector to prosper on the world stage. Central to both the prejudice and ideology of Thatcherism, therefore, is this predisposition in favour of the market.

In conformity with its market philosophy, one of the initial acts of the Thatcher government in the autumn of 1979 was to abolish exchange controls. A substantial outflow of investment followed. Whereas only 8.7 per cent of the total investments of pension funds had been invested overseas in 1979, by 1982 this proportion had risen to 28.5 per cent. Similarly, the overseas investments of insurance companies rose from 6 per cent of total investment in 1979 to 22 per cent in 1982. In terms of net external assets the abolition of exchange control produced a spectacular growth from some £10 billion in 1978 to over £70 billion in 1984 (*The Times*, 16 August 1985).

The impact of the international market was equally apparent on the exchange rate. Unlike those governments between 1945 and 1971 which tried to stabilize exchange and interest rates in accordance with Keynesian techniques, the government after 1979 chose to let the market primarily determine the exchange rate. Mrs Thatcher enthusiastically accepted what the Labour government in 1976 had reluctantly been forced to accept: that the sheer weight, size and mobility of currency transactions negated effective government action. Indeed, according to William Keegan (1984, p. 44), one of the major 'milestones on the road to the Thatcher administration's monetarism' was the Labour government's decision to allow the pound to float to protect its published monetary targets. In this manner, monetarism and the *laissez-faire* operation of the international monetary markets become inextricably linked. Market confidence in sterling subsequently is seen to reflect the belief of international traders in the sanctity of the money supply and government borrowing figures as the major indicators of economic vibrancy. Of necessity, governments have to react to this belief by controlling both sets of figures. In a real sense, therefore, 'the *laissez-faire* element of monetarism was the policy of the City, the result of the way the City markets operated' (Coakley and Harris, 1983, p. 213). The very operation of the international markets, the model for the Thatcher strategy, led logically to the Conservative government's open embrace of monetarism.

In the search for 'monetary conditions that will ... bring down inflation' (N. Lawson, quoted in *The Times*, 22 June 1985), interest rates have become an essential ingredient in the policy mix of Chancellors since 1979. From August 1981 until January 1985 the government had no official interest rate policy. The suspension of the Minimum Lending Rate ended the Bank of England's discretionary control of interest rates. Thereafter, market mechanisms were supposed to determine short-term rates. In practice, however, the Treasury and the Bank of England still guided interest rates and came to do so with increasing sensitivity to exchange rates. Nevertheless, the freedom of the credit market was greater and more volatile than at any stage in the post-war period. This volatility is in itself a reflection of the impact of world markets upon the domestic economy. Modern British governments have been unable to escape the international constraints within which the domestic economy has to operate. As we noted above, the last Labour government adopted monetary targets and public expenditure reductions as a direct result of the priorities it accorded to sustaining Britain's international financial standing. Yet its pragmatic monetarism fitted uneasily with its domestic policies – its interventionist pretensions, its industrial strategy and its Social Contract. The mismatch between its micro-economic policies and its internationally focused macro-economic policies became ever more apparent and contradictory.

The true significance of the Thatcher government is that it has brought a unity to economic and industrial policy. There are now few pretences that the two can be separated or that British industrial capital can escape the full rigour of international competition. The achievement, if that is the right word, of Mrs Thatcher has been to integrate the British economy more firmly into the world economy. The need to re-align domestic policy to the liberal foreign economic policy has been one of the main themes of the present government. Monetary and financial policies, as we noted above, have been attuned to this aim. More specifically, an industrial 'strategy' has been designed to undermine those forces which seek to insulate industry from international competition, or to mitigate its effects. British industry is to be made to compete, whether it likes it or not. Hence, the problem of modernizing and restructuring manufacturing industry has been set unambiguously within an international context. Those industries which were already internationally competitive and those with transnational operations were lauded by the Prime Minister. Those industries which were not competitive in world markets were largely left to feel the full effects of international competition. The logic of the Thatcherite strategy was, as Andrew Gamble (1985, p. 195) has cogently argued, that 'the attempt to secure prosperity for the whole national economy was implicitly abandoned'. The government has accepted a massive contraction in Britain's manufacturing base as the price of economic salvation. Thus, under Mrs Thatcher's administration, domestic manufacturing weakness has not been rectified, whilst multinational and internationally oriented firms have been strengthened. The result is, again in Gamble's words (1985, p. 226), 'a lopsided pattern of British integration in the world economy ... there is a declining national economy and a thriving multinational economy side by side'. A logical consequence of this pattern is domestic 'de-industrialization'. For the first time in its industrial history, Britain has a government ready to accept the logic of this position and to resign itself, and its people, to the destruction of much of its manufacturing base.

The essence of Thatcherism's negative approach to industry was set out in the 1979 manifesto in the section 'Industry, commerce and jobs'. There a general responsibility was claimed for government to establish the conditions in which industrial modernization could occur, but primary responsibility for success or failure was seen to rest with individual firms themselves. In the words of the manifesto, 'government cannot do industry's job for it'; 'government strategies and plans cannot produce revival nor can subsidies'. Nationalization and interference by governments had only served to curb entrepreneurial spirit by placing too much emphasis on attempts to preserve existing jobs and placing too little emphasis upon creating new jobs in small businesses. Explicit within the manifesto, therefore, was an outright rejection of Labour's industrial strategy. Indeed, Sir Keith Joseph came to the Department of Industry in 1979 boasting of not having an industrial policy and astounded his officials by asking, 'Why [do] we need a Department of Industry?' (quoted in Holmes, 1985, p. 155). Although Sir Keith and his successors rediscovered the 'need' for the department over time, none the less the underpinning philosophy remained essentially negative. State disengagement from industry and the reversal of the interventionist role of the state has remained a consistent preoccupation of Conservative Secretaries of State for Industry since 1979.

That this preoccupation has not reached its full objective is revealed in the increased public expenditure devoted to industry between 1978–79 and 1984–85. In this period, public expenditure on industry increased by 1.2 per cent in real terms (*Guardian*, 4 July 1985). Throughout, the Thatcher government has displayed a contradictory stance towards selective intervention in industry. Nowhere are these contradictions better epitomized than in the granting of financial assistance to British Leyland.

Support was granted to BL in December 1979 and renewed in January 1981, even though, as Wilks (1983, p. 146) points out, 'this subsidy was clearly in total contravention of Conservative ideology'. The social and industrial ramifications of BL's demise upon the West Midlands, and the short-term costs which would be incurred by the Treasury persuaded the Cabinet to intervene. At this stage in the Thatcher administration the possible electoral consequences of its economic policy still weighed fairly heavily with the government. Nevertheless, Sir Keith actually counselled the Cabinet to reject his own department's case for intervention (see Keegan, 1984, p. 176). Similarly, in Sir Keith's eyes, support for Harland & Wolff, the British Steel Corporation, the National Coal Board, International Computers Limited and Meriden all pointed to the un-doubted failure of the non-interventionist strategy of the Conservative government in its early years. However, a condition of government aid was invariably the restoration of profitability on the part of assisted firms. Short-term concessions were made by the government in the prospect of the longer-term restructuring of the industries concerned. Initial subsidies were thus to be paid for in the long run by 'rationalization' and job loss. Hence, the corporate plans for BSC, NCB and BL, for example, all entailed the mutilation of the corporations and their workforces. Clearly, jobs were no longer a priority of the Thatcher government.

This negative approach is echoed throughout other areas of interaction between government and industry. Regional policy, for long a mainstay of governments' attempts to reduce unemployment in the depressed regions, has been severely pruned. In June 1979 the scope of assisted area status was reduced from 44 to 27 per cent of the population. In November 1984 the designation of the areas eligible for aid was redefined and a further £300 million was cut from the financial aid available to the remaining areas. Regional policy as a form of 'spatial Keynesianism' became a casualty of Thatcherism's wider rejection of Keynesianism. Correspondingly, the present government has sought to dismantle the institutional structure of its predecessor's planning and industrial strategy. Although the NEB, unlike the IRC in 1970, was not immediately abolished, it was none the less instructed to restore some £130 million of its assets to the private sector, to abandon its responsibility for extending public ownership, and to hand over its control of BL and Rolls-Royce to the Department of Industry. Eventually, in 1981, the NEB merged with the National Research Development Corporation to form the British Technology Group with a focus upon securing innovation and investment in the 'sunrise' industries. After the 1983 election, the Conservative government went still further and terminated the NEB-type functions of the BTG.

The NEDC escaped the onslaught upon the instruments of 'socialist planning'. It was retained, but has come to symbolize the Conservatives' rejection of economic planning and their determination to reduce organized labour's contribution to the formulation of state policy. Some senior representatives of industry have, for instance, openly acknowledged that 'the NEDC structure, composition and aims ... are incompatible with the present government's approach to the development of a social market economy' (G. Mather, quoted in *The Times*, 2 March 1984). From the trade unions' perspective, membership of the NEDC has increasingly taken on the appearance of 'loitering without intent in the corridors of power' (K. Gill, quoted in *The Times*, 6 September 1984). In effect, therefore, the necessary consensus for the operation of the tripartite structure of the NEDC was an early victim of Mrs Thatcher's style of commitment politics.

This style of politics openly disavowed the interventionist philosophy and procedures of the Social Contract. In particular, incomes policies were denounced for their tendency to enable unions

> 'to demand and obtain policies in exchange for restraint which either damage the national interest as a whole ... or which they hope will further their own interests at the expense of the rest of the community. The basic bargain is likely to mean that the government promises to do things that ought not to be done ....' (The Right Approach, 1976, pp. 37–8)

Even when these promises were unfulfilled, as between 1974 and 1979, they were sufficient to alarm capital. Industrialists began to express openly a belief that 'Mrs Thatcher's government is all that stands between us and a rapid slide into a down-market version of the German Democratic Republic' (see Leys, 1985, p. 17). The control by capital over the production process, and more generally its abilities to influence state policy, were perceived to have been threatened by the corporatist structures developed under the Labour government. Defusing this threat has been a major priority of the Thatcher administration.

The tripartism and planning systems of Labour's social democratic modernization strategy have been countered by the emphasis placed upon free markets and disengagement in the neo-liberal modernization strategy. Indeed, a significant achievement of the Thatcher strategy has been to elevate the impersonal market mechanism to the status of a 'commonsense' proposition. Popular perceptions of Britain's economic and industrial problems have subsequently come to be framed more within a market philosophy, a key element of which has been the government's abrogation of its responsibility for unemployment. Hence, the Thatcher government has been the first post-war administration that has not explicitly committed itself to the preservation of manufacturing jobs. This has been because the philosophy of the social market economy maintains that jobs cannot be preserved while trade unions price their members out of work. Higher wages lead to higher prices, and, in the *laissez-faire* operations of international markets, customers are driven 'to buy from other countries, forcing thousands of employers out of business and hundreds of thousands of workers out of jobs' (The Conservative Manifesto, 1983, p. 13). The trend towards unemployment has also been exacerbated further by the activities of politicized trade unions 'associated with Luddism' (Sir Keith Joseph, quoted in Holmes, 1985, p. 37). Unemployment, in this view, is thus no more than an 'inevitable' result of the monopolistic power of trade unions in the labour market and their capacity to obstruct changes in the process of production.

In apportioning blame to the trade unions in this manner, the government has sought to legitimize its attack upon the fundamental rights of organized labour in terms of removing the 'rigidities' of the labour market. Undoubtedly, widespread unemployment and its demoralizing consequences for the workforce has assisted this attack: fear has been a consistent element of the Conservatives' 'commonsense' stance on unemployment. Indeed, fear has eased the acceptance of policies designed to remedy unemployment but which in practice have served only to exacerbate job loss. The paradoxes of the government's strategy on unemployment are all too depressingly self-evident. Yet, its strategy has been successful in gaining a widespread acceptance that the market, not government, carries the responsibility for employment. The recession and unemployment have often been presented as 'acts of God', as world forces beyond the control of government. If opinion polls are to be believed, a majority of the electorate by 1983 also seemingly subscribed to the same view. Importantly, at the level of public perceptions and ideology, Thatcherism has successfully attained the goal of linking external and internal policy – of linking the operation of the domestic labour market to the vagaries of the international trading markets.

■ Thatcherism and manufacturing: closure and resistance

It has been argued that the economic rationale of the Thatcher government is 'extremely simple: it amounts to crashing the economy' (Harrison, 1982, p. 19). However, such kamikaze intent is not the basis of the Thatcher strategy. Rather, the analogy to be drawn is with a pilot trained on bi-planes attempting to fly Concorde. In true early-Biggles style, Mrs Thatcher has assumed control of the flight deck only to declare that the sophisticated instruments so far developed to steer, monitor and control the economy have proved defective in the past. Therefore, they should be ignored. In their place old skills and techniques are to be utilized, with only the guiding light of M3 money supply figures needed to illuminate the control panel. Flying by the seat of one's pants, with the speed and direction of economic progress determined by the winds of international market conditions, is the new style. To press the analogy still further: to

Table 1.1 Growth of industrial production, 1957–76. (Source: *National Institute Economic Review*, no. 77, 1976, NIESR, p. 80.)

	Annual growth of industrial production (%)	Total growth of industrial production (%)
UK	2.27	57.8
France	5.03	151.2
W. Germany	4.93	146.6
Italy	6.41	219.6
EEC (the Six)	5.32	160.4

ensure that the working-class passengers aboard the state airline do not seek to disturb this exhilarating experience, the crew have sought to strap them firmly into their seats – either through the restraint of industrial relations legislation or through invoking the fear of being sucked out of the economic cabin in the rapid depressurization of recession. Should labour venture to object, then increased stewarding of the aisles (albeit with riot gear if necessary!) has been provided by the governmental air crew. If Thatcherism has not sought to crash the economy, it has certainly put it into a steep dive.

Undoubtedly, the actions of the Thatcher government have exacerbated Britain's industrial position, but many of its policies have only added a short-term recession onto the underlying long-term decline of manufacturing. 'Thatcherism' alone cannot provide a simple explanation of Britain's industrial malaise in the 1980s. In many ways the Thatcher strategy is as much a consequence as a cause of industrial decline. This is not to absolve Mrs Thatcher's government of blame, for the economic effects of its decisions have been truly disastrous, but only to argue that its policies are a logical, if perverse, culmination of some of the long-run tendencies within state–industry relations in Britain.

To set what has happened since 1979 in context, it is necessary to appreciate both the extent of Britain's comparative industrial weakness and also the domestic weakness of manufacturing within the British economy over time. In comparative terms, Britain's industrial malaise has been apparent for some considerable time. In terms of annual growth rates in industrial production and the overall share of trade in manufactures, Britain has increasingly lagged behind her major competitors (see Tables 1.1 and 1.2).

The domestic weakness of British manufacturing was less apparent until the 1970s. Until then, manufacturing output had increased by about 30 per cent per decade since the 1930s. By the mid-1960s, however, the rate of industrial growth began to lag behind the general growth in

Table 1.2   Shares in the value of world exports of manufactures (%). (Sources: A. Gamble, *Britain in Decline*, 2nd edn, 1985, p. 17; *National Institute Economic Review*, no. 118, 1986, NIESR, p. 102.)

	1950	1960	1970	1975	1979	1980	1981	1982	1983	1984	1985
UK	25.5	16.5	10.8	9.3	9.7	10.2	8.8	8.4	7.8	7.6	7.8
France	9.9	9.6	8.7	10.2	10.4	9.9	9.0	9.0	8.9	8.5	8.5
W. Germany	7.3	19.3	19.8	20.3	20.7	19.8	18.3	19.6	19.0	18.0	18.6
Japan	3.4	6.9	11.7	13.6	13.6	14.7	17.8	17.2	18.4	20.0	19.7
USA	27.3	21.6	18.5	17.7	15.9	17.1	18.8	18.0	17.2	17.4	16.8

economic output. In the period 1966–79, although GDP increased by 29 per cent, the growth in manufacturing output was only 11 per cent. Indeed, industrial production peaked in 1973; thereafter there was a significant downturn. Industrial output had, therefore, begun to decline absolutely before 1979 (see Table 1.3).

Similarly, employment in manufacturing had shown a steady decline well before the return of the Conservative government in 1979. In 1970 employment in manufacturing stood at 97 per cent of its 1966 level (the highest level of manufacturing employment). In 1973 this figure was down to 91 per cent and it declined to 84 per cent in 1979. Between 1979 and 1982 manufacturing employment fell from 7 197 000 to 5 776 000, a 20 per cent drop in three years, so that employment in manufacturing stood at 67 per cent of the 1966 total. Yet, the effects of the Thatcher-induced recession were more keenly felt by manufacturing employees than those in other sectors of the economy (see Table 1.4).

If industrial output and employment were in decline before 1979, the recession after 1979 certainly steepened the trajectory of decline. In the first year of the Thatcher government, manufacturing output fell by 15 per cent. Rowthorn (1983, p. 73) compares this slump with a fall in output of

Table 1.3   Index of output in British manufacturing industries (1980 = 100). (Source: CSO, *Economic Trends*, Annual Supplement, 1986 edn, HMSO.)

1950	56.8	1975	105.0	1981	94.0
1960	77.2	1976	106.9	1982	94.2
1965	90.1	1977	109.0	1983	96.8
1970	103.4	1978	109.7	1984	100.6
1973	114.2	1979	109.5	1985	103.9
1974	112.7	1980	100.0		

Table 1.4   Wage earners by activity, 1979–84 (%).
(Source: OECD, *Labour Force Statistics 1964–1984*, 1986, pp. 452–3.)

	1979	1980	1981	1982	1983	1984
Agriculture	1.6	1.6	1.6	1.7	1.7	1.6
Mining and quarrying	1.5	1.6	1.6	1.6	1.5	1.4
Manufacturing	31.4	30.2	28.4	27.5	26.6	26.0
Electricity, gas, water	1.5	1.5	1.6	1.6	1.6	1.5
Construction	5.4	5.5	5.2	4.9	4.8	4.6
Trade: wholesale, retail, catering	17.6	18.0	18.2	18.6	19.0	19.6
Transport, storage and communication	6.4	6.5	6.5	6.4	6.3	6.2
Finance, insurance, business services, etc.	7.0	7.3	7.8	8.2	8.5	8.8
Community, social and personal services	27.6	28.0	29.0	29.5	30.1	30.3
Total	100.0	100.0	100.0	100.0	100.0	100.0

5.5 per cent in the worst year of the Great Depression between 1878 and 1879 and a fall of 6.9 per cent in 1930–31. In this context even the industrial giants, such as ICI, took a pounding. So great was the downturn that in the third quarter of 1980, ICI announced a loss. The shock within the company led to the unprecedented step of the chairman going to Downing Street to inform the Prime Minister personally of the effects of her government's policies upon manufacturing industry (see Keegan, 1984, p. 155). As ICI floundered, other smaller and less competitive manufacturers capsized, sinking their entire labour forces in the trough of the recession. Significant sectors of manufacturing industry were submerged, particularly in the traditionally depressed regions. Thus, in the Merseyside Special Development Area, 384 plants, with more than ten employees, closed between 1979 and 1982. 25 511 jobs were subsequently lost (HC Debates, 14 November 1983, vol. 48, col. 316). In Scotland, between June 1979 and June 1984, 613 closures of manufacturing firms were notified to the Manpower Services Commission (HC Debates, 5 December 1984, vol. 49, col. 206); 164 000 jobs were lost as a result. In Wales, 576 manufacturing plants closed in the period 1978–84 (HC Debates, 1 March 1984, vol. 55, col. 294). More generally, 577 foreign-owned plants closed in the period January 1979–June 1984, with a loss of 106 510 jobs in the UK (HC Debates, 2 May 1984, vol. 59, col. 178; 6 June 1984, vol. 61, col. 179).

With closure on this scale, and with one-third of total job losses since 1979 resulting from closure, the politics of plant closure was forced on to the public agenda. What needs to be explained is how the state attempted to foreclose, pre-empt and depoliticize this issue: for, within the space of a decade, the state has systematically, and largely successfully, undermined resistance to closure. One observable change in this period has been the response of governments to unemployment. Even the precursor of the Thatcher government, the Conservative administration of the early 1970s, was firmly locked into the social democratic consensus and had a major and 'emotional' concern with the problem of unemployment (Holmes, 1982, pp. 44–8). Indeed, the rise in unemployment to one million in 1972 triggered the famous 'U-turns' in Heath's neo-liberal strategy.

One of the most famous of Heath's 'U-turns' came with the granting of state aid to Upper Clyde Shipbuilders. Whereas in June 1971 the government had declared its intention of liquidating UCS as the basis for restructuring the company, by February 1972 this decision had been reversed and £35 million was injected into the newly formed Govan Shipbuilders (see Young, 1974, pp. 155–63). The importance of the UCS work-in for our purposes is that the Heath government was unable to counter the arguments of the UCS shop-stewards concerning the catastrophic employment prospects of closure in an area where there was already considerable unemployment. The work-in underscored the legitimacy of the *right* to work: a right that had been secured in the post-war consensus. So entrenched was this right that support for the UCS workforce galvanized 100 000 people to stop work and 50 000 to join a demonstration in Glasgow on 24 June 1971; two months later, on 18 August, 200 000 strikers and 80 000 marchers demonstrated in support of UCS (Hardy, 1985, p. 17). Indeed, the very scale of local support for the UCS workforce and real fears of widespread public disorder in Glasgow contributed to the U-turn (Holmes, 1982, p. 44). In the early 1970s, therefore, the state was thus both ideologically and institutionally unprepared to deal with workforce resistance to its modernization strategy. Political leaders were psychologically unprepared to contemplate mass unemployment and the forces of law and order were operationally unprepared to deal with widespread industrial resistance. By the return of the Conservative government in 1979, however, the state apparatus had been geared for confrontation (see Jeffrey and Hennessy, 1983) and the new political leadership was ideologically predisposed to accept high levels of unemployment.

Staying for the moment with the effects of the UCS work-in, it ushered in a brief period, between 1970 and 1975, when factory occupations became a fairly common way for groups of workers to resist closure. These 'sit-ins' or 'work-ins' appeared to many in the labour movement to be a more effective weapon against closure than the strike, since they prevented the disposal of the assets concerned and demonstrated the commitment of the employees to the plant concerned. In this period there were around 200 factory occupations, involving 150 000 workers (see Clarke, 1979). However, as Hardy (1985, p. 17) has noted, this phase of opposition to closure lasted only until around 1975 and, thereafter, the factory occupation became a far less common tactic – with occasional notable exceptions, such as the struggle of women workers at the Lee Jeans factory in Greenock in 1981 and at Plessey in Bathgate in 1982.

The resistance to closure has been eroded by structural failings within the trade union movement; by the attrition of management strategies and by the actions of the state itself. [...]

The state was directly confronted with [the] need for acclimatization [of the workforce to manufacturing closure] after the 1973–74 oil-generated world recession spotlighted the weakness of British manufacturing industry. After this date the contradictions of the post-war social democratic consensus were apparent in the simple fact that the time at which state intervention and expenditure was needed marked the very time that the state appeared unable to afford such expenditure. Callaghan's statement to the 1976 Labour Party conference revealed the extent to which even a Labour government had abandoned the Keynesian consensus: 'We used to think you could spend your way out of recession, and increase employment by cutting taxes and boosting government spending. I tell you in all candour that that option no longer exists' (Labour Party, 1976, p. 188).

In jettisoning Keynesian demand-management, as explained earlier, Callaghan's government demonstrated the dominance of external policy and the inescapability of monetarism in the face of the operation of the international financial markets. Increasingly, ministers fitted the intractability of Britain's economic and industrial problems within this world frame. Shirley Williams, for example, admitted the government's helplessness in a speech in February 1977: 'We are seeing the increase in unemployment throughout the industrial world, and it is a problem for which we still have no real answer' (quoted in Coates, 1980, p. 71). Similarly, Jim Callaghan, in his foreword to the 1979 manifesto, attempted to set Labour's record within the context of the 'worldwide unemployment crisis'. The manifesto proceeded to declare Labour's commitment to employment protection within a 'healthy and expanding economy'. Although Callaghan was pressed by the left within his party to resolve the mismatch between internal and external policies, through the adoption of the Alternative Economic Strategy and its insulation of British industry from the international order, he chose to define a 'healthy' economy in terms of its internationally competitive position. Given this emphasis, unemployment was portrayed as inescapable, as but an intrinsic part of the new international industrial order. From this basis the rhetoric of Thatcherism merely completed a logical circle: if unemployment was the product of international forces, there was little that British governments could achieve. Unemployment was thus deemed to be a 'natural' consequence of Britain's manufacturing international competitive weakness.

Resistance to closure in the early 1970s was also facilitated by the fact that no government could be said to have developed a coherent, or explicitly stated, policy on closure. The Heath government hinted at such a policy in its Selsdon phase but failed to enact the necessary measures when confronted by their consequences. Increased public expenditure was ultimately preferred to higher levels of unemployment by the 1970–74 government. Similarly, the Labour government came to office in 1974 committed to maintaining jobs. Indeed, under the direction of Tony Benn at the Department of Industry, a structure within which closure could be fought was developed in the assistance provided to three workers' cooperatives, at Meriden (Triumph Motor Cycles), Kirkby (Fisher-Bendix), and Glasgow (Scottish Daily Express). Significantly, even though the sums of public money provided were relatively small (some £10 million), the response from the Treasury and the 'establishment' was determinedly obstructive (see Benn, 1980, pp. 158–9). More generally, the antipathy of the Treasury and financiers towards Labour's industrial programme perverted its original aims of job enhancement and creation into state-sponsored rationalization and job destruction. By the end of their term in office, Labour ministers had been obliged 'to add their own voices to those of management, in the call to subordinate industrial policy to the dictates of the world market, and transformed even radical ministers into the most adamant proponents of industrial competitiveness' (Coates, 1980, p. 131). Thus, even before Mrs Thatcher came into office in 1979, the foundations of a 'Thatcherite' industrial strategy were embedded within state policies!

Nevertheless, it is important to stress the particular contribution made by Thatcherism to the legitimization of closure and unemployment. Although the logic of its economic policy was inevitably to abandon the attempt to preserve jobs, the 1979 administration, as noted above, was sufficiently wary of the electoral implications to continue, in selected cases, the policy of government assistance to declining industries. However, as the policy consequences inevitably began to work through and the rate of closures (and unemployment) rose, the government was forced to underpin its strategy with a consistent legitimization explaining such factors in terms of, on the one hand, the necessity of short-term suffering for long-term gain and, on the other, the impact of worldwide recession. Thus unemployment was presented as a universal phenomenon amongst Western nations and hence unavoidable.

But the post-war consensus on full employment, established over many years, could not be discarded quite so easily. The volatility of voting behaviour over the last twenty years, which has been the subject of considerable debate (see Alt, 1978; Crewe and Sarlvik, 1983), can, at least partly, be ascribed to the failure of successive governments to manage the

Table 1.5   Unemployment rate (% of total labour force).
(Source: OECD, *Labour Force Statistics 1964–84*, 1986, pp. 496–7.)

1970	2.2	1980	6.6
1972	3.2	1981	9.8
1974	2.2	1982	11.7
1976	5.2	1983	12.1
1978	5.5	1984	12.1
1979	5.1	1985	12.3

economy successfully. The rapid rise in unemployment after 1979 seemed to have a similar effect on the Thatcher administration as opinion polls showed its ratings in 1981 to be amongst the lowest for a post-war government. The supreme irony was that the issue which decisively swung public opinion behind Thatcherism – the Falklands War – illustrated so clearly the imperialist legacy which has been so destructive in economic terms. The popular sentiment and jingoism aroused by a military victory over a foreign nation disputing Britain's claim to territory half-way across the world was to underpin Thatcherism's relentless pursuit of the destruction of jobs in manufacturing.

Thus the Conservative electoral triumph of 1983 was taken as the signal for full steam ahead. Unemployment continued to rise inexorably (see Table 1.5). This massive and unrelenting increase meant that a greater proportion of public expenditure had to be devoted to unemployment and social security benefits. For example, between 1979 and 1984, government expenditure on unemployment benefits rose by 163 per cent in real terms (*Guardian*, 4 July 1985). In consequence, public expenditure was skewed still further towards welfare benefits and away from capital investment. In particular, under central direction, local authority spending on construction, especially on housing, plummeted. Indeed, the deterioration of Britain's infrastructure so worried the CBI that it issued a warning in November 1985 that the inadequacy and continued degeneration of basic infrastructure was a contributory factor in maintaining British industry's high production costs (CBI, 1985). Another twist to the spiral of under-investment and the declining competitiveness of manufacturing industry was thus added by the Thatcherite public expenditure policies.

Resistance to closure in this climate seemed futile. It is in this context that the miners' strike of 1984–85 assumed such symbolic importance. The claim of the National Union of Mineworkers that jobs in the industry were as much the property of those who worked in it as of their employer struck at the heart of Thatcherism. In particular, it challenged three basic tenets of the strategy – the social market philosophy which declared that only the market should determine profitability and employment levels, the position of the government as the employer, and its ability to remove the influence of unions as a market distortion. The centrality of this challenge explains the significance of the Chancellor's claim that, whatever the price of the miners' strike, it was a price worth paying. If Thatcherism was to remain intact, it was a conflict the government could not afford to lose. Thatcherism, then, can be seen in both its domestic and external dimensions, as but an extreme development of some of the policy options used by British capital and the state throughout Britain's industrial development.

References

Aaronovitch, S. (1981) 'The relative decline of the UK', in S. Aaronovitch and R. Smith, *The Political Economy of British Capitalism* (Maidenhead: McGraw-Hill).

Alt, J. (1978) *The Politics of Economic Decline* (Cambridge: CUP).

Anderson, P. (1964) 'Origins of the present crisis', *New Left Review*, 23, pp. 26–53.

Bacon, R. and Eltis, W. (1978) *Britain's Economic Problems: Too Few Producers* 2nd edn (London: Macmillan).

Benn, A. (1980) *Arguments for Socialism* (Harmondsworth: Penguin).

Bowers, J., Deaton, D. and Turk, J. (1982) *Labour Hoarding in British Industry* (Oxford: Blackwell).

Cairncross, A. (1985) *Years of Recovery: British Economic Policy 1945–51* (London: Methuen).

Calvocoressi, P. (1979) *The British Experience 1945–75* (Harmondsworth: Pelican).

CBI (1985) *Fabric of the Nation II* (London: CBI Publications).

Chandler, G. (1984) 'The political process and the decline of industry', *The Three Banks Review*, 141, pp. 3–17.

Clarke, T. (1977) 'The raison d'être of trade unionism', in T. Clarke and L. Clements (eds), *Trade Unions under Capitalism* (Glasgow: Fontana).

Clarke, T. (1979) 'Redundancy, worker resistance and the community', in C. Craig, M. Mayo and N. Sharman (eds), *Jobs and Community Action* (London: Routledge and Kegan Paul).

Cmnd 6527 (1944) *Employment Policy* (London: HMSO).

Coakley, J. and Harris, L. (1983) *The City of Capital* (Oxford: Blackwell).

Coates, D. (1980) *Labour in Power?* (London: Longman).

Coates, D. (1985) 'The character and origin of Britain's economic decline', in D. Coates and G. Johnston (eds), *Socialist Strategies* (Oxford: Martin Robertson).

Crewe, I. and Sarlvik, B. (1983) *Decade of Dealignment* (Cambridge: CUP).

Crouch, C. (1977) *Class Conflict and the Industrial Relations Crisis* (London: Heinemann Educational Books).

Crouch, C. (1979) *The Politics of Industrial Relations* (Glasgow: Fontana).

Crouzet, F. (1982) *The Victorian Economy* (London: Methuen).

Eatwell, J. (1982) *Whatever Happened to Britain?* (London: Duckworth).

Gamble, A. (1985) *Britain in Decline*, 2nd edn (London: Macmillan).

Gamble, A. M. and Walkland, S. A. (1984) *The British Party System and Economic Policy 1945–83* (Oxford: Clarendon Press).

Grant, W. (1982) *The Political Economy of Industrial Policy* (London: Butterworths).

Hall, S. (1984) 'The state in question', in G. McLennan, D. Held and S. Hall (eds), *The Idea of the Modern State* (Milton Keynes: Open University Press).

Hardy, C. (1985) 'Responses to industrial closure', *Industrial Relations Journal*, 16, pp. 16–24.

Harrison, J. (1982) 'Thatcherism: is it working?' *Marxism Today*, pp. 19–25.

Hobsbawm, E. (1968) *Industry and Empire, from 1750 to the Present Day* (Harmondsworth: Pelican).

Holmes, M. (1982) *Political Pressure and Economic Policy: British Governments 1970–74* (London: Butterworths).

Holmes, M. (1985) *The First Thatcher Government 1979–83* (Brighton: Wheatsheaf Books).

Jeffrey, K. and Hennessy, P. (1983) *States of Emergency: British Governments and Strikebreaking* (London: Routledge and Kegan Paul).

Jessop, B. (1980) 'The transformation of the state in post-war Britain', in R. Scase (ed.), *The State in Western Europe* (London: Croom Helm).

Keegan, W. (1984) *Mrs Thatcher's Economic Experiment* (Harmondsworth: Penguin).

Kilpatrick, A. and Lawson, T. (1980) 'On the nature of industrial decline in the UK', *Cambridge Journal of Economics*, 4, pp. 85–102.

Labour Party (1973) *Annual Conference Report* (London: Labour Party).

Labour Party (1976) *Annual Conference Report* (London: Labour Party).

Leys, C. (1983) *Politics in Britain* (London: Heinemann Educational Books).

Leys, C. (1985) 'Thatcherism and British manufacturing: a question of hegemony', *New Left Review*, 151, pp. 5–25.

Longstreth, F. (1979) 'The City, industry and the state', in C. Crouch (ed.), *State and Economy in Contemporary Capitalism* (London: Croom Helm).

Martin, R. L. and Hodge, J. S. C. (1983) 'The reconstruction of British regional policy: the crisis of conventional practice', *Environment and Planning C: Government and Policy*, 1, pp. 133–52.

Morris, D. J. and Stout, D. K. (1985) 'Industrial policy', in D. Morris (ed.) *The Economic System in the UK*, 3rd edn (Oxford: OUP).

Musgrave, P. W. (1967) *Technical Change, the Labour Force, and Education* (Oxford: Pergamon Press).

Nairn, T. (1982) *The Break-Up of Britain*, 2nd edn (London: NLB).

Panitch, L. (1976) *Social Democracy and Industrial Militancy* (London: Cambridge University Press).

Panitch, L. (1979) 'Social democracy and the Labour Party: a reappraisal', in R. Miliband and J. Saville (eds), *The Socialist Register* (London: Merlin).

Pollard, S. (1983) *The Development of the British Economy*, 3rd edn (London: Edward Arnold).

Pollard, S. (1984) *The Wasting of the British Economy*, 2nd edn (London: Croom Helm).

Right Approach (1976) *A Statement of Conservative Aims* (London: Conservative Central Office).

Rowthorn, B. (1983) 'The past strikes back', in S. Hall and M. Jacques, *The Politics of Thatcherism* (London: Lawrence and Wishart).

Singh, A. (1977) 'UK industry and the world economy: a case of de-industrialization?', *Cambridge Journal of Economics*, 2, pp. 113–36.

Smith, K. (1984) *The British Economic Crisis* (Harmondsworth: Penguin).

Warwick, P. (1985) 'Did Britain change? An enquiry into the causes of national decline', *Journal of Contemporary History*, 20, pp. 99–133.

Wilks, S. (1983) 'Liberal state and party competition: Britain', in K. Dyson and S. Wilks (eds), *Industrial Crisis: A Comparative Study of State and Industry* (Oxford: Martin Robertson).

Young, S. (1974) *Intervention in the Mixed Economy: The Evolution of British Industrial Policy 1964–72* (London: Croom Helm).

Chapter 2

De-industrialization in Britain

R. E. Rowthorn

■ Introduction

This chapter is [...] primarily concerned with manufacturing employment in Britain since the Second World War, although there is some discussion of industrial employment as a whole. We show how Britain has experienced an enormous reduction in manufacturing employment over the past thirty years – greater than in almost any other advanced capitalist country – and we consider various hypotheses which might explain this phenomenon. Three main hypotheses are identified which for convenience we label: the Maturity Thesis, the Trade Specialization Thesis and the Failure Thesis. All three hypotheses, it turns out, have considerable evidence in their favour and all three help to explain what has happened to manufacturing employment in Britain.

The present chapter draws heavily upon material contained in a longer and more comprehensive study by Rowthorn and Wells (1986). Of necessity, many of the arguments are presented in a condensed form and many of the details have been left out. Anyone desiring a more comprehensive treatment should consult the longer study.

■ Britain's post-war record in an international context

Figure 2.1 shows what has happened to employment in the major sectors of the British economy since the Second World War. There has been an

Source: R. E. Rowthorn (1986) 'De-industrialisation in Britain', in *The Geography of De-Industrialisation*, R. Martin and R. E. Rowthorn (eds), Macmillan, London and Basingstoke, pp. 1–27.

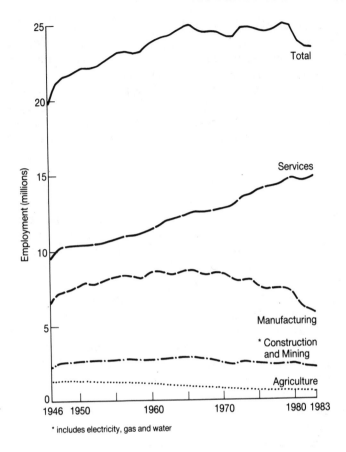

Figure 2.1 Employment in the UK by sector, 1946–83 (millions). (Source: based on historical data from Ministry of Labour and Department of Employment.)

almost continuous fall in the number of people employed in agriculture, from around 1.8 million in 1946 to under 1 million in 1983. Over the same period employment in the service sector has risen dramatically, from just under 10 million to over 14 million. In the so-called 'production' industries – manufacturing, mining, construction and public utilities – the picture is more complex. In the immediate post-war years, under the impetus of reconstruction and a government-sponsored export drive, employment in these industries increased rapidly. Then, in the 1950s, the pace of expansion slackened. Employment continued to rise in manufacturing and construction, though at a slower pace than before; while coal mining began to shed labour as pits were closed because of competition from oil. For a time the new jobs created in manufacturing and construction more than offset those lost in mining, with the result that industrial employment, as a whole, carried on rising right through into the 1960s. However, this expansion came to a halt in 1966 when, following a major sterling crisis, the Labour government of the day imposed a deflationary budget on the economy. Since that time industrial employment of all kinds – mining, construction and manufacturing alike – has fallen dramatically. From an all-time peak of 11.5 million in 1966, the total number of people employed in industry had fallen to less than 7 million by 1984. Over the same period manufacturing employment alone fell from 8.7 million to 5.4 million. About half of this enormous decline took place before the present Thatcher government took office in 1979, while the rest has occurred since.

The picture is much the same if we look at relative shares rather than absolute numbers, although the timing is somewhat different (see Figure 2.2). After rising strongly immediately after the war, the share of industry in civil employment reached a peak in 1955 of around 48 per cent. In that year approximately one-third of the entire population between the ages of 15 and 64 were employed as industrial workers, while most of the rest were students, housewives and service workers. These figures for industrial employment have rarely been equalled and certainly never surpassed in the whole of British history. Moreover, they are almost without equal in the experience of other capitalist countries. This last point can be verified from Table 2.1, which compares Britain's employment structure in 1955 with that of other highly industrialized economies at an equivalent stage in their development. In the entire history of world capitalism the all-time peak of industrialization was probably achieved by Germany in 1970 and Switzerland in 1963. In each case industry accounted for 47–48 per cent of civil employment – which is virtually identical to the figure reached in Britain in 1955. Thus, in employment terms, the British economy in 1955 was one of the most highly industrialized economies the capitalist world has ever seen. Never before, nor since, in any capitalist country, at any time, has industrial employment been significantly more important than it was in Britain in 1955. Yet no sooner had this pre-eminence been achieved than the process went into reverse. Industrial employment began declining in importance, at first slowly and then with gathering speed. By 1984 the share of industry in civil employment had fallen to 34 per cent, and that of manufacturing alone to 26 per cent. To illustrate the scale of the transformation which has occurred since 1955, consider the relationship between industry and the services which is implied by this transformation. In 1955 there were more workers employed in industry than in all of the services combined, both public and private. By 1983 there were almost two service workers for each industrial worker, and the public services alone employed about three-quarters as many people as the whole of manufacturing put together (4.3 million as compared to 5.8 million). Under ideal

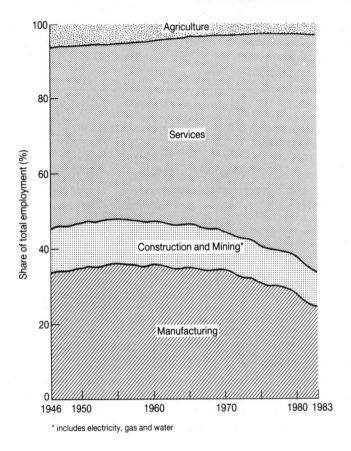

Figure 2.2 Employment in the UK by sector, 1946–83 (percentage shares). (Source: based on historical data from Ministry of Labour and Department of Employment.)

conditions of prosperity and full employment, such a transformation over such a short period of time would have been disruptive. Under the actual conditions of stagnation and unemployment it has been traumatic.

Let us now consider the experience of other countries over the past thirty years. We shall concentrate on the manufacturing sector, but our remarks apply with only minor qualifications to the industrial sector as a whole, including mining and construction. Tables 2.2 and 2.3 show what has happened to manufacturing employment in the advanced capitalist countries over the past thirty years. Wherever possible the figures shown go back to 1955 or even before, although there are gaps caused by a lack of

Table 2.1 Comparative employment structure in the West's most industrialized economies. (Source: OECD – the dates in parentheses refer to the year in which industrial employment reached its all-time peak as a share of civil employment in the country concerned.)

	Industrial employment as % of		Manufacturing employment as % of	
	Civil employment	Population aged 15–64	Civil employment	Population aged 15–64
Belgium (1957)	47.0	26.9	36.0	20.6
Germany (1970)	48.5	33.1	37.7	25.8
Luxemburg (1966)	46.9	28.8	35.8	22.0
Switzerland (1963)	47.6	n.a.	38.5	n.a.
UK (1955)	47.9	32.8	36.1	24.7

reliable information. Table 2.2 shows the average annual growth rate in manufacturing employment in three distinct periods: 1955–66, 1966–73 and 1973–83. Looking at these growth rates the following points stand out. In the first period manufacturing employment increased in every country shown, often at an extremely high rate. In the second period growth continued in most countries, although at a slower pace; moreover there were a few countries in which manufacturing employment began to fall. Finally, in the third period there was an almost universal decline in manufacturing employment with only three minor exceptions: Finland, Iceland and New Zealand. Thus, the first period is one of general expansion in manufacturing employment, the second is a period of transition and the third is one of general contraction. Comparing Britain's performance with that of other countries, we find that between 1956 and 1966 manufacturing employment grew more slowly in Britain than in any other country shown in Table 2.2; between 1966 and 1973 it fell by more than in any other country with the exception of Sweden; and between 1973 and 1983 it fell by more than in any other country with the exception of Belgium. Taking the period 1955–83 as a whole, or even the subperiod 1966–83, we find that Britain has experienced the greatest percentage decline of manufacturing employment of any Western country.

Looking at relative shares the picture is not quite so clear as in the case of absolute numbers. Between 1955 and 1981 the share of manufacturing in civil employment in Britain fell by 9.7 percentage points, from 36.1 per cent to 26.4 per cent. This is certainly a much greater reduction than occurred in most of the other countries shown in Table 2.3. However,

Table 2.2 Manufacturing employment in the advanced capitalist countries.

	Annual percentage change			Cumulative percentage change	
	1955–66	1966–73	1973–83	1955–66	1966–83
Italy	1.0	2.0	−0.9	10.3	5.3
Japan	3.9	2.9	−0.4	47.3	18.3
Finland	n.a.	1.6	0.5	n.a.	17.5
Austria	n.a.	n.a.	−0.6	n.a.	n.a.
Iceland[1,2]	1.5[1]	2.1	2.8	15.6	52.1
France	0.8	0.6	−1.9	8.7	−14.0
Norway	n.a.	n.a.	−0.9	n.a.	n.a.
Denmark[2]	2.2	−1.2	−1.9	24.5	−24.4
Canada	2.4	1.4	−0.4	26.5	6.7
Luxemburg[1]	1.3[1]	0.9	−2.3	14.3	−15.5
Germany	1.2	0.2	−1.9	12.2	−16.2
Sweden[1]	1.0[1]	−1.3	−1.2	10.7	−18.8
Switzerland[1]	1.7[1]	−0.2	−2.0	18.5	−19.9
New Zealand[1]	n.a.	1.9	0.4	n.a.	18.9
Netherlands	1.0	−0.8	−2.4	11.0	−25.7
Australia	n.a.	1.7	−2.7	n.a.	−14.3
Belgium[2]	0.6	−0.3	−3.4	7.1	−30.8
USA	1.3	0.7	−0.4	13.5	0.6
UK	0.4	−1.2	−3.1	4.1	−33.2

[1] Initial date is 1957, estimate for cumulative change 1955–66 is based on annual growth rate 1957–66.
[2] Terminal date is 1981, estimate for cumulative change 1966–83 is based on annual growth rates for 1966–73 and 1973–81.

enormous though it is, even greater reductions were recorded in Australia and Belgium, where the share of manufacturing fell by 10.2 and 10.6 percentage points respectively. Thus, if we take as our index the share of manufacturing in civil employment, the extent of de-industrialization over the thirty years has been much greater in Britain than in most other advanced capitalist countries, although slightly less than in Australia and Belgium.

Table 2.3   Share of manufacturing in civil employment, 1950–81.
(Source: diverse OECD publications and Bairoch (1968).)

	Percentage share					Change
	1950	1955	1966	1973	1981	1955–81
Italy	n.a.	20.0	25.8	28.5	26.1	+6.1
Japan	n.a.	18.4	24.4	27.4	24.8	+6.4
Finland[3]	n.a.	21.3	22.8	25.4	26.1	+4.8
Austria[1]	n.a.	29.8[1]	29.8	29.7	29.7	−0.1
Iceland[3]	21.5	23.7	25.5	25.2	26.3	+2.6
France	n.a.	26.9	28.7	28.3	25.1	−1.8
Norway	22.0	23.1	23.7	23.5	20.2	−2.9
Denmark	n.a.	27.5	29.0	24.7	21.3	−6.2
Canada	24.9	24.1	23.9	22.0	19.4	−4.7
Luxemburg[2]	n.a.	33.2	35.8	33.8	27.4	−5.8
Germany	n.a.	33.8	35.2	36.7	33.6	−0.2
Sweden[2]	n.a.	31.7	31.2	27.5	23.3	−8.4
Switzerland[3]	n.a.	36.1	37.8	35.0	32.0	−4.1
New Zealand[3]	n.a.	23.7	25.4	25.7	24.0	+0.3
Netherlands	29.3	29.3	28.9	25.7	21.1	−8.2
Australia[3]	n.a.	29.6	28.6	25.6	19.4	−10.2
Belgium	35.0	35.3	33.6	31.8	24.7	−10.6
USA	27.9	28.5	27.8	24.8	21.7	−6.8
UK	34.8	36.1	34.8	32.3	26.4	−9.7

[1] Initial date is 1956, figure in the final column refers to 1956–81.

[2] Figure in second column is for 1957, figure in the final column refers to 1957–81.

[3] Figure in second column is for 1959, figure in the final column refers to 1959–81.

■ Towards an explanation: three theses

Whether we consider relative shares or absolute numbers the decline in manufacturing employment in Britain has been spectacular. What accounts for it? Why did this decline begin so much earlier in Britain than in most other countries and why has it been so great? In this chapter we shall examine three potential explanations for what has happened. For convenience we shall call these: the Maturity Thesis, the Specialization Thesis, and the Failure Thesis.

☐ The Maturity Thesis

The first thesis locates Britain's own historical experience within a more general theory of economic development and structural change. This theory asserts that, in any country which develops, the structure of employment undergoes the following sequence of transformations. When development first gets under way the share of industry in total employment rises rapidly. After a time this share stabilizes. Then, at a certain point, it starts to fall. An economy which has reached this final stage is said to be 'mature'. The reason why the share of industry falls in the final stage of development can be readily appreciated by means of a diagram. Figure 2.3 shows in a stylized form what happens to the structure of employment in the course of development. From the diagram we can see how development is accompanied by a continuous rise in the share of services in total employment. We can also see how the impact of this on the industrial sector depends on what stage of development the economy has reached. When development first gets under way, services grow at the expense of agriculture, and their share in total employment rises while that of agriculture falls. Meanwhile the share of industrial employment rises. Thus, in relative terms, both industry and the service sector increase their share at the expense of agriculture. In the intermediate stage of development the share of industry stabilizes, while the share of services continues to rise at the expense of agriculture. Eventually, in the final stage of development, the share of industry starts to fall. The reason for this is obvious from Figure 2.3. In the final stage only a small fraction of the labour force is employed in agriculture and the vast majority work in industry or the services. Under these conditions any major rise in the share of services in total employment must be at the expense of industry. As a matter of arithmetic the share of industry must fall. There is simply no other way in which the service sector can continue to increase its share in total employment.

Thus, at first the service sector increases its share at the expense of agriculture. Later, as the potential for this kind of expansion is exhausted, the services increase their share at the expense of industry. Here in a nutshell is the maturity thesis. It explains why in a mature economy the share of industry in total employment falls in the course of time. The entire argument rests, of course, on the assumption that the share of services in total employment rises continuously as the economy develops. There is considerable evidence for this assumption, some of which is reviewed below.[1] Note that the Maturity Thesis is primarily about relative shares

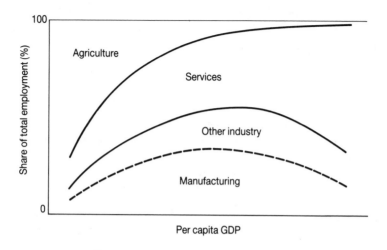

Figure 2.3   Employment structure and economic development.

and not absolute numbers. The absolute number of people employed in the industrial sector depends on the behaviour of total employment. Where total employment is growing rapidly the relative share of industry may fall by a considerable amount without any reduction at all in the absolute number of people employed in this sector. Indeed, this number may actually rise.[2] On the other hand, where total employment is increasing slowly, any major reduction in the relative share of industry will be accompanied by an absolute fall in industrial employment.

One cannot lay down a mechanical rule to determine exactly when any particular economy will reach maturity as there are many different factors which can influence the turning-point. However, from evidence considered elsewhere, it seems that the typical capitalist economy reaches maturity when per capita GDP is in the region of 4000 US dollars (at 1975 prices).[3] At this stage agriculture normally accounts for between 5 and 10 per cent of total employment, although the figure may be higher, depending on the economy concerned and its pattern of specialization.

The maturity thesis is of obvious relevance to Britain in the 1950s. At that time Britain was still one of the most advanced countries in the world and was just approaching maturity. Per capita income in 1955 was $3305 (at 1975 prices), which is not far short of the turning-point at which the share of industry in total employment starts to fall. Moreover, agriculture accounted for only 5 per cent of total employment, so any substantial rise in the share of services, however caused, could only come at the expense of industry. The situation was very different in other

Table 2.4   Employment structure and stage of development.

	Percentage share of civil employment				Change		
	1955	*1966*	*1973*	*1981*	*1955–73*	*1973–81*	*1955–81*
Agriculture							
Group A (immature)	31.0	20.6	14.1	9.9	−16.9	−4.2	−21.1
Group B (transitional)	14.6	9.3	7.0	5.8	−7.6	−1.2	−8.8
UK (mature)	5.4	3.6	2.9	2.6	−2.5	−0.3	−2.8
Manufacturing							
Group A (immature)	23.8	26.2	26.6	25.0	+2.8	−1.6	+1.2
Group B (transitional)	30.5	30.8	28.9	24.7	−1.6	−4.6	−5.8
UK (mature)	36.1	34.8	32.3	26.4	−3.8	−5.9	−9.7
Industry							
Group A (immature)	33.0	36.6	37.2	34.9	+4.2	−2.3	+1.9
Group B (transitional)	40.7	41.2	38.6	33.7	−2.1	−4.9	−7.0
UK (mature)	47.9	46.3	42.6	35.7	−5.3	−6.9	−12.2
Services							
Group A (immature)	36.0	42.8	48.7	55.2	−12.7	+6.5	+19.2
Group B (transitional)	44.7	49.5	54.4	60.5	+9.7	+6.1	+15.8
UK (mature)	46.7	50.1	54.5	61.7	+7.8	+7.2	+15.0

Note   The group figures refer to an unweighted average of the countries concerned. Group A contains those advanced capitalist countries in which the share of agriculture in civil employment was greater than 21.0 per cent in 1955, viz. Italy, Japan, Finland, Austria, Iceland, France, Norway and Denmark. Group B contains those countries in which the agricultural share was between 9.7 and 18.0 per cent in 1955, viz. Canada, Luxemburg, Germany, Sweden, Switzerland, New Zealand, Netherlands, Australia, Belgium, and the USA. The UK, with an agricultural share of 5.4 per cent in 1955, is the only advanced capitalist country not in one of these groups.

Western countries. Some were still relatively poor and had enormous reserves of labour in agriculture. These countries were nowhere near mature, and there was ample room for services to increase their share of employment at the expense of agriculture without significantly affecting the share of industry. Others were more advanced, but even in these countries the share of agriculture in total employment was considerably higher than in the UK, and in this respect their economies were less mature.

The contrast in experience between Britain and other countries can be seen from Table 2.4 which shows how the structure of employment has

Table 2.5 Summary of employment changes, 1955–81 (change in percentage share). (Source: last column of Table 2.4.)

	Group A (immature)	Group B (transitional)	UK (mature)
Agriculture	−21.1	−8.8	−2.8
Industry	+1.9	−7.0	−12.2
Services	+19.2	+15.8	+15.0
	0.0	0.0	0.0

evolved since 1955, the year in which the share of manufacturing, and that of industry as a whole, reached a peak in Britain. Countries have been divided into three groups, depending on how agrarian they were in 1955. At one extreme are the 'immature' economies in group A, all of which were still agrarian in character in 1955, having more than 21 per cent of their employed labour force in agriculture. At the other extreme is the UK which forms a group of its own, being the least agrarian economy in the world in 1955 with just over 5 per cent of its labour force in agriculture. Between these two extremes lie the transitional economies of group B, all of which were still moderately agrarian in character in 1955, with agriculture accounting for between 9 and 18 per cent of total employment.

From Table 2.4 we can see how the share of services has risen dramatically in all of the countries shown since 1955. In the immature economies of group A this increase has been matched by an almost equal reduction in the share of agriculture; as a result the share of industry has hardly altered. This can be seen from Table 2.5 which summarizes some of the information given in Table 2.4. Between 1955 and 1981 the share of services in total employment rose from 36.0 per cent to 55.2 per cent in the immature economies of group A – a rise of 19.2 points. Over the same period the share of agriculture fell from 31.0 per cent to 9.9 per cent – a fall of 21.1 points. Meanwhile the share of industry rose very slightly, from 33.0 per cent in 1955 to 34.9 per cent in 1981. At the other extreme is the UK, where the relative expansion of services has been almost entirely at the expense of industry. Between 1955 and 1981 the share of services in total employment rose from 46.7 per cent to 61.7 per cent in the UK – an increase of 15.0 points. There was some decline in agriculture, whose share fell by 2.8 points, but the vast bulk of service expansion was at the expense of industry, whose share fell by 12.2 points. This is hardly surprising. Given the small size of the agricultural sector at the beginning of the period (5.4 per cent) it was mathematically impossible for this sector to shrink sufficiently to offset a 15.0 per cent rise in the share of services. As a matter of arithmetic, such a rise in the *share* of services could only be at the expense of industry, whose *share* was bound to fall.

Thus, at one extreme are the immature economies of group A where, as a rule, services have increased their share at the expense of agriculture, leaving industry largely unaffected.[4] At the other extreme is the UK, which had virtually no agricultural employment in 1955, and where the relative expansion in services has been almost entirely at the expense of industry. Between these two extremes are the transitional economies of group B. These countries were moderately agrarian to start with and on average the increased share of services since 1955 has been at the expense of both agriculture and industry, almost equally (see Table 2.5).[5]

To explore this point a little further let us go back to Tables 2.2 and 2.3. The countries shown in these tables are arranged in a definite order, being ranked according to the share of agriculture in total employment in 1955. Thus, at the top of the list is Italy where the share of agriculture was 40.8 per cent in 1955; at the bottom is the UK where the share was only 5.4 per cent. Looking at the tables we find a clear pattern. The more agrarian economies, towards the top of the list, have normally experienced either faster growth, or a smaller fall, in manufacturing employment. Conversely, the least agrarian economies towards the bottom of the list have experienced the greatest fall in manufacturing employment, either absolutely or as a share of total employment. This is exactly what we should expect from our discussion about maturity and structural change. In every economy service employment expands either absolutely or relatively in the course of development. In agrarian economies this expansion is at the expense of agriculture, while in mature, non-agrarian economies it is mainly at the expense of manufacturing and other industrial sectors. This explains why in agrarian economies, economic development will be accompanied by an increase in manufacturing employment, either absolutely or as a share of total employment; while in non-agrarian economies the opposite will normally be the case.

Quite apart from the light they throw on structural change in general, Tables 2.2 and 2.3 tell us something about the British economy. As the least agrarian economy Britain lies at the bottom in each table, and this in itself helps to explain why the fall in manufacturing employment, both absolutely and relatively, has been so great. Here, then, we have a possible explanation for the fall in industrial employment so early in Britain and why the decline has been so intense. By the mid-1950s the British economy was already close to maturity. The share of agriculture in total employment was already very small, and any major rise in the share of services – however caused – could only be at the expense of industry. The situation in most other capitalist countries was quite different. Many of them still had enormous reserves of labour in agriculture; they had not yet reached the stage of development in which economic growth involves an absolute or relative decline in industrial employment. Thus, from the evidence we have examined so far the maturity thesis looks quite convincing. It certainly helps to explain why the decline in industrial employment began earlier in Britain and has been more extensive than in most other countries. It is further supported by the fact that many other capitalist countries began to experience a similar decline in industrial employment in the 1960s and 1970s, as their reserves of agricultural labour were depleted and they reached the stage of maturity where the service sector increases its share of employment at the expense of industry.

□   The Trade Specialization Thesis

A second potential explanation for the decline in manufacturing employment in Britain is concerned with foreign trade, with the huge changes which have occurred over the past thirty years in Britain's role in the international division of labour. These changes are described at length in [Rowthorn and Wells, 1986], so here we shall only outline their main features.[6] By the time post-war recovery was complete in 1950 Britain had become a highly specialized 'workshop' economy, importing vast amounts of food and raw materials, and also oil, in return for manufactured exports. This can be seen from Figure 2.4, which shows what has happened to Britain's trade in manufactures and non-manufactures (including services) since 1950. In the years 1950–52 there was a surplus on manufacturing trade equal to some 10 per cent of GDP on average, while on non-manufacturing trade there was an even larger deficit. These are truly remarkable figures which have never been equalled, before or since, in British history and never surpassed elsewhere, not even in those archetypal 'workshop' economies of Germany and Japan. The reasons for such a remarkable situation are, briefly, as follows. On the non-manufacturing side global scarcities in the aftermath of the Second World War had forced up to unprecedented levels the cost of items which Britain had always imported in bulk, such as food and raw materials. Moreover Britain's previously massive income from service activities, such as shipping and the City of London, had fallen substantially, while receipts from her once considerable coal exports had almost vanished. This combination of inflated import prices and lost export earnings explains why the deficit on non-manufacturing trade was so large in the early 1950s. To cover this deficit Britain had no alternative but to export manufactured goods. Her profits from foreign investments had been greatly reduced by the enforced wartime sale of her overseas assets and her ability to borrow was limited. So, to finance the huge trade deficit in non-manufactures Britain required a surplus of roughly equal proportions in her manufacturing trade. This surplus she achieved through a vigorous combination of industrial protection and export promotion.

The early 1950s marked the high point of Britain's role as a

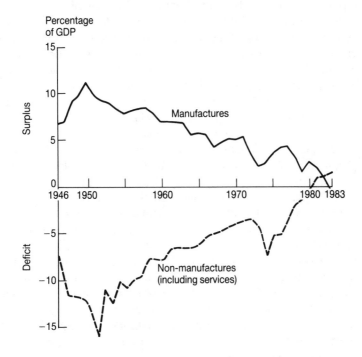

Figure 2.4   UK balance of trade, 1946–83 (as a percentage of GDP). (Source: adapted from Rowthorn and Wells (1986).)

workshop economy. Since then the picture has been transformed beyond recognition. In non-manufacturing trade the old deficit has disappeared completely to be replaced by a small surplus, of around 1 per cent of GDP in 1981–83; in manufacturing trade the opposite has occurred and the old surplus has been replaced by a small deficit (see Figure 2.4). This transformation is often cited as evidence of Britain's industrial decline, of the failure of her manufacturing industry to compete internationally. However, such an interpretation is largely unfounded. Certainly the performance of manufacturing industry has been very poor over the past thirty years, but this is not what explains the dramatic transformation which has occurred in the structure of trade. The origins of this transformation are to be found in events largely unrelated to the country's industrial performance. Since the early 1950s there has been a whole stream of autonomous developments on the non-manufacturing side whose cumulative impact on Britain's trade structure and pattern of specialization has been enormous.

Imports of food and raw materials have become much cheaper in real terms; increased domestic food production has reduced the need for food imports; new methods of production and a changing composition of output has reduced the need for imported raw materials; service exports in such areas as civil aviation, construction and finance have risen; finally, the discovery of North Sea oil has turned Britain into a major oil-producer. Between them, these developments explain why the balance in non-manufacturing trade has improved so much over the past thirty years. They also explain why the balance of trade in manufactures has deteriorated so much over this period. In the early 1950s Britain was a 'workshop' economy because she had to be. To finance the huge deficit in non-manufacturing trade the country required a huge surplus on manufacturing trade. There was simply no other way to remain solvent. Nowadays, however, the situation is quite different. The deficit on non-manufacturing trade has disappeared and with it has gone the need for a huge surplus on manufacturing trade. Hence the deterioration in the manufacturing balance. Britain is no longer a massive net exporter of manufactures because she no longer needs to be, and industrial performance has only a marginal bearing on the matter. The marked decline in Britain's manufacturing surplus over the past thirty years is not a symptom of industrial failure, but is mainly a response to autonomous developments elsewhere in the economy. Autonomous developments in non-manufacturing trade have led to a new pattern of specialization, a new role for Britain in the world economy, of which the loss of a formerly huge manufacturing surplus is but one expression.

Now, for obvious reasons, a country's internal pattern of employment depends on its pattern of specialization, on its role in the international division of labour. *Ceteris paribus*, a 'workshop' economy such as that of Britain in the early 1950s, with her huge surplus of manufactured exports, will have a much larger manufacturing sector than a country such as the USA, whose trade structure is more balanced. Moreover, when an economy ceases to be a workshop economy and develops a new, less specialized pattern of trade its manufacturing sector is likely to contract, relatively, if not absolutely. Here then is a potential explanation for what has happened to manufacturing employment in Britain over the past thirty years. In the early 1950s, Britain was a highly specialized industrial producer, perhaps the most extreme example of a workshop economy the world has ever seen. This in itself helps to explain why such a large fraction of her labour force was employed in the manufacturing sector. Since those days, however, because of autonomous developments in non-manufacturing trade, the British economy has become much less specialized. Britain no longer requires a large surplus on her manufacturing trade and, as a result, no longer needs to employ anything like such a large fraction of her labour force in manufacturing. Moreover, no other country has experienced such a massive transformation in its pattern of trade over the past thirty years. No other country, not even Australia or Norway, has experienced such a vast improvement in its non-manufacturing balance over the period, nor such a deterioration in its manufacturing balance. This may help to explain why the decline in manufacturing employment has been so much greater in Britain than in most other countries.

□   The Failure Thesis

So far we have considered two explanations for the decline of manufacturing employment in Britain. There was the maturity thesis, which located our industrial decline within the framework of a general theory of development and structural change. Britain, it argued, was the first country to reach the stage of development known as 'maturity', in which the share of manufacturing in total employment starts to fall. This in itself helps to explain why the decline in manufacturing employment began so much earlier in Britain than elsewhere and has been so much greater. A very different explanation was put forward by the trade specialization thesis. According to this thesis the decline in manufacturing employment is merely an internal consequence of Britain's changing external relations with other countries, of the huge improvements which have occurred in the realm of non-manufacturing trade since the early 1950s. Thus, one thesis argues that a fall in manufacturing employment was inevitable given the stage of development Britain had reached by the 1950s, while the other argues that improvements in non-manufacturing trade are responsible for this decline.

There is, however, a third possible explanation – the failure thesis. As its name suggests, this thesis sees the decline of manufacturing employment as a symptom of economic *failure*: of a growing failure on the part of manufacturing industry to compete internationally or to produce the output required for a prosperous and fully employed economy. The failure thesis can be summarized in the following propositions:

1. Britain's economic record in the realm of incomes and employment has been poor.
2. This is largely explained by the weak performance of manufacturing industry.
3. If the manufacturing sector had been much stronger, output in the sector would have been much greater.
4. This would have stimulated the non-manufacturing side of the economy and led to the creation of more employment in services and other non-manufacturing activities.
5. Finally, if the manufacturing sector had been much stronger, neither the absolute number of people employed in manufacturing, nor the

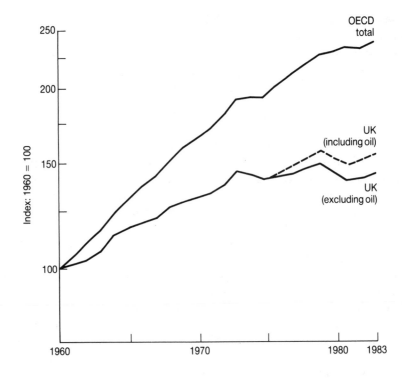

Figure 2.5   GDP in the UK and OECD, 1960–83. (Sources: OECD and *Economic Trends.*)

share of this sector in total employment, would have fallen anything like so fast as they have done.

Many of these propositions are uncontroversial and are universally accepted by economists of all persuasions. Even so, let us examine them briefly.[7]

Consider the question of Britain's economic record. Here the evidence is overwhelming. By international standards, real incomes have risen slowly in Britain. Moreover since 1973 the growth in GDP has been entirely the result of North Sea oil-production; indeed, between 1973 and 1983 non-oil GDP actually fell by 2 per cent (Figure 2.5). The cumulative effect of slow growth on Britain's position in the international hierarchy can be seen from Table 2.6. In 1953 she was among the half-dozen richest countries in the world. By 1983, of all the advanced capitalist countries, Britain was among the poorest. In the realm of employment the picture is much the same. In the 1950s there was almost full employment in Britain, and the bulk of her population had never enjoyed greater economic

Table 2.6   GDP per head in selected countries ($ US 1975).[1] (Source: OECD.)

	1953	1963	1973	1983	Percentage growth per annum, 1953–83
Canada	3896	4688	7030	7701	2.3
USA	4946	5503	7371	8037	1.6
Japan	1054	2245	4974	6010	5.8
Australia	3074	3884	5337	5611	2.0
Austria	1735	3031	4785	5610	3.9
Belgium	2499	3384	5253	5860	2.8
France	2432	3476	5437	6280	3.2
Germany	2319	3866	5628	6291	3.3
Italy	1814	2903	4363	4600	3.1
Netherlands	2694	3639	5502	5815	2.6
Norway	3067	4058	5716	7347	2.9
Sweden	3536	4993	6769	7311	2.4
Unweighted average	2756	3806	5680	6373	2.8
UK	3125	3855	5097	5506	1.9

[1] Exchange rates are based on purchasing-power parity.

security. By 1983 well over 3 million people were out of work and, of all the advanced capitalist countries, only Belgium had a greater fraction of her labour force unemployed (see Table 2.7). Not since the 1930s have so many British people faced such a bleak and insecure future.

What about the role of manufacturing in all this? Here again the evidence is overwhelming. By international standards the performance of British manufacturing industry has been very poor, especially since the oil crisis of 1973, and even more so since the Thatcher government took office in 1979. Prior to 1973 both output and productivity rose quite fast in Britain in comparison with past historical experiences, but they rose even faster in many other countries. As a result, despite moderately fast industrial growth, Britain was overtaken by many of her foreign rivals during this period, and by the time the world crisis broke at the end of 1973 she was no longer a first-rank industrial power. Thus, up to 1973, the decline of British manufacturing was relative rather than absolute. Since then, however, Britain's decline has become absolute. Manufacturing industry has experienced a large fall in output, most of which has occurred

Table 2.7   Unemployment rates in selected OECD countries[1] (percentage of total labour force). (Source: OECD, *Economic Outlook* and *Main Economic Indicators*.)

	1964–73	1974–9	1980	1981	1982	1983	1984
USA	4.4	6.6	7.0	7.5	9.5	9.5	7.4
Germany	0.8	3.2	3.0	4.4	6.1	8.0	8.6
France	2.2	4.5	6.3	7.3	8.1	8.3	9.7
Italy	5.5	6.6	7.4	8.3	9.0	9.8	10.2
Canada	4.7	7.2	7.5	7.5	10.9	11.8	11.2
Australia	1.9	5.0	6.0	5.7	7.1	9.9	8.9
Belgium	2.2	3.8	9.0	11.1	12.6	13.9	14.0
Netherlands	1.4	3.8	4.9	7.5	11.4	13.7	14.0
Japan	1.2	1.9	2.0	2.2	2.4	2.6	2.7
Norway	1.7	1.8	1.7	2.0	2.6	3.3	3.0
Sweden	2.0	1.9	2.0	2.5	3.1	3.5	3.1
Austria	1.5	1.6	1.9	2.5	3.5	4.1	4.0
Unweighted average	2.5	4.0	4.9	5.7	7.2	8.2	8.1
UK	3.1	5.0	6.9	11.0	12.3	13.1	13.2

[1] Standardized to accord with the International Labour Organization definition of unemployment.

since 1979. Meanwhile output has continued to rise in other major OECD countries, albeit irregularly (see Figure 2.6). Between 1973 and 1982 manufacturing output in the major six fell by 18 per cent on average.[8] In the realm of labour productivity Britain's performance has also been poor by international standards since 1973. Despite a spectacular labour shake-out in vehicles, steel and certain other industries after 1979, output per person-hour in British manufacturing rose by only 2.0 per cent per annum over the decade 1973–83, as compared with an average of 3.0 per cent per annum in the six major OECD countries. Although accurate comparisons in this field are notoriously difficult, available statistics establish beyond doubt that labour productivity in manufacturing industry is now much lower in Britain than elsewhere in the advanced capitalist world.

The weakness of manufacturing industry is certainly the main reason why Britain has become a relatively poor country, why per capita incomes in Britain are now the lowest in northern Europe. It also helps to explain why the unemployment rate is so high. Consider what it would mean if Britain's manufacturing industry were much stronger and more competi-

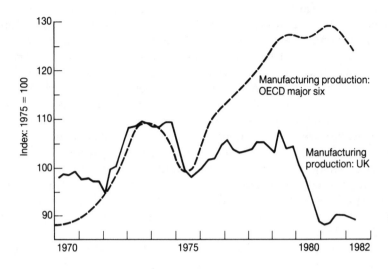

Figure 2.6   Manufacturing output in the UK and the OECD, 1970–82. (Sources: OECD and *Economic Trends*.)

tive than it is at present, having more equipment, using more advanced methods of production, and producing a wider range of higher quality output. For a start, manufacturing output would obviously be much greater. Part of this additional output would go directly to meet domestic requirements, and part would be exported in payment for goods and services purchased from other countries. Some of these additional imports would be non-manufactures, such as raw materials or services; but there would also be a large increase in manufactured imports. Taking account of both the additional supplies from domestic industry and the additional imports from elsewhere, the total amount of manufactured goods available for home use would rise considerably. Since the production and distribution of manufactured goods involves a wide range of complementary activities, output would also rise in such areas as construction, mining, consulting finance, transport and retail distribution. Moreover, real incomes would be higher and, consequently, consumers' expenditure of almost every kind would be greater; as, indeed, would public expenditure on items such as health and education. Thus, with a stronger manufacturing sector, output would be greater in almost every sector of the economy.

What about employment? Would it also be greater? In considering this question we must distinguish between total employment in the economy as a whole and employment in particular industries or sectors. Taking the economy as a whole, there is no doubt that total employment would be greater than it is, if Britain's manufacturing industry had been stronger and had performed better over the past thirty years. The weakness of manufacturing industry has been responsible for the inflation and balance-of-payments crisis which have plagued the country over this period. In the face of these problems successive governments, Tory and Labour alike, have imposed deflationary measures which reduce employment in the short term and inhibit its longer-term growth. With a stronger manufacturing industry, there would have been less need for such measures. Inflationary pressures would have been weaker, because more output would have been available to meet the competing claims of workers, employers and the state; and the balance of payments would have been stronger because British industry would have been more competitive in world markets. Thus, governments could have pursued more expansionary policies without jeopardizing their targets for inflation and the balance of payments and, as a result, the overall level of employment would have been much higher.

How would this increase in total employment have been distributed between one sector of the economy and another? In particular, how would employment in the manufacturing sector itself have been affected, and what would have happened to the share of this sector in total employment? To answer these questions by means of *a priori* argument is not easy, and specific numerical estimates are required if one is to go beyond the most general of observations. Such estimates are provided in the longer study mentioned at the beginning of this chapter, but here we must be content with a few general remarks.

If manufacturing industry had performed much better over the past thirty years we can assume that almost every major sector of the economy, including manufacturing itself, would have gained some of the extra jobs; either new jobs would have been created or old jobs saved. As a result more people would now be employed in construction, the services and, of course, in manufacturing itself.[9] Thus, employment would be greater than it now is in both manufacturing and non-manufacturing alike. However, this still leaves open several possibilities. Suppose the superior performance in manufacturing had been accompanied by an enormous rise in labour productivity. Then relatively few additional jobs would have been created in the manufacturing sector itself, despite a massive increase in the output of this sector; and most of the additional employment would have been in non-manufacturing, especially the services. In this case the *share* of manufacturing in total employment would have fallen as fast or even faster than it has actually done in reality. Conversely, suppose the superior performance in manufacturing industry had been accompanied by only a modest increase in labour productivity – an unlikely, but logically conceivable, combination. Then many of the additional jobs would have been in the manufacturing sector itself. As a result the *share* of manufacturing in total employment would by now be much larger than it is; and over the past thirty years this share would have fallen much less than it has done. Both these scenarios are logically conceivable and on *a priori* grounds alone there is no way of choosing between them. However, simulations by the author suggest that the former scenario is closer to the truth. According to these simulations industrial failure is of minor importance in explaining the fall in manufacturing employment. Had manufacturing industry been stronger, employment in this sector would still have fallen dramatically, and only a few hundred thousand jobs would have been saved. Moreover, the share of manufacturing in total employment would have fallen even more than it has done in reality. If these simulations are any guide the dramatic decline in manufacturing employment is not the result of poor industrial performance. It is almost entirely the result of other factors and would have occurred no matter how good the performance of British industry.

■ Concluding remarks

The preceding discussion may be summarized as follows. Britain was the first country to reach the stage of 'maturity' at which services increase their share of employment at the expense of manufacturing and other 'production' industries. Moreover the country has experienced massive changes in her pattern of trade specialization. Because of huge improvements in non-manufacturing trade she no longer needs such a large surplus on her manufacturing trade, and fewer people are now required to produce this surplus than was formerly the case. Between them these two factors – maturity and trade specialization – account for virtually all of the decline in manufacturing employment. Poor industrial performance is of only minor importance in explaining this decline. Had manufacturing industry been stronger, manufacturing employment would still have fallen dramatically. For a more detailed assessment of the quantitative influence of the various factors considered in this chapter the reader is referred to Rowthorn and Wells (1986).

Notes

1. For a more extensive treatment of this subject see Rowthorn and Wells (1986) ch. 1.
2. For example, in the USA, the number of people employed in manufacturing rose by 5.2 per cent between 1970 and 1981. However, total employment rose by 27.6 per cent over the same period, so the share of manufacturing fell considerably, despite an increase in the absolute number employed in this sector. The USA is unusual in this respect. In most other countries a falling

share of manufacturing in total employment has been accompanied by a decline in the absolute number of people working in this sector.

3. See Rowthorn and Wells (op. cit.) ch. 1.
4. An exception to this rule is Denmark, which belongs to group A, but has also experienced a big fall in the share of industry in total employment.
5. The principal exception here is Germany, where the share of industry hardly changed at all between 1955 and 1981.
6. See Rowthorn and Wells (op. cit.) chs 5 and 6.
7. For a clear statement of the Failure Thesis see Singh (1977) or Thirlwall (1982).
8. The six major OECD countries referred to here are: the USA, Canada, Japan, France, Germany and Italy.
9. See Rowthorn and Wells (op. cit.).

References

Bairoch, P., *et al.* (1968) *The Working Population and its Structure,* (Université Libre de Brussel, Institut de Sociologie).

Rowthorn, R. E., and Wells, J. R. (1986) *De-industrialisation and Foreign Trade: Britain's Decline in a Global Perspective,* (Cambridge: Cambridge University Press).

Singh, A. (1977) 'UK industry and the world economy: a case of de-industrialisation?', *Cambridge Journal of Economics,* **1**, 2, pp. 113–36.

Thirlwall, A. P. (1982) 'De-industrialization in the United Kingdom', *Lloyds Bank Review* (April), pp. 22–37.

Chapter 3

Fordism and Post-Fordism

R. Murray

During the first two centuries of the industrial revolution the focus of employment shifted from the farm to the factory. It is now shifting once more, from the factory to the office and the shop. A third of Britain's paid labour force now works in offices. A third of the value of national output is in the distribution sector. Meanwhile 2.5 million jobs have been lost in British manufacturing since 1960. If the Ford plants at Halewood and Dagenham represented late industrialism, Centrepoint and Habitat are the symbols of a new age.

The Right portrayed the growth of services as a portent of a post-industrial society with growing individualism, a weakened state and a multiplicity of markets. I want to argue that it reflects a deeper change in the production process. It is one that affects manufacturing and agriculture as well as services, and has implications for the way in which we think about socialist alternatives. I see this as a shift from the dominant form of 20th-century production, known as Fordism, to a new form, post-Fordism.

Fordism is an industrial era whose secret is to be found in the mass-production systems pioneered by Henry Ford. These systems were based on four principles, from which all else followed:

1. Products were standardized; this meant that each part and each task could also be standardized. Unlike craft production – where each part had to be specially designed, made and fitted – for a run of mass-produced cars, the same headlight could be fitted to the same model in the same way.

2. If tasks are the same, then some can be mechanized; thus mass-production plants developed special-purpose machinery for each

Source: R. Murray (1989) 'Fordism and Post-Fordism', in *New Times*, S. Hall and M. Jacques (eds), Lawrence & Wishart, London, pp. 38–53.

model, much of which could not be switched from product to product.

3. Those tasks which remained were subject to scientific management or Taylorism, whereby any task was broken down into its component parts, redesigned by work-study specialists on time-and-motion principles, who then instructed manual workers on how the job should be done.

4. Flowline replaced nodal assembly, so that instead of workers moving to and from the product (the node), the product flowed past the workers.

Ford did not invent these principles. What he did was to combine them in the production of a complex commodity, which undercut craft-made cars as decisively as the handloom weavers had been undercut in the 1830s. Ford's Model T sold for less than a tenth of the price of a craft-built car in the USA in 1916, and he took 50 per cent of the market.

This revolutionary production system was to transform sector after sector during the 20th century, from processed food to furniture, clothes, cookers, and even ships after the Second World War. The economies came from the scale of production, for although mass production might be more costly to set up because of the purpose-built machinery, once in place the cost of an extra unit was discontinuously cheap.

Many of the structures of Fordism followed from this tension between high fixed costs and low variable ones, and the consequent drive for volume. First, as Ford himself emphasized, mass production presupposes mass consumption. Consumers must be willing to buy standardized products. Mass advertising played a central part in establishing a mass-consumption norm. So did the provision of the infrastructure of consumption – housing and roads. To ensure that the road system dominated over rail, General Motors, Standard Oil and Firestone Tyres bought up and then dismantled the electric trolley and transit systems in 44 urban areas.

Second, Fordism was linked to a system of protected national markets, which allowed the mass producers to recoup their fixed costs at home and compete on the basis of marginal costs on the world market, or through the replication of existing models via foreign investment.

Third, mass producers were particularly vulnerable to sudden falls in demand. Ford unsuccessfully tried to offset the effect of the 1930s depression by raising wages. Instalment credit, Keynesian demand and monetary management, and new wage and welfare systems were all more effective in stabilizing the markets for mass producers in the postwar period. Hire purchase and the dole cheque became as much the symbols of the Fordist age as the tower block and the motorway.

The mass producers not only faced the hazard of changes in consumption. With production concentrated in large factories they were also vulnerable to the new 'mass worker' they had created. Like Taylorism, mass production had taken the skill out of work, it fragmented tasks into a set of repetitive movements, and erected a rigid division between mental and manual labour. It treated human beings as interchangeable parts of a machine, paid according to the job they did rather than who they were.

The result was high labour turnover, shopfloor resistance, and strikes. The mass producers in turn sought constant new reservoirs of labour, particularly from groups facing discrimination, from rural areas and from less developed regions abroad. The contractual core of Taylorism – higher wages in return for managerial control of production – still applied, and a system of industrial unions grew up to bargain over these wage levels. In the USA, and to an extent the UK, a national system of wage bargaining developed in the postwar period, centred on high-profile car industry negotiations, that linked wage rises to productivity growth, and then set wage standards for other large-scale producers and the state. It was a system of collective bargaining that has been described as implementing a Keynesian incomes policy without a Keynesian state. As long as the new labour reservoirs could be tapped, it was a system that held together the distinct wage relation of Fordism.

Taylorism was also characteristic of the structure of management and supplier relations. Fordist bureaucracies are fiercely hierarchical, with links between the divisions and departments being made through the centre rather than at the base. Planning is done by specialists; rulebooks and guidelines are issued for lower management to carry out. If you enter a Ford factory in any part of the world, you will find its layout, materials, even the position of its Coca Cola machines, all similar, set up as they are on the basis of a massive construction manual drawn up in Detroit. Managers themselves complain of de-skilling and the lack of room for initiative, as do suppliers who are confined to producing blueprints at a low margin price.

These threads – of production and consumption, of the semi-skilled worker and collective bargaining, of a managed national market and centralized organization – together make up the fabric of Fordism. They have given rise to an economic culture which extends beyond the complex assembly industries, to agriculture, the service industries and parts of the state. It is marked by its commitment to scale and the standard product (whether it is a Mars bar or an episode of *Dallas*); by a competitive strategy based on cost reduction; by authoritarian relations, centralized planning, and a rigid organization built around exclusive job descriptions.

These structures and their culture are often equated with in-dustrialism, and regarded as an inevitable part of the modern age. I am suggesting that they are linked to a particular form of industrialism, one that developed in the late 19th century and reached its most dynamic expression in the postwar boom. Its impact can be felt not just in the economy, but in politics (in the mass party) and in much broader cultural fields – whether American football, or classical ballet (Diaghilev was a Taylorist in dance), industrial design or modern architecture. The technological *hubris* of this outlook, its Faustian bargain of dictatorship in production in exchange for mass consumption, and above all its destructiveness in the name of progress and the economy of time – all this places Fordism at the centre of modernism.

Why we need to understand these deep structures of Fordism is that they are embedded, too, in traditional socialist economics. Soviet-type planning is the apogee of Fordism. Lenin embraced Taylor and the stopwatch. Soviet industrialization was centred on the construction of giant plants, the majority of them based on Western mass-production technology. So deep is the idea of scale burnt into Soviet economics that there is a hairdresser's in Moscow with 120 barbers' chairs. The focus of Soviet production is on volume and because of its lack of consumer discipline it has caricatured certain features of Western mass production, notably a hoarding of stocks, and inadequate quality control.

In social-democratic thinking, state planning has a more modest place. But in the writings of Fabian economists in the 1930s, as in the Morrisonian model of the public corporation, and Labour's postwar policies, we see the same emphasis on centralist planning, scale, Taylorist technology, and hierarchical organization. The image of planning was the railway timetable, the goal of planning was stable demand and cost-reduction. In the welfare state, the idea of the standard product was given a democratic interpretation as the universal service to meet basic needs, and although in Thatcher's Britain this formulation is still important, it effectively forecloses the issue of varied public services and user choice. The shadow of Fordism haunts us even in the terms in which we oppose it.

■ The break-up of Fordism

Fordism as a vision – both Left and Right – had always been challenged, on the shopfloor, in the political party, the seminar room and the studio. In 1968 this challenge exploded in Europe and the USA. It was a cultural as much as an industrial revolt, attacking the central principles of Fordism, its definitions of work and consumption, its shaping of towns and its overriding of nature.

From that time we can see a fracturing of the foundations of predictability on which Fordism was based. Demand became more volatile and fragmented. Productivity growth fell as the result of workplace resistance. The decline in profit drove down investment. Exchange rates were fluctuating, oil prices rose and in 1974 came the greatest slump the West had had since the 1930s.

The consensus response was a Keynesian one, to restore profitability through a managed increase in demand and an incomes policy. For monetarism the route to profitability went through the weakening of labour, a cut in state spending and a reclaiming of the public sector for private accumulation. Economists and politicians were re-fighting the battles of the last slump. Private capital, on the other hand, was dealing with the present one. It was using new technology and new production principles to make Fordism flexible, and in doing so stood much of the old culture on its head.

In Britain, the groundwork for the new system was laid not in manufacturing but in retailing. Since the 1950s, retailers had been using computers to transform the distribution system. All mass producers have the problem of forecasting demand. If they produce too little they lose market share. If they produce too much, they are left with stocks, which are costly to hold or have to be sold at a discount. Retailers face this problem not just for a few products, but for thousands. Their answer has been to develop information and supply systems which allow them to order supplies to coincide with demand. Every evening Sainsbury's receives details of the sales of all 12 000 lines from each of its shops; these are turned into orders for warehouse deliveries for the coming night, and replacement production for the following day. With computerized control of stocks in the shop, transport networks, automatic loading and unloading, Sainsbury's flowline make-to-order system has conquered the Fordist problem of stocks.

They have also overcome the limits of the mass product. For, in contrast to the discount stores which are confined to a few, fast-selling items, Sainsbury's, like the new wave of high-street shops, can handle ranges of products geared to segments of the market. Market niching has become the slogan of the high street. Market researchers break down market by age (youth, young adults, 'grey power'), by household types ('dinkies' [double income, no kids], single-gender couples, one-parent families), by income, occupation, housing and, increasingly, by locality. They analyse 'lifestyles', correlating consumption patterns across commodities, from food to clothing, and health to holidays.

The point of this new anthropology of consumption is to target both product and shops to particular segments. Burton's – once a mass producer with generalized retail outlets – has changed in the 1980s to being a niche market retailer with a team of anthropologists, a group of segmented stores – Top Shop, Top Man, Dorothy Perkins, Principles and Burton's itself – and now has no manufacturing plant of its own. Conran's Storehouse group – Habitat, Heals, Mothercare, Richards and BHS (all geared to different groups) – offers not only clothes, but furniture and furnishings, in other words entire lifestyles. At the heart of Conran's organization in London is what amounts to a factory of 150 designers, with collages of different lifestyles on the wall, Bold Primary, Orchid, mid-Atlantic and the Cottage Garden.

In all these shops the emphasis has shifted from the manufacturer's economies of scale to the retailer's economies of scope. The economies come from offering an integrated range from which customers choose their own basket of products. There is also an economy of innovation, for the modern retail systems allow new product ideas to be tested in practice, through shop sales, and the successful ones then to be ordered for wider distribution. Innovation has become a leading edge of the new competition. Product life has become shorter, for fashion goods and consumer durables.

A centrepiece of this new retailing is design. Designers produce the innovations. They shape the lifestyles. They design the shops, which are described as 'stages' for the act of shopping. There are now 29 000 people working in design consultancies in the UK, which have sales of £1600 million per annum. They are the engineers of designer capitalism. With market researchers, they have steered the high street from being retailers of goods to retailers of style.

These changes are a response to, and a means of shaping, the shift from mass consumption. Instead of keeping up with the Joneses, there has been a move to be different from the Joneses. Many of these differences are vertical, intended to confirm status and class. But some are horizontal, centred around group identities, linked to age, or region or ethnicity. In spite of the fact that basic needs are still unmet, the high street does offer a new variety and creativity in consumption which the Left's puritan tradition should also address. Whatever our responses, the revolution in retailing reflects new principles of production, a new pluralism of products and a new importance for innovation. As such it marks a shift to a post-Fordist age.

There have been parallel shifts in manufacturing, not least in response to the retailers' just-in-time system of ordering. In some sectors, where the manufacturers are little more than subcontractors to the retailers, their flexibility has been achieved at the expense of labour. In others, capital itself has suffered, as furniture retailers like MFI squeeze their suppliers, driving down prices, limiting design, and thereby destroying much of the mass-production furniture industry during the downturns.

But the most successful manufacturing regions have been ones which have linked flexible manufacturing systems with innovative organization and an emphasis on 'customization' design and quality. Part of the flexibility has been achieved through new technology, and the introduction of programmable machines which can switch from product to product with little manual resetting and downtime. Benetton's automatic dyeing plant, for example, allows it to change its colours in time with demand. In the car industry, whereas General Motors took nine hours to change the dyes on its presses in the early 1980s, Toyota has lowered the time to two minutes, and has cut the average lot size of body parts from 5000 to 500 in the process. The line, in short, has become flexible. Instead of using purpose-built machines to make standard products, flexible automation uses general-purpose machines to produce a variety of products.

■ Japanization

Manufacturers have also been adopting the retailers' answer to stocks. The pioneer is Toyota, which stands to the new era as Ford did to the old. Toyoda, the founder of Toyota, inspired by a visit to an American supermarket, applied the just-in-time system to his component suppliers, ordering on the basis of his daily production plans, and getting the components delivered right beside the line. Most of Toyota's components are still produced on the same day as they are assembled.

Toyoda's prime principle of the elimination of wasteful practices meant going beyond the problem of stocks. His firm has used design and materials technology to simplify complex elements, cutting down the number of parts and operations. It adopted a zero-defect policy, developing machines which stopped automatically when a fault occurred, as well as statistical quality-control techniques. As in retailing, the complex web of processes, inside and outside the plant, were coordinated through computers, a process that economists have called systemation (in contrast to automation). The result of these practices is a discontinuous speed-up in what Marx called the circulation of capital. Toyota turns over its materials and products ten times more quickly then Western car producers, saving material and energy in the process.

The key point about the Toyota system, however, is not so much that it speeds up the making of a car. It is that, in order to make these changes, it had adopted quite different methods of labour control and organization. Toyoda saw that traditional Taylorism did not work. Central management had no access to all the information needed for continuous innovation. Quality could not be achieved with de-skilled manual workers. Taylorism wasted what they called 'the gold in workers' heads'.

Toyota, and the Japanese more generally, have broken the industrial unions in the 1950s, have developed a core of multi-skilled workers whose tasks include not only manufacture and maintenance, but the improvement of the products and processes under their control. Each breakdown is seen as a chance for improvement. Even hourly-paid workers are trained in statistical techniques and monitoring, and register and interpret statistics to identify deviations from a norm – tasks customarily reserved for management in Fordism. Quality circles are a further way of tapping the ideas of the workforce. In post-Fordism, the worker is designed to act as a computer as well as a machine.

As a consequence, the Taylorist contract changes. Workers are no longer interchangeable. They gather experience. The Japanese job-for-life and corporate welfare system provides security. For the firm it secures an asset. Continuous training, payment by seniority, a breakdown of job demarcations, are all part of the Japanese core wage relation. The lead of the Electrical, Electronic, Telecommunication and Plumbing Union (EETPU) in embracing private pension and medical schemes (e.g. BUPA), internal flexibility, union-organized training and single-company unions are all consistent with this path of post-Fordist industrial relations.

Not the least of the dangers of this path is that it further hardens the divisions between the core and the peripheral workforce. The cost of employing lifetime workers means an incentive to sub-contract all jobs not essential to the core. The other side of the Japanese jobs-for-life is a majority of low-paid, fragmented peripheral workers, facing an underfunded and inadequate welfare state. The duality in the labour market, and in the welfare economy, could be taken as a description of Thatcherism. The point is that neither the EETPU's policy nor that of Mrs Thatcher should be read as purely political. There is a material basis to both, rooted in changes in production.

There are parallel changes in corporate organization. With the revision of Taylorism, a layer of management has been stripped away. Greater central control has allowed the decentralization of work. Day-to-day autonomy has been given to work groups and plant managers. Teams linking departments horizontally have replaced the rigid verticality of Fordist bureaucracies.

It is only a short step from here to subcontracting and franchising. This is often simply a means of labour control. But in engineering and light consumer industries, networks and semi-independent firms have often proved more innovative than vertically integrated producers. A mark of post-Fordism is close two-way relations between customer and supplier, and between specialized producers in the same industry. Cooperative competition replaces the competition of the jungle. These new relationships within and between enterprises and on the shopfloor have made least headway in the countries in which Fordism took fullest root, the USA and the UK. Here firms have tried to match continental and Japanese flexibility through automation while retaining Fordist shopfloor, managerial and competitive relations.

Yet in spite of this we can see in Britain a culture of post-Fordist capitalism emerging. Consumption has a new place. As for production the keyword is flexibility – of plant and machinery, as of products and labour. Emphasis shifts from scale to scope, and from cost to quality. Organizations are geared to respond to, rather than to regulate, markets. They are seen as frameworks for learning as much as instruments of control. Their hierarchies are flatter and their structures more open. The guerrilla force takes over from the standing army. All this has liberated the centre from the tyranny of the immediate. Its task shifts from planning to strategy, and to the promotion of the instruments of post-Fordist control – systems, software, corporate culture and cash.

On the bookshelf, Peters and Waterman replace F. W. Taylor. In the theatre, the audience is served lentils by the actors. At home, Channel 4 takes its place beside ITV. Majorities are transformed into minorities, as we enter the age of proportional representation. And under the shadow of Chernobyl even Fordism's scientific modernism is being brought to book, as we realize there is more than one way up the technological mountain.

Not all these can be read off from the new production systems. Some are rooted in the popular opposition to Fordism. They represent an alternative version of post-Fordism, which flowered after 1968 in the community movements and the new craft trade unionism of alternative plans. Their organizational forms – networks, workplace democracy, cooperatives, the dissolving of the platform speaker into meetings in the round – have echoes in the new textbooks of management; indeed capital has been quick to take up progressive innovations for its own purposes. There are then many sources and contested versions of post-Fordist culture. What they share is a break with the era of Ford.

Post-Fordism is being introduced under the sway of the market and in accordance with the requirements of capital accumulation. It validates only what can command a place in the market; it cuts the labour force in two, and leaves large numbers without any work at all. Its prodigious productivity gains are ploughed back into yet further accumulation and the quickening consumption of symbols in the postmodern market place. In the UK, Thatcherism has strengthened the prevailing wind of the commodity economy, liberating the power of private purses and so fragmenting the social sphere.

To judge from Kamata's celebrated account, working for Toyota is hardly a step forward from working for Ford. As one British worker in a Japanese factory in the North-East of England put it, 'they want us to live for work, whereas we want to work to live'. Japanization has no place in any modern *News from Nowhere*.

Yet post-Fordism has shaken the kaleidoscope of the economy, and exposed an old politics. We have to respond to its challenges and draw lessons from its systems.

■ Political consequences of post-Fordism

Firstly there is the question of consumption. How reluctant the Left has been to take this on, in spite of the fact that it is a sphere of unpaid production, and, as Gorz insists, one of creative activity. Which local council pays as much attention to its users as does the market research industry on behalf of commodities? Which bus or railway service cuts queues and speeds the traveller with as much care as retailers show to their just-in-time stocks? The perspective of consumption – so central to the early socialist movement – is emerging from under the tarpaulin of production: the effects of food additives and low-level radiation, of the air we breathe and the surroundings we live in, the availability of childcare and community centres, or access to privatized city centres and transport geared to particular needs. These are issues of consumption, where the social and the human have been threatened by the market. In each case the market solutions have been contested by popular movements. Yet their causes and the relations of consumption have been given only walk-on parts in party programmes. They should now come to the centre of the stage.

Secondly, there is labour. Post-Fordism sees labour as the key asset of modern production. Rank Xerox is trying to change its accounting system so that machinery becomes a cost, and labour its fixed asset. The Japanese emphasize labour and learning. The Left should widen this reversal of Taylorism, and promote a discontinuous expansion of adult education inside and outside the workplace.

They should also provide an alternative to the new management of time. The conservative sociologist Daniel Bell sees the management of time as the key issue of post-industrial society. Post-Fordist capital is restructuring working time for its own convenience: with new shifts, split shifts, rostering, weekend working, and the regulation of labour, through part-time and casual contracts, to the daily and weekly cycles of work. Computer systems allow Tesco to manage more than 130 different types of labour contract in its large stores. These systems of employment and welfare legislation should be moulded for the benefit, not the detriment, of labour. The length of the working day, of the working week, and year, and lifetime, should be shaped to accommodate the many responsibilities and needs away from work.

The most pressing danger from post-Fordism, however, is the way it is widening the split between core and periphery in the labour market and the welfare system. The EETPU's building of a fortress round the core is as divisive as Thatcherism itself. We need bridges across the divide, with trade unions representing core workers using their power to extend benefits to all, as IG Metall have been doing in Germany. A priority for any Labour government would be to put a floor under the labour market, and remove the discriminations faced by the low paid. The Liberals pursued such a policy in late 19th-century London. Labour should reintroduce it in late 20th-century Britain.

Underlying this split is the post-Fordist bargain which offers security in return for flexibility. Because of its cost, Japanese capital restricts this bargain to the core: in the peripheral workforce flexibility is achieved through insecurity. Sweden has tried to widen the core bargain to the whole population, with a policy of full employment, minimum incomes, extensive retraining programmes, and egalitarian income distribution. These are the two options, and Thatcherism favours the first.

Could Labour deliver the second? How real is a policy of full employment when the speed of technical change destroys jobs as rapidly as growth creates them? The question – as Sweden has shown – is one of distribution. There is the distribution of working time: the campaign for the 35-hour week and the redistribution of overtime should be at the centre of Labour policy in the 1990s. There is also the distribution of income and the incidence of tax. Lafontaine's idea of shifting tax from labour to energy is an interesting one. Equally important is the need to tax heavily the speculative gains from property, the rent from oil, and unearned and inherited income. finally, taxes will need to be raised on higher incomes, and should be argued for not only in terms of full employment, but in terms of the improvements to the caring services, the environment, and the social economy which the market of the 1980s has done so much to destroy. Full employment is possible. It should be based on detailed local plans, decentralized public services and full employment centres. It cannot be delivered from Westminster alone.

Thirdly, we need to learn from post-Fordism's organizational innovations, and apply them within our own public and political structures. Representative democracy within Fordist bureaucracies is not enough. What matters is the structure of the bureaucracy and its external relations. In the state this means redefining its role as strategist, as innovator, coordinator, and supporter of producers. In some cases the span of coordination needs to be extended (notably in integrating public transport and the movement of freight): in others production should be decentralized and the drive for scale reversed (the electricity industry, education and health have all suffered from over-centralized operations). Public services should move beyond the universal to the differentiated service. Nothing has been more outrageous than the attack on local government as loony Leftist, when councils have sought to shape policies to the needs of groups facing discrimination. Capitalist retailers and market researchers make these distinctions in the pursuit of sales, and socialists should match them in pursuit of service. If greater user control and internal democracy were added to this, then we would be some way towards the dismantling of mass-produced administration, and the creation of a progressive and flexible state.

Lastly, there is private industry. In many sectors both industry and public policy are frozen in Fordism, even as the leading edge of competition has shifted from scale to product, and from costs to strategy. In spite of the restructuring that has taken place in the 1980s, largely at the expense of labour, manufacturing competitiveness continues to decline. By 1984 only five out of 34 major manufacturing sectors did not have a negative trade balance.

The Left's response to this decline has been couched largely in terms of macro policy: devaluing the pound, controlling wage levels and expanding investment. Industrial policy has taken second place, and centred on amalgamations and scale and the encouragement of new technology. This has been Labour's version of modernization.

The fact remains that size has not secured competitiveness. Neither has a declining exchange rate with the yen, nor wage levels which have made the UK one of the cheap labour havens of Europe. The changes are much deeper than this.

An alternative needs to start not from plans but from strategies. Strategic capacity within British industry is thin, and even thinner in the state and the labour movement. Sector and enterprise strategies need to take on board the nature of the new competition, the centrality of skilled labour, the need for specialization and quality, and for continuous innovation.

What public policy should do is to find ways of ensuring that the resultant restructuring takes account of social priorities: labour and educational reform is one part of this; industrial democracy another; environmental and energy saving a third; user concerns about quality and variety a fourth. Some of these will require new laws; others incentive schemes; others collective bargaining. They all need to be a part of strategic restructuring.

In each sector there will be giants barring the path towards such a programme. One will be the stock market. A priority for a Labour government will be to reduce the stock market's power to undermine long-term strategic investment (in this we need to follow the example of the Japanese). Another will be multinationals which dominate so many industrial and service sectors in the economy. The urgent task here is to form coalitions of states, unions and municipalities across the European Community to press for common strategic alternatives at the European level. A third will be the retailers. In some cases retailers will be important allies in restructuring industry progressively (the Co-op has a role here); in others the conduct of retailers is destructive, and a Labour government should take direct measures against them.

At the same time, Labour needs to develop a network of social industrial institutions – decentralized, innovative and entrepreneurial. For each sector and area there should be established one or more enterprise boards. They would be channels for long-term funds for new technology, for strategic support across a sector, for common services, and for initiatives and advice on the social priorities.

Public purchasing should be coordinated and used not just to provide protection in the old manner, but as supporters of the sectoral programme, as contributors to the improvement of quality, and as sources of ideas. New technology networks should also be set up, linking universities and polytechnics with the sectors and unions (this is an effective part of Dukakis's Massachusetts programme).

In short, we need a new model of the public economy made up of a honeycomb of decentralized, yet synthetic institutions, integrated by a common strategy, and intervening in the economy at the level of production rather than trying vainly to plan all from on high. The success of the Italian consortia and the German industrial regions has been centrally dependent on such a network of municipal and regional government support.

A key role in taking forward this industrial programme should be played by the unions. Restructuring has put them on the defensive. They have found their power weakened and their position isolated. Few have had the resources to develop alternative strategies and build coalitions of communities and users around them. Yet this is now a priority if unions are to reclaim their position as spokespeople of an alternative economy rather than defenders of a sectional interest. Research departments should be expanded, and commissions given to external researchers. There should be joint commissions of members, and users and other related groups, as well as supportive local authorities. The production of the policy would itself be a form of democratic politics.

Mrs Thatcher has led an attack on the key institutions of Fordism: on manufacturing, on the centralized state, on industrial unions and on the national economy. She has opened up Britain to one version of post-Fordism, one that has strengthened the control of finance and international capital, has increased inequality and destroyed whole areas of collective life.

There is an alternative. It has grown up in the new movements, in the trade unions, and in local government over the past twenty years. It has broken through the bounds of the Left's Fordist inheritance, in culture, structure and economics. From it can develop – as is already happening in Europe – an alternative socialism adequate to the post-Fordist age.

Chapter 4

Changing Working Patterns: How Companies Achieve Flexibility to Meet New Needs

J. S. Atkinson and N. Meager

■ Introduction

This report is about flexibility in UK firms. In particular, it is intended to take forward our understanding of the extent and nature of recent changes in working practices in large UK companies ostensibly aimed at securing greater workforce flexibility. The research is designed to explore how far changes to manning practices have been introduced, what kind of changes they are and under what conditions different practices have emerged. [...]

The study is based on three sources of information: first, an extensive literature review; secondly, interviews with representative organizations such as employer and trade associations, trade unions, etc. in each of the sectors chosen for the fieldwork; and thirdly, interviews with managers and trade unionists in 72 large firms in four sectors (engineering, food and drink manufacturing, retail distribution and financial services). [...] For the moment we should note that the firms chosen for interview were all large ones (between them they employed some 660 000 full- and part-time workers) and were all faced with the need to accommodate substantial market or technological change in recent years. Thus the sample focuses on organizations which economic orthodoxy suggests are least flexible (large ones) when faced with a need to respond to change. In other respects, such as location and subsectoral characteristics, the sample

Source: J. S. Atkinson and N. Meager (1985) 'Introduction and summary of main findings' in *Changing Working Patterns*, J. S. Atkinson and N. Meager (eds), National Economic Development Office, London, pp. 2–11. Reproduced with the permission of the Controller of Her Majesty's Stationery Office.

is more balanced, but we can make no claims for its representativeness for all firms nor for companies in other sectors of industry (an area perhaps for further research). It was possible in only a few cases to interview local trade union representatives and thus it would be unwise to view their responses as necessarily representative of all the trade unions in the sectors studied.

The 'flexibility debate' has been widespread in the UK and the rest of Europe over the last two years. For this reason, and because flexibility itself is a notoriously slippery concept, we begin with a brief overview of the issues to which this research is addressed, before proceeding [...] to outline its main findings.

■ Why flexibility? The pressures for change

A full account of the factors influencing British employers and their perceptions of the need to change manning practices and obtain greater flexibility from the workforce would require a detailed economic history of at least the last 20 years. It is, however, clear from the research to date (see particularly CBI 1985, Institute of Manpower Studies 1985, OECD 1981) that three key pressures to innovate can be identified, one or more of which is invariably cited by employers.

Consolidating productivity gains. This first factor is associated with greater competitive pressures during both the recent recession and the subsequent upturn in trade. These have given rise to a need to improve productivity and cut unit labour costs and more particularly to develop policies and practices which consolidate and sustain higher productivity levels to meet current and future market conditions.

Market volatility and uncertainty. The second factor stems from the changing nature of market conditions experienced by employers. It appears that many firms now face markets which not only exhibit greater pressure of competition (domestic and international) but are also characterized by greater volatility and uncertainty. In this situation firms apparently feel a need to develop manning practices which enable them to adjust to larger and increasingly unpredictable fluctuations.

Technological change. The third factor arises from the increased pace of technological change, which has given companies the need for:

- new manning practices to match today's technology, and
- new manning policies or strategies to enable them quickly to introduce practices appropriate for tomorrow's technology.

■   Why now? Facilitators and constraints

But are these pressures themselves sufficient to explain the developments in working practices observed in recent years? Certainly these pressures have intensified lately, but it can nevertheless be argued that they have been present to some extent for many years prior to the recent recession. Such evidence as is available indicates that recent years have seen the relaxation of two important constraints, permitting new employment practices aimed at flexibility (and the extension of old practices into new areas). These are the constraints of labour market conditions and the industrial relations climate.

Labour market conditions.   The growth of unemployment to historically high levels, and its persistence at those levels despite the recovery in output, are well documented. Such high unemployment levels and the absence of generalized skill shortages have meant that employers can generally be more certain of obtaining the kind of labour they require on the local labour market as and when they need it, and consequently they have less need to retain labour during troughs in their workload. At the same time workers may be more inclined to accept the pattern of jobs so produced, either because it gives rise to the part-time jobs which they want or because they can find no alternative employment opportunities.

Industrial relations climate.   The growth of unemployment has also had an effect on internal labour markets, in the sense that the experience and/ or fear of redundancy and unemployment influence the industrial relations climate and the ability of companies to obtain from their workforces greater acceptance of new manning practices.

On balance, it remains unclear from existing evidence how important these labour market and industrial relations developments have been in facilitating the observed changes in working practices, and this was accordingly identified as a topic for further investigation in the present study. The key question must be: if the new practices depend on these changes in the environment, how sustainable will they be in the face of further changes in that environment?

■   What is flexibility? The employers' perspective

It is useful here to consider the model of the 'flexible firm' developed at the IMS. The model is helpful, not because it describes the situation of any actual organization, but because it contains all the main parameters of change observed in the research work to date. It draws into a simple framework the new elements in employers' manpower practices, bringing out the relationships between the various practices and their appropriateness for different companies and groups of workers. The model is therefore used here as an analytical tool. Its purpose is to identify different types of flexibility, to demonstrate how employers tend to seek those different types of flexibility from different groups of workers and to suggest that employers are reorganizing their workforces into different categories according to their own (possibly unique) needs for flexibility.

The model identifies four types of flexibility, as follows:

Numerical flexibility. This is concerned with enhancing firms' ability to adjust the level of labour inputs to meet fluctuations in output. There is a variety of practices which companies may adopt to achieve numerical flexibility, according to their own particular circumstances, but those most often reported are either the use of additional or supplementary labour resources to meet changes in the level of output, such as part-time, temporary, short-term contract and casual workers, or the alteration of the working time patterns of existing labour resources to meet changes in the level of output, which might again involve the use of part-timers or of varied shift patterns, overtime, 'annual hours', etc.

Functional flexibility. This relates not to changes in the number of workers, but to changes in what they do. It consists of a firm's ability to adjust and deploy the skills of its employees to match the tasks required by its changing workload, production methods and/or technology. It is concerned with the versatility of employees and their working flexibility within and between jobs.

Distancing strategies. This third category involves the displacement of employment relationships by commercial ones, as employers may opt, for example, to subcontract rather than reorganize their internal manning practices.

Pay flexibility. This final category is concerned with the extent to which a company's pay and reward structure supports and reinforces the various types of numerical and/or functional flexibility which are being sought.

The 'flexible firm', then, has geared itself up to achieve these flexibilities. Atkinson (1985) and the IMS (1985) give a detailed account of the flexible firm, whose essentials are summarized in Figure 4.1. It consists of a 'core' group of employees surrounded by peripheral groups of workers who may or may not be employees. The peripheral groups, with appropriate

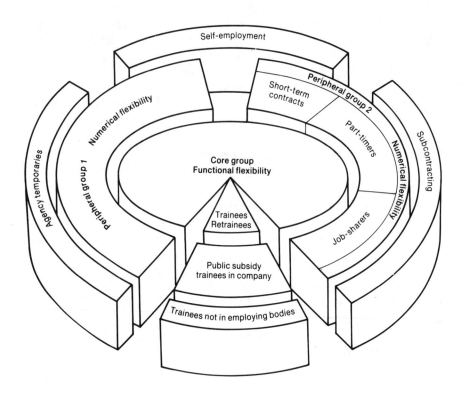

Figure 4.1   The flexible firm. (Source: IMS.)

contracts and conditions of service, provide numerical flexibility. Functional flexibility is achieved in the core, supported by appropriate incentives and rewards, possibly including enhanced employment security. In theory, this is possible because the peripheral groups soak up numerical fluctuations in demand. The core is the centre of the diagram; the surrounding ring is the periphery whose ready expansion and contraction achieves numerical flexibility; and the outer ring (of commercial sub-contractors, specialist self-employed workers on project or fee-based contracts, etc.) represents the adoption of distancing strategies.

Finally, we re-emphasize that the flexible firm is an analytical construct, which brings together into a common framework the changes which are occurring (often on a fragmented basis) and reveals their commonalities and the relations between them. It is presented neither as an example of a type of organization which already exists nor as an ideal for organizations to aim at. A key question for this research is to ask how far such changes are actually taking place and how far they represent a conscious strategy to restructure the workforce into core and periphery.

■ Flexibility in firms: who benefits?

So far the discussion has been conducted from the point of view of the employer, but it is clear that many of the changes outlined cannot be unambiguously regarded as being in the mutual interest of employers and employees alike. Indeed, there are emerging notable differences of opinion as to the objectives and effects of such changes, and there is considerable potential for industrial relations conflict over both the fact and the manner of their introduction. For example, trade union and some academic commentators (TUC 1985, European Trade Union Institute 1985, Rubery, Wilkinson and Tarling 1981) have questioned whether such developments in working arrangements and practices are indeed associated solely with a need for greater flexibility or whether they are also (or even primarily) pursued for some of the 'extrinsic' benefits they confer on employers (including weakening of trade union influence and power). Moreover, unions have objected to the methods by which such changes have been achieved – the argument being that the new practices have been unilaterally imposed rather than jointly determined by negotiation. agreement and consent, and are opportunistic in taking advantage of current weakness in trade union bargaining power and high levels of unemployment. It is further argued that such an approach is short-sighted and destructive of harmonious industrial relations and that the new practices will be unsustainable in the longer run. The issue of mutuality of interest between employers and employees is therefore one of those which we seek to address in the research.

■ Summary of main findings

The research for the present study was conducted in order to illuminate some of these issues; in particular, to explore the extent to which more flexible working practices had been introduced, to ascertain under what circumstances particular kinds of change might be found, to consider how permanent they might be and to look at their implications for employers, workers and job-seekers. The main findings are summarized in the following paragraphs.

■ Business strategies

Changes in manning practices reflect in large part changes in business strategies. The research identified great differences between the four sectors in the 'typical' business strategies being implemented by firms, and it is worth noting these at the outset.

In food and drink manufacturing firms, the typical business strategy involved a shift to low-cost, high-volume, continuous-production plant, often involving rationalization on fewer, product-specific sites. Such plant was intended to exploit new technology, to improve quality and process control and to build in a capacity for quick switches between similar product lines. Respondents were either shifting to high value-added products and establishing their brand name as a market leader or securing volume through an orientation towards 'own label' products for the big food retailing multiples. For most, this strategy involved the deployment of a high-productivity, full-time workforce to secure the most cost-effective use of new technology with minimum downtime. As a result, many firms placed strong emphasis on functional flexibility among process and maintenance workers. Work scheduling typically involves attempts to reduce seasonal/market fluctuations if possible, or otherwise to use temporary seasonal workers. At the same time, we found a strong move towards contracting out non-hygiene related ancillary services where it was cost-effective to do so.

The engineering firms demonstrated greater diversity and a wider range of strategies but these often entailed a shift to a decentralized business organization, frequently involving the concentration of pro-duction on fewer, best-practice sites. Firms were seeking to maximize the use of new technology within functions and where possible to integrate these functions through new technology. Most firms were attempting to promote 'build-to-order' methods, increasing variety and quality and reducing stockholding, while orientating production towards export markets. This led them to emphasize functional flexibility among skilled groups of workers, and to shed peripheral functions where cost-effective.

In retail distribution, firms were either trying to increase the value added per square foot of sales floor or promoting price competitiveness (particularly in food retailing) as the main method of expanding market share. The latter strategy sought to secure price competitiveness through exploiting economies of scale (larger units), buying power and containing labour costs. All respondents were seeking to lower costs by reducing stockholding, coordinating sales and stocks and, most importantly, by reducing the number of employees in post through new technology. Most were intent on varying opening hours to meet the local trading pattern.

In financial services, most of our respondents were seeking to exploit their existing physical network of branches and to diversify into other financial and non-financial services while reducing unit costs. This was leading them to reorganize the corporate structure to promote diversification where needed. Typically, firms were trying to maintain the network cover at reduced cost through the use of new technology, branch reorganization, merger and six-day trading. All were intent on raising labour productivity through increasing the use of existing new technology to take up output growth. Diversification plus greater use of new technology was leading firms to improve the calibre of professional employees while systematizing the jobs of clerical and branch staff.

We did not encounter any company in any of the four sectors which exhibited *all* the features illustrated in the IMS 'flexible firm – core/periphery' construct, and we found no evidence of *de jure* job security for core workers. Three common themes linking business strategies to manning practices were observed: a perceived need to improve the responsiveness of all factors of production to changes in business requirements; a shift towards decentralization as a means of doing so; and a reluctance to increase the number of employees in the process. All three gave rise to pressures to increase workforce flexibility. We now consider how far the respondents demonstrated the types of flexibility discussed above.

■ Numerical flexibility

Numerical flexibility is defined as the ability of firms to adjust the number of workers, or the level of worked hours, in line with changes in the level of demand for them. Nine out of every ten respondents had introduced changes to manning practices since 1980 designed to increase numerical flexibility. These changes were of four main types: temporary workers, part-timers, overtime and new shift patterns, and flexible working hours. The incidence of these four types of change varied greatly from sector to sector, with, broadly speaking, part-time employment of more importance among service sector respondents, temporary working more important in manufacturing, and flexible working hours more an aspiration than a reality, save among part-time workers. We now consider them in turn.

☐ Temporary work

Among the respondents increasing numerical flexibility, temporary workers were employed in three out of every four cases. Temporary working had increased among 42 per cent of these respondents since 1980, yet traditional (seasonal, holiday and absence cover) temporary work appears to have changed little. We found that the increased use of temporary work in food and drink and engineering was associated with the creation of a buffer peripheral workforce as a hedge against market uncertainty, while in financial services it was more often employed as a hedge against any future job loss resulting from the impact of new technology. In retail distribution little pressure for change was noted, save for the use of Youth Training Scheme trainees as a form of peripheral workforce. Temporary work was largely restricted to unskilled and semi-skilled jobs and/or to jobs requiring non-company-specific skills, as firms declined to meet substantial training costs for temporary workers. We found that the increasing use of temporaries was opposed by trade unions more strongly in those firms without a tradition of using them. In most cases this opposition had conditioned the terms, but not the fact, of their use. Hence, except in retailing, most temporary workers received the same basic pay rates, but less favourable conditions of employment, than permanent workers.

☐   **Part-time working**

Among the firms increasing numerical flexibility, part-time workers were employed in three out of every four cases. Fewer than one in every ten manufacturing firms had increased their use of part-timers, while in financial services two-thirds, and in retailing nine out of every ten, were making greater use of part-timers than they had in 1980. The two main factors underlying the growth of service-sector part-time working were a desire to match manning levels more precisely to fluctuating customer patterns during the working day and the reduction of labour costs through substituting part-time labour (with significantly lower non-pay costs) for full-time labour. Opening hours in retailing which would attract premium rates for full-time staff were more likely to be covered using part-timers on non-premium rates (where possible). Like temporary working, the increased use of part-time workers was generally limited to unskilled and semi-skilled jobs requiring minimal training. This permitted substantial use in retailing and restricted their use in financial services. However, job systematization, associated with new technology, was believed to have reduced this constraint in both sectors, particularly in financial services.

☐   **Overtime and new shift patterns**

Overtime working was common in all sectors except financial services. In the manufacturing sectors the use of overtime had increased among three-quarters of our engineering firms, but among only 12 per cent of food and drink firms. However, in both these sectors we observed a move to reduce systematic overtime, to increase managerial control of overtime and to construct shift systems which did not incorporate overtime. In the service sector the picture was quite different. In the (few) firms using overtime in financial services, its incidence had been increasing, largely to cope with Saturday opening. However, although more heavily used in retailing, only a quarter of retailing firms reported increasing their use of overtime since 1980. In fact, overtime working among part-time workers in retailing had grown considerably, but it was not classed as overtime by our respondents as much of it attracted no premium rate. We saw no evidence of any similar shift away from premium payments for overtime in manufacturing.

Eight out of every ten manufacturing firms increasing numerical flexibility had changed their shift systems to achieve it, but among service sector firms changes to shift patterns were most common among part-time workers, with new, and generally shorter, shifts emerging.

☐ **Flexible working time**

Only one firm (in food and drink) had moved to a system of contractual annual hours. Elsewhere, flexible working hours were restricted to part-time workers, whose working time patterns were increasingly defined as minima with additional hours to be supplied as required, or as a fixed number of hours with the distribution of those hours within the week to be determined as required. In general, service sector respondents were very reluctant to require full-time staff to work flexible hours, or indeed to roster worked days. Flexitime was generally seen as a 'perk' for employees.

■ Functional flexibility

Functional flexibility is defined as the ability of firms to reorganize the competences associated with jobs so that the job-holder can deploy such competences across a broader range of tasks. This may involve horizontal enlargement of competences at roughly the same skill level (e.g. electrical/ electronic craft skills) or vertical enlargement, which may be either upwards (e.g. operator/quality control) or downwards (e.g. maintenance/ operator).

We found that a shift towards greater functional flexibility was restricted largely to manufacturing firms. Nine out of every ten manufacturing respondents had been seeking to increase the functional flexibility of their workforces since 1980. This falls to two in ten in retail distribution and just over that figure in financial services.

Among these manufacturing respondents we observed three main types of increased functional flexibility:

1. Horizontal enlargements within maintenance areas,
2. Vertical and horizontal enlargements within process and operator areas,

3.   Vertical enlargements between different areas.

Within maintenance three-quarters of our respondents seeking to increase functional flexibility had achieved a limited overlap between maintenance craftsmen, only one-third had achieved dual-skilling even within electrical and mechanical trade groups and only 15 per cent had achieved it across the electrical/mechanical divide. However, in process and operator areas, all those firms who had sought it had increased the mobility of operators between jobs at similar skill levels (30 out of 31 firms). Fewer firms had achieved functional flexibility across group boundaries, particularly where this involved different status or union membership, although new test, inspection and monitoring equipment had enabled operators both to move into inspection roles and to conduct routine maintenance tasks. The main constraints to functional flexibility identified in manufacturing were union demarcation, training implications and (much less often) health and safety considerations.

Among service sector respondents, the situation was radically different. Achieving increases in functional flexibility was not generally reckoned to be an important priority for our service sector firms. They either had it by tradition or they could get it relatively easily.

In food retailing, we found a high level of mobility between tasks among shop staff where jobs were unskilled. This was traditional and had not changed significantly in recent years. Department stores and non-food chainstores were more constrained and generally sought to build up expertise within departments, but many had developed floating staff trained to move between such departments. New technology had increased the potential for such low-level mobility by systematizing jobs but increasing use of part-time workers had correspondingly reduced it. In financial services there remains a substantial amount of traditional functional flexibility, but this was being undercut through increasing levels of part-time work and increasing recruitment of specialist senior staff. As in retailing, new technology has increased the potential for clerical level job mobility in financial services, and with lower levels of part-time working than in retailing the net effect has been to increase such mobility.

■ Distancing

Distancing is defined as the displacement of employment contracts by commercial contracts, as exemplified by subcontracting. It is an alternative to flexibility rather than another form of flexibility. Seven in every ten respondents had increased their use of distancing since 1980. Of these, 90 per cent had increased their use of subcontracted ancillary services, 51 per cent had increased their use of subcontracting in non-ancillary areas and 22 per cent had increased their use of self-employed workers. Increased distancing was associated with a wish to concentrate corporate resources on areas of comparative advantage, to find cheaper ways of undertaking non-core activities, to shift the burden of risk and uncertainty elsewhere and to reduce (or contain) formal headcount and wage bill.

■ Pay flexibility

Pay flexibility is defined as the ability of firms to adjust pay structures to encourage functional flexibility, match market rates for scarce skills and/or reward individual performance. We found that about two-thirds of our firms had changed their pay structures to secure greater pay flexibility.

In manufacturing, pay flexibility mainly involved the introduction of new pay systems to encourage the acquisition and deployment of the additional skills associated with functional flexibility. These were of two types: a multigraded structure reflecting and encouraging skill acquisition and a simplified structure with fewer, broad grades. The first was often reported to be a transitional phase towards the latter. We found very few cases (six out of 26 reporting changes) where 'individual' restructuring had been introduced in manufacturing.

Although increases in pay flexibility were less common in the service sector, they were by contrast principally concerned to encourage individual performance through such devices as merit pay, commission payments, performance assessment, etc. However, diversification within financial services had led to the creation of new pay systems for subsidiaries in different subsectors in order to avoid the constraints of an inappropriate pay structure.

■ Corporate strategies

Having considered the extent and nature of these observed changes in manning practices, we go on to ask how far they derive from conscious and long-term corporate employment strategies. We found that the impact of recession had generally heightened awareness, at all levels in firms, of a need to change working practices to maintain competitiveness. This varied directly with the impact of recession on organizations and was therefore less evident in the service sector. Combined with increased management communication direct to the workforce and (in a few cases) the erosion of union bargaining rights and organization on site, the net effect had been to reduce union opposition to change.

Firms tended not to have long-term manpower strategies comparable with their business strategies, save in cases where the latter entailed major technological change. Observed changes in working practices in manufacturing in particular were therefore much more likely to have been devised and initiated at site level than centrally. Further, while most of the observed changes could not truly be represented as enforced, they had often been secured because of a shift in collective bargaining strength towards the employers, resulting from (real or threatened) job loss associated with recession. This was particularly true in manufacturing. Neither union nor management respondents generally regarded this situation as permanent. Indeed, most management respondents in manufacturing relied heavily on the permanence of that imbalance in collective bargaining strength, and on the continuation of high levels of unemployment, to maintain the changes in working practices they had achieved. Few thought the former likely, and while most thought the latter more likely few saw it as sufficient on its own either to maintain the changes already achieved or to permit further changes.

Changes to pay structures, the impact of new investment and greater stress on direct communication with workers were widely regarded by managers as ways of maintaining the achieved changes. Single-status terms and conditions and explicit employment security agreements were neither widely observed nor mentioned in this context.

The main constraints to achieving greater flexibility observed were:

1. Inadequate skill levels and training resources, which slowed the pace and limited the extent of change towards functional flexibility;

2. Status differences, both staff/manual and union membership differences, which constrained movement and, where combined, often prevented it.

Legislative and other institutional factors were generally regarded as much less important than internal, domestic ones. Our service sector respondents were generally less constrained by either of these factors.

Firms' orientation towards securing greater flexibility was generally inward-looking, and distancing initiatives had been strongly constrained by operational and cost considerations to particular, usually ancillary or support, activities such as cleaning, catering, security, transport, etc. Retailing, with the growth of concessions, franchises and 'store-in-store' trading, was the only significant exception.

The changes observed in firms provide some confirmation about the growth of segmentation in the labour market. At any given level of skill our respondents were likely to require both functional and numerical flexibility, but as skill levels rose so did the emphasis on functional flexibility. As a result, this differential emphasis was producing markedly different contractual, working time, pay and job content regimes between groups of workers.

■ Flexibility and workers

Peripheral forms of employment such as temporary and part-time jobs had grown among our respondents since 1980. Such forms entailed 'intrinsic' or unavoidable shortcomings for workers; in particular, they tended to lack employment continuity and security. In addition, as such jobs were inclined to require only low-level skills, and their peripheral status tended to inhibit investment in training from employers, workers in them were unlikely to enjoy substantial opportunities for advancement on internal labour markets. These shortcomings were accentuated because they were often overlaid with 'extrinsic' or avoidable ones, which apparently had little to do with achieving flexibility and more to do with reducing employment costs. In particular, most peripheral status workers enjoyed substantially worse provision of non-pay benefits than did their core counterparts and, although most respondents paid *pro rata* hourly rates for peripheral workers, the actual administration of pay tended to disadvantage them, particularly in regard to part-time work and overtime premia.

We found that the advantages sometimes claimed to flow from peripheral status were likely to be enjoyed by very small numbers of freelance professionals in shortage occupations. Significant advantages did accrue to core workers, however. In particular, access to retraining, job enlargement and the acquisition of higher skills had begun to open up some 'career' movement for manual workers which they had not previously enjoyed. Although full-blown staff status was rare for manual workers, most core workers had enjoyed some piecemeal progress towards harmonization since 1980. However, explicit employment security agreements for core workers were not observed. Most often, particularly in manufacturing, any change towards security entailed no more than a reduction in the threat of job loss rather than anything more positive.

Looking at the wider labour market, the growth of segmentation seems likely to increase the volatility of employment patterns, giving rise to more short-term interrupted employment while at the same time reducing access to core status jobs. In addition, we would expect firms to shift their recruitment orientation to workers not aspiring to core status, particularly if service sector employment continues to grow.

Firms saw a potential problem arising out of 'poaching' of reskilled manual workers. In addition, they were increasingly reluctant to train peripheral workers, yet widely feared that nobody else would either. However, this was not generally regarded by our management respondents as a problem for most peripheral workers, save in the case of subcontracted specialist work (e.g. pattern making, jig and tool making, etc.).

■ Flexibility reconsidered

In the light of the findings of the research, we reconsider some of the issues raised in the introduction.

First, we need to ask how far the initiatives being introduced are likely to promote the desired end of a more flexible and responsive workforce. This research demonstrates that, despite their lack of long-term employment strategies, our respondents had generally introduced changes explicitly aimed at securing the different manning implications of their business strategies. Most respondents saw achieving greater flexibility as a necessary, but not a sufficient, condition for securing their business plans. Although the changes were extensive (viewed across firms), they did not often represent qualitative breaks with previous manning practices within individual firms nor did the changes to manning practices observed encompass major changes to existing company cultures.

We should therefore also consider how far the changes achieved can persist under different internal and external conditions. We conclude that to achieve change most manufacturing respondents had relied heavily on a shift in the balance of collective bargaining strength, which they believed to be temporary. This reliance was less marked in the service sector. Very few firms had instituted employee relations strategies intended to sustain, far less to extend, their initiatives, save where substantial capital investment had occurred.

An important issue is whether segmentation is increasing as firms seek different flexibilities from different workers. We conclude that segmentation had increased among our respondents precisely because the type of flexibility they sought varied between skilled and unskilled groups. As a result, peripheral workers (particularly part-time ones) were confined to low-skilled jobs as access routes upwards through internal labour markets were denied them.

A major concern of some commentators is the possibility that the growth of peripheral workforces implies a 'low skill – low tech – low productivity' workforce. This research confirms that firms who had strongly committed themselves to the use of substantial proportions of supplementary peripheral workers in order to achieve numerical flexibility (primarily our retailing respondents) had found their ability to secure versatility from their workforces inhibited. However, where functional flexibility had been the dominant aim, firms tended to rely on traditional practices like overtime and shiftworking to secure numerical flexibility. Further, peripheral forms of employment were, in general, found only in occupations where employers had not sought, and did not expect to need, much versatility or a high level of skill. We conclude that employers have not sought to introduce low-skill low-tech jobs so that they can be filled with workers employed on a peripheral basis, but rather that where such jobs exist anyway employers have seen advantages in so filling them.

Finally, we need to consider whether employers' needs for flexibility can be secured in a fashion consistent with the interests of workers. We conclude that the reskilling often implied by functional flexibility is generally in the interests of employer and employee alike, but that some of the extrinsic shortcomings associated with peripheral status do not contribute to flexibility. Rather, they represent attempts to cut labour costs.

Note

This chapter is taken from the report published in 1986 entitled *Changing Working Patterns: How Companies Achieve Flexibility to Meet New Needs*. It was prepared by the Institute of Manpower Studies for the National Economic Development Office in association with the Department of Employment. John Atkinson and Nigel Meager were the researchers on the project.

References

Atkinson, J. S. (1985) 'Flexibility: planning for an uncertain future', *Manpower Policy and Practice*, vol. 1, Summer.

CBI (1985) *Managing Change: the Organization of Work*, London.

European Trade Union Institute (1985) *Flexibility and Jobs – Myths and Realities*, Brussels.

Institute of Manpower Studies (1985) *New Forms of Work Organization*, IMS Manpower Commentary no. 30, Brighton.

OECD (1981) *Manpower and Social Aspects of Positive Adjustment Policies*, Manpower and Social Affairs Committee, Paris.

Rubery, J., Wilkinson, F. and Tarling, R. (1981) *Flexibility in the Use of Labour and Fixed Wage Costs*, EEC Labour Market Studies 81/23, Brussels.

TUC (1985) *New Jobs, Economic Adjustment and the Labour Market*, (NEDC(85)19), Mimeo, London.

Chapter 5

Flexible Specialization, Work Organization and Skills: Approaching the 'Second Industrial Divide'

A. J. Phillimore

It is becoming commonplace to argue that the advanced industrialized countries are currently living in an era of great transformation. Whether it be the onset of 'The Third Wave', the 'Farewell to the Working Class', or the 'End of Organized Capitalism', the post-1945 world of cheap energy, US-dominated trade and Keynesian demand management is recognized as having ended [1]. Its symptoms are high and persistent unemployment, a rapidly changing balance of international economic power, and a political and economic convergence by governments of East and West alike towards more reliance on market forces, less government intervention and the widespread adoption of new, microelectronics-based technology.

It was into this debate that Piore and Sabel introduced their own 'era of transformation' book, *The Second Industrial Divide*. They argue that the 'present deterioration in economic performance results from the limits of the model of industrial development that is founded on mass production: the use of special-purpose (product-specific) machines and of semi-skilled workers to produce standardized goods' [2]. The advanced industrial economies now face a choice between building on the organization of mass production, or shifting to an era based on flexible specialization (FS). This 'epochal redefinition of markets, technologies and industrial hierarchies' [3] will have different implications for industries, regions, national economies,

Source: A. J. Phillimore (1979) 'Flexible specialisation, work organisation and skills: approaching the "second industrial divide" ', *New Technology, Work and Employment*, 1979, pp. 79–91.

consumers and workers, depending upon what choices are made, when, and by whom.

Piore and Sabel's book is important for a number of reasons. First, it summarized a great deal of material that had been gathered about the renaissance of the small firm, the entrepreneur, and the growing 'industrial districts' based on these successful firms. Second, it linked changes at the level of production (which had already been noted in many European analyses under the rubric of neo-Fordism [4]), with the macro-economic and global crises and shifts of power. Third, and perhaps most importantly, it sounded a distinctly optimistic tone: the future was *not* determined; choices did exist. Politics reassumed a central role, with the recognition that particular technologies, the organization of production and even whole technology systems, were not 'given', but *socially* determined and, in the present era, 'up for grabs'.

This optimistic tone was perhaps the primary cause of the controversy which the book aroused at all points on the political spectrum. On the positive side, the book was seen as a 'tour de force' [5]. FS was seen as a 'third way' for the Left between monetarism and Keynesianism [6], and as a possible avenue of advance for small and Third World countries who could build upon their craft traditions through the judicious use of new technology [7]. On the negative side, Piore and Sabel were seen as 'incurably romantic' [8]; going from one nostalgia (the mass-production worker) to another (the craft worker) [9]; FS was seen to 'spell a return to the worst excesses of industrial capitalism', and to be 'bad news for the trade unions' and the labour movement in general [10].

The Second Industrial Divide covers a vast area, ranging from the global economic regulatory system to shop-floor industrial relations. The focus of this article will be more narrow in scope. It will concentrate on the changes occurring at the level of production, and in particular on the application and implications of FS on the organization of work and on the labour force. This concentration on production is, however, crucial to Piore and Sabel's thesis, for their basic starting point is that changes at the level of production are the primary determinants of the current economic crisis at all levels. As one set of critics caustically points out, 'seldom in the history of intellectual endeavour, can so much have been built on the foundation of one opposition' – that is, the opposition between mass production (or Fordism) and FS (neo-Fordism) [11].

■ The concept of flexible specialization (FS)

Even confined to the level of production, FS is an elusive, if not elastic, concept, with no single defining feature. To some, the technology used in production is the key; to others, it is the smaller size of the production unit, or of the production run. Still other analysts focus on the labour requirements (both in terms of skills and of numbers), while some see innovatory management as most important. In essence, however, FS is a relative concept, defined in relation to another, different type of production system – mass production, or Fordism. Table 5.1 summarizes ten of the principal differences between Fordism and FS.

According to Piore and Sabel, the shift from mass production to FS arose from two main factors. The first was the increasing labour unrest of the late 1960s and early 1970s. This encouraged firms to decentralize their production processes, through 'splitting up' their in-house production to geographically dispersed plants, and through 'putting out' aspects of production to sub-contractors. This strategy in turn led to the development of a significant number of small, technologically advanced firms, often founded by skilled workers originally displaced from the large firm.

The second factor was the changing nature of market demand. As the market for standardized, mass-produced goods became saturated in the 1960s, two developments opened the way to FS. First, increased competition (both from other advanced countries and from the newly industrialized countries) forced large firms to cut costs (especially labour and fixed capital costs – with the splitting-up and putting-out strategies noted above). Second, consumers' tastes became more diverse as 'basic' needs were increasingly satisfied, and the resulting market differentiation enabled many 'First World' producers to profitably enter 'market niches' for low-volume, high-quality goods for which mass production was unsuited and for which high-wage, high-skill labour was an asset rather than a cost.

In addition to these two factors, the development of new technology – such as computer aided design (CAD), computer aided manufacture (CAM) and computer numerical control (CNC), etc. – enabled small firms to produce efficiently in competition with large firms. Also, new technology enabled the integration of production, distribution, and marketing to an extent previously unattainable. This was the basis of Benetton's success, for example. Finally, the success of Japanese producers in world markets, with their use of production methods such as just-in-time, total quality control, flexible work patterns and extensive use of sub-contractors provided an example of a new form of manufacturing 'best practice' to which other firms should strive.

■ Three views about FS

There are a number of different views about the overall importance and 'progressiveness' of FS. For convenience, we can distinguish between three schools of thought: the optimists, the pessimists, and the sceptics.

The 'optimists' regard FS as the new paradigm of production, which

Table 5.1 Fordism and flexible specialization (FS) compared. (Source: adapted from Poon [12].)

	Fordism	FS
1. Production concept	Mass production; economies through fixed capital and labour productivity within the production process	FS/flexible automation; economies through working capital productivity between production processes and in distribution
2. Technology	Machines purpose-built and dedicated; R & D functionally separate and discontinuous	General-purpose and adaptable machinery; importance of design
3. Products	Limited range of standardized products	Specialization, product variety; 'niche' markets
4. Inputs	Materials and energy-intensive	Materials and energy-saving; information-intensive
5. Work process and skills	Fragmented and standardized tasks; strict division between mental and manual labour; semi-skilled workers	Open-ended tasks/closer integration of manual and mental tasks/core of multi-skilled workers linked to sub-contract and semi-skilled labour
6. Payment system	Rate for the job; formalized pay bargaining	Payment for person; rising income for skilled core; more informal wage settlement
7. Organization and management	Managerial hierarchies; centralization; multi-divisional corporation	Flatter hierarchies; centralized information and planning systems, decentralized production, networks, franchising, sub-contracting
8. Markets and customers	Domination of manufacturers over retailers, producers over users; one-way relations/mass advertising	Domination of retailing/two-way relations between customer and manufacturer; firm rather than product advertising
9. Suppliers	Arm's length/stocks held 'just in case'	Two-way relations/stocks arrive 'just in time'
10. Competitive strategy	Compete by full capacity utilization and cost-cutting; tends to over production, stockpiling, mark downs	Compete by innovation; respond to falling market through diversification, innovation, sub-contracting or lay-off

contains positive features for capital and labour [13]. Many of them draw upon the experience of the clothing and engineering sectors in the so-called 'Third Italy', where regional clusters of small, innovative firms have been very successful in terms of increased growth, export performance, income and employment by the use of advanced computer technology in production, distribution and marketing. The optimists also include advocates of Japanese-style production methods and industrial relations (especially in vehicle manufacturing – the archetypal Fordist industry), with their emphasis on quality, low inventories, multi-skilling, etc.

The optimists see FS as challenging mass production, by providing opportunities for small companies (and regions based on clusters of such small firms, the so-called 'industrial districts') to compete with the large mass-production firms, and by allowing large firms to decentralize their operations and incorporate more skill, quality and variety into their organization of production so as to compete more effectively against low-wage mass producers in the Third World. They also consider 'niche' production as being of some potential to minority consumer groups, whose needs were neglected by the mass producers.

The 'pessimists' to a great extent share the views of the optimists about the significance of FS's challenge to Fordist production methods [14]. However, by contrast, they regard the development with much more trepidation. Aware of its origins in the industrial relations struggles of the late 1960s, they see FS as having disproportionate benefits for capital, by dividing labour and intensifying the labour process more thoroughly than mass production ever did. They also doubt that small, innovative firms such as those highlighted by studies of the 'Third Italy' will necessarily be the dominant feature of an era of flexible production. Much more typical, they argue, are the dependent sub-contractors, or homeworkers – 'sweatshop' labour with poor working conditions and low job security. In addition, the minority tastes which FS caters to are likely to be luxury tastes, ignoring the needs of the majority.

The 'sceptics' doubt the significance of FS at all [15]. Some argue that, quantitatively, mass production is still very much more important than FS, which is at present confined to relatively few regions and industries. Also, mass production is much more 'flexible' than critics give it credit for – market segmentation and product choice in the 'mature' consumer goods industries has increased markedly since the 1950s, under a mass-production regime. Others argue that the spread of Fordism itself has been exaggerated, and that FS is in fact more common in those sectors which were resistant to Fordism, such as batch engineering. Still others argue that the whole debate misses the point [16]. FS enthusiasts are manufacturing enthusiasts – but manufacturing is declining in significance and thus FS is not the wave of the future. However, although this concentration on manufacturing is true of some FS proponents, such as Piore and Sabel, it is not exclusively so. Poon, for example, in her work on the tourism sector, has argued that FS may in fact be even *more* applicable to services (as mass-production techniques are less prevalent there) [17].

These schools of thought are by no means exclusive, of course. Many of the pessimists agree with the points raised by the sceptics – but they are still more alarmed by the threat of FS to organized labour. Many of the optimists are in fact 'guarded optimists', who recognize the negative potentialities of FS, especially if government support for labour is not forthcoming [18]. Piore and Sabel also emphasize the need for such support. And almost all optimists note that FS will flourish much better with growing market demand, to make the transition from mass production easier and to avoid competition between FS firms being based on cutting costs (and therefore wages), rather than on innovation [19]. Many FS advocates are also coming to terms with some of the sceptics' arguments about the continued resilience of mass production. FS is increasingly regarded as 'a modifying factor for mass production which develops from the old, very conventional Ford style ... into a new type that produces a range of high-quality products' [20].

■ FS, work organization and skills

Work organization and skills are of special importance to the whole debate surrounding FS, for a number of reasons. First, the defining characteristic of mass production is seen by most as the hierarchically organized production process, with its extensive division of labour into fragmented and standardized tasks requiring a minimum of skills. FS, if it is a true alternative paradigm to mass production, should differ from it in this respect at least. Second, the different perceptions of the implications of FS for labour constitute the major dividing line between the optimists and the pessimists in their attitude towards FS.

For the optimists, FS offers an opportunity to reclaim the craft traditions of a bygone age. New technology and changed market conditions now enable the craft paradigm to re-assert itself, offering more control over the labour process for workers, a renewed emphasis on skills, more job security, less alienation and better working conditions. For the pessimists, FS represents an intensification of work, further divisions of the workforce (and consequent problems for unions) and at best a neutral effect on workers' skills. Whether FS is seen positively or negatively, the issues of work organization and skills have major policy implications for government.

Before discussing these policy issues, the evidence from a number of industry sectors influenced by FS will be presented. At the outset, it should be recognized that the empirical evidence on the skill implications of FS is not yet very substantial. Most studies have either simply asserted the importance of skilled labour to FS, or instead concentrated on the effects of FS on unionization, work conditions, labour unity or left political strategy rather than on skills *per se*.

■ Clothing and textiles

Until recently, the clothing and textiles industry was considered to be 'the most mature of the mature industries' [21]. Low-wage Third World producers had increasingly outcompeted advanced industrial countries in producing low-cost, mass-produced garments for world markets. Any substantial industry left in the advanced industrial countries was either heavily protected through tariffs or quotas, or resembled Third World countries with sweatshop labour and low productivity. In short, it was the archetypal 'sunset' industry.

The success of the Benetton group (and of the Emilia-Romagna region of Italy in general), and of similarly organized companies in Britain such as Burton, Next, and Richards, has altered this perception markedly [22]. High-quality, innovative design and a new marketing and distribution system which reduces inventories to a minimum has enabled 'First World' producers to compete more effectively and to regain much of their lost market share. The 'Emilian model' is regarded as a prime example of an FS success story – high growth rates, high exports, low unemployment, a disproportionately high number of small firms, a low degree of vertical integration between firms, modern technology, reliance on quality, customized goods produced in short series, etc. [23].

Assessments of the implications of this model for work organization and skills are generally enthusiastic. Brusco, for example, considers it a 'certitude that this system is rich in opportunities for all, ... everyone is ultimately the master of his own fate' [24]. Solinas, though less rapturous, still considers that 'good jobs' predominate [25].

The evidence, however, is less clear cut. Both Brusco and Solinas acknowledge the existence of substantially different types of firms and conditions of work. Firms in the 'primary' sector – the vertically integrated, large batch producers – differ substantially from those in the 'secondary' sector – the small firms with small batch production. The former tend to be heavily unionized, to respect labour laws, to have stable employment, high wages, etc. They have a variety of skilled and unskilled workers.

The secondary sector is much less unionized, labour laws are commonly flouted (or do not apply) and it is much more flexible in its output, wage and employment levels. In fact, this flexibility is crucial as 'all attempts to impose rigidity on the secondary sector would immediately reverberate on the system as a whole' [26].

Within this secondary sector, at least three types of production unit are identified. Sub-contracting firms undertake a single, intermediate stage of manufacture. 'Independents' are firms with access to the consumer market who produce individual styles and high-quality products (in fact, many only produce prototypes and sub-contract out the production). Homeworkers have a similar function to the sub-contractors, but work at home, often to evade taxes and to enable employers to avoid welfare payments. There are also the more seasonal and temporary workers, such as pensioners, students, 'moonlighters' and married women.

The implications of this type of industrial structure for skills are ambiguous, and depend to a great extent upon which type of firm is being considered. Craft skills – the type most commonly associated with the 'Third Italy' – are not evenly distributed between firms, or between groups of workers. Artisans (who predominate in the 'independents' sector) are mainly older men, while production-line workers (who predominate in the sub-contractor sector) and homeworkers tend to be women, younger men or newcomers to the region. Production-line workers in small firms tend to be more skilled than those in large firms, often as a result of fewer job demarcations which allow small-firm workers to acquire a wider variety of skills and to have more individual responsibility. However, opposing this is the lack of any real career structure within the small firm, and the greater degree of job insecurity [27].

Solinas and Brusco also point out the extent to which 'good jobs' depend on strong product demand, which provides incentives for employers and employees to acquire skills. Should recession set in, the system would falter, as job mobility to higher skill opportunities would cease.

The situation outside the 'core' firms is quite different. Work by Mitter and the Greater London Council has shown the sweatshop nature of what remains of London's clothing industry, where skills are deemed to be 'inherent' in the (overwhelmingly) female (and immigrant) labour force and where training, job security and living wages are a rarity [28]. Mitter argues that 'the rise of homeworking ... is currently playing an important role in the global restructuring of capital', and that any evidence of improved skills and conditions in, for example, Benetton are mirrored (and indeed dependent on) the decentralization of the less skilled parts of the production process to sub-contractors. Thus, Benetton employs only 1500 workers directly, but another 10 000 indirectly – and the latter's job skills and conditions are unlikely to be comparable to those of the 'core' workers [29].

The evidence from the clothing industry poses a number of crucial issues for FS. First, is the dualistic nature of the industry endemic or transitory? Piore and Sabel, for instance, argue that at the beginning of the FS movement the Italian small-firm sector *was* analogous to turn-of-the-century sweatshops. But, they insist, such dependence was not permanent: 'dependent subcontractors ... used their collective capacities to devise innovative products and processes that gave them increasingly independent access to markets' [30]. Solinas supports this interpretation by remarking that dependent, low-quality sub-contractors are 'small in number and much less representative'. However, he then goes on to acknowledge that the subordination of other regions (which could include the UK producers discussed by Mitter) is a determining factor in providing the 'good jobs' in the core region [31].

Second, are the 'sweatshops' of the UK part of the FS production system, or of an old production system which is being *overrun* by FS? Mitter, to some extent, argues both. Without more quantification of the links and distribution of output, employment and skills between different types of firm, it is not possible to conclude definitively which is the case.

Third, the situation is not static. Purposive action by firms and governments can change things. Robin Murray, for example, and the GLC's *London Industrial Strategy* argue that the London clothing sector (and others) could change from a vicious circle of low skills, low wages and low productivity to a more virtuous circle along Italian lines, with the aid of judicious investments in technology and a different marketing and production strategy [32]. Such a strategy would result in enhanced skills and training. But the problems of the overall impact on jobs and skills, and of the core–periphery dilemma would remain. For example, is the aim simply to shift London to the core, and by implication create other, peripheral workers elsewhere?

■ Machine tools and machine shops

The machine tool sector of the economy is distinctive because, despite its importance, it has traditionally been one of the least 'Fordist' in its production methods [33]. Small batch production has predominated and craft workers, often organized in strong unions, have maintained significant control over the production process.

The introduction of NC and CNC tools triggered a debate, begun by Braverman [34], about the extent to which the machine tool sector was becoming 'Fordist', in the sense of workers being de-skilled and losing control over production to management. The success of the Italian, West German and Japanese industries has led to speculation that principles of FS are supplanting any nascent tendencies towards de-skilling and the application of Fordist principles to the machine tool sector. For example, the Japanese machine tool industry (the most successful in the general-purpose machine market) is comprised of vertically disintegrated, specialized firms, able to shift quickly from one line of product to another using broadly skilled employees [35].

The craft skills of workers in the West German and Italian machine tool industries are also being used, in conjunction with the new technology, to transform production along FS lines with subsequent successes in international markets [36].

However, there are dissenting voices to this generally rosy picture. First, there are clear examples of where the new technologies have been used to de-skill workers in machine shops, rather than re-skill them, although the commercial wisdom of such a policy is being increasingly questioned. British industry has been singled out for this in many studies [37]. Second, there are those who criticize even the success stories. F. Murray, in his study of the Italian machine tool sector, echoes many of the criticisms of the 'Third Italy' clothing industry by noting the differentiated nature of skills and employment conditions between the elite workers (usually male) with skills and the rest of the workforce. Murray argues that alienated, low-skill labour is much more widespread than is commonly perceived [38].

■ Motor vehicles

The motor vehicle industry, in contrast to machine tools, constitutes mass production *par excellence*. 'Fordism', with its assembly line, strict subdivision of jobs and workers, and long production runs, was perfected in this industry. By the 1970s, however, the giant automobile manu-facturers of the US and Western Europe were all faced with serious problems from a combination of changed consumer markets and tastes, government regulation and increased competition from Japan and other, Third World, producers.

The Japanese challenge was particularly significant because of its basis in a different philosophy of production organization. Concepts of total quality control and just-in-time production were utilized to achieve astonishing productivity improvements compared with traditional mass production. This Japanese strategy depended crucially on flexibility in all aspects of production [39].

The Japanese system of production is based, like that of Benetton, on a core–periphery distinction of firms and workers, with the latter bearing the major brunt of the risks in order to make the system suitably flexible. The 'core' firms, in order to maximize their own flexibility, ensure that their workers are sufficiently trained to undertake a variety of tasks. Life-time employment contracts are an important incentive for workers to acquire such skills.

The UK car industry, under threat from increased competition and with a long history of industrial relations problems, has now begun its own 'Japanization' strategy. Established companies like British Leyland and Ford have cut back on their 'core' workforce, reduced their inventories, begun to dismantle skill and job demarcations and, in general, have striven to instil flexibility and quality into their production processes. Nissan, which entered production in Britain unencumbered by existing work practices, has adopted Japanese production standards to an even greater extent [40].

Using a drastically reduced number of formal skill hierarchies, the trend is to combine teamwork and flexibility to establish a 'multi-skilled' workforce, organized by a one-union deal (as opposed to over twenty in Ford UK's plants) [41]. The extent of such multi-skilling is, however, a moot point: critics argue that the job rotation and enlargement aspect of Nissan's operations are in reality forms of work intensification, in which downtime is reduced, and 'skills' can be acquired in a few days. As one worker put it, 'the jobs are just the same as before, you just do more of 'em' [42]. The control of the whole work process, meanwhile, is more effectively centralized in the hands of management away from the 'teams' who can only affect small parts of a plant's total production.

■ Printing

Printing provides an example of an industry where skill levels were maintained for a long time, despite the threats and intrusions from new technology and the potential of mass production. Print unions, in the UK at least, managed to hold onto their craft skills and their control of production until very recently, and also managed to extend this control virtually throughout the industry, despite the overwhelming numerical dominance of small firms.

However, recent developments in new print technology and the market offensive of print franchise companies have enabled a growing number of independent small companies to produce high (or acceptable) quality work without the use or sanction of skilled labour organized in trade unions. As such, instant print is being established 'as the "cutting edge" of an "alternative", non-union, printing industry' [43]. Goss's study of the instant print industry shows that the skill levels required in this sector are very low, and training is 'denied workers where possible'. Most workers are young, inexperienced, previously unemployed, and unable to withstand employer pressure. The success of instant print is regarded as important both in itself, as a growing sector of the total printing industry, and as 'a model and a material asset' to employers in the wider printing industry 'in the struggle to reassert control over labour' [44].

■ Summary

Perhaps the strongest impression to be gleaned about the effects of FS on skills and work organization from these brief industry case studies is that of confusion and uncertainty. This is the result of a number of factors. The first is that if we *are* moving into an era of FS, it is still very much in its early period, and the implications of FS for jobs, work organization and skills are by no means mapped out definitively.

Second, most empirical and theoretical discussion of the FS concept has been centred around private sector manufacturing industry. However, this sector employs a minority of workers. The application of FS to services and the public sector has received less attention and its prospects in these areas are also not yet clear.*

Third, just as the extent to which particular industrial sectors and countries could be categorized as 'Fordist' differed quite markedly, so too it is likely that differences will appear in their tendency towards an FS regime [49]. Countries and sectors with a stronger craft tradition and a ready supply of high-skilled labour (such as West Germany and the clothing regions of the 'Third Italy') are more likely to adopt FS principles than those steeped in Fordist traditions (such as the US and Britain). This has been demonstrated in a number of comparisons between West Germany and Britain, for example [50].

Fourth, and perhaps most importantly, the criteria of what constitutes an FS production system, or an FS firm, are far from settled. Small size, decentralized production, quality and design conscious products in niche markets, new technology, a skilled workforce – all have been cited, yet exceptions to each exist. An attempt to clarify terms has been made by Atkinson and Meager with their distinction between numerical and functional flexibility [51]. The former refers to the ability of a firm to adjust its employment levels to changes in the level of demand, while the latter

---

* Because the Fordist or mass-production paradigm was developed for manufacturing industry, some critics have argued that FS is inapplicable to the services sector [45]. Others argue, however, that the increasing use of 'flexible' workers, such as temporary and part-time staff, and the 'putting out' to specialist firms of many services formerly performed in-house (ranging from legal and insurance services to cleaning and catering) indicate otherwise. Hirschhorn's study of a large bank in the US tells a familiar tale, for example. He found that the bank 'broadened line jobs, . . . increased the sophistication of certain specialist jobs, [and] . . . increased its use of part-time workers' [46]. Similar experiences were found in a recent study by the Institute of Manpower Studies of major UK service industry employers [47]. The role of the public sector has been even less scrutinized, although it has been argued that, in Britain at least, FS tendencies (in particular moves towards numerical flexibility [see below]) have been more prominent in the public than in the private sector [48].

refers to the ability of employees to perform a variety of tasks according to changes in the composition of demand.

Numerical flexibility gives a clearer idea of the core–periphery distinction. As reduction of the firm's exposure to uncertainty becomes the most important organizational motive (as distinct from the reduction of costs *per se*), workers and activities which are not deemed essential to the firm's core business are hived off to the periphery [52]. The growth in the number of temporary and part-time workers and of industrial services is given as evidence of this trend.

It is the notion of functional flexibility, however, that is central to the skills debate. Atkinson and Meager found, for example, that the most important occupational changes accompanying new forms of work organization were 'not the changing balance between occupational groups ... but the changes to job content within occupational groups' [53]. It is in this context that many of the optimistic views about FS have been formed.

The claim that 'de-skilling' is an inevitable consequence of management strategy and of technological change has been extensively debated and will not be reviewed here [54]. However, there is an increasing consensus that, for 'core' workers at least, re-skilling is possible and in fact becoming more common. The growing need for flexibility in production in response to rapidly changing market demands has, especially in combination with the introduction of new computer-based technologies, resulted in a different perception on behalf of management about the skill requirements of the workforce [55]. It is becoming essential for all 'core' workers to have 'a better knowledge of the production process and more responsibility' [56]. The distinction between blue and white collar work (the basis of the separation of the conception and execution of work) is becoming increasingly blurred and simple 'craft' notions of skill are being challenged [57].

Efforts by firms to attain functional flexibility appear to involve an increase in the responsibility and skills of their 'core' workforce. In some cases, this has involved a vertical integration of skills, with workers undertaking tasks of a higher level of competence which had previously been done by a specialist, more highly skilled group of workers. This has been the case with some multi-skilled machine operators. More common, however, has been a horizontal integration of skills, involving tasks at similar levels of competence – such as bricklayers becoming competent in joinery, plastering and painting [58]. This latter type of re-skilling is also more typical of the car industry [59].

On the periphery, the picture is quite different. We can distinguish between two types of peripheral firms (and workers). The first is the relatively independent, specialist, skill-based firm providing quality goods to niche markets or 'producer services' to larger, 'core' firms. This type of peripheral firm corresponds to the 'independents' of the Italian clothing sector, the craft-based machine tool firms of Japan and Western Europe, and the growing number of software, computing, legal and other professional consultancy firms. Their skill profiles are, if anything, higher than those of the 'core' firms they service.

By contrast, there is a much larger 'poor periphery', represented by the dependent clothing sub-contractors, the instant print shops, the growing part-time and temporary workforce composed mainly of domestically committed women, students and other minority or deprived groups, and of course homeworkers. In this part of the periphery, skills and training are not encouraged, employment security is minimal and wages variable.

It would appear, then, that both the 'optimists' and 'pessimists' of the FS debate have valid points to make. Some workers' skills *are* being enhanced – both at the core and in the specialist periphery. On the other hand, many people are being marginalized by being assigned to the 'poor periphery'.

The likely balance between these opposing tendencies is difficult to ascertain (giving support to the 'sceptics'!). As we have seen, the situation varies by region, country and industry and much more empirical work is required before any definitive conclusions can be made. The onus is on the proponents of FS (whether from an optimistic or pessimistic viewpoint) to produce stronger empirical support than they have up to now, to avoid the criticism that 'their vision of a future … dominates their analysis of the present' [60].

One thing does seem fairly certain, however: 'core' jobs will not be the dominant mode of work in the future. Even FS proponents have noted how 'paradoxically, the better use production makes of the quality of labour, the smaller the quantity required' [61]. Only a massive reduction in working hours, but with a maintenance of employment protection, can overcome the increasingly segmented nature of the labour market [62].

Within the periphery, the numerical balance between the specialist and the poor periphery is more problematic. The re-emerging craft paradigm, the basis of Piore and Sabel's FS thesis, is as yet restricted to only a few products and countries. Its ability to be extended appears constrained by FS's need for numerical flexibility, which implies a ready supply of low-skill, low-security labour. Indeed, even the specialist peripheral firms rely on a flexible labour supply to enable them to adjust to changing demand conditions [63].

■ Implications for training policy

Training policy is moving to the centre stage of political debate in many advanced industrialized countries [64]. The FS debate is likely to reinforce this, implying as it does the potential of a renewed demand for high-level skills. If it proves to be the case that we are moving towards an FS regime, the implications for training could be profound for management and government. They would also provide a strong challenge to trade unions.

For employers, the creation of a 'core' workforce has been accompanied by an increasing preparedness to provide resources for extensive retraining and upgrading of their workers' skills to ensure functional flexibility. However, as yet, most re-skilling (in Britain) has been add-on in nature and has not involved the definition of a new, core-skill requirement, reflecting the pragmatic rather than strategic attitude of most firms to their skill requirements [65]. This appears to be in contrast to the case in West Germany, where a much more integrated approach to skill training, work organization, investment in new technology and revised product market strategy has been taken [66].

A longer-term problem for employers has been highlighted by Atkinson and Meager. Currently, core or peripheral status is normally allocated on the basis of posts, rather than postholders; yet most firms regard an individual (core) worker's behavioural characteristics as more important than the 'job' they are currently doing. In fact, the essence of a flexible workforce (and workplace) is that in principle everyone is capable of doing every job. The need to ensure that the core workforce is composed of the 'right' workers will require a new approach to recruitment, selection, training and severance policies [67]. The attraction of 'green field' start-ups, to overcome the rigidities and limitations of current practices, will also increase.

The in-house nature of training for core workers also means that skills acquired through training will become increasingly firm-specific, and their transferability on the external labour market will decline. Combined with the static or reduced number of positions within the firm, workers could find themselves 'trapped'. While some regard this as a 'feudalization' of the employment relationship [68], others are more positive, and cite the Japanese experience of life-time employment approvingly [69].

For smaller firms, especially the skill-based, specialist firms, training represents a dilemma. The innovativeness and growth of these firms depends on a steady supply of skilled labour, but limited resources and competitive pressures make provision of the requisite training for current or future employees problematical. Government training assistance is vital to ensure the future provision of a skilled workforce [70].

The government's role is even more crucial in the case of peripheral workers, for whom firms are actively opposed to the provision of anything other than minimal training. The highly concentrated nature of workers in the peripheral sector (i.e. women, young people) also makes this a legitimate and pressing area for public policy, if such groups are to obtain access to the 'core' job market. Protection of peripheral workers' conditions of employment and assistance for the transitional costs of 'numerical flexibility' is also a state responsibility which has, however, been neglected or actively downgraded. If anything, current policy in

Britain seems to be reinforcing peripheral status on young people through such schemes as the Youth Training Scheme [71]. Atkinson and Meager also noted how large firms rarely use government Jobcentres for filling core-job vacancies [72].

■ Conclusion

Towards the end of their book, Piore and Sabel pose two possible scenarios for the future. One is a restricted FS regime, where 'isolated communities of producers ... seek their fortune in disregard of the fate of their rivals, ... where an island of craftsmen, producing luxury goods ... [is] surrounded by a subproletarian sea of misery'. The alternative is one where 'the local community structures [are] coordinated by national social-welfare regulation, and [where] the provision ... of research facilities and training [is] ... partly a public responsibility' [73]. Given the failure of governments to ensure a more equitable distribution of core jobs and better conditions for peripheral workers, and (in Britain) the attacks on local government, this latter scenario of an 'artisans' republic' seems wildly optimistic.

However, Piore and Sabel's insistence that the future is not determined is salutary in this context. Which scenario results will depend on a number of factors: government ideology and policies, the existing industrial structure, the corporate strategies of firms, evidence from successful examples elsewhere, etc. A potentially crucial factor will be the role played by the trade union movement.

Any move towards FS will pose severe challenges to unions [74]. By establishing core–periphery relationships between firms, FS threatens to further divide workers. By fragmenting production into smaller, dispersed units, it makes union organization more difficult. In Britain, these tendencies are aggravated by the structure of unions, organized as they are along craft and general union principles, rather than by industry. Multi-skilling and the general move towards functional flexibility threaten existing union boundaries and allow employers to play unions off against each other, as the recent debate over the proposed Ford Dundee plant indicates. Single union deals have become the yardstick of union flexibility, but are proving difficult to achieve. In such circumstances, even the work conditions of 'core' workers are threatened, either by non-unionization or by shifting production to other more 'amenable' countries.

The focus on teamwork, quality and innovation, and the new personnel policies inherent in FS, encourage identification by workers with the company. Placing responsibility on workers for production is a novel concept which blurs the lines between 'them' and 'us' and calls into question the traditional basis of British unionism [75].

FS also highlights the need for unions to organize among peripheral workers and firms, to prevent exploitation. This will require a broader perspective and more solidarity to overcome barriers and conflicts between different groups of workers [76].

Such a solidaristic and forward looking strategy is more evident in unions in countries such as Sweden, West Germany and Austria than in Britain. It must be recognized that these countries enjoy a strong legislative basis conducive to consensual decision-making and 'holistic' industrial relations in the face of technological and organizational change. Such a favourable legislative backdrop is unlikely in Britain in the foreseeable future, and it is therefore imperative that unions adopt a more strategic approach to the challenge of FS than the 'confused and generally aimless' approach they have adopted so far [77]. The outcome of Britain's 'Second Industrial Divide' may depend on them.

References

1.　Toffler, A., *The Third Wave*, Pan, 1980; Gorz, A., *Farewell to the Working Class: An Essay on Post-Industrial Socialism*, Pluto Press, 1982; Lash, S. and Urry, J., *The End of Organized Capitalism*, Polity, 1987.

2.　Piore, M. J. and Sabel, C. F., *The Second Industrial Divide – Possibilities for Prosperity*, Basic Books, 1984.

3.　Sabel, C. F., *Work and Politics: the Division of Labour in Industry*, Cambridge University Press, 1982.

4.　Blackburn, P., Coombs, R. and Green, K., *Technology, Economic Growth and the Labour Process*, Macmillan, 1985; Coriat, B., The restructuring of the assembly line: a new economy of time and control, *Capital and Class* 11, 1981, pp. 34–43.

5.　Webber, A. W., Socialization and its discontents, *Harvard Business Review* 63 (3), 1985, pp. 38–54.

6.　Murray, R., Benetton Britain: the new economic order, *Marxism Today* November 1985, pp. 28–32.

7.　Poon, A., *Flexible Specialisation and Small Size – The Case of Caribbean Tourism*, SPRU, 1988.

8.　Williams, K., Cutler, T., Williams, J. and Haslam, C., The end of mass production? *Economy and Society* 16 (3), 1987, pp. 405–439.

9.　Block, F., Economy and nostalgia, *Dissent* 32, Fall 1985, pp. 498–501.

10.　Murray, F., Flexible specialisation in the 'Third Italy', *Capital and Class* 33, 1987, pp. 84–96.

11.　Williams et al., *op. cit.*

12.　Poon, *op. cit.*

13.　Brodner, P., Towards an anthropocentric approach in European manufacturing, *Vocational Training Bulletin* no. 1, 1987, pp. 30–39; Brusco, S., The Emilian model: productive decentralisation and social integration, *Cambridge Journal of Economics* 6 (2), 1982, pp. 167–184; Friedman, D., Beyond the age of Ford: the strategic basis of the Japanese success in automobiles, in Zysman, J. and Taylor, L. (eds), *American Industry in International Competition: Government Policies and Corporate Strategies*, Cornell University Press, 1983; Hirschhorn, L., The post-industrial economy: labour, skills and the new mode of production, *The Service Industries Journal* 8(1) 1987, pp. 19–38; Murray, R., *op. cit.*; Piore and Sabel, *op. cit.*; Sorge, A. and Streeck, W., Industrial relations and technical change: the case for an extended perspective, in Hyman, R. and Streeck, W. (eds), *New Technology and Industrial Relations*, Blackwell, 1988; Wobbe, W., Technology, work and employment – new trends in the structural change of society, *Vocational Training Bulletin* no. 1, 1987, pp. 3–6; Wickens, P., *The Road to Nissan: Flexibility, Quality, Teamwork*, Macmillan, 1987.

14. Gough, J., Industrial policy and socialist strategy: restructuring and the unity of the working class, *Capital and Class* 29, 1986, pp. 58–81; Holloway, J., The red rose of Nissan, *Capital and Class* 32, 1987, pp. 142–164; Hyman, R., Flexible specialization: miracle or myth?, in Hyman and Streeck, *op. cit.*; Mitter, S., Industrial restructuring and manufacturing home work: immigrant women in the UK clothing industry, *Capital and Class* 27, 1986, pp. 37–80; Murray, F., *op. cit.*; Sayer, A., New developments in manufacturing: the just-in-time system, *Capital and Class* 30, 1986, pp. 43–72.

15. Pollert, A., The 'flexible firm': fixation or fact?, *Work, Employment and Society* 2 (3) 1988, pp. 281–316; Williams et al., *op. cit.*; Wood, S., Between Fordism and flexibility? The US car industry, in Hyman and Streeck, *op. cit.*

16. Block, *op. cit.*; Kuttner, R., The shape of things to come, *The New Republic*, January 7–14, 1985, pp. 84–96.

17. Poon, *op. cit.*

18. Murray, R., *op. cit.*; Sorge and Streeck, *op. cit.*

19. Piore and Sabel, *op. cit.*; Brusco, *op. cit.*

20. Wobbe, *op. cit.*

21. Piore and Sabel, *op. cit.*

22. Murray, R., *op. cit.*

23. Brusco, *op. cit.*

24. *ibid.*

25. Solinas, G., Labour market segmentation and workers' careers: the case of the Italian knitwear industry, *Cambridge Journal of Economics* 6 (4), 1982, pp. 331–352.

26. Brusco, *op. cit.*

27. Solinas, *op. cit.*

28. Mitter, *op. cit.*; Greater London Council, *The London Industrial Strategy*, GLC, 1987.

29. Murray, R., *op. cit.*

30. Piore and Sabel, *op. cit.*

31. Solinas, *op. cit.*

32. Murray, R., *op. cit.*; GLC, *op. cit.*

33. Wood, S. (ed.), *The Degradation of Work? Skill, Deskilling and the Labour Process*, Hutchinson, 1982.

34. Braverman, H., *Labor and Monopoly Capital*, Monthly Review Press, 1974.

35. Piore and Sabel, *op. cit.*

36. *ibid.*
37. Wood, 1982, *op. cit.*
38. Murray, F., *op. cit.*
39. Friedman, *op. cit.*
40. Holloway, *op. cit.*; Wickens, *op. cit.*
41. Sayer, *op. cit.*; Wickens, *op. cit.*
42. Turnbull, P.J., The limits to 'Japanisation' – just-in-time, labour relations and the UK automotive industry, *New Technology, Work and Employment* 3(1) 1988, pp. 7–20.
43. Goss, D., Instant print: technology and capitalist control, *Capital and Class* 31, 1987, pp. 79–91.
44. *ibid.*
45. Block, *op. cit.*
46. Hirschhorn, *op. cit.*
47. Atkinson, J. and Meager, N., *New Forms of Work Organisation*, Institute of Manpower Studies, 1986.
48. Pollert, *op. cit.*
49. Piore and Sabel, *op. cit.*
50. Lane, C., Capitalism or culture? A comparative analysis of the position in the labour process and labour market of lower white-collar workers in the financial services sector of Britain and the Federal Republic of West Germany, *Work, Employment and Society* 1(1) 1987, pp. 57–83; Lane, C., Industrial change in Europe: the pursuit of flexible specialisation in Britain and West Germany, *Work, Employment and Society* 2 (2) 1988, pp. 141–168; Sorge and Streeck, *op. cit.*
51. *ibid.*
52. Hirschhorn, *op. cit.*
53. Atkinson and Meager, *op. cit.*
54. Wood, 1988, *op. cit.*; Hyman and Streeck, *op. cit.*; Knights, D. and Willmott, H. (eds), *New Technology and the Labour Process*, Macmillan, 1988.
55. Atkinson and Meager, *op. cit.*; Sayer, *op. cit.*
56. Heinz, W.R., The future of work, *Vocational Training Bulletin* no. 1, 1987, pp. 13–18.
57. Wobbe, *op. cit.*
58. Atkinson and Meager, *op. cit.*
59. Turnbull, *op. cit.*
60. Wood, 1988, *op. cit.*
61. Brodner, *op. cit.*
62. *ibid.*
63. Brusco, *op. cit.*
64. OECD, *The Future of Vocational Education and Training*, OECD, 1983.
65. Atkinson and Meager, *op. cit.*
66. Lane, C., 1988, *op. cit.*
67. *ibid.*; Sayer, *op. cit.*
68. Heinz, *op. cit.*
69. Senker, P., The Technical and Vocational Education Initiative and economic performance in the United Kingdom: an initial assessment, *Journal of Education Policy* 1 (4) 1986, pp. 293–303.

70.   Piore and Sabel, *op. cit.*

71.   Goss, *op. cit.*; Jarvis, V. and Prais, S.J., *Two Nations of Shopkeepers: Training for Retailing in France and Britain*, NIESR, 1988.

72.   Atkinson and Meager, *op. cit.*

73.   Piore and Sabel, *op. cit.*

74.   Murray, F., The decentralisation of production – the decline of the mass-collective worker?, *Capital and Class* 19, 1983, pp. 74–99; Rainbird, H., New technology, training and union strategies, in Hyman and Streeck, *op. cit.*; Sayer, *op. cit.*; Sorge and Streeck, *op. cit.*; Wickens, *op. cit.*

75.   Turnbull, *op. cit.*; Wickens, *op. cit.*

76.   Lash and Urry, *op. cit.*

77.   Atkinson and Meager, *op. cit.*

Chapter 6

Mass Unemployment Returns

K. Roberts

■ The spread of joblessness

The oil price spirals of the 1970s created world-wide inflation. Governments responded by plunging the entire Western economy into recession. In Britain, output and employment in manufacturing declined sharply. In 1981–82 production was no higher than during the three-day week enforced by the 1973–74 coal-miners' strike. Public spending and consequently the growth of service sector employment were restrained in 1976. These restraints were intensified under the 1979 Conservative government's monetarist policies. Throughout the 1970s the labour force was growing owing to the long-term inflow of married women and increasing numbers of school-leavers, the consequence of a rising birth-rate from 1955 to 1965. A net loss of jobs coupled with increasing numbers seeking work sent unemployment soaring more rapidly than ever before in Britain's history, to over 3 000 000 in 1982.

   The initial rise of unemployment was accompanied by debate as to whether involuntary joblessness was really spreading as rapidly as the statistics suggested. Were redundancy payments and earnings-related benefits enabling the unemployed to delay and search for the right jobs instead of settling for whatever was immediately available? Had the separation of social security claims from the Jobcentre service eased former pressures on claimants to apply for notified vacancies? (Layard, 1979). There were suggestions that employment protection legislation might have destroyed jobs by making employers reluctant to hire. However, by the time unemployment had reached 2 000 000 no-one believed that the above influences were more than marginal. The folklore of work-shy scroungers was easily ridiculed. The plain fact was that Britain had many more would-be workers than jobs.

Source: K. Roberts (1984) *School-Leavers and their Prospects*, The Open University Press, Milton Keynes, ch. 4, pp. 45–60.

Table 6.1 Unemployment rates by age-group: Great Britain, October 1982.

	Males	Females	Total
Under 18	24.9	32.1	27.6
18–19	29.9	25.4	27.8
20–24	22.5	16.8	20.1
25–34	14.5	9.7	12.7
35–44	11.5	5.1	9.1
45–54	11.0	5.1	8.5
55–59	13.3	5.9	10.4
60+	20.5	0.7	15.5
All ages	16.0	10.0	13.5

During the 1980s, 3 000 000 out of work has invited comparison with the 1930s. There are many similarities, including some social and personal consequences of prolonged joblessness, but there are also important differences (Tomlinson, 1982). Firstly, Britain in the 1980s is faring worse, not better, than her competitors. Opinions differ, needless to say, on whether this is due to the incompetence of the 1980s governments or to the low productivity, investment and profit margins, coupled with high inflation inherited from previous administrations.

Secondly, unemployment in the 1980s is a national malaise, less concentrated within severely depressed regions than in the 1930s. Unemployment is still well above average in regions dependent on older manufacturing industries like shipbuilding and textiles, vulnerable to international competition and technological change, and now in decline. But some growth industries of the 1950s, including steel and motor vehicles, have joined the older industries in shedding labour. Areas in the West Midlands, recently a boom region, have become industrial waste-lands. In the still relatively prosperous south-east, unemployment black-spots have appeared, many in inner cities where the natural decline of older industries has been accelerated by urban re-development. The intention was to improve the environment. The consequences have often included the spread of social and economic blight. However, unemploy-ment blackspots are not all close to city centres. During the 1970s and 1980s many of the 1950s' new industrial estates, built for that generation's expanding industries, have been devastated by factory closures, creating extremely high unemployment in adjacent housing areas.

Thirdly, the 1980s unemployment is more concentrated among vulnerable groups, especially the unskilled and young people. Between

1972 and 1977 general unemployment rose by 45 per cent, and unemployment among 16–17-year-olds by 120 per cent. In 1977 there were 1 500 000 unemployed, 6 per cent of the workforce, but the unemployment rate for 16–18-year-olds was 8.8 per cent. In some regions it was considerably higher: 12.4 per cent on Merseyside, and in blackspots such as Knowsley (which includes Kirkby) it was 37.1 per cent. After 1977, despite the rapid expansion of special measures, the gap between youth and adult unemployment continued to widen. In October 1982, with general unemployment of 13.5 per cent, the rate for 16–19-year-olds was 28 per cent (see Table 6.1). Programmes to alleviate youth unemployment seemed to be waging a despairing battle against economic tides.

During the 1930s unemployment among young people was higher than for the adult workforce, but the gap was narrower than opened in the 1970s. In their 1910 survey of York, Rowntree and Lasker (1911) were surprised to find as many as 12.4 per cent of the 14–18-year-olds unemployed for over six months. It was believed at the time that school-leavers found jobs relatively easily, albeit juvenile jobs with low pay, and that their risks of unemployment were greatest as blind alleys closed around age 18, when they became eligible for adult rates. This older pattern may be reappearing in the 1980s, with government policies having held down school-leavers' wage levels making them more attractive to employers, and with training and educational schemes aimed primarily at 16-year-old school-leavers. During the early 1980s joblessness began to spread rapidly among 20–24-year-olds, to 20 per cent in October 1982, but throughout the rise of unemployment towards 3 000 000, teenagers suffered more acutely than any other age groups.

■ Why have young people's jobs disappeared?

The recession of the 1970s and 1980s has victimized young people in three ways. First, when firms trim workforces, recruitment is reduced or halted, which is particularly frustrating for newcomers to the labour market, like school-leavers. Natural wastage can sound a painless way of shedding labour. It is less likely to encounter trade union opposition than redundancies. Existing workers are protected, but individuals without jobs, including school-leavers, are penalized when vacancies dry up.

Second, when profit margins are squeezed, training is often one of the 'luxuries' to be pruned. Firms realize that this economy threatens their long-term prospects, but when short-term survival is at risk all possible cutbacks are considered. In the 1960s, 40 per cent of males leaving school at 16 or earlier were apprenticed. By 1980 this proportion had been halved. In 1968 there were 236 000 apprentices in manufacturing industry, but only 100 000 in 1982 (Manpower Services Commission, 1982).

Third, when general unemployment is high, young job-seekers face strong competition from older experienced workers. Some school-leavers' jobs, including apprenticeships, are 'sheltered' because adults are ineligible. Other jobs are closed to young people who are considered immature and irresponsible, unsuited to heavy work, excluded by health, safety and other protective legislation, or because alcohol, driving and/or shifts are involved. The majority of jobs open to young people are also open to adults, and the latter often win the favour of employers, many of whom [. . .] have become highly critical of school-leavers (National Youth Employment Council, 1974; Colledge *et al.*, 1977).

[. . .] some employers' complaints are at variance with the facts. On any assessment, educational standards have risen. Studies that have recorded the usual complaints when employers were questioned about young people in general have found the same firms expressing complete satisfaction with their own young workers (Yates and Hall, 1982; Ashton *et al.*, 1982). Employers' criticisms may sometimes be attempts to disclaim responsibility for denying young people employment, but whatever firms' motives and however unjustified some may appear, the removal of unskilled manual jobs from youth labour markets seems to be a long-term trend that was accentuated, not instigated, by the onset of recession in the mid-1970s. Throughout the 1960s, there was a decline in demand for unskilled teenagers, which more than offset the trend towards 'staying on' at school, and raising the school-leaving age in 1973 (National Youth Employment Council, 1974). Larger companies with scope for choice began restricting recruitment to semi and unskilled jobs to the over-18s, or even over-21s. New technologies which allow few opportunities for school-leavers to learn the ropes, the fact that teenagers had ceased to be cheap, market pressures on firms to reduce labour costs, the spread of shift systems, now covering over a third of male manufacturing jobs, and the availability of cheap, part-time female labour could have been responsible. Whatever employers' motives, the 1970s recession accelerated the withdrawal of school-leavers' jobs.

■ Local labour markets

Beginning workers do not face equal risks of unemployment. Individuals' prospects depend not on national or even regional rates, but on the levels of unemployment in local labour markets, the areas within which, for practical purposes, their search for work is confined. The geographical shape and size of school-leavers' labour markets depends, among other things, on public transport networks. City centres are usually accessible from all suburbs whereas public transport to adjacent out-lying districts may be inconvenient. A Youthaid (1979) study of 250 school-leavers in London, Northumberland and Newcastle-upon-Tyne found that the average distance travelled to work was under three miles. Public transport is expensive. Teenagers cannot afford to commute long distances on the wages they are likely to be offered, unless their families are able and willing to subsidize the young people's employment. This is one reason why levels of youth unemployment can vary considerably within regions, even within the same towns and cities, and how young people in out-lying towns, villages and rural areas become trapped in local labour markets offering very limited opportunities. Acquiring a car or motorbike widens individuals' employment prospects, but once again, unless they have prosperous and generous parents, school-leavers and the young un-employed can rarely afford these assets. Once young adults have been able to save and purchase private transport, they can seek jobs further afield, and which involve starting and finishing work at unsocial hours. This is one way in which individuals escape from the 'trash jobs' paying 'slave wages' to which many school-leavers are confined.

Only nine respondents in the Youthaid study moved away from home in their search for work. Six of these entered the armed forces. Residential mobility is not a real option for most school-leavers unless they wish to join and are accepted by the armed services or in other occupations like nursing where accommodation is normally available along with the job. Beginning workers cannot afford independent flats and houses. Giving young people access to the national labour market will require the provision of cheap housing for all young single persons, not just full-time higher education students.

■ Qualifications

Within local labour markets, school-leavers' chances of gaining employ-ment invariably depend upon their qualifications. Rising unemployment has implications for all beginning workers including university graduates. The latter have found their scope for choice narrowing. Instead of deciding which jobs to accept, many have been obliged to take whatever is offered. Instead of fixing jobs prior to graduation, some have remained un-employed for months, and have then been obliged to take temporary stop-gap vacancies. But graduates rarely become long-term unemployed. They can always move down the labour market if necessary, into formerly non-graduate occupations like local government, banking and insurance. There are now more graduate recruits into the executive than the administrative civil service grades. Trading down occurs at all levels. In most parts of the country, 'O'-levels are now demanded for craft apprenticeships. It is school-leavers without useful qualifications, who would have obtained unskilled jobs in the relatively buoyant labour markets of the 1960s and who have nowhere downwards to trade, who tend to be left without any jobs. A 1977 national survey found that 53 per cent of the young unemployed had no qualifications, at a time when only a fifth of young people left school in this condition (Colledge et al., 1977).

The most modest qualifications can enhance school-leavers' prospects. At the same time, even 'A'-levels and degrees carry no guarantee. There are no jobs where recruitment is wholly on the basis of educational attainments. When employers pay attention to qualifications, they invariably use additional criteria, including personal qualities, such as maturity and appearing keen to work (Ashton et al., 1982). Moreover, the value of a given level of qualification depends on the state of the labour market in which it is traded. When jobs were plentiful, CSEs enabled school-leavers to enter office jobs and apprenticeships. When the level of unemployment means that there are always better-qualified applicants even for unskilled jobs, lower-grade CSEs cease to be useful. This is why experiences and opinions among teachers and young people differ so sharply on the value of paper credentials.

Furthermore, a given level of qualification can enhance a group of school-leavers' prospects without being any use whatsoever to most members. Two CSEs rather than no qualifications may mean that 20 rather than 10 per cent of male school-leavers obtain craft apprenticeships or avoid joblessness completely, depending on the state of the local labour market. In either event, 80 per cent find that their qualifications are 'no use'. Teachers who advise pupils that qualifications will strengthen their chances in the labour market are telling the truth. At the same time they are increasing the likelihood of the young people finding cause to complain of 'broken promises'.

Pupils and parents react in diverse ways, depending on their predispositions, as unemployment devalues qualifications. The standard advice offered by middle-class and other aspiring parents is to 'try even harder'. Young people who take this advice battle on, sometimes as 'new sixth-formers' and equip themselves with additional CSEs, 'O'-levels, and sometimes 'A'-levels before entering the labour market. These tactics are sometimes successful, but risky. Qualifications do not always carry the same weight at age 18 as at 16. 'Staying on' can make modestly qualified school-leavers too old for craft apprenticeships (Lee and Wrench, 1981).

Among young people from unskilled working-class homes, a more common reaction to unemployment appears to be that 'even qualifications are no use'. Teachers are unable to motivate these pupils with the threat of unemployment and the carrot of qualifications. In districts where these attitudes are widespread, unemployment makes schooling seem more pointless, and teaching a more thankless task than ever. Pupils become restless, disillusioned and indifferent, when they are in attendance. It has been suggested that for these young people truanting can be a useful preparation for street life on the dole (Adams and Sawdon, 1978).

■ Contacts

In addition to their places of residence and qualifications, school-leavers' prospects depend upon their contacts. Informal job-finding and recruitment are as widespread as ever. Being 'spoken for' is still an advantage, and often decisive when seeking a good job. This applies at all levels of employment. Social class origins are irrelevant to students' performances within higher education, but discriminate at the point of entering the workforce. Graduates from middle-class homes are advised when and how to apply for jobs in prestigious professions such as law and accountancy (Kelsall *et al.*, 1972). Offering the right references, displaying a recognized school tie, speaking in the interviewer's accent and already being known by the right people add weight to job applications.

Equivalent processes operate in the competition for craft apprenticeships and, indeed, all 'worthwhile' jobs. Many young people who are left jobless, particularly the long-term unemployed, owe this fate to lacking useful contacts. In 1977, when youth unemployment was rising rapidly, a Manpower Services Commission (MSC) survey found that 19 per cent of the young unemployed came from families with other members out of work, at a time when adult unemployment was 6 per cent, and 79 per cent had unemployed friends when unemployment among 16–18-year-olds was 8.8 per cent (Colledge *et al.*, 1977). The long-term young unemployed are concentrated in families and communities whose members are not the 'right people'. Some social backgrounds act as millstones: 'No-one from Liverpool 8 need apply' (Wilson and Womersley, 1977).

Research among the young unemployed has clarified how labour markets operate and how contacts work. Large firms' existing workforces are said to function as 'internal labour markets'. Competition for firms' better jobs is often limited to existing employees. These internal labour markets become 'extended' to non-employees with contacts that make them potential recruits (Manwaring, 1982). The barriers that divide potential recruits from other individuals may be invisible but they are extremely powerful. Within localities, these barriers segment all workers, in employment and jobless, into numerous labour markets, divided vertically and horizontally (Ashton and Maguire, 1982).

Why do large, otherwise highly bureaucratized enterprises persist with informal recruitment? It is inexpensive. The costs of placing and replying to adverts are avoided. It enables local managements to respond flexibly to novel problems and opportunities. Most important of all, firms discover that informal recruitment 'works'. It enables them to exclude the 'unacceptable' and recruit non-troublesome labour (Jenkins, 1982). The costs are borne by individuals who would be competent but lack contacts. Young people from unskilled homes and the ethnic minorities (Lee and Wrench, 1981) are often trapped in this situation, excluded from the better jobs, and confined to 'slave labour', government schemes and unemployment.

■ Ethnic minorities

Every study to compare their prospects has found that black and brown school-leavers are less successful than whites in the quality of jobs obtained and avoiding unemployment (Allen and Smith, 1975; Brooks and Singh, 1978; Manchester City Council Planning Department, 1979; Ipswich National Union of Teachers Working Party, 1979; Watts, 1980; Dex, 1982). Unemployment among young people of West Indian origin, the most frequently researched minority, is two to three times as high as among whites.

Discrimination in the labour market is not the sole explanation. Racial disadvantage is multi-dimensional. Britain's non-white minorities are concentrated in high unemployment, inner-urban areas. The first generation immigrants settled in these 'twilight' districts where the majority have remained. Economic and cultural barriers have impeded their dispersal. West Indian pupils, but not Asians, under-achieve at school compared with the white population (Swann Report, 1981). Young people from all minority backgrounds tend to lack the contacts that facilitate entry into apprenticeships and other jobs worth keeping (Lee and Wrench, 1981). Asian youth sometimes retreat into family businesses, a course which is usually considered second-best (Fowler *et al.*, 1977). Entrepreneurial activity has been less common within West Indian communities; their young people often retreat into unemployment.

Discrimination in the labour market is piled on top of other racial disadvantages. Before 1968, discrimination was blatant and widespread. 'Coloureds' were excluded or subject to quotas in many firms. The 1968 Race Relations Act, strengthened in 1976, has made discrimination illegal, but the practice persists. Studies of identically qualified applicants for the same jobs always find that, overall, blacks are less successful than whites (Smith, 1977). Individual acts of discrimination are difficult to prove. Non-white youth may not always realize when they are being victimized (Allen and Smith, 1975). The thin stream of complaints reaching the Commission for Racial Equality (CRE) is evidence that existing legislation simply does not work, rather than that the law has changed behaviour. Immigration has not been a cause of rising unemployment. Since the 1960s the inflow has been reduced to a trickle, exceeded by emigration. The ethnic minorities who filled Britain's labour shortages during the 1950s and 1960s have simply borne the costs of subsequent economic failures.

On paper the battery of government-sponsored measures to achieve parity of treatment appears formidable. In addition to enforcing statutes forbidding discrimination, the CRE, supported by the Race Relations Employment Advisory Service within the Department of Employment, plays an educational role. Inner-city programmes and, insofar as they are aimed at disadvantaged groups, the MSC's training schemes for young people and adults, are intended to benefit ethnic minorities. Race relations is now covered in the initial training of all teachers and careers officers. Special language classes are offered in schools and further education. The MSC supports language training at places of employment. Yet despite all these measures, the spread of unemployment has been particularly rapid among ethnic minority youth. Between 1973 and 1976, when youth employment was creeping upwards, the proportion of ethnic minority youth among the young jobless rose from 2.8 to 4.6 per cent. By the early 1980s, in many inner cities, over a half of all young blacks were out of work (Roberts *et al.*, 1981).

Ethnic divisions are strengthened during work entry. Despite multi-racial education, on leaving school black and Asian youth are not assimilated, but forced back into ethnic sub-cultures. West Indian and Asian youth face higher rates of unemployment even when, as is often the case, they leave school better qualified than local whites (Driver, 1980; Fuller, 1980; Roberts *et al.*, 1981). The superior performances of ethnic minority youth in many inner-city schools are not difficult to explain. Inner-city whites are a residue, many families with the means and motivation having departed. In contrast, the parents of present-day Asian and West Indian school-leavers are mostly first generation immigrants, and include many talented and ambitious people. Why else would they have crossed the oceans? Since settling in Britain they have been under-employed in unskilled jobs. They were told that they lacked relevant qualifications and skills, but many are determined that their children should succeed. They may not be able to provide the knowledgeable support available in middle-class homes, but Asian and West Indian parents are no less keen that their children should do well. The pupils are encouraged to study and enrol in examination courses. Ethnic minority families want education to lead to qualifications that lead to jobs, and often display little interest in alternative, multi-cultural curricula (Stone, 1981).

Asian pupils are now equalling whites' performances. West Indian pupils atill lag well behind their white population in general, but often out-perform whites from their own neighbourhoods and schools, which usually means entering the labour market with CSEs rather than completely unqualified. Ethnic minority youth leave better qualified and, on average, more ambitious than their white classmates (Gupta, 1977, Roberts *et al.*,

1981), but there are no grounds for describing their ambitions as unrealistic. The jobs to which most aspire are within the young people's abilities. They are not all demanding employment as brain surgeons and airline pilots. Most boys seek trades and training. The girls hope to work in offices, libraries, as receptionists and community workers. They are not demanding 'the best', but many are determined to avoid servile jobs. West Indian and Asian school-leavers are rarely content to accept 'anything'.

Ambitious West Indian and Asian youth are not necessarily keen to leave the neighbourhoods where they were reared. It is ordinarily taken for granted that aspiring whites from inner-city backgrounds hope to move to better areas. This is what 'getting on' is taken to mean. Ethnic minority families would appreciate better houses and surroundings. Nevertheless, given the prevailing social climate, many are ambivalent about leaving known people and places. Would they be accepted elsewhere? The wider society's deprived areas have become black youth's swinging places, their refuges and spiritual homes (Pryce, 1979). Many want better houses, education and employment prospects while they remain in Britain's Brixtons and Moss Sides. Does the wider society even understand this kind of ambition?

Asian and West Indian youth's qualifications and ambitions are rewarded with well-above-average rates of unemployment. Another difference is that minority youth have an obvious explanation for all their labour market difficulties – racial injustice. They are arrested by the same social class disadvantages faced by local whites. But no matter how strenuously and frequently sociologists argue their importance, social class divisions remain invisible. It is much easier to see skin pigmentation, and to many unemployed blacks and Asians, the explanation for their predicament is as clear as daylight – they are non-white citizens in a white society that is intent on holding them down, forcing them back. Black and Asian youth are less likely than whites to attribute their unemployment to 'bad luck', or accept it stoically as a fact of life, like the geographical terrain. Researchers have noted that black youth are among the most radical members of their entire generation (Rex and Tomlinson, 1979). Many, especially those influenced by Rastafarian doctrines (Garrison, 1979; Cashmore, 1979), are no longer seeking assimilation, or 'submersion'. They are turning inwards, drawing upon their own cultures, and looking to their own community organizations to help realize their ambitions.

Unemployment is not uniting black and white youth to address a common problem. It deepens racial divisions, and obstructs policies for racial equality. Ethnic minority youth's unemployment rates make the case for 'positive action', delivering better education, training and job opportunities. Blacks and Asians obtain their fair share of special measures (Stares et al., 1982), which would be reassuring if these opportunities always led to good jobs. The ethnic minorities are not seeking equality with their disadvantaged white neighbours. The latter's jobs and unemployment rates will not assuage the minorities' grievances. Why should they rest content with opportunities considered adequate only for the least privileged whites? Yet it would obviously be inflammatory to offer opportunities to inner-city blacks and Asians that were denied to their white neighbours. Positive discrimination and affirmative action in favour of women and ethnic minorities were originally proposed in the context of full employment, economic expansion and growing opportunities for upward mobility.

■ Gender

The growth of female participation in the workforce has helped to generate pressures for equal pay and opportunities. At the beginning of the century only one in ten married women held paid employment. Women whose working lives were brief interludes before marriage may have conceded male breadwinners' prior claims in the competition for good jobs. Females' standards of living depended primarily on the occupations of their male heads of households – their fathers, then husbands. Employers saw no reason to waste training on female school-leavers who would attach greater importance to motherhood.

Today well over a half of married women are in employment. The majority of today's female school-leavers can expect to work outside their homes for the greater part of their adult lives. Even if their spouses are employed, women's earnings will be major, not marginal determinants of their families' living standards. Moreover, a third of today's marriages are expected to end in divorce or separation. Women can no longer rely upon marriage to deliver lifetime economic security. This is the background against which women won rights to equal pay for equal work, conferred by the 1970 Equal Pay Act, and to equal treatment in hiring and promotion in 1975.

It is common knowledge that these laws have yet to reshape the labour force. On average, women still earn a third less than men. Labour markets remain segmented. Female school-leavers are mainly recruited as office workers, shop assistants and factory operatives, when jobs are available. Management, jobs requiring scientific and technical qualifications, the prestigious professions and skilled trades remain male-dominated. Gender legislation has not changed employers' habits (Ashton and Maguire, 1980). They still regard women as cheap and flexible, suitable for jobs requiring little training but manual dexterity. Firms are still reluctant to invest in training young women.

Overt sex discrimination is disappearing from education. More girls than boys now enter 'O'-levels. Females are still under-represented in the universities, but their numbers are growing, to 37 per cent of under-graduates in 1982, and they are just as likely as males to enter some form of higher education. Colleges of Education recruit more women than men. Girls are still the less likely to succeed in maths and the physical sciences. A hidden curriculum which defines science as masculine and endorses teachers' acquiescence when clever girls fail to progress still operates. But schools and colleges are havens of equality compared with the labour market where their confinement to low-paid jobs perpetuates the idea that women's earnings are secondary and that husbands' careers should take precedence. While passing equal opportunity laws, governments have preserved social security regulations which treat married women as dependants.

Female school-leavers rarely allege unfair treatment (Allen and Smith, 1975). Individual acts of discrimination against women and ethnic minorities are equally difficult to prove. Until now, however, most girls have appeared satisfied with their inferior opportunities. Boys' and girls' vocational aspirations differ. Homes and schools separate the sexes' aspirations like the labour market divides their opportunities. Girls still see their futures primarily in terms of marriage. Their occupational horizons are short-term (Wilkins, 1955; Douvan and Adelson, 1966; Closs et al., 1977). The sexes' aspirations are less divided than their actual occupations, but girls are still more likely than boys to abandon first choices and lower their sights when obstacles arise. An American study of unsuccessful medical school applicants found that women were less likely to reapply and more likely to abandon medicine for less prestigious careers (Weisman et al., 1976).

If women's own aspirations were decisive there would be a trend towards equal representation throughout the occupational structure. Women doctors, managers, solicitors and motor mechanics would increase in number. But women's own wishes do not shape the entire labour market. Many employers still prefer to train males. Furthermore, male employees display little inclination to escape from their own enclaves and share women's work, unless the latter is upgraded, sometimes with shift premiums as in Lancashire textile mills. It is rare to encounter male school-leavers seeking jobs as typists, canteen assistants and switchboard operators. Men who perform women's work, whether by choice or necessity, may be regarded as 'odd'. Male nurses are considered unambitious and unattractive (Hesselbart, 1977). Males face greater difficulty in gaining acceptance in female occupations than women in formerly masculine jobs.

Between the wars, many studies of youth unemployment ignored girls; their lack of jobs and confinement to blind alleys were considered 'less of a problem'. It was believed that girls could withdraw into their homes without loss of face, occupy themselves with domestic duties and prepare for marriage. Women who did not marry and remained in employment were considered failures. Until World War I it was common for girls to be kept off school performing domestic duties during family emergencies, such as the illness of younger siblings. School Board officials sometimes turned a blind eye to these 'necessary' absences. After 1945, studies of school-leavers often concentrated upon boys. The latter's entry into employment was treated as a major status transition. Marriage and motherhood were regarded as the feminine equivalents. We do not know how earlier generations of girls felt about this role-typing, but recent female school-leavers have shared boys' worries about unemployment.

Youth unemployment has become equally prevalent among girls and boys. Competition from experienced married women and labour cut-backs in the light manufacturing industries that once recruited large numbers of female school-leavers have reduced girls' opportunities. During periods out of work, many girls still retreat into their homes, but few revel in the enforced domesticity (Donovan and Oddy, 1982). It is considered less acceptable for girls than boys to hang about in pubs, clubs, arcades and on the streets. Girls who are 'kept in' helping their mothers usually resent their confinement. They resent their isolation from youth scenes; their inability to dress in the latest fashions, attend discos and socialize with workmates (Roberts *et al.*, 1981).

There is anecdotal evidence, nothing more, of some unemployed girls drifting into the sex industries. Doctors and youth workers report instances of unemployed girls opting for early motherhood, thereby qualifying for more generous social security payments and independent housing, and establishing themselves in adult roles (Harold Francis, *Guardian*, 30 December 1982). Will unemployment halt any trend towards equality and force women back into the domestic role? The latter has always concealed massive female unemployment. Some contemporary politicians regard domesticity for women as a solution to the wider society's unemployment problem. Many generations of teenage girls, confined to routine office and factory jobs, have seen marriage and motherhood as escape routes. Unemployment may be entrenching these preferences among some girls, but it seems unlikely that high levels of youth unemployment will provoke a general trend towards younger marriage and parenthood. In the full employment era, among young women, settling quickly in a chosen occupation was related to early marriage (Dex, 1982). Unemployment is more likely to impede than accelerate other aspects of social development. Moreover, male unemploy-ment makes the traditional female role, supported by a male breadwinner, less accessible. In 1980 there were only three-fifths as many pregnancies among 15–19-year-olds as in 1971. There is further anecdotal evidence of some women, usually highly educated, refusing to 'retire' temporarily from employment for fear that they may never recover their jobs and occupational status. Males' and females' reactions to unemployment seem to vary by social class, like responses to educational and employment opportunities. These reactions may be helping to create an increasingly divided society. The number of households with both husbands and wives in well-paid jobs could increase, alongside a growth of families with neither partner in employment.

Government programmes to alleviate unemployment have catered equally for boys and girls, but are the schemes equally useful to the latter? Like jobs, training opportunities are still divided according to gender. Moreover, government measures appear designed to facilitate male careers in which, following initial training, individuals establish themselves in worthwhile jobs during their twenties. At this point in the life cycle, women tend to withdraw from the labour market. On what terms, if any, will young women who have recently retired to become parents be able to re-enter the workforce? Many will be unable to impress employers with their prior experience. Adult education and training, rather than pro-grammes aimed at teenagers, may be more effective in preventing women's disadvantages mounting while youth unemployment persists.

■ Cyclical and structural problem?

The rise of unemployment has been accompanied by a debate on the respective contributions of cyclical and structural factors. This controversy has more than academic significance. Prescriptions based on incorrect diagnoses will not deliver the intended cures.

Cyclical unemployment rises at troughs in the business cycle then disappears when the economy recovers. Structural unemployment is a term covering a variety of conditions which share in common only their intransigence in the face of general economic recovery. Simply 'throwing money at unemployment' is of no avail when the problem is structural. The decline of older industries such as textiles results in structural unemploy-ment when firms shed workers, many of whom cannot be absorbed into expanding industries like banking and telecommunications, because either they lack relevant qualifications and skills or they live in the wrong parts of the country.

All analysts agree that cyclical and structural factors have con-tributed during the rise of unemployment since the mid-1970s. The entire Western economy entered a period of recession. National governments were reluctant to expand their economies for fear of pulling in imports, upsetting their trade balances, destroying the value of their currencies and stoking inflation, thereby building more serious problems for the future. The international community proved unable to act in concert, so the recession deepened, and accelerated structural changes including, in Britain, the decline of older industries with out-dated technologies. Where it exists, structural unemployment accentuates cyclical movements. With a permanent pool of job-seekers, employers can lay off workers in the knowledge that later recruitment will be no problem. This is one reason why high levels of unemployment and job mobility sometimes co-exist (White, n.d.).

Writers who allege that contemporary youth unemployment is structural accept that its growth has been accelerated by cyclical forces. Their argument is that straightforward reflation, if and when it arrives, will not re-absorb all the young unemployed; that technological trends and the changing shape of the occupational structure will perpetuate young people's exclusion from jobs. Most job losses of the 1970s and early 1980s were caused by recession, not new technologies (Yates and Hall, 1982). Nevertheless, it is argued, reflection and new investment are now more likely to produce capital intensification, and higher output with labour forces of current or smaller sizes than increased employment (White, n.d.; Sawdon and Taylor, 1980).

Silicon chips could revolutionize work patterns in most offices and factories. Their applications are neither job- nor industry-specific. Robots can service assembly lines. Information can be stored and transmitted through microcircuits instead of by clerks. Rational decisions can be entrusted to computers instead of managers. The replacement of human workers by machines is not new. The internal combustion engine made horses and blacksmiths redundant. Mechanization and the container revolution have decimated dock workforces. It is possible to argue that forecasts of mass technological unemployment are not new and that the Luddites, then the later generation who believed that assembly-line methods would cost factory jobs, were proved mistaken. In the past new technologies have always led to new products, greater prosperity and more jobs than formerly. Optimists declare that today's new technologies will also increase employment once economic growth resumes, and provided we cease struggling to preserve old jobs and concentrate upon developing new products and services incorporating the latest techniques and components.

The problem with this strategy is that even if the diagnosis eventually proves correct, restoring full employment could take a long time, too long to benefit the 1970s', 1980s', and even the 1990s' school-leavers. Western economies seem unable to stimulate the investment and sustained growth to eradicate their current pools of unemployment. Predictions which link 'realistic' expectations of economic growth, maybe 2 per cent per year on average, with anticipated technological trends' implications for the demand for labour and the likely size of the workforce, lead to 'alarmist' forecasts of up to 6 million unemployed in Britain at the end of the century. In the long-term, new technologies may create additional employment, but we can be more confident that their short-term impact will be to destroy old jobs, and the gap before unemployment declines could span decades.

Insofar as new technology jobes are created, will 16-year-old school-leavers be able to perform them? If the jobs are within the young people's capacities, will they stand any chance in the competition for entry? If general unemployment remains high, what are young people's prospects, given employers' preference for older, experienced workers? Analyses which suggest that young people's problems are structural lead to proposals for structural remedies, and governments have grown increasingly receptive to these ideas. A series of special, temporary measures that could be dismantled when the recession ended, were governments' initial responses to rising youth unemployment. Current measures, including the Youth Training Scheme, are designed to last.

[NB: Since the original publication of this chapter, GCE 'O'-levels and CSEs have been replaced by the GCSE.]

References

Adams, D. and Sawdon, D. (1978) 'In and out of work', *Actions*, January 1978.

Allen, S. and Smith, C. R. (1975) 'Minority group experience and the transition from school to work', in Brannen, P. (ed.) *Entering the World of Work*, London, HMSO.

Ashton, D. N. and Maguire, M. J. (1980) 'Young women in the labour market: stability and change', in Deem, R. (ed.) *Schooling for Women's Work*, London, Routledge & Kegan Paul.

Ashton, D. N. and Maguire, M. J. (1982) 'The organization of local labour markets: dual markets or market segments'; paper presented to workshop on the Management and Mismanagement of Labour, Loughborough University.

Ashton, D. N., Maguire, M. J. and Garland, V. (1982) *Youth in the Labour Market*, Research Paper 34, London, Department of Employment.

Brooks, D. and Singh, K. (1978) *Aspirations versus Opportunities*, London, Commission for Racial Equality.

Cashmore, E. (1979) *Rastaman*, London, Allen and Unwin.

Closs, J., Downs, S. and Willoughby, J. (1977) 'Me Tarzan, you Jane', *Careers Quarterly*, 28, 4, 24–31.

Colledge, M., Llewellyn, G. and Ward, V. (1977) *Young People at Work*, London, Manpower Services Commission.

Dex, S. (1982) *Black and White School-leavers*, Research Paper 33, London, Department of Employment.

Driver, G. (1980) 'How West Indians do better at school (especially the girls)', *New Society*, 17 January 1980.

Donovan A. and Oddy, M. (1982) 'Psychological aspects of unemployment: an investigation into the emotional and social adjustment of school leavers', *Journal of Adolescence*, 5, 15–30.

Douvan, E. A. and Adelson, J. (1966) *The Adolescent Experience*, New York, John Wiley.

Fowler, B., Littlewood, B. and Madigan, R. (1977) 'Immigrant school-leavers and the search for work', *Sociology*, 11, 65–85.

Fuller, M. (1980) 'Black girls in a London comprehensive school', in Deem, R. (ed.) *Schooling for Women's Work*, London, Routledge & Kegan Paul.

Garrison, L. (1979) *Black Youth, Rastafarianism and the Identity Crisis in Britain*, London, Acer Project.

Gupta, Y. P. (1977) 'The educational and vocational aspirations of Asian immigrant and English school-leavers', *British Journal of Sociology*, 28, 185–198.

Hesselbart, B. (1977) 'Women doctors win and male nurses lose', *Sociology of Work and Occupations*, 4, 49–62.

Ipswich National Union of Teachers Working Party (1979) *Job Opportunities in Ipswich for Black School Leavers*, Ipswich, National Union of Teachers.

Jenkins, R. (1982) 'Acceptability, suitability and the search for the habituated worker'; paper presented to workshop on the Management and Mismanagement of Labour, Loughborough University.

Kelsall, R. K., Poole, A. and Kuhn, A. (1972) *Graduates: the Sociology of an Elite*, London, Methuen.

Layard, R. (1979) 'Have the Jobcentres increased unemployment?', *Guardian*, 5 November 1979.

Lee, G. L. and Wrench, K. J. (1981) *In Search of a Skill*, London, Commission for Racial Equality.

Manchester City Council Planning Department (1979) *School-leavers and Jobs*, Manchester City Council.

Manpower Services Commission (1982) *Youth Task Group Report*, London, HMSO.

Manwaring, T. (1982) 'The extended internal labour market'; paper presented to a workshop on the Management and Mismanagement of Labour, Loughborough University.

National Youth Employment Council (1974) *Unqualified, Untrained and Unemployed*, London, HMSO.

Pryce, K. (1979) *Endless Pressure*, Harmondsworth, Penguin.

Rex, J. and Tomlinson, S. (1979) *Colonial Immigrants in a British City*, London, Routledge & Kegan Paul.

Roberts, K., Duggan, J. and Noble, M. (1981) *Unregistered Youth Unemployment and Outreach Careers Work, Part One, Non-registration*, Research Paper 31, London, Department of Employment.

Rowntree, B. S. and Lasker, B. (1911) *Unemployment: a Special Study*, London, Macmillan.

Sawdon, A. and Taylor, D. (1980) *Youth Unemployment*, London, Youthaid.

Smith, D. J. (1977) *Racial Disadvantage in Britain*, Harmondsworth, Penguin.

Stares, R., Imberg, D. and McRobie, J. (1982) *Ethnic Minorities*, London, Manpower Services Commission, Research and Development Series 6.

Stone, M. (1981) *The Education of the Black Child in Britain*, London, Fontana.

Swann Report (1981) *West Indian Children in our Schools: Committee of Inquiry into the Education of Children from Ethnic Minority Groups*, Interim Report, London, HMSO.

Tomlinson, J. (1982) 'Unemployment and policy in the 1930s and 1980s', *The Three Banks Review*, 135, 17–33.

Watts, A. G. (1980) *Work Experience Programmes – the Views of British Youth*, Paris, OECD.

Weisman, C. S. *et al.* (1976) 'Sex differences in response to a blocked career pattern among unaccepted medical school applicants', *Sociology of Work and Occupations*, 3, 187–208.

White, S. (n.d.) 'Unemployment on Merseyside', unpublished manuscript.

Wilkins, L. T. (1955) *The Adolescent in Britain*, London, Central Office of Information.

Wilson, H. and Womersley, L. (1977) *Getting a Job*, London, Department of the Environment.

Yates, J. and Hall, B. (1982) *What Chance Work?*, Cheshire County Council Careers Service.

Youthaid (1979) *Study of the Transition from School to Working Life*, London, Youthaid.

Chapter 7

Gender and the Experience of Employment

K. Purcell

Gender is an attribute which individuals of both sexes bring to the workplace as a component of their identity, which influences the sort of work they do, where and with whom they work and how they are treated by their workmates, supervisors, managers and others with whom they interact in the course of their employment. As such, gender is a central component of experience at work, as of most social interaction, both implicitly and explicitly, but gender is not *simply* an extrinsic attribute which is a component of the supply characteristics of employees and employers. Precisely because employment relationships are concerned with the distribution of task and authority and these are most often segregated according to sex, the workplace, as the site of tertiary socialization for most people, is the main arena where they learn to play adult gender roles, to develop and modify their performance and interpret the significance of gender in the structure and interaction of the organization and its wider setting (Purcell, forthcoming). Perhaps the most important aspect of this tertiary socialization is learning the conventions and limits of 'normal' adult gender, including sex-appropriate occupations, tasks and performances.

Brown (1976) has made the point that, prior to the 1970s, most industrial and occupational sociology studies failed to recognize that gender and gender relationships are important dimensions of both the way in which employment is structured and the way in which work is experienced. The majority of writers and researchers have tended either to assume that all 'workers' are male or that their gender is not a relevant variable. Some have gone to the other extreme and seen gender as a

Source: K. Purcell (1989) 'Gender and the experience of employment', in *Employment in Britain*, D. Gallie (ed.), Blackwell, Oxford, pp. 157–186.

primary variable which divides workers into the binary division of 'workers' and 'women workers', taking it as axiomatic that most women in paid work have orientations to work and extrinsic constraints which are different from those of most men.

In this chapter, the evidence for differences in male and female attitudes to work will be reviewed, the sexual division of labour and explanations of why gendered occupational segregation has evolved and is sustained will be considered, as will the extent to which established patterns have been changing. Using recent research findings, the chapter concludes by focusing on the gender process, arguing that it is a key aspect of workplace interaction, industrial relations and, thus, the experience of work.

■ Gender and attitude to work

The gender stereotypes and domestic division of labour between the sexes which implicitly define the parameters of debates about women's employment and occupational segregation have more often been assumed than investigated. Furthermore, the underlying assumptions made about *men's* orientations to paid work, domestic work and childrearing are even more questionable. Certainly, male gender has been subjected to less research scrutiny and, where male employees' orientations to work have been investigated, it has been with reference to a different scale of values and range of options to those against which women's motivations are assessed. The finding that certain groups of male manual workers have had extrinsic orientations to work and derived their main sense of identity from their patterns of consumption and privatized home lives (Goldthorpe *et al.*, 1968) or attach more importance to work connected with their leisure interests (Moorhouse, 1984) is not analogous to the often unsubstantiated assumption that women's 'central life interests' are invested in their family roles and domestic responsibilities. The former relate primarily to individual satisfactions whereas the latter concerns other-directed activity. Sociologists have asked male workers why they choose to work on a conveyor belt rather than in a craft workshop, or invited them to evaluate the relative job satisfaction or skills involved in different jobs they have experienced. They have rarely asked *why* men have a job, whether they would prefer to work part-time, requested that they rank parenthood and employment in terms of importance to their identity or, most importantly, inquired whether they feel that being a man affects either their ability to do their job or the attitudes of workmates, bosses and clients towards them.

To some extent, it is obvious why this is the case. Women are perceived to have a career option which men do not have: marriage and motherhood. This reflects Wadel's (1979) observation that folk concepts and economists' concepts of what constitutes work vary and vary systematically with gender. For women, the family provides an alternative *work* role identity in a way that is less the case for men (Purcell, 1978). However, the evidence cited [by Dex (1988)] conclusively demonstrates that these aspects of identity and the workload which they generate are no longer experienced by the majority of women as alternatives to employment, but as complements to it. But like all successful ideological constructs, the notion of women's choice has just enough truth in it to remain a powerful influence on gender stereotypes and, through stereotypes, on people's expectations and behaviour.

The debates on the extent to which work is experienced as a 'central life interest' (Dubin, 1956) have tended to juxtapose real situations where work roles manifestly lack scope for intrinsic satisfaction with a somewhat idealized notion of craftworking fulfilment. British research evidence concerning work attitudes and orientations to work has been evaluated and summarized by Brown *et al.* (1983), who concluded that while most employees' attachment to work is primarily calculative and may be more so during a period of recession, men as well as women cite the social aspects of work – working conditions, work environment and the social relations encountered there – as major considerations in determining their degree of satisfaction. As Daniel (1969: 373) pointed out, most surveys show that nearly all workers are comparatively satisfied with their jobs. The more interesting question is whether they are satisfied *in* their jobs or *with* the job.

Goldthorpe *et al.* (1968: 178) recognized that 'wants and expectations are culturally determined variables, not psychological constructs'. Responses to questions about satisfaction with employment have to be evaluated in relation to the alternatives available. For most women, the choice is between the boredom and domestic isolation of housework, and boring paid work which provides some opportunities for social interaction and companionship. Research findings frequently appear to show that social relations and convenience factors are more important for females than for males and that most females give lower priority to opportunities for promotion and training than most men (Brown *et al.*, 1983; Ballard, 1984; Martin and Roberts, 1984). Previous studies (e.g. Dubin *et al.*, 1976) have found women to be more satisfied with less objectively satisfactory employment, which may well reflect their realistically lower expectations of fulfilment, interest and good wages. To put it bluntly, if employees working in low skilled repetitive jobs are asked what they like about their work, it should not be surprising if the answer is given in terms of earnings, as in *The Affluent Worker* studies (Goldthorpe *et al.*, 1968). The remuneration of the majority of women in employment does not put them, relatively speaking, in the 'affluent' category, so that their only *possible* sources of satisfaction are going to be in relationships with workmates or variables such as convenience in terms of proximity to home or hours which fit in with other responsibilities. Similarly, men in badly paid unfulfilling work and men who work part-time have been found to cite 'social' reasons and convenience as the main sources of satisfaction at work (Nichols and Armstrong, 1976).

For those women with formal occupational qualifications, the choice they are faced with tends to be limited to either such routine jobs or to higher-status, generally more pleasant jobs at the lower levels of career structures. This is particularly the case if they require part-time employment. The fact that many women, particularly after a career break, are overqualified for the jobs they are doing, makes it unlikely that they will *expect* a high level of satisfaction. In addition, the finding that women less often invest in post-experience training and career development (Crompton and Jones, 1984) and more often experience downward occupational mobility when they return to work after periods of childrearing (Elias and Main, 1982; Martin and Roberts, 1984) is consistent with women's different *structural* relationship to the family and to employment. Elias (1988a) found the career profiles of highly qualified women and women who do not have children most closely approximate to those of similarly qualified men. Conversely, part-time women employees' prioritizing of convenient hours and proximity to home, along with their lack of concern with promotion prospects and training (Ballard, 1984; Brown *et al.*, 1983) is indicative both of the fact that paid work is a less substantial component of their lives, which is undertaken as additional to, and required to accommodate, other responsibilities, and realistically recognizes that part-time employees are virtually never given the opportunity to develop their human capital at work (Ballard, 1984).

Part-time employment in Britain is normally undertaken by people (overwhelming married women) who are primarily economically dependent on someone else. While alleviating married women's financial dependency, it arguably ultimately reinforces unequal roles and economic power in the family and in employment. It has been recognized (Diamond, 1980) that women's earnings are vital in raising many family incomes above the poverty line and are an increasingly significant determinant of living standards. Polarization between two-earner and no-earner families is encouraged by occupational segregation – particularly in the concentration of women in part-time jobs – and by social policy, particularly relating to unemployment and social security benefit payments (Pahl, 1984; Morris, 1985). Research among women employees in the early 1970s indicated that they regarded redundancy with a certain degree of impunity, in the belief that they would be able to find alternative employment without difficulty (Wood, 1981; Pollert, 1981). More recent work on redundant manual working women suggests that they approach impending loss of jobs with considerably more pessimism (Coyle, 1984; Martin and Wallace, 1984), realistically assessing their chances of immediate re-employment as slight. Both these studies found that the majority of employed women's attachment to paid work was similar to men's, in so far as they defined employment as a necessary and natural component of their lives, whether their employment was full-time or part-time.

■ Sources of gender segregation

As the data cited by Dex (1988) indicate, the overall pattern of gender segregation in British employment has remained surprisingly stable, despite the increase in female economic activity rates, the introduction of equal opportunities legislation, occupational diversification and industrial restructuring. Explanations for the existing pattern of gender segregation in employment can be superficially divided into two basic categories: those which derive from the sexual division of labour in the family and those which derive from the organization of employment itself (Stacey, 1981). These tend in practice to be mutually reinforcing.

The model of households headed by a complementary partnership of man-the-breadwinner and woman-the-homemaker continues to provide the template for family law, fiscal policy and social policy legislation, whose combined effect is to reinforce women's dependence (Beechey and Whitelegg, 1986). Substantially different rates of pay for 'men's jobs' and 'women's jobs' reinforce both occupational segregation and women's dependency in the family and thus, as well as domestic roles constraining employment, gender roles in the household have been reinforced by opportunities in the labour market (Garnsey, 1978).

The range and content of work carried out in both the public sphere of employment and the private sphere of the household have an important impact on women's economic activity, most importantly in the extent to which labour-intensive tasks have become automated and work previously undertaken on an unpaid basis in the home has been transformed by mass production. Changes such as the decline in domestic service and the expansion of public and personal services may not be exactly two sides of the same coin but they are intimately related. Similarly, the reduction of commodities and services produced in the home, such as food and clothing, and the expansion in completed goods and market services brought into the household as alternatives has meant that the range of tasks carried out in the household has diminished while the demand for labour in manufacturing and the collective provision of services has increased. Despite an increased interest in do-it-yourself home development and maintenance and, for some sections of society at least, in self-provisioning and the rediscovery of traditional crafts and domestic skills (Gershuny,

1978), most households have been moving away from, rather than towards, self-sufficiency. As Pahl's (1984) research on the Isle of Sheppey illustrated, engaging in such domestic 're-skilling' is a luxury which is only easily available to people with a comfortably high household income from the formal economy, predominantly those in dual-earner households.

In addition, although most research on the domestic division of labour in households where the 'breadwinner' is unemployed reveal that, if anything, gender roles and males' lack of participation in household tasks are reinforced rather than challenged (McKee and Bell, 1985; Pahl and Wallace, 1985; Morris, 1985), there is evidence that women's employment in two-earner households does tend to facilitate, if not a more egalitarian sexual division of labour, at least a proportionately higher level of male participation in childcare and housework (Martin and Roberts, 1984: 100–2; Pahl, 1984: 110). Data from time budget studies suggest that, in general, men's participation in these activities has steadily increased over the last two decades (Gershuny, 1987). But both those and detailed studies of housework, childcare and domestic divisions of labour (Pahl, 1984; Oakley, 1974; Derow, 1982; Hertz, 1986) reveal that even in households where both partners are in full-time employment, the domestic division of labour is more likely to be asymmetrical than symmetrical and that such symmetries as exist are more likely to be balanced upon a traditional gendered than androgynous basis. As a reflection of the fact that full-time employment, parenting and domestic efficiency are incompatible without third-party support (Delphy, 1976: 161), two-earner households most often survive by co-opting paid or unpaid helpers to carry out these latter, traditionally 'female' tasks; and these helpers are almost invariably women (Yeandle, 1984: 156; Martin and Roberts, 1984; Rapoport and Rapoport, 1976; Hertz, 1986: 162 ff.).

The asymmetry in the distribution of 'caring' responsibilities which has evolved in the patriarchal sexual division of labour in the household and the wider community (Finch and Groves, 1983; Cunnison, 1986) is also symptomatic of the power differential which arises from women's economic dependency and has promoted the institutionalization of a 'deferential dialectic' as part of 'normal' gender interaction (Bell and Newby, 1976). The fact that gender adds a particular dimension to relations of authority and subordination is illustrated by male reluctance to work for female supervisors (Kanter, 1977: 197–205) and the belief that men make 'better' bosses (Wacjman, 1983: 173). The classic example of such institutionalized deference in employment is the personal secretary–boss relationship, where deference and 'femininity' are an important part of the job training of aspiring secretaries (McNally, 1979: 57–9; Valli, 1986) and where the workload of such women is frequently assumed to have boundaries encompassing tasks which have more 'caring' than clerical content (Benet, 1972; McNally, 1979: 70).

☐   **The gendering of jobs**

Gender differentiation is implicit in the segmentation of occupations, which have been revealed at workplace level to be more segregated by sex than aggregate figures suggest, both at the level of job and tasks allocated (Martin and Roberts, 1984; Craig et al., 1984; Bielby and Baron, 1986; Crompton and Sanderson, 1986). In the 1981 Women and Employment survey, only 42 per cent of full-time and 30 per cent of part-time female employees did similar jobs to male workmates. Women working in segregated occupations or environments, particularly those who worked part-time, were more likely to see their work as 'women's work' than those who were employed in workplaces where men did similar work. A parallel tendency for men employed in workplaces where women did similar work to be less likely to see their work as 'men's work' than men in sex-segregated occupations was revealed by the responses of husbands interviewed for the survey. But there was an important difference in the types of reasons men and women gave for regarding their own work as more appropriate for their own sex. The men believed on the whole that women *could not* do their work for practical reasons – physical limitations, lack of skills or training, working conditions – whereas women more often saw men as not so much incapable as unlikely to do their jobs for social or economic reasons – the fact that such jobs were widely regarded as being 'women's work' and, accordingly, low paid (Martin and Roberts, 1984: 30–1). These responses highlight the different labour market conditions under which, by and large, men and women sell their labour.

Women's labour has been used in a very much wider range of occupations than those in which they are currently employed. It has been argued that the separation of home and work effected by the industrial revolution narrowed the range of opportunities available to women, particularly married women, to participate both formally and informally in production and civic activities (Clark, 1919; Thirsk, 1985), so that gender segregation in employment crystallized and progressively increased throughout the eighteenth and nineteenth centuries. In jobs where they might generally be expected to perform less efficiently than men due to physiological differences, such as coalmining and heavy industry, women's participation, like children's, was ultimately precluded in Britain on moral rather than utilitarian or economic grounds (Hewitt, 1958; Johns, 1984; Pinchbeck, 1981), reflecting the presumed desirability of women's confinement to the private sphere. The participation and survival of women in 'traditionally male' jobs during and after the two world wars in Britain (Braybon, 1981; Summerfield, 1984; Riley, 1984) were explicitly restrained by patriarchal views about 'women's place' and the presumed interests of 'the family'. Contrary to the belief that gendered barriers were overthrown in the interests of wartime expediency, employers and government were slow to introduce shifts and childcare arrangements to facilitate women's participation in employment, even when faced with acute labour shortages in the wake of male conscription.

However, beliefs about women's 'proper sphere' and the attributes which are presumed to equip them for it, have also been seen by employers as positive incentives to recruit female labour for certain types of jobs. Ideas about 'natural' differences between the aptitudes, roles and orientations to work of women and men permeate the sexual divisions of labour in employment. Women are often credited with the possession of skills which are assumed to derive directly from female physiological and psychological characteristics – manual dexterity, gentleness, caring and acquiescence – and, because their 'central life interest' is assumed to be the family rather than employment, a greater tolerance of boredom and repetition at work, less ambition and less willingness to take responsibility and exert authority. An excellent example of the way in which ideology, management strategies and specific cultural variables interact is provided by Dunning (1986: 160–1) who cited a Japanese manager's experience of attempting to replicate Japanese recruitment strategies in a British subsidiary:

> 'We started off by recruiting female school leavers but found them undisciplined, bad timekeepers and lacking motivation. In Japan, they would have been trained to be housekeepers. Nowadays we prefer to employ 20–25 aged married women. They often need the money, have learned to manage their own house, and have a greater sense of responsibility . . .'

Pearson's (1986) analysis of multinational export-manufacturing firms indicates that, like the company discussed by Dunning, their recruitment practices demonstrate a marked preference for 'green' female labour for most production and assembly work, even where there is a surplus of male labour, but they are prepared to modify their selection criteria in the light of local and cultural variables. Different cultures have different constraints – patriarchal, religious, in terms of family-building norms and fecundity – which affect the supply of labour, particularly female labour. Thus, in Malaysia, the preferred female operative appears to be young and childless, whereas in Barbados she is an older, post-childbearing mother. Pearson cites research indicating systematic differences in recruitment patterns of different industries in the same locality and similar industries in different localities, concluding that although it is possible to identify common objectives pursued by employers through gendered occupational segregation policies, the tactics they use in the recruitment and deployment of labour will ultimately depend on the pool of labour available and the cultural, political and technical environment in which they are operating.

Studies of the link between technology and the type of labour used go some way towards explaining the process involved in gendered occupational segregation. A fascinating analysis by Glucksmann (1986) of the 'new' manufacturing industries which developed in Britain in the inter-war years (electrical engineering, the car and aircraft industries, chemicals, synthetic fibres, food processing, etc.) suggests that the availability of young women, eager to reject the constraints, humiliations and low wages of domestic service in favour of employment in the new factories, was a factor in determining the work-force recruited. She concludes, however, that their main attractions to employers were their youth, which endowed 'suppleness of fingers' and the aptitude and energy to do repetitive, precise assembly work efficiently, quickly and cheaply; and their sex, which, given demographic norms and the sexual division of labour in marriage and the family, ensured a conveniently high turnover of those whose youth and efficiency were running out, encouraged by the formal or informal operation of a marriage bar in most sectors of employment. She sees the demand for new types of employee – fewer craftsmen and more semi-skilled process workers – as being a far more important determinant of women's employment patterns than any inherent characteristics or preferences of women themselves. Thus employer's *beliefs* about gender and the relative cheapness of female labour, rather than technology, are the primary causal variables in the allocation of such work to women rather than men.

Custom and practice may go some way towards explaining current patterns of occupational segregation, given that sex stereotyping tends to be self-perpetuating for social as well as economic reasons, but only detailed historical analysis at cultural, occupational, industrial and organizational levels can reveal how particular jobs originally came to be seen as the prerogative of one sex or the other (Crompton, 1987). The most illuminating studies carried out recently have attempted to analyse the evolution and interrelationships of occupational and organizational hierarchies and divisions of labour. At a comparative level, Crompton's (1988) analysis of the age and gender distribution of clerks across different industries enabled her to identify the extent to which such occupations have become increasingly feminized and indicates that some industries and organizations have been more impervious to change in the sexual division of labour than others. Focusing on one particular industry, Siltanen's (1986) analysis of the gendered occupational distribution of postal delivery workers and telephonists indicates a complex interaction of supply and demand factors. Her research revealed that insufficient male applicants for delivery work and female applicants able and willing to work 'unsocial hours' as telephonists led to the dilution of previously rigidly gendered occupational groups. She records the Union of Post Office Workers' (UPW) temporarily successful resistance to the recruitment of women for delivery work in defence of it as a breadwinner (or what she calls a 'full wage' as opposed to 'component wage') occupation, and assesses the reasons why equal opportunities legislation has had less impact on recruitment to these jobs than might have been expected. She argues that concentrating on gender divisions in employment reifies 'gender' as part of the construction of occupational categories and task allocation in a way that may obscure how such categories have evolved and how they are maintained. It deflects attention from underlying variables which are correlated, but not synonymous with, sex and gender; for example, financial need, alternative responsibilities or opportunities and the earnings potential of specific jobs.

The implication of this is that focusing exclusively on gender or on the part-time/full-time distribution may confuse rather than clarify why jobs come to be allocated to different categories of employee. Once jobs have come to be seen as 'female' rather than 'male' or ungendered they are more likely to be seen by employers as amenable to part-time organization. Thus the initial conditions which generate gender segmentation may be shortage or availability of male or female labour, but once the job becomes identified with one sex, perception of it as a potential job for members of the other sex is less likely and its gendered character is consolidated by custom. Beechey and Perkins (1987: 37) make the point that where 'male' jobs have characteristics which might, in terms of economic rationality, lead employers to organize employment on a part-time basis, the required flexibility and accommodation of uneven workloads over the working day or week tends to be achieved by other means; for example, by overtime or complex shiftworking arrangements.

■ Changes in patterns of gender segregation

At the level of particular organizations, there is some evidence that gendered occupational and task segregation may have been increasing in manual work (Westergaard and Restler, 1975: 103; Craig et al., 1984; Trades Union Congress, 1983: 7). Cockburn (1986) carried out case studies in three types of employment: pattern-making and cloth-cutting in the clothing industry, warehousing in mail-order firms and X-ray departments in hospitals. She wanted to investigate the extent to which technology which substantially alters the skill and task range of previously gendered jobs might lead to the breaking down of occupational demarcations and gender barriers, thus redistributing employment between the sexes, and to explore the criteria applied in allocating completely new jobs with no gendered custom and practice. In all three of the selected sectors, she found an element of de-skilling and, in the case of clothing and mail order, loss of 'female' jobs, but her main finding was the extent to which gender permeated the organization of employment and the division of labour in the workplaces she studied. She concluded that the ideological context in which labour is supplied, demanded and deployed reinforces and perpetuates gender segregation, erecting and sustaining 'invisible barriers' between male and female jobs and skills which derive momentum from the expectations and prejudices of the participants: men and women, employers and employees. The predominant direction of influence she identifies, in what is intrinsically a reflexive relationship between policy and practice, is of custom and practice upon policy: thus, her conclusion that 'opportunity is not enough' (Cockburn, 1986: 187).

Game and Pringle (1983) have suggested that, as traditional bases of skill distinctions are being eroded by changing technology and other organizational innovations, gender has frequently become a scarcely disguised basis for differentiating job grades. After studying gender at work in a variety of very different industries – banking, 'white goods' manufacturing, retailing, computing, health care and housework – they concluded that the sexual division of labour is remarkably flexible in terms of the tasks which men and women actually perform in the course of employment. The only invariable aspect of all the employment situations they investigated was that there *were* distinctions between work regarded as primarily or exclusively appropriate for either men or women. Where existing distinctions had been eroded by changes in technology or work organization, new distinctions were found to have been made to distinguish 'men's' and 'women's' jobs, or one or other sex had been allocated different tasks. They argue that slight differences between job content are used to rationalize different job grading and to reassure men of their superiority by distinguishing what they do from 'women's work'. 'The distinction lies not in the inherent quality of the work but almost entirely on the meaning given to it in particular contexts' (Game and Pringle, 1983: 31). This endorses Crompton and Jones's (1984) finding that the non-manual labour force is systematically divided by gender. While acknowledging the greater overall investment in training and career development of males, they observed that many women carried out comparatively high level, responsible tasks, of which they concluded that 'if a *man* had been occupying these positions, he would be in a "promoted" grade' (Crompton and Jones, 1984: 244).

Thus the structure of the labour force, from national and industrial to establishment and workshop level, is systematically gendered. Despite the exhortations of the Equal Opportunities Commission and other interested parties to break down gender segregation in employment and career choice, the recruitment and distribution of males and females throughout the labour force suggests that most employers, employees and careers advisory staff continue to regard most occupations as either exclusively or predominantly male or female, and occupational segregation patterns are perpetuated by recruitment and promotion practices. Service sector employment growth has included a tiny but growing minority of women acquiring professional qualifications and entering professions and occupations previously overwhelmingly dominated by men. There have been successive initiatives at a national level to encourage girls to consider training and occupations in which they have been underrepresented in the past, particularly engineering, technical and scientific areas of employment (Engineering Council, 1985; Kelly, 1987). A number of women have thus been enabled to train as engineers (Newton, 1987) but this was clearly despite being handicapped by the prejudices of employers, superiors and male colleagues (Breakwell and Weinberger, 1987: 17–18), who regarded 'token women' as liable both to experience and cause problems. This compares interestingly with the experiences of men who work in environments where they are in a minority, who appear to derive occupational and psychological benefit from being 'token men'. Even men in gender atypical jobs, such as male nurses, have been found to be in an advantageous position to their female colleagues: more likely to be promoted and to be taken seriously by doctors and other superordinates (Wharton and Baron, 1987: 576).

As entry to 'service class' careers – including the management of industry – becomes increasingly dependent upon possession of formal credentials (Goldthorpe, 1982: 18; Abercrombie and Urry, 1983: 150), discriminatory recruitment and employment policies become more difficult to maintain. However, even in occupations where there are no formal barriers to sex equality, such as teaching and banking, vertical gender imbalances exist to a degree that suggests segregation mechanisms operate more or less explicitly, although vertical barriers may be more permeable than the barriers to horizontal integration. For example, Llewellyn (1981) described how her research in banking uncovered the different criteria applied, and career development envisaged, for male and female school leavers who were ostensibly recruited to the same trainee grade. Crompton and Jones (1984: 145) found that management in the finance sector often actively discouraged women from acquiring post-entry qualifications which would have equipped them for promotion. Crompton and Sanderson (1986), discussing the career patterns of women with professional occupational qualifications, suggest that current trends in such employment indicate both the possibility of increasing convergence between male and female career paths and some evidence of the development of gendered 'niches' within professions.

Legge (1987) provides an illuminating discussion of one such area of relatively high female employment in a predominantly 'male' career: the personnel specialism within management in Britain. She discusses how the personnel function developed from 'employee welfare' concerns in the nineteenth century: the 'caring' aspect of management which was, perhaps unsurprisingly, predominantly allocated to women. In 1927, membership of the professional association of personnel specialists was 420, of whom fewer than twenty were men, but she argues that, as the personnel function came to be regarded as more important and closely related to productive efficiency, the proportion of male personnel specialists increased, to 40 per cent by 1939, and to over 80 per cent by 1970 (Legge, 1987: 34–42). In addition, there is evidence that women in the profession were more likely to be in subordinate positions and confined to the welfare and administrative rather than industrial relations and policy-making functions (Long, 1984), a pattern which is reflected throughout management (Hunt, 1975; Kanter, 1977; Hennig and Jardim, 1978) and the professions generally (Crompton and Mann, 1986; Spencer and Podmore, 1987). Legge reflects that, as the personnel function is seen as increasingly peripheral in the context of 1980s managerial 'strategic realism', women may be expected to form an increasing proportion of the occupational membership, since she takes personnel management to be a paradigmatic example of the inverse relationship between the perceived power of an occupational group and the proportion of women employed. However, there are significant differences among organizations in terms of their attitudes to equal opportunities and job segregation. Crompton and Jones (1984: 189–92) found that the organizations which they studied were characterized by distinctive 'organizational cultures' which were more or less conducive to equal opportunities. Clearly, women stood less chance of recruitment and career development in the organization where the manager tended to think in terms of recruiting 'a good left back' rather than simply an underwriting clerk (Crompton and Jones, 1984: 190).

It is unlikely that women's experience in the late 1980s will be characterized by greater equality of opportunity, although in the short term there are likely to be more new jobs for women than men, particularly in personal and miscellaneous services (Institute for Employment Research, 1987; Elias and Purcell, 1988). Many of these jobs, however, are likely to be insecure, low-paid and part-time. In manufacturing, where women's share of skilled work has been decreasing throughout this century in Britain, semi-skilled and unskilled jobs are disproportionately vulnerable to displacement by technology, as is also the case in low-skilled clerical occupations. Recent work on the trends in part-time and full-time working (Elias, 1988b), covering the period 1971–86, shows that there has been a steady and significant decline in the proportion of part-time employees in most of the manufacturing sector, particularly in areas which have traditionally used female part-time employees for manual assembly or packing work (e.g. electronic engineering). Increased productivity in manufacturing has been pursued by 'hard' changes in production technologies, but also by 'soft' changes in the organization of work (Massey and Meegan, 1982). It has been argued that one of the more important changes in the latter category has been the shift from the formal to informal economy in the last ten years (Murray, 1983) and that this has particularly been true of the clothing industry, an important sector of women's employment with implications for the measurement of female economic activity rates (Mitter, 1986: 44). Although there is disagreement about the dimensions of the 'hidden work-force', it is widely recognized that officially recorded female activity rates considerably underestimate women's paid work, particularly in the provision of personal services such as childcare, domestic service and in the clothing industry, which is largely comprised of small units of production which often rely on networks of outworkers and homeworkers. Official estimates suggest that, while the manufacturing sector has been diminishing overall, the use of outworkers – whose work is done solely or mainly away from their employer's premises (Hakim, 1985: 66) – has been increasing.

Both the decline in manufacturing homeworking (Rubery and Wilkinson, 1981; Allen and Wolkowitz, 1987) and the utility to employees of 'hi-tech' homeworking (Huws, 1984; Bisset and Huws, 1984) have been questioned, suggesting that trends in neither area of employment are likely to lead to an improvement in women's employment prospects or conditions of employment, or to change in the sexual division of labour. Hakim (1987: 93) estimates that one-quarter of males and half of all females currently in the labour force are employed in relatively insecure or temporary work and that there has been a parallel substantial growth in self-employment without employees, particularly among women (Creigh et al., 1986) which is more a reflection of lack of employment opportunities than spontaneous entrepreneurial growth.

As long as the occupational structure remains segmented along gendered lines and social policies reinforce rather than challenge a segregated sexual division of labour in the family, gender is likely to remain an important determinant and restraint in workplaces. Neither women's nor men's experience of employment can be understood without reference to gender relations outside work, but much can be learned about gender divisions in society as a whole by considering, as well as the evolution of gendered employment structures, the process of gender relations in employment.

■ Gender and social interaction at work

Ethnographic research (Purcell, 1982, forthcoming) carried out among semi-skilled manual workers in an engineering firm (NICO) in the north of England in the early 1980s, illustrates the significance of gender in workplace organization and interaction. Earlier research on manual workers' attitudes and experience with regard to the sexual division of labour at work had led to the finding that gender was apparently a less important variable in influencing employees' political attitudes and behaviour than factors such as plant size, industry and occupation (Purcell, 1984), although it had been observed that, quite apart from the gendered allocation of task and status within workplaces, a great deal of work-related and other forms of social interaction at work were defined, restricted and expressed in terms of gender.

In examining the relevance of gender at work it is useful to distinguish between two broad categories of actions, interactions and events: those which exhibit formally organized, taken-for-granted differences between men and women, as exemplified by the sexual segregation of occupations, which is not intrinsically related to sex although defined by gender and can be termed *implicit* gender; and actions, interactions and events which are specifically related to, or draw attention to, sex differences – such as real or mock flirtation – which constitute *explicit* gender. The two are, of course, situated on the same continuum, but it may be useful to separate them analytically. Cockburn's research drew attention to the barriers which implicit gender maintain and her interviews elicited statements from employers which revealed these implicit assumptions. Participant observation research enables researchers to analyse explicit gender interaction and its relationship to the implicit structures which underlie the process of gender at work which, because of its subjective and sensitive nature, is less amenable to more structured methods of research and analysis.

Gender is suffused with beliefs about sex differences and sexuality, and is defined by what are believed to be sex-related characteristics and potentials. It is, like colour, age and physiological attributes, part of the immediately visible presentation of self and a primary identifying characteristic. This is so much the case that it is difficult for men and women to have relationships with each other, from the most casual, transitory public encounters to the most intimate friendship, without awareness of their gender being part of the relationship. Simmel (1950) claimed that consciousness of gender is a constant aspect of female experience to a greater extent than is the case for men, which may be an accurate observation of experience in patriarchal cultures where women tend to be objectified in popular culture (Berger, 1972; Goffman, 1976). In fact, the observations at NICO suggest that a major reinforcement of women's perpetual gender consciousness is the fact that, in the factory at least, they were rarely allowed to forget that they were women. They were addressed, responded to and handled, both literally and metaphorically, as women rather than as people or as workers.

Thus implicit gender was an attribute which defined people's place in the structure and their roles in the processes of work. Clearly, gender is an important attribute which employees bring to the workplace, which often determines their type of employment and rate of pay. Explicit gender determined that awareness of gender identity and sex differences were an integral dimension of work experience. Throughout the course of the working day, the women's gender was frequently referred to, acknowledged or implied, mediated by flirtation, exaggerated chivalry and teasing. The men's gender was less often explicitly drawn attention to by the women and was more often implicitly or explicitly revealed by male-initiated gender interaction. This is not to argue that gender is a less important dimension of work experience for men than for women: indeed, the reverse may be the case. The point is that for most men, gender interaction and the reinforcement of male identity at work is generally a positive experience, promoting social and personal integration rather than drawing attention to role conflict and status ambiguity. Pollert (1981: 79) perceptively noted that women who are employed in factory work are deviating from 'appropriate' gender roles. Men in repetitive, unfulfilling factory work can at least derive satisfaction from the knowledge that they are doing 'men's work' (Willis, 1977: 99) but women in factories cannot derive analogous satisfaction: factory work is not a 'feminine' occupation.

It is instructive to consider the collective identities of male and female factory workers. Men may be referred to as 'the lads', but the endowment of such membership is more an accolade than – as is usually the case with 'the girls' – a diminution (Westwood, 1984: 24–5) and is less imbued with notions of sex and gender. A woman may be referred to as 'one of the lads' with approval, whereas to regard a man as 'one of the girls' would definitely diminish him and cast doubts on his virility. The 'old boys' network' and similar male camaraderie reinforces male bonding in higher status employment and has a similar effect of excluding and marginalizing women (Kanter, 1977). Given the extent to which people experience and respond to one another according to the categories to which their attributes appear to assign them, allied to the fact that in essentially patriarchal societies, sex is not only a binary distinction but also hierarchical, this is not surprising. What is, perhaps, surprising, is the extent to which the dynamics of gender relations have been virtually overlooked as a variable in workplace interaction, organizations and the labour process itself in the development of industrial and organizational sociology.

Gouldner (1957: 285), discussing the complexities of social roles, observed that 'many sociologists give little indication of the fact that the people they study in offices, factories, schools or hospitals are also males and females'. To some extent, a significant proportion of more recent sociology, while taking account of gender, continues to underestimate its importance. The way in which gender defines and restricts women's experience as factory workers has recently received incisive exploration (Pollert, 1981; Cavendish, 1982; Westwood, 1984) but even in these feminist analyses, the *process* of gender (cf. Thompson, 1965: 357 on the process of class), while recognized to be a crucial dimension of work experience, is rarely scrutinized in its own right. In particular, the importance of the sexual aspect of gender has been subsumed within a consideration of power differences, without detailed analysis of how sex, as a component of gender, is mobilized in the exercise and deflection of power.

Freudian psychology sees sex as a central preoccupation of humanity and sexuality as perhaps the most important dimension of the self, yet industrial psychology has had little to say about gender and sex in workplace interaction. This is not to argue that sex is literally the lowest common denominator of life or of work experience, but sex and its cultural interpretation, gender, are such overwhelming and inescapable aspects of experience and identity that it is difficult to see how an adequate account of social action can be given without reference to the gender of the participants and the implications for that of their interaction (cf. Morgan, 1986). These implications have more often been assumed with reference to gender stereotypes than observed. The significance of gender within the context of what actually happens at work is so much part of the implicit experience of employment that dramatized depictions of workplace interaction are full of gendered ritual, social exchange and relationships.

Paradoxically, women's assumptions of roles and statuses tradition-ally filled by men makes the gendered content of work roles and relationships more visible, in so far as the significance of *women's* sex, on both how she operates and how she is responded to, tends to be subjected to scrutiny in a way that 'normal' gendered hierarchical relations are not. The most vivid illustrative example is perhaps Mrs Thatcher, whose sex is seen to be a relevant consideration for political analysts to take account of when assessing her performance and, indeed, has been alleged to be an important aspect of her leadership tactics:

> 'Her sex has helped shape her style of government. In the early days, according to John Hoskyns, she used the fact that she was a woman very powerfully to get her own way. She was deliberately unreasonable, emotional, excitable, instead of being calm and consensus-seeking.' (Harris, 1988: 18).

Such stereotype-laden comment illustrates the extent to which professional behaviour and interaction are observed and interpreted as gendered; perhaps particularly in a context where the gender of the actor concerned is regarded as marginally inappropriate. Mrs Thatcher's professional and political identity is intimately bound up with her identity as a woman. She has been praised, criticized, parodied and manipulated for propaganda purposes as alternatively 'tough' (and therefore atypical of women in that she appears not to be inhibited by 'normal' female 'weaknesses') and 'caring' (the good housekeeper and mother who understands the really important things in life and whose gender therefore equips her particularly well for humane and thrifty leadership).

Where the gender dimension of work relationships has been examined by sociologists, it has usually been in the context of discussion of the informal systems which operate in work environments. Banter about sex and the objectification of women have frequently been recorded as being among the main topics of everyday conversation in male work groups (Brown *et al.*, 1973; Roy, 1974; Burawoy, 1979; Cockburn, 1983; Morgan, 1987) and equivalent ribaldry has been observed among female workers (Wilson, 1963; Morgan, 1969; Pollert, 1981; Cavendish, 1982; Cunnison, 1983; Westwood, 1984). Mock flirtation and gendered joking behaviour have been noted by all the above authors and subjected to detailed ethnographic analysis in a Glasgow printworks by Sykes (1966), who concluded that such exaggerated role playing and symbolic behaviour serves the function of controlling sexuality in mixed sex workplaces; an objective, according to Burrell (1984), which is also a major formal preoccupation of bureaucracy. Sykes's analysis, however, assumes that the formal and informal systems of the factory are separate and that 'joking behaviour' and 'real' relationships between people are also distinct and unambiguous, which is questionable. Perhaps the clearest exposure of the ambiguities involved has been provided by those who have studied gender interaction in offices, particularly between bosses and secretaries (Benet, 1972; McNally, 1979; Crompton and Jones, 1984). Their studies have revealed not only how sex-typed interaction ritual and the gender hierarchy structure work relationships; but also how the place of employment is seen by the participants to provide opportunities for 'real' romantic and sexual partnerships and encounters.

Roy (1974) has carried the analysis forward both by considering the wider spectrum of sexual and gender interaction and monitoring the impact of gender relations on work group behaviour and productivity. He argues that the formal and informal systems in the workplace are spatially and temporally interlocked and are effectively part of the same system. This leads him to incorporate aspects of workplace interaction not normally taken account of in industrial sociological analysis. He observed that:

> 'When a situation is one of men and women working side by side or sharing a task that calls for team work, Eros may infiltrate the production line to evoke attachments of various qualities and durations of affection, ranging from the protracted attentions of true love to ephemeral ardencies of the opportune moment.' (Roy, 1974: 46).

Quinn (1977) indicates that such infiltration is not confined to the production line, citing examples from commercial and medical work institutions. Such British evidence as there is suggests that a substantial minority of people first meet their marriage partner in the course of training or employment and that the workplace may be the most common place for love affairs, illicit or otherwise, to begin (Hearn and Parkin, 1987: 14).

Roy's observations and discussions with his workmates, however, indicate that the workplace is not simply a recruitment source for leisure or domestic partnerships; the very fact that such liaisons are negotiated and carried out both during work and outside it means that they are also part of work situations, with implications not only for those directly involved but for the whole work group and the conduct of work. This leads him to postulate, in the light of cases he observed, that the sexual dynamics of an attachment between two people who work together may have a cyclical effect on productivity. During the initial stage of courtship, productivity and congenial relations throughout the group appeared to be enhanced; once relationships became established, there was some evidence of wider harmony being threatened by the exclusiveness of the romantic dyad – particularly since the 'factory wife', like the 'office wife' (Benet, 1972), tended to be of subordinate status to her 'spouse' and her intimacy with him was observed to cause, or be assumed to cause, favouritism and consequent jealousies; and, not surprisingly, the decline of relationships tended to cause disruption, tensions, absenteeism and a variety of problems which disrupted the flow and efficiency of production. Quinn (1977) also documented positive and negative impacts of romantic attachments in organizations, but concluded that such relationships are potentially more dangerous for women than for men in the long run, since problems arising from them were more likely to result in the woman's employment being terminated than the (usually higher status and therefore more occupationally secure) man's. Roy's findings among manual workers confirm this.

Sexual harassment, ranging from mild verbal innuendo to sexual molestation and rape, has been more often alluded to than systematically researched in Britain, but surveys indicate that cases brought to industrial tribunals represent a very small proportion of women for whom it has been a problem (Leeds TUCRIC, 1983; Sedley and Benn, 1982). McKinnon (1979) cites numerous examples of women's sexuality being assessed as part of job specifications, of favours being offered and threats being made by men, often in superordinate positions, to women at work. Roy's (1974) research leads to the bleak conclusion that, although the myth of 'true love' may have had some currency among the population he studied, his 'factory wives' were largely used and abused by the men in a calculative way which degraded both parties, with the women almost always regarded as sex objects rather than people.

Sykes (1966) concluded that the most gendered teasing in the printworks where he conducted his research took place between 'old' men (defined as over 25 and/or married) and 'young' women (under 25 and/or unmarried) and thus, he hypothesized that it served to control sexuality at work by ritualizing interaction between potential but taboo sex partners. Observations at NICO, where most of the interaction was among 'old' women and 'old' men according to Sykes's definitions, led to the conclusion that it was not sexuality that was thus controlled, but women, whose gender was constantly drawn attention to. Thus, participant observation revealed that the distinction between the sexist 'joking behaviour' directed largely at women by men, described by Sykes, and sexual harassment, is very slim.

Burrell (1984) suggests that sexual relations at work represent a major frontier of control and resistance in organizations. It is in the interests of the formal organization to minimize the impact of variables which are extrinsic to its objectives. Burrell argues that the survival of sexuality as an important variable in the workplace represents resistance to such bureaucratic control. While it is clearly true that the full range of heterosexual attachments identified earlier in this chapter by Roy are found in work organizations, ethnographic studies suggest that Burrell's analysis may be somewhat optimistic, particularly from women's point of view. Although most of the males and some of the females involved may be resisting tedium and the depersonalizing straitjacket of bureaucratic control, on the whole, the expression of and reference to sexuality and gender differences in the workplace more often indicate male attempts to control and restrict women (Pollert, 1981; Cavendish, 1982; Westwood, 1984; Purcell, forthcoming). Whether gender interaction at work is characterized by hostility and harassment or by chivalry and flirtation, the net effect is to remind women of their subordinate gender and, usually, occupational status and, in the case of women in 'male' environments or occupations, of their essential marginality and vulnerability in 'male' territory. In a recent survey (Leeds TUCRIC, 1983) it was found that women who worked in gender-atypical work environments were twice as likely to report having experienced sexual harassment at work than women who worked in traditionally 'female' areas of employment.

Although women are far from being passive victims and, collectively and individually, have been observed to exhibit a wide variety of protective responses and counter-assaults to exert countervailing control, they are generally coerced into responding in terms defined by men (Webb, 1984). Observational research at the NICO engineering firm revealed that even in amicable intergender exchanges such as real or mock flirtation, the interaction was invariably initiated by the man, whether verbal or tactile, with the woman forced to respond according to a prescribed pattern. Thus an arm would be thrown proprietorially around a women's shoulder or a hand would grasp her knee or thigh as she worked at her bench and she would be expected to respond with warmth or at least wit; or, walking through a 'male' work area, she would be wolf-whistled at or subjected to a running commentary about her possession, or lack, of physical charms. The only successful defence observed was humorous counter-attack which played along with the initiated ritual, but even in this there tended to be tension, as is characteristic of joking behaviour (Radcliff-Brown, 1952). Women who responded coldly by attempting to ignore the 'game' or refusing to play along with it were subjected to increasingly hostile teasing and personal criticism. Women who responded warmly tended to be 'led on' and ultimately ridiculed. There appeared to be no 'correct' response which would guarantee immunity from such joking or harassment, but it was observed that the older women tended to be better at deflecting attention from themselves and that they often came to the defence of their younger colleagues.

The other conclusion reached with regard to gendered joking behaviour was that, far from suppressing or repressing sexuality on the shopfloor, such interaction enflamed and encouraged the development of both public and clandestine relationships. Marriages, long-term extramarital affairs and 'ardencies of the opportune moment' were observed or alleged to have been initiated on the NICO shopfloor. As is characteristic of research on socio-sexual behaviour, direct observational data were limited and subjects' reports have to be treated with caution, although the fact that allegations were made about illicit relationships indicates at least the symbolic significance of sexuality and its importance as an item of conversational currency in the workplace. The problem for sociologists wishing to understand the labour process, and for employers and employees, is that such concerns and activities are a central component of employment experience and cannot be regarded as extrinsic factors which can be excluded from organizational analysis.

■ Gender, power and industrial relations

An important implication of the gendered structure and processes of employment for organizational sociologists is that not only have women been socially inhibited and discouraged from deviating from their appropriately gendered tasks and role playing, they have also been discouraged from exercising full citizenship rights (Marshall, 1950) in the workplace, particularly in the sphere of industrial relations. As is discussed [by Winchester (1988)] trade union membership in Britain has been declining in recent years and the only substantial area of expansion of both employment and union recruitment has been among female non-manual employees. Consequently, it might be expected that trade unions would be increasingly concerned with equal opportunities and other issues relating to women's employment, particularly the terms and conditions of employment of part-time workers. The Donovan Commission (1968: 91–2) drew attention to the underutilization of women's potential as employees and the failure of the trade unions to promote their interests. This coincided with the new wave of feminist consciousness in the late 1960s and increasing economic activity and recruitment to trade unions of married women, all of which, allied to international developments, combined to generate conditions conducive to the introduction of equal opportunities and sex discrimination legislation. Since then the TUC and individual unions, particularly those with a high proportion of female members, have become increasingly concerned with equal opportunities and 'women's issues' but this has often been a formal rather than enthusiastic concern, particularly at local and shopfloor level, tempered by ambivalence about the relative virtues, and incompatibility of, support for 'the family wage' and equal pay (Barrett and McIntosh, 1980; Campbell, 1982) and underlying beliefs about the sexual division of labour in the private and the public spheres.

In 1979, the TUC published a ten-point charter to promote equality for women within trade unions in affiliated unions, but it was found to have had what was euphemistically referred to as 'a mixed response' among unions (Equal Opportunities Commission, 1983; Coote and Kellner, 1980) with little evidence of change in ratios of women and men appointed to union posts. Many unions continued to discriminate against women within their own ranks, and those unions which did take significant action to promote the interests of their female members were almost exclusively confined to white-collar unions with large numbers of women members: the National Association of Teachers in Further and Higher Education, the National Union of Teachers (NUT), National Association of Local Government Officers (NALGO), National Union of Journalists (NUJ), Banking Insurance and Finance Union (BIFU), National Union of Public Employees (NUPE) and the Administrative Clerical and Technical Section of the Transport and General Workers Union (ACTS) (Boston, 1987: 329 ff.; Cockburn, 1987: 12–14).

It should also be noted that part-time employees are less likely than full-timers to have access to, or belong to, trade unions. 69 per cent of full-time employees, but only 50 per cent of part-time employees interviewed in the Women and Employment Survey had access to union membership in their employment and 51 per cent of full-time, but only 28 per cent of part-time employees, were union members. The proportion of women who were union members was inversely related to the number of hours per week worked, with only 17 per cent of those who worked less than 16 hours per week belonging to a union (Martin and Roberts, 1984: 56–59). Differences in union membership between male and female employees have often been assumed to illustrate women's lesser commitment to paid work and greater political conservatism, but an examination of the distribution of male and female union membership and political attitudes reveals that the organization and market situation of the industry, plant size and hours of work are more reliable correlates of union membership and political attitudes than gender itself (Purcell, 1984; Elias and Bain, 1988).

Furthermore, Cockburn (1987) points out that while it is true that women in employment have less often been shop stewards, voted in union elections, been to union meetings or taken industrial action, and that their attitudes towards both political parties and trade unions tends to be more suspicious, their political orientation in terms of response to particular issues and moral absolutes is often to the left of their male colleagues (Cockburn, 1987: 20). She argues that the majority of women may refuse to engage with, or identify with, organized politics at national and workplace levels because of the preponderance of men within such organizations and what she alleges to be the 'male' adversarial approach to internal procedure and political action which tends to predominate.

Research in work organizations suggests that Cockburn may be correct in her diagnosis that many women in employment effectively boycott trade-union activities because of its apparent irrelevance to their day-to-day experience at work. None of the women at NICO were active in the union, although all were union members and Labour voters, who belonged to the union because they believed in workers' representation and their own responsibility to be members; but most of them also agreed with the statement that 'the unions have too much power in this country' and all of them were cynical about the motives and work capacities of those who *were* active in the union locally. These contradictions are not an unusual finding (Beynon and Blackburn, 1972; Pollert, 1981; Cavendish, 1982; Westwood, 1984) and are not confined to women in employment. Cavendish (1982: 136) commented on the union at UMEC, the factory where she worked as a participant-observer:

> 'The women on the line were pretty negative about the union's activities in the factory. They said they were never told what was going on, and only learnt about decisions after they affected the wage packet. They were kept in the dark, their views weren't properly represented, and the dues of 30p a week were too high for the service they got.'

Only a minority of employees tend to be active union members and both Burawoy (1979) and Palm (1977) make the explicit point that most employees refer to 'the union' as if it is something separate from them. Conversely, Cavendish notes that while women were negative about union *activities* they were strongly committed to the union in principle 'and often said that they, the women on the line, were the union' (Cavendish, 1982: 137). This illustrates Cockburn's point that disenchantment with union practice and politics is not synonymous with lack of radicalism. It is only when a particular conflict arises that trade union members tend to become aware of their collective interests and, in instances of industrial action involving women, there is plenty of evidence that women have been as committed to defence of their jobs, the redressal of grievances and support for fellow workers, as men (Purcell, 1984; Wacjman, 1983). Women's support groups during the miners' strike of 1984–86 were acknowledged to be a radicalizing and pivotal force which had a major impact upon solidarity within most of the mining communities (Loach, 1985). The extent to which women tend to be more passive and exploitable as employees than men reflects their concentration in low-skilled, low-paid, part-time and expendable jobs rather than their gender, since men in similar jobs exhibit similar orientations to work and attitudes to trade unions (Lupton, 1963; Purcell, 1984).

In their study of a food factory employing full-time and part-time workers of both sexes, Beynon and Blackburn (1972: 122), while labelling women as having 'lower commitment, to work and trade-union membership', observed that the full-time women were the most vociferous group in terms of raising grievances with supervisors and management. They noted that 'grievances which may analytically be defined as "individual" – such as being moved from one job to another – became defined within the work group as collective' (1972: 113). Such solidarity is at odds with the more usual picture of individualistic, privatized, apolitical women which, in fact, Beynon and Blackburn anticipated in their initial classification of the expected orientations to work of men and women (1972: 9).

Nevertheless, if Cockburn is correct that women have a more consensual, albeit radical approach to politics and industrial relations, as has been argued by feminist psychologists to be a feature of gender difference in contemporary Western cultures (Miller, 1976; Gilligan, 1982), it may be that they have different ways of handling conflict at work. Raising a grievance collectively, without recourse to union intervention, may be a politically more astute, diplomatic and effective way of exerting control. Observations at NICO revealed several instances of work group negotiation and resolution of conflict between employees and management involving both male and female employees' grievances, all of which were initiated and led by women (Purcell, forthcoming). Perhaps the more important observation, particularly in the light of such action, was the way in which the women's union representatives and management did not *expect* the women to be involved or interested in formal industrial relations events or issues. During the participant observation period at NICO, instances were observed of a pension fund election being presented to the women as something they were unlikely to be interested in; of them being told after the event, rather than consulted before, about an overtime ban and other industrial action; of them invariably having to ask the (male) shop steward in their workshop about what had happened at major meetings concerning pay negotiations and the disbanding of the joint negotiating committee; and ambiguity on their own, the union and the management's parts about who exactly *was* their union representative – the 'lady shop steward' in another workshop or the male one in their own. Pollert (1981) describes similar ambiguities and 'oversights' at the tobacco factory where she carried out her research.

At NICO the 'lady shop steward' complained when interviewed that she was often not consulted, not told about meetings and not taken seriously by fellow union officers and management, an accusation which was substantiated during interviews with managers and other union activists. Imray and Middleton (1983: 17–18) cite a classic example of a female shop steward being chivalrously marginalized by her male colleagues despite her concern to become fully involved in her union. Other union women have reported similar lack of encouragement (Coote and Kellner, 1980) and such evidence demonstrates that an important reason for women's generally low profile and lack of activism in trade unions is clearly overt and more subtle male exclusionary tactics, even in the case of women who have been manifestly prepared to participate in traditional 'adversarial' industrial relations politics.

■ Conclusion

Research on gender and the experience of employment suggests that it is impossible to understand the gendered structure of employment or the processes in workplaces which sustain it, without reference to the sexual division of labour in British society as a whole, its historical evolution and the social and economic policies which currently underpin it. Theoretical analysis of the interrelationships between patriarchy and capitalism (for example, Hartmann, 1979; Beechey, 1987; Walby, 1986) has stimulated much debate and research, but, in itself, is limited to the construction of hypotheses about why men and women do the jobs they do and share domestic responsibilities and childcare to a more or less egalitarian degree. Empirical research, examining both employment trends and practice in particular industries, occupations and organizations, is increasingly clarifying the hidden structures and dynamics of gender relationships in employment and other social institutions (Cockburn, 1986; Siltanen, 1986; Beechey and Perkins, 1987; Crompton, 1987). In the same way as the relative advantages and disadvantages to girls and boys of single-sex and coeducational schooling have been observed and debated (Deem, 1978; Kelly, 1987; Arnot, 1986; Stanworth, 1981), it would be illuminating to observe the positive and negative effects for employers and employees of mixed and single-sex work groups, same and different sex supervision and the presence or absence of occupationally successful women in organizations as role models to motivate ambition and achievement in women lower down the career structure. Where change, particularly the encouragement of women to achieve occupationally higher status and more skills, is being initiated, it is very often handicapped by the failure to recognize the extent and pervasiveness of gender inequalities both in the workplace and the home. The unequivocal evidence of the twelve years following the enactment of equal opportunities legislation is that the provision of formal equality of opportunity in training and employment makes an impact on, but does not radically alter, gender segregation and occupational inequalities. A clearer understanding is required of the links between gender stereotyping, group behaviour and the dynamics of organizations – particularly the significance of sexuality, which can have a major stabilizing or destabilizing influence on work relationships.

Acknowledgements

I am indebted to Peter Elias, without whose practical suggestions, encouragement and diplomacy, this chapter would be considerably less coherent or even unpublished, and to John Purcell, without whose willingness to bear a ridiculously asymmetrical domestic workload over an unreasonably long period it would never have been written at all.

References

Abercrombie, N. and Urry, J. 1983. *Capital, Labour and the Middle Classes*. London: George Allen & Unwin.
Allen, S. and Wolkowitz, C. 1987. *Homeworking: Myths and Realities*, London: Macmillan.
Argyris, C. 1957. *Personality and Organisation*. New York: Harper & Row.
Arnot, M. 1986. 'State education policy and girls' educational experiences'. *Women in Britain Today*, eds V. Beechey and E. Whitelegg. Milton Keynes: Open University Press.
Ballard, B. 1984. *Employment Gazette*, 92 (September), 409–16. London: Department of Employment.
Barrett, M. and McIntosh, M. 1980. 'The family wage: some problems for socialists and feminists'. *Capital and Class*, 11 (Summer), 51–72.
Beechey, V. 1987. *Unequal Work*. London: Verso.
—— and Whitelegg, E. 1986. *Women in Britain Today*. Milton Keynes: Open University Press.
—— and Perkins, T. 1987. *A Matter of Hours*. Cambridge: Polity.
Bell, C. and Newby, H. 1976. 'Husbands and wives: the dynamics of the deferential dialectic'. *Dependence and Exploitation in Work and Marriage*, eds Barker, D. L. and Allen, S. London: Longman.
Benet, M. K. 1972. *Secretary*. London: Sidgwick and Jackson.
Berger, J. 1972. *Ways of Seeing*. Harmondsworth: Penguin.
Beynon, H. and Blackburn, R. M. 1972. *Perceptions of Work*. Cambridge: Cambridge University Press.
Bielby, W. T. and Baron, J. N. 1986. 'Men and women at work: sex segregation and statistical discrimination'. *American Journal of Sociology*, 91, 759–99.
Bisset, L. and Huws, U. 1984. *Sweated Labour: Homeworking in Britain Today*. London: Low Pay Unit.
Blackburn, R. M. and Mann, M. 1979. *The Working Class in the Labour Market*. London: Macmillan.

Boston, S. 1987. *Women Workers and the Trade Unions*. London: Lawrence and Wishart.

Braybon, G. 1981. *Women Workers in the First World War: The British Experience*. London: Croom Helm.

Breakwell, G. and Weinberger, B. 1987. 'Young women in 'gender-atypical' jobs'. Research paper No. 49. London: Department of Employment.

Brown, R. K. 1976. 'Women as employees: some comments on research in industrial sociology'. *Dependence and Exploitation in Work and Marriage*, eds Barker, D. L. and Allen, S. London: Longman.

—— Brannen, P., Cousins, J. and Samphier, M. 1973. 'Leisure in work: the "occupational culture" of shipbuilding workers'. *Leisure and Society in Britain*, eds Smith, M. A., Parker, S. and Smith, C. London: Allen Lane.

—— Curran, M. and Cousins, J. 1983. 'Changing attitudes to employment?'. Research Paper no. 40. London: Department of Employment.

Burawoy, M. 1979. *Manufacturing Consent*. Chicago: University of Chicago Press.

Burrell, G. 1984. 'Sex and organisational analysis'. *Organisation Studies*, 5: 2, 97–118.

Campbell, B. 1982. 'Not what they bargained for'. *Marxism Today* (March).

Cavendish, R. 1982. *Women on the Line*. London: Routledge & Kegan Paul.

Clark, A. 1919. *Working Women of the 17th Century*. London: G. Routledge and Sons Ltd.

Cockburn, C. 1983. *Brothers: Male Dominance and Technological Change*. London: Pluto Press.

—— 1985. *Machinery of Male Dominance*. London: Pluto.

—— 1986. 'Opportunity is not enough'. *The Changing Experience of Employment*, eds Purcell, K., Wood, S., Waton, A. and Allen, S. London: Macmillan.

—— 1987. *Women, Trade Unions and Political Parties*. London: Fabian Society.

Coote, A. and Kellner, P. 1980. *Hear This Brother: Women Workers and Union Power*. London: New Statesman report 1.

Coyle, A. 1984. *Redundant Women*. London: The Women's Press.

Craig, E., Garnsey, E. and Rubery, J. 1984. 'Payment structures and smaller firms: women's employment in segmented labour markets'. Research Paper no. 48. London: Department of Employment.

Creigh, S. *et al.* 1986. 'Self-employment in Britain: results from the Labour Force Survey 1981–84'. *Employment Gazette*, 94 (June), 183–94. London: Department of Employment.

Crompton, R. 1987. 'Gender, status and professionalism'. *Sociology*, 21 (August), 413–28.

—— 1988. 'The feminisation of the clerical labour force since the Second World War'. *The Feminisation of Office Work*, ed. G. Anderson. Manchester: Manchester University Press.

—— and Jones, G. 1984. *White-Collar Proletariat*. London: Macmillan.

—— and Mann, M. 1986. 'Women and the service class'. *Gender and Stratification*. Cambridge: Polity Press.

—— and Sanderson, K. 1986. 'Credentials and careers: some implications of the increase in professional qualifications amongst women'. *Sociology*, 20 (February), 25–42.

Cunnison, S. 1983. 'Participation in local union organisation: school meals staff: a case study'. *Gender, Class, and Work*, eds Gamarnikow, E., Morgan, D., Purvis, J. and Taylorson, D. London: Heinemann.

—— 1986. 'Gender, consent and exploitation among sheltered housing wardens'. *The Changing Experience of Employment*, eds Purcell, K., Wood, S., Waton, A. and Allen, S. London: Macmillan.

Daniel, W. W. 1969. 'Industrial behaviour and orientation to work'. *Journal of Management Studies*, 6: 3, 366–75.

Deem, R. 1978. *Women and Education*. London: Routledge & Kegan Paul.

Delphy, C. 1976. 'Continuities and discontinuities in marriage and divorce'. *Dependence and Exploitation in Work and Marriage*, eds D. L. Barker and S. Allen. London: Longman.

Derow, E. 1982. 'Childcare and employment: mothers' perspective'. *Strategies for Integrating Women into the Labour Market*, eds Hvidtfeldt, K., Jorgensen, J. and Nielsen, R. Denmark: Women's Research Centre in Social Sciences.

Dex, S. 1988. 'Gender and the labour market'. *Employment in Britain*, ed. Gallie, D. Oxford: Blackwell.

Diamond. 1980. Royal Commission on the Distribution of Income and Wealth. *Report*. London: HMSO.

Donovan 1968. Royal Commission on Trade Unions and Employers' Associations 1965–8 *Report*. Cmnd 3623. London: HMSO.

Dubin, R. 1956. 'Industrial workers' worlds: a study of the "central life interest" of industrial workers'. *Social Problems*, 3, 131–42.

—— Hedley, R. A. and Taveggia, T. C. 1976. 'Attachment to work'. *Handbook of Work, Organisation and Society*, ed. Dubin, R. Chicago: Rand-McNally College.

Dunning, J. 1986. *Japanese Participation in British Industry*. London: Croom Helm.

Elias, P. 1988a. 'Family formation, occupational mobility and part-time work'. *Women and Paid Work*, ed. Hunt, A. London: Macmillan.

—— 1988b. 'Sectoral trends in full-time and part-time employment'. Project Report to the Department of Employment. Coventry: Institute for Employment Research, University of Warwick (unpublished).

—— and Main, B. 1982. *Women's Working Lives*. Coventry: Institute for Employment Research, University of Warwick.

—— and Bain, G. 1988. 'The dynamics of trade union membership'. Coventry: Institute for Employment Research, University of Warwick.

—— and Purcell, K. 1988. 'Women and paid work: prospects for equality'. *Women and Paid Work*, ed. Hunt, A. London: Macmillan.

Ellis, V. 1981. *The Role of Trade Unions in the Promotion of Equal Opportunities*. Manchester: Equal Opportunities Commission and Social Science Research Council.

Engineering Council 1985. *Career Breaks for Women*. London: Engineering Council.

Equal Opportunities Commission 1983. *Women and Trade Unions: A Survey*. Manchester: EOC.

Finch, J. and Groves, D. (eds) 1983. *A Labour of Love: Women, Work and Caring*. London: Routledge & Kegan Paul.

Gamarnikow, E., Morgan, D., Purvis, J. and Taylorson, D. (eds) 1983. *Gender, Class and Work*. London: Heinemann.

Game, A. and Pringle, R. 1983. *Gender at Work*. Sydney: Allen & Unwin.

Garnsey, E. 1978. 'Women's work and theories of class and stratification'. *Sociology*, 12: 2.

Gershuny, J. 1978. *After Industrial Society? The Emerging Self-service Economy*. London: Macmillan.

—— 1987. 'Daily life, economic structure and technical change'. *International Social Science Journal*, 11 (August), 337–42.

Gilligan, C. 1982. *In A Different Voice*. Cambridge, Mass.: Harvard University Press.

Glucksmann, M. 1986. 'In a class of their own? Women in the new industries in inter-war Britain'. *Feminist Review*, 24 (Autumn), 7–37.

Goffman, E. 1976. *Gender Advertisements*. London: Macmillan.

Goldthorpe, J. H. 1982. 'On the service class, its formation and future'. *Social Class and the Division of Labour*, eds Giddens, A. and McKenzie, G. Cambridge: Cambridge University Press.

—— Lockwood, D., Bechhofer, F. and Platt, J. 1968. *The Affluent Worker: Industrial Attitudes and Behaviour*. Cambridge: Cambridge University Press.

Gouldner, A. 1957. 'Cosmopolitans and locals: towards an analysis of latent social roles'. *Administrative Science Quarterly*, 2, 218–306.

Hakim 1985. 'Employers' use of outwork: a study using the 1980 Workplace Industrial Relations Survey and the 1981 National Survey of Homeworking.' Research Paper no. 44. London: Department of Employment.

—— 1987. 'Homeworking in Britain'. *Employment Gazette*, 95 (February), 99–104. London: Department of Employment.

Harris, R. 1988. 'Prima donna inter pares'. *The Observer* (3 January), 18–19.

Hartmann, H. 1979. 'Capitalism, patriarchy and job segregation by sex'. *Capitalist Patriarchy and the Case for Socialist Feminism*, ed. Eisenstein, Z. New York: Monthly Review Press.

Hearn, J. and Parkin, W. 1987. *'Sex' at 'Work'*. Brighton: Wheatsheaf.

Hennig, M. and Jardim, A. 1978. *The Managerial Woman*. London: Marion Boyars.

Hertz, R. 1986. *More Equal Than Others: Women and Men in Dual Career Marriages*. Berkeley and Los Angeles: The University of California Press.

Hewitt, M. 1958. *Wives and Mothers in Victorian England*. London: Rockliff.

Humphries, J. 1977. 'Class struggle and the persistence of the working class family'. *Cambridge Journal of Economics* (September).

Hunt, A. 1975. *Management Attitudes and Practice Towards Women at Work*. London: HMSO.

Huws, U. 1984. 'The new homeworkers'. *New Society* (March).

Imray, L. and Middleton, A. 1983. 'Public and private: marking the boundaries'. *The Public and the Private*, eds Gamarnikow, E., Morgan, D., Purvis, J. and Taylorson, D. London: Heinemann.

Institute for Employment Research 1987. *Review of the Economy and Employment*. Coventry: IER, University of Warwick.

Johns, A. 1984. *Coalmining Women: Victorian Lives and Campaigns*. Cambridge: Cambridge University Press.

Kanter, R. 1977. *Men and Women of the Corporation*. New York: Basic Books.

Kelly, A. (ed.) 1987. *Science for Girls?* Milton Keynes: Open University Press.

Leeds TUCRIC, 1983. *Sexual Harassment of Women at Work*. Leeds: Leeds TUCRIC.

Legge, K. 1987. 'Women in personnel management: uphill climb or downhill slide?'. *In A Man's World*, eds Spencer, A. and Podmore, D. London: Tavistock.

Llewellyn, C. 1981. 'Occupational mobility and the use of the comparative method'. *Doing Feminist Research*, ed. Roberts, H. London: Routledge & Kegan Paul.

Loach, L. 1985. 'We'll be here right to the end ... and after: women in the miners' strike'. *Digging Deeper*, ed. Beynon, H. London: Verso.

Long, P. 1984. *The Personnel Specialists: A Comparative Study of Male and Female Careers*. London: IPM.

Lupton, T. 1963. *On the Shopfloor*. London: Pergamon.

McKee, L. and Bell, C. 1985. 'Marital and family relations in times of male unemployment'. *New Approaches to Economic Life*, eds Finnegan, R., Gallie, D. and Roberts, B. Manchester: Manchester University Press.

McKinnon, C. 1979. *Sexual Harassment of Working Women*. New Haven and London: Yale University Press.

McNally, F. 1979. *Women For Hire: A Study of the Female Office Worker*. London: Macmillan.

Marshall, T. H. 1950. *Citizenship and Social Class*. Cambridge: Cambridge University Press.

Martin, J. and Roberts, C. 1984. *Women and Employment: A Lifetime Perspective*. London: HMSO.

Martin, R. and Wallace, J. 1984. *Working Women in Recession*. Oxford: Oxford University Press.

Massey, D. and Meegan, R. 1982. *The Anatomy of Job Loss*. London: Methuen.

Miller, J. B. 1976. *Towards a New Psychology of Women*. Boston: Beacon Press.

Mitter, S. 1986. 'Industrial restructuring and manufacturing homework: immigrant women in the UK clothing industry'. *Capital and Class*, 27 (Winter), 37–80.

Moorhouse, H. F. 1984. 'The work ethic and hot rods'. Paper given at the British Sociological Association Conference at Bradford University, April.

Morgan, D. 1986. 'Gender'. *Key Variables in Social Investigation*, ed. Burgess, R. London: Routledge & Kegan Paul.

Morgan, D. H. J. 1969. 'Theoretical and conceptual problems in the study of social relations at work: an analysis of differing definitions of women's roles in a northern factory'. Ph.D thesis, University of Manchester.

—— 1987. ' "It will make a man of you": notes on national service, masculinity and autobiography'. *Studies in Sexual Politics* no. 17. Manchester: Department of Sociology, University of Manchester.

Morris, L. D. 1985. 'Renegotiation of the domestic division of labour in the context of male redundancy'. *Restructuring Capital*, eds Newby, H. *et al*. London: Macmillan.

Murray, F. 1983. 'The decentralisation of production – the decline of the mass-collective worker'. *Capital and Class* (Spring).

Newton, D. 1987. 'Women in engineering'. *In A Man's World*, eds Spencer, A. and Podmore, D. London: Tavistock.

Nichols, T. and Armstrong, P. 1976. *Workers Divided*. London: Fontana.

Novarra, V. 1981. *Men's Work, Women's Work*. London: Marion Boyars.

Oakley, A. 1974. *The Sociology of Housework*. Oxford: Martin Robertson.

Pahl, R. E. 1984. *Divisions of Labour*. Oxford: Basil Blackwell.

—— and Wallace, C. D. 1985. 'Household work strategies in an economic recession'. *Beyond Employment*, eds Redclift, N. D. and Miginone, E. Oxford: Basil Blackwell.

Palm, G. 1977. *The Flight From Work*. Cambridge: Cambridge University Press.

Pearson, R. 1986. 'Female workers in the first and third worlds: the "greening" of women's labour'. *The Changing Experience of Employment*, eds Purcell, K., Wood, S., Waton, A. and Allen, S. London: Macmillan.

Pinchbeck, I. 1981. *Women Workers and the Industrial Revolution*. London: Virago.

Pollert, A. 1981. *Girls, Wives, Factory Lives*. London: Macmillan.

Purcell, K. 1978. 'Working women, women's work and the occupation of being a woman'. *Women's Studies International Quarterly*, 1 (Summer).

—— 1982. 'Female manual workers, fatalism and the reinforcement of inequalities'. *Rethinking Inequality*, eds Robbins, D. *et al*. Farnborough: Gower.

—— 1984. 'Militancy and acquiescence amongst women workers'. *Women in the Public Sphere*, eds Siltanen, J. and Stanworth, M. London: Hutchinson.

—— (forthcoming). *Gender at Work*. Oxford: Oxford University Press.

Quinn, R. E. 1977. 'Coping with cupid: the formation, impact and management of romantic relationships in organisations'. *Administrative Science Quarterly*, 22 (March), 30–45.

Radcliff-Brown, A. K. 1952. *Structure and Function in Primitive Society*. London: Cohen and West.

Rapoport, R. and Rapoport, R. 1976. *Dual Career Families Re-examined*. London: Martin Robertson.

Riley, D. 1984. *War in the Nursery*. London: Virago.

Roy, D. F. 1974. 'Sex in the factory. Informal heterosexual relations between supervisors and work groups'. *Deviant Behaviour*, ed. Bryant, C. D. Chicago: Rand McNally.

Rubery, J. and Wilkinson, F. 1981. 'Outwork and segmented labour markets'. *The Dynamics of Labour Market Segmentation*, ed. Wilkinson, F. London: Academic Press.

Sedley, A. and Benn, M. 1982. *Sexual Harassment at Work*. London: National Council for Civil Liberties (NCCL).

Siltanen, J. 1986. 'Domestic responsibilities and the structuring of employment'. *Gender and Stratification*, eds Crompton, R. and Mann, M. Cambridge: Polity Press.

Simmel, G. 1950. *The Sociology of George Simmel*. Trans., ed. and introduced by Wolff, K. H. Glencoe, Ill.: The Free Press.

Spencer, A. and Podmore, D. (eds) 1987. *In a Man's World: Essays on Women in Male-dominated Professions*. London: Tavistock.

Stacey, M. 1981. 'The division of labour revisited or overcoming the two adams'. *Practice and Progress: British Sociology 150–80*, eds Abrams, P., Deem, R., Finch, J. and Rock, P. London: George Allen & Unwin.

Stageman, J. 1980. 'Women in trade unions'. Occasional Paper no. 6. Hull: Industrial Studies Unit, Adult Education Department, University of Hull.

Stanworth, M. 1981. *Gender and Schooling*. London: Hutchinson.

Summerfield, P. 1984. *Women Workers in the Second World War: Production and Patriarchy in Conflict*. London: Croom Helm.

Sykes, A. G. M. 1966. 'Joking relationships in an industrial setting'. *American Anthropologist*, 68, 188–93.

Thirsk, J. 1985. Foreword. *Women in English Society 1500–1800*, ed. Prior, M. London: Methuen.

Thompson, E. P. 1965. 'The peculiarities of the English'. *The Socialist Register*, eds Miliband, R. and Saville, J. London: The Merlin Press.

Trades Union Congress (TUC), 1979. *Equality for Women Within Trade Unions*. London: TUC.

—— 1983. *Women in the Labour Market*. London: TUC.

Valli, L. 1986. *Becoming Clerical Workers*. Boston and London: Routledge & Kegan Paul.

Wacjman, J. 1983. *Women in Control*. Milton Keynes: Open University Press.

Wadel, C. 1979. 'The hidden work of everyday life'. *Social Anthropology of Work*, ed. Wallman, S. London: Academic Press.

Walby, S. 1986. *Patriarchy at Work*. Cambridge: Polity.

Webb, S. 1984. 'Gender and authority in the workplace'. *Looking Back: Some Papers From The BSA 'Gender and Society Conference'*. Studies in Sexual Politics no. 1. Manchester: Department of Sociology, University of Manchester.

Westergaard, J. 1970. 'The rediscovery of the cash nexus'. *The Socialist Register*, eds Miliband, R. and Saville, J. London: The Merlin Press.

—— and Restler, H. 1975. *Class in a Capitalist Society*. London: Heinemann.

Westwood, S. 1984. *All Day, Every Day*. London: Pluto.

Wharton, A. S. and Baron, J. 1987. 'So happy together? The impact of gender segregation on men at work'. *American Sociological Review*, 52 (October), 574–87.

Willis, P. 1977. *Learning to Labour*. London: Saxon House.

Wilson, C. S. 1963. 'Social factors influencing industrial output. A sociological study of a factory in North West Lancashire'. Ph.D. thesis, University of Manchester.

Winchester, D. 1988. 'Sectoral change and trade-union (*sic*) organization', in *Employment in Britain*, ed. Gallie, D. Oxford: Blackwell.

Wood, S. 1981. 'Redundancy and female unemployment'. *Sociological Review*, 29: 4.

Yeandle, S. 1984. *Women's Working Lives*. London: Tavistock.

Chapter 8

Discrimination and Equal Opportunity in Employment: Ethnicity and 'Race' in the United Kingdom

R. Jenkins

This chapter focuses upon the manner in which forms of social identification concerned with ethnicity and 'race' figure in labour recruitment and employment in the United Kingdom. There are three central themes: first, the nature of ethnic and 'racial' discrimination; secondly, the relationship between labour-market disadvantage and formal educational or skill qualifications; and thirdly, strategies and problems in the pursuit of greater equality of opportunity. First, however, it is necessary to clarify the definitions of a number of basic concepts which will be used throughout.

What, for example, is meant by 'ethnicity'? In the most basic definition, drawing on the work of social anthropologists such as Barth (1969) and Cohen (1978), ethnicity is simply the social organization of cultural diversity. In this approach, which can legitimately trace its roots back to the classic formulations of Weber (1978: 385–99), ethnic identity and the boundaries of ethnic groups are situationally defined by the actors concerned, subject to negotiation and redefinition within the constraints of history and present circumstances. Among the elements of culture which make up ethnicity are language, religion, kinship, patterns of residence and the mundane routines of everyday life and subsistence. In the United Kingdom, the ethnicity approach has informed a number of empirical

Source: R. Jenkins (1988) 'Discrimination and equal opportunity in employment: ethnicity and 'race' in the United Kingdom', in *Employment in Britain*, D. Gallie (ed.), Blackwell, Oxford, pp. 310–343.

studies of work and employment (see, e.g., the essays collected in Wallman, 1979).

The ethnicity paradigm has come in for criticism from a number of directions. Rex, for example, has argued that it is important to distinguish 'race' – social identity based upon folk or commonsense 'racial' categories – from ethnicity, because of the more restricted set of situations which are characterized by 'race relations' and the higher levels of conflict which they engender (1973: 184). Authors working within an ethnicity framework, many of them coming from the structural-functionalist tradition of British social anthropology, have tended to stress 'ethnicity as a social resource' at the expense of an analysis of inter-ethnic conflict. Nor have anthropological analyses of ethnicity paid much attention to relationships of power and domination. In addition, as Bourne and Sivanandan have argued (1980: 35), too strong an emphasis upon the culture, values and orientations of ethnic minorities themselves can appear to be 'blaming the victims' for their own disadvantage.

Despite such criticisms, however, a recognition of the role of ethnicity in inter-group relations remains important. In stressing social processes, the approach discourages overly deterministic analyses. The intrusion of irrelevant biological models of 'race' is also discouraged by the stress placed upon the social construction of ethnic and 'racial' categories by those working within a theoretical framework concerned with ethnicity. Finally, the emphasis upon actors' own definitions of the situation is a healthy safeguard against ethnocentrism.

The concept of 'race' is equally problematic. Throughout this chapter the word will remain within inverted commas in order to signify its contested status. In particular, it must be stressed that no biological reference is denoted by its use. It simply refers to popular models of 'racial' differentiation. There are no grounds for suggesting that 'real' differences between 'races' are the cause of 'racial' differentiation (Rex, 1986: 15–17; Stone, 1985: 9–33). There are, however, good grounds for insisting upon a clear definition of racism. An historically specific facet of ethnicity characterizing situations of ethnic subordination and domination, racism is typically the categorization of 'them', as opposed to the ethnic identification of 'us' (Banton, 1983: 10). Two other aspects of racism are important in the definition proposed here. First, racism categorizes the 'other' as inherently different and typically inferior (whether culturally or biologically), and denies the possibility of egalitarian coexistence. Secondly, racism involves the disadvantageous treatment of the 'other', whether intentionally or not (Jenkins, 1986: 4–6). This definition is in broad agreement with writers such as Barker (1981) in insisting that neither prejudice nor intentionality are necessary aspects of racism.

The final concept which must be defined at this stage is 'discrimination'. Put at its simplest, this is no more than telling the difference (or *a* difference) between people or things; a less general definition would imply an element of choice or evaluation. Looked at in this way, discrimination is basic to the 'freedom' of the capitalist labour market: workers choose which jobs to apply for, recruiters adjudicate between competitive job candidates in order to choose one and reject the others. In much popular usage, however, the word has acquired a more pejorative meaning. Discrimination is largely taken to mean a choice between people on the basis of criteria which are inadmissable, either *tout court* or in a specific context. Discrimination has come to mean *unfair* discrimination. Unless otherwise indicated, this is the sense in which the word will be used in the discussion which follows.

In looking at ethnic discrimination in employment in the United Kingdom, there is a range of possibilities from which to select topics and data. In the main, this chapter will concentrate upon two subjects: black workers in Great Britain and the distinction between Catholic and Protestant workers in Northern Ireland. There is a considerable amount of argument as to whether or not it is appropriate to use the category 'black' to include both people whose origins line in the Caribbean region and those with antecedents in the Indian subcontinent. Inasmuch as both sets of people, in addition to the important cultural and historical factors which serve to differentiate them, share a similar experience of racist discrimination in the British context, and in the absence of any better nomenclature, this inclusive usage will be maintained here. Where appropriate, of course, specific black ethnic minorities will be identified and discussed as such. The reader should, however, remember that the term 'black' is a personal choice of the author, and not without its critics.

■   Black and white workers in Great Britain

As recent historical scholarship has demonstrated, a small population of black people has been present in the British Isles for centuries (Fryer, 1984; Ramdin, 1986; Visram, 1985; Walvin, 1984). It was only in the post-war period, however, that black migrant workers arrived in large numbers, settling as permanent communities in most of Britain's industrial areas. The legal and political framework within which this movement of population occurred was the 1948 British Nationality Act, which established the right of people from British colonies and the Commonwealth countries to settle and work in Britain. Between the arrival of the SS *Empire Windrush* from the West Indies in 1948 and the introduction of the Commonwealth Immigration Act in 1962, which heralded the end of mass New Commonwealth immigration, something of the order of half a million black people arrived in Britain (Deakin, 1970: 44–55; Jones and Smith,

1970: 5–17). Since then most of the expansion in the black population has reflected either natural increase or family reunification. By 1985, according to the Labour Force Survey, the black population of Great Britain was 2.4 million (approximately 4.4 per cent of the total population), made up of just over a million Asians, just over half a million Afro-Caribbeans and over half a million people from other ethnic minorities (Department of Employment, 1987: 19).

By and large, the motivation for this migration was largely economic (Watson, 1977: 6–7). To simplify the matter considerably, perhaps to oversimplify it, the 'push' factors were underemployment and poverty in the countries of origin, the 'pull' factor, labour shortages in Britain. A major exception to this broad generalization was the movement of Asian families from East Africa in the late 1960s and early 1970s as a result of political developments in Kenya and Uganda. The jobs which most migrants entered were typically unskilled or semi-skilled, comparatively low paid, disproportionately likely to involve shift working and were mainly in the manufacturing sector (Daniel, 1968: 57–62; Deakin, 1970: 72–82).

To characterize these migrations as primarily economic is not, however, to exhaust the explanatory possibilities. There is, for example, some debate as to how the employment of the early generations of black workers in post-war Britain should be understood in the context of the development of the national economy. Peach, for example, writing about migration from the Caribbean, conceptualizes black workers as 'replacement labour', drawn in to fill the labour-market niches deserted as undesirable by local workers during a period of economic growth (Peach, 1968). Duffield, however, in his study of Punjabi labour in the foundry industry argues that black labour, particularly in situations where trade unions were weak, moved into new (and unskilled) occupational niches created by the technological restructuring of the labour process (Duffield, 1985, 1988).

The two explanations are, of course, not necessarily contradictory. Both processes are likely to have been at work in different contexts. The merit of Duffield's analysis, however, is that it draws our attention to the importance of the resistance offered by white workers, both informally and formally through their unions, as a factor limiting the access of black migrant workers to 'better' jobs and occupations (Phizacklea and Miles, 1987; Wrench, 1987). Racist discrimination is not the prerogative of employers. Whatever the precise nature of the discrimination, however – and this will be discussed in more detail later – there is little doubt that black workers in the 1950s and 1960s did not end up located in the bottom reaches of the labour market because of *their* occupational goals or social aspirations (Jenkins, 1986: 8–13).

During this period, continental Europe, particularly France, Germany, Switzerland and the Benelux countries, was also experiencing labour immigration. Some of the new arrivals were from colonies or ex-colonies; others, the larger proportion, were drawn as 'guest workers' (*gastarbeiter*) from the underdeveloped margins of the Mediterranean – Southern Italy, Yugoslavia, Turkey, Greece, North Africa and the Iberian peninsula (Berger and Mohr, 1975; Castles, Booth and Wallace, 1984; Castles and Kosack, 1985; Edye, 1987; Paine, 1974). While there are some similarities between the British and European cases, the comparison should not be overdrawn. First, the European countries differ substantially from each other in law and policy. Secondly, the swingeing – although, in time, moderated – legal constraints upon *gastarbeiter*, and the political goal of maintaining them as strictly temporary sojourners, renders their position very different to ex-colonial migrants in Britain with partial or full rights of citizenship and settlement.

The most comprehensive recent information about the labour-market position of black workers in Britain comes from the 1985 Labour Force Survey (Department of Employment, 1987). Looking at the employment status of those in work, the most obvious difference relates to self-employment: 14.0 per cent of white male workers were self-employed, as compared to 8.5 per cent of West Indians, 23.7 per cent of Indians, 21.4 per cent of Pakistani or Bangladeshis and 22.9 per cent of East African Asians. For women workers, the figures are white workers 6.6 per cent, West Indians 0.9 per cent, Indians 9.4 per cent and East African Asians 11.9 per cent. The Labour Force Survey figures for Pakistani or Bangladeshi women are – for all categories of economic activity – too small to be reliable.

There are also differences with respect to industrial distribution: 23.5 per cent of white males who are in paid employment or on government schemes work in manufacturing, compared to 30.4 per cent of ethnic minority males. For construction, the percentages are 11.7 and 5.2 respectively; for distribution, hotels, catering and repairs, 15.8 and 25.1; and for transport and communications, 8.0 and 12.4. The pattern for women workers is different: women ethnic minority workers are disproportionately represented in manufacturing (21.9 per cent, as compared to 14.9 per cent of white women workers) and the health service (16.8 per cent, as against 10.5 per cent). They are *under*represented in education (6.0 per cent compared to 11.4 per cent). The overrepresentation of black workers in manufacturing has rendered them particularly sensitive to changes in the economic climate and more vulnerable to redundancy and lay-offs than white workers.

Perhaps the most striking difference between black and white workers revealed by the Labour Force Survey is, in fact, their propensity to suffer unemployment. Taking the overall view, the unemployment rate for white workers (10 per cent) is half that for ethnic minorities. The situation of young workers is most severe: 16 per cent of economically active white young people between 16 and 24 years were unemployed, compared to 33 per cent of ethnic minorities. The minority groups worst affected were Pakistanis and Bangladeshis (31 per cent), followed by West Indians (21 per cent) and then Indians (17 per cent).

A largely similar picture is painted by the other major source of data, the Policy Studies Institute's *Black and White Britain* survey (Brown, 1984). The successor to the famous Political and Economic Planning surveys (Daniel, 1968; Smith, 1974, 1977), the PSI study provides clearer information than the Labour Force Survey concerning certain aspects of the labour-market disadvantage experienced by black workers. For example, there are clear ethnic differences with respect to occupational level. Whereas 23 per cent of white men in the PSI survey were in non-professional or non-managerial white-collar jobs, this was true for only 10 per cent of West Indians and 13 per cent of Asians. In semi-skilled manual jobs, however, the figures are 13 per cent of white men, 26 per cent of West Indian men and 34 per cent of Asian men. In the unskilled manual category, the percentages are 3 per cent, 9 per cent and 6 per cent respectively. For women workers, the results for semi-skilled manual jobs are white women 21 per cent, West Indians 36 per cent and Asians 44 per cent. In non-manual jobs the figures are broadly comparable for white and West Indian women (55 and 52 per cent), with Asian women at 44 per cent.

The PSI findings also reveal the extent of important ethnic differences with respect to conditions of employment. For instance, Asians and West Indians (both men and women) are appreciably more likely than white workers to work shifts. Despite this, however, ethnic minority men, in particular, earned on average approximately twenty pounds a week less than white workers at the time of the survey (1982). In some regions and at some job levels, the earnings differential was much greater than this; at *all* occupational levels the average wage for black workers was below that for white workers.

The 1982 PSI survey provides a useful point of comparison with the earlier PEP surveys. Such a comparison throws light on the extent and nature of the impact of the recession upon black workers (Brown, 1984: 173–83). At the risk of oversimplifying, the position can be summarized thus: while there has been no convergence of the labour-market situations of black and white workers with respect to industrial or occupational concentration, job levels, pay or working patterns, the marked gap between them with respect to unemployment has widened.

Among the reasons for this deteriorating situation are the following. First, because of the manner of their incorporation into the labour force in the 1950s and 1960s – something which will be discussed in more detail later – black workers are disproportionately more likely to be in industries (manufacturing and the health service, for example), occupations (un-skilled and semi-skilled manual jobs) and locations (inner-city areas and the declining industrial areas of the West Midlands and the North) which are particularly severely affected by unemployment (Massey and Meegan,

1982). Factors such as these are probably the most influential in determining the disproportionate distribution of unemployment between white and black workers (Rhodes and Braham, 1987). Secondly, there is some evidence to suggest that, just as there is discrimination *against* black people in recruitment, so there may also be discrimination in doubtful *favour* of them when it comes to choosing workers for redundancy or other kinds of involuntary severance (Smith, 1981: 67–93). Racism, it seems, operates at ports of entry *and* exit. Once unemployed, black workers are, as a consequence, likely to experience particular problems in the job search. Thirdly, deliberate discrimination aside, employers are likely to discriminate unfavourably against workers with interrupted labour-market careers. For the reasons which have just been discussed, black workers are more likely to experience such an employment pattern. Thus a vicious cycle of insecure employment and unemployment is created. Finally, some research has suggested that recession-related changes in recruitment procedures, in particular an increased propensity to use internal recruitment and 'word of mouth' networks (Ford *et al.*, 1984; Jenkins *et al.*, 1983; Manwaring, 1984), are particularly disadvantageous for black workers (Jenkins, 1984). More recent research, however, has cast some doubt on the general thesis about the impact of the recession upon recruitment practices (Ford *et al.*, 1986). 'Word of mouth' recruitment and the internal labour market will be discussed further below.

Although black workers in general are disproportionately vulnerable to unemployment, it is clear that young black people are most severely affected. So much so, in fact, that some commentators have talked about 'black youth in crisis' (Cashmore and Troyna, 1982). This topic will be considered further in the discussion of education and its relationship to employment. Suffice it to make two points here. First, the evidence that young black people are systematically and seriously disadvantaged within the Youth Training Scheme and other government schemes is overwhelming (Cross, 1987; Cross and Smith, 1987; Lee and Wrench, 1987; Pollert, 1985). Among the most important reasons for this are racist discrimination and unchallenged commonsensical assumptions about the goals and training needs of black young people. Secondly, while accepting the central importance of policing practices and policies as the seeds of disorder, there can be little doubt that black youth unemployment was one factor underlying the disorders ('the riots') of 1981 and 1985 in British cities (Benyon and Solomos, 1987; Solomos, 1985, 1986). Despite subsequent public commitments by various state and other agencies to addressing the problem of black youth unemployment, the situation does not seem to have changed much for the better.

The connection between violent conflict and unemployment is often mooted. It should, however, only be made with caution and in the context of other factors and relationships. This is particularly the case with respect to inter-ethnic relations in Northern Ireland, the next topic to be discussed.

■ Catholic and Protestant workers in Northern Ireland

In the opening discussion, reference was made to Rex's remark that one reason for distinguishing conceptually between ethnicity and 'race' was that 'race relations' give rise to more serious conflict than do ethnic relations. Northern Ireland is an interesting exception to this generalization, although there has been some academic controversy relating to whether the situation there can be conceptualized as a situation of 'racial' conflict (Moore, 1972). Following the line of argument put forward by Sarah Nelson (1975), the current social science consensus is that it is not appropriate to analyse Northern Ireland within a 'race relations' framework. This is the view adopted in this discussion.

While there is no space here for an extensive discussion of the Northern Ireland situation, such as those available in the volumes edited by Boal and Douglas (1982) and Darby (1983), for example, some background material may be useful. Two ethnicities in conflict – Protestant and Catholic – were established by the sixteenth-century plantation of the north of Ireland by English and Scottish (Protestant) settlers and the consequent economic dispossession and political exclusion of the Irish (Catholic) population. The resulting ethnic hierarchy of advantage and disadvantage was consolidated during the nineteenth-century industrial revolution, when the north-eastern end of the island developed into an urban industrial centre on a par with Clydeside and Merseyside. Catholics migrated from rural areas to undertake unskilled work in the cities and towns of Ulster. Sectarian ethnicity was manipulated as an industrial relations strategy by local employers, and turned to advantage by the Protestant work-force. The twentieth century has been marked by political conflict, as a consequence of the partition of Ireland in 1921 and the creation, within the United Kingdom, of a six-county state – Northern Ireland – dominated by Protestant interests. The current 'troubles' began in the late 1960s, arising out of Catholic civil rights agitation and the violent Protestant response to those demands, and have coincided with a period of marked economic decline, part of the wider national and international recession. In 1972 direct political control of Northern Ireland was assumed by the United Kingdom government, although the province remains legally and administratively distinct from Great Britain.

One of the most recent sources of information relating to ethnic disadvantage in employment in Northern Ireland is the 1983–84 Continuous Household Survey (Department of Finance and Personnel, 1985). Looking at employment status, the difference between Catholics and Protestants surveyed is striking: 35 per cent of Catholic men and 17 per cent of Catholic women were unemployed, by comparison with 15 per cent of Protestant men and 11 per cent of Protestant women. Looking at those in the sample who were unemployed, it is clear that long-term unemployment is more prevalent in the Catholic community: 44 per cent of unemployed Catholics had been out of work for more than two years, compared to 33 per cent of unemployed Protestants. Of those interviewed who had been unemployed for less than a year, 54 per cent of Protestants had suffered only one or two spells of unemployment in the previous two years, as compared to 43 per cent of Catholics. In summary, Catholics are more likely to be unemployed and they are more likely to be unemployed in the long term (see also Osborne and Cormack, 1986).

This sorry situation is, given the well-attested relationship between occupation and vulnerability to unemployment, at least in part a reflection of the occupational structure of the two communities. The relationship between education and labour-market disadvantage will be examined in a later section. The Continuous Household Survey reveals that while 38 per cent of Protestants were in professional, managerial or other non-manual occupations, this was true of only 27 per cent of Catholics. At the other end of the spectrum, 37 per cent of Catholics were in unskilled or semi-skilled manual occupations, by comparison with 31 per cent of the Protestants interviewed. Bearing in mind this relatively small differential between the two populations with respect to unskilled and semi-skilled employment, an obvious implication is that occupational factors can only account for a small part of their difference with respect to unemployment. Looking at the situation of young workers, research suggests not only that, as elsewhere in the United Kingdom, young people are most severely affected by unemployment, but that Catholic young people are particularly vulnerable (Cormack and Osborne, 1983; Murray and Darby, 1983). This is, at least in part, a consequence of demographic factors. The Catholic community, in reflection of differential fertility rates, is a younger population than the Protestant community, although the significance of this is offset to some extent by higher levels of emigration among Catholics (Compton, 1982: 99–102).

A further useful source of information is the official consultative paper on equal opportunity in Northern Ireland (Department of Economic Development, 1986). Drawing on a variety of data sources, and discussing gender and disability as well as ethnicity, this report supplies some extra detail not available elsewhere. Looking at increases in unemployment with the recession, while the overall Protestant unemployment rate rose from 6 per cent at the 1971 census to 10 per cent in 1981, the equivalent figures for the Catholic population are 14 per cent and 25 per cent. Although the degree of differential unemployment between the two communities varies from place to place, its existence is widespread throughout the province.

This situation of Catholic disadvantage in employment has persisted since the nineteenth century (Hepburn, 1983). Similar patterns are revealed in analyses of data deriving from the 1971 census and the Irish Mobility Study (Aunger, 1983; Miller, 1983, 1986). As we have seen, there is little indication that the gap between the two populations in this respect is closing, despite the fact that Protestant workers have, with the deepening of recession since the late 1970s, become more likely to suffer unemployment (Cormack and Osborne, 1987; Miller and Osborne, 1983). Employment has always, even during periods of comparative prosperity such as the 1960s, been a scarce resource. Sectarian ethnicity has served to maintain the relative economic advantage experienced by Protestants, although there is evidence of improving Catholic employment profiles in the public sector (Osborne, 1987).

To round out the picture further, it must be noted that while Northern Irish welfare benefits are in line with British scales, average wages in the province are lower and the cost of living higher. The result, particularly for the long-term unemployed in Northern Ireland – who are, it should be remembered, disproportionately Catholic – is family poverty at a level markedly higher than that found on the other side of the Irish Sea (Black et al., 1980; Evason, 1985). Such a conclusion is supported by the 1983–84 Continuous Household Survey: 29 per cent of Catholic households 'frequently' or 'always' experienced difficulty in paying the rent, as opposed to 21 per cent of Protestant households (and the latter is, itself a high enough proportion to cause concern). Similarly, the Survey reveals significantly lower ownership levels of telephones, fridges, freezers and cars among Catholic households.

There has been a fair amount of lively academic controversy about whether Catholic disadvantage in employment is due to discrimination or other factors. This controversy should be viewed in the context of a wider debate relating to the 'troubles': to what degree can the conflict be related to the economic and other grievances of Northern Irish Catholics – caused, so much conventional wisdom would have it, largely by discrimination – and to what degree is it the result of Irish nationalism?[1] Doherty, for example, has suggested (1982) that higher levels of unemployment among Catholics can *in part* be explained by their greater concentration in rural areas west of the River Bann, away from centres of industrial employment. More controversially, Compton (1982, 1986) argues that higher Catholic fertility rates and larger families may account in large part for Catholic unemployment and lower-class status. Broadly similar arguments have been put forward by Hewitt (1981) and Kelley and McAllister (1984), who, along with Whyte (1983), have also reviewed the evidence for the presence of discrimination against Catholics prior to the 'troubles' and suggested that it was less prevalent than has been often supposed.

This, by now considerable, body of revisionist scholarship is impressive. It is, however, subject to a number of important criticisms. First, and probably most important, even when factors such as geographical location, class status and family size are controlled for, there is a significant ethnic factor apparently working to the economic advantage of Protestants (Miller, 1986: 226). In Belfast, for example, 27 per cent of the variation in unemployment rates may be attributed to ethnicity (Doherty, 1982: 242). Secondly, in explaining away Catholic disadvantage as due to family size or father's occupational status, for example, these factors are treated as independent variables. In fact, they are themselves likely to be dependent upon past or present discrimination (Kennedy, 1973). Thirdly, much of the revisionist argument relies for its force on a crude model of blatant discrimination, ignoring the subtleties of 'indirect' forms of discrimination, as discussed in the next section. Finally, and this will also be discussed later, there is, in fact, good evidence of sectarian discrimination before the introduction of direct rule from Westminster in 1972, and some evidence for its subsequent persistence.

The research reviewed above suggests that, while the Northern Ireland situation is one of 'ethnic' not 'race' relations, it has much in common with the state of affairs in Great Britain described in the previous section. Catholic disadvantage in employment is an interrelated compound of – among other things – the following ingredients: the history of their incorporation into the labour market, locational factors, demography, the occupational structure of the Catholic labour force and discrimination. This latter, perhaps the most important single factor in many people's eyes, is the subject of the next section.

■ The nature of discrimination

Discrimination has already been defined in such a way as to stress a process of unfair differentiation between people. At this point it is important to reiterate that, in the word's non-perjorative sense, recruitment into employment is of necessity discriminatory: applicants are either accepted or rejected. On what basis does this decision-making process operate? What are employers doing in the recruitment process?

Research in both Northern Ireland and Britain has suggested that employers routinely use two different kinds of selection criteria: *suitability* and *acceptability* (Jenkins, 1983: 101–13; 1986: 46–70). Both types of criteria are related to the efficient functioning of the worker and the workplace, as perceived by management. Suitability is functionally specific, inasmuch as it is concerned with the individual's ability to perform the tasks required by the job. Criteria of suitability might include physique, particular experience or formal educational, trade or professional qualifications. Acceptability is functionally non-specific, concerned with the general control and management of the organization: will the recruit 'fit in' to the context in question; is he or she 'dependable', 'reliable' and hard working; will the new worker leave after a short time? Criteria of acceptability, highly subjective and dependent upon managerial perceptions, include appearance, 'manner and attitude', 'maturity', gender, labour-market history and age and marital status. The basic distinction between acceptability and suitability – and in practice it is not always clear cut – has been taken up by other researchers concerned with discrimination (e.g. Curran, 1985: 30–1; Lee and Wrench, 1987: 88). In one of the most sophisticated discussions of the issue, Jewson and Mason have further suggested that to criteria of suitability and acceptability should be added *collectivist* and *individualist* principles of recruitment, to produce four modes of discrimination: determinism, rational-legality, particularism and patronage (1986a: 44–8). Which versions of suitability (determinism or rational-legality) or acceptability (particularism or patronage) are of most importance in a particular context may, according to their argument, have implications for the promotion of equal opportunity policies.

Criteria of suitability are undoubtedly influential in recruitment, particularly during the early stages, in shortlisting, for example. Acceptability is, however, important in determining final selection outcomes, particularly – although by no means exclusively – in manual and routine non-manual occupations (Ashton, Maguire and Garland, 1982; Blackburn and Mann, 1979; Silverman and Jones, 1976). The issue of suitability will be discussed in the following section.

To look at acceptability here, there is a considerable amount of evidence to suggest that black workers are systematically disadvantaged by selection criteria of this kind. First, managerial concern with the capacity to 'fit in', for example, may be racist in a fairly straightforward fashion: 'the lads' won't like it' has been frequent justification for refusing employment to black applicants (Commission for Racial Equality, 1981). It should also be recognized, of course, that there is considerable truth in this: the lads *don't* like it. Trade unions have been, and are, a major brake – as democratic organizations representing the interests of the majority of their members – upon the pursuit of ethnic equality in employment (Phizacklea and Miles, 1987; Rolston, 1980; Wrench, 1987). Secondly, the implicit nature of many criteria of acceptability, their informality and taken-for-grantedness, allows racism to slip unremarked upon into the recruitment process. To digress for a moment, it is clear that direct racist discrimination remains a problem for black workers. This has been amply demonstrated in recent 'discrimination tests' or 'situation tests', which document the responses of employers offering job vacancies when contacted by candidates of differing ethnic identities. In Nottingham in the late 1970s, 48 per cent of the employers tested discriminated against West Indian and Asian applicants (Hubbuck and Carter, 1980). In tests in London, Birmingham and Manchester in 1984 and 1985, the equivalent figure was 37 per cent (Brown and Gay, 1985). The difference between the two studies may, in part, reflect the wider range of occupations surveyed in the more recent study.

Other aspects of the notion of acceptability may also systematically disadvantage black job-seekers, albeit without any necessarily prejudicial intent on the part of the recruiter (Jenkins, 1986: 80–115). Stereotypes of the acceptable worker interact with widely held ethnic stereotypes to the detriment of black candidates. Given the demographic structure of the black population, biased, as a recently migrant population, towards the youthful end of the spectrum (Department of Employment, 1987: 19), criteria such as 'maturity' or male age and marital status – 'a married man with two kids, a mortgage and a car' – will, at the present time, exclude disproportionately more black than white candidates. More generally, the routine ethnocentrism of notions of acceptability and the diagnostic cues upon which they rest is likely subtly to load the dice in favour of applicants whose verbal and non-verbal cultural repertoires harmonize with those of recruiters (Akinnaso and Seabrook Ajirotutu, 1982; Gumperz, 1982). Since most recruiters are white and British, this means applicants who are also white and British.

One of the original contexts within which the distinction between suitability and acceptability was formulated was research into young people and the labour market in Belfast (Jenkins, 1983: 101–13). With respect to selection criteria of acceptability and ethnic discrimination in Northern Ireland, there is little in the way of directly comparable research evidence. Common sense and everyday experience suggests that many Protestant employers regard Catholics as less acceptable, as lazy, disloyal or 'shifty', for example. Such is the nature of Northern Irish ethnic stereotypes (O'Donnell, 1977). There is, however, evidence of past sectarian discrimination of a more straightforward kind (e.g. Barritt and Carter, 1972: 93–108; Fair Employment Agency, 1983b: pp. i–xi). The persistence of such discrimination at the present time is less easy to document directly, in the absence of situation testing or investigative qualitative research. Such research and evidence as there is, however, points, by strong implication, towards its continued significance (Fair Employment Agency, 1983a: 7–10; 1984: 25–31; Miller, 1986: 227–30; Osborne, 1982).

There is one important dimension of recruitment – directly related to notions of acceptability and ethnic discrimination – where comparable material does exist. 'Word of mouth' recruitment through informal social networks has been documented in Britain (Brooks and Singh, 1979; Jenkins, 1986: 135–50; Lee and Wrench, 1983) and Northern Ireland (Cormack and Osborne, 1983; Jenkins, 1983: 114–28; Maguire, 1986). This, and other evidence,[2] demonstrates the importance to employers of personal recommendations and informal recruitment channels, both because of their relative cheapness and convenience, but also as a source, in managers' eyes, of more acceptable recruits. As a form of closure and channel of participation, they also frequently attract the support of trade unions. Recruitment procedures of this kind are often disadvantageous to black workers in Britain and Catholics in Northern Ireland, for a number of reasons. Their informality, for example, provides for the operation of nepotism, sectarianism and racism. Less obviously, the flow of vacancy information is generally restricted within the networks of the existing work-force of a given establishment. If this work-force is overwhelmingly of a particular ethnicity or 'race', it is likely to remain so (Commission for Racial Equality, 1982). This is an important mechanism serving, whether by force of inertia or exclusionary intent, to maintain ethnic employment hierarchies and differentials and produce labour-market closure (Kreckel, 1980). The undoubted importance of 'word of mouth' recruitment is a barrier to equality of opportunity in Britain and Northern Ireland.

Banton, in the course of developing a rational choice model of ethnic relations, has distinguished between *categorical* and *statistical* discrimination (1983: 274). Categorical discrimination entails treating someone in a particular way simply because they are, for example, black (or a member of any specified category). Statistical discrimination, however, involves treating someone in a particular fashion because it is believed that, as members of a socially specified category, they are more or less likely to possess a valued or stigmatized attribute.

Categorical discrimination, therefore, includes the straightforward racist discrimination discussed above. A leading American economist has described this as a 'taste for discrimination'; in the conventional neo-classical model of the labour market, their taste for discrimination is something which employers seek to indulge to the maximum (Becker, 1971: 13–17). Fevre, in his study of the Yorkshire wool textiles industry, offers a broadly similar argument when he says that white employers have an *absolute* belief in the total inferiority of black workers in *all* jobs, only employing them when there is no other choice (1984: 106–25, 147–56). Although there is no need to review them in detail here, there are a number of criticisms, both empirical and conceptual, to which the 'taste for discrimination' model is vulnerable (Joll *et al.*, 1983: 131–53; Sloane, 1985).

Statistical discrimination corresponds to the discrimination resulting from the use of criteria of acceptability. Black workers, for example, are less likely to be recruited because – for whatever reasons – they are believed to be less likely than whites to prove reliable, manageable, or whatever. If black workers or Catholics are believed to be less likely than whites or Protestants to be suitable in particular contexts, because a greater proportion lack the required training or experience perhaps, this is also an example of statistical discrimination. The point is that statistical discrimination does not mean that the recruiter views *all* blacks or *all* Catholics as less suitable or acceptable than whites or Protestants. It is simply that a greater proportion of the stigmatized than the non-stigmatized group is believed to be deficient in these respects. It is, therefore, rational behaviour on the part of the employer, albeit based upon faulty information or stereotypes, to discriminate against them as a collectivity.

From the discussion so far, it should be clear that statistical and categorical discrimination interact in the recruitment process to the systematic disadvantage of black workers in Britain and Catholics in Northern Ireland. They are complementary explanations rather than alternatives. The distinction is important inasmuch as the notion of statistical discrimination lays bare the situational logic of the 'some of my best friends are black, but ...' rationalization for ethnic discrimination. This is a useful contribution to an understanding of the way in which individuals can vehemently deny being racist or sectarian, but continue to discriminate knowingly against black people or Catholics. It is also an explanation of the recruitment of token – and highly visible – members of ethnic minorities: 'so-and-so's all right, but ...'. Whatever else ethnic discrimination may be, it is rarely just straightforward, i.e. categorical racism or sectarianism. The notion of statistical discrimination takes the discussion beyond simple models of prejudice and relates employment discrimination to the rational goals of managers and recruiters.

Another way of conceptualizing discrimination is the legal distinction between *direct* and *indirect* discrimination created by the 1975 Sex Discrimination Act and the 1976 Race Relations Act (section 1(i)(b)). Drawing directly upon American experience, this categorization has no equivalent in Northern Irish fair employment law, so the discussion will be confined to Great Britain. Direct discrimination is quite straightforward: it involves the intent to discriminate on ethnic or 'racial' grounds.[3] Indirect discrimination, a concept which is in some respects similar to the idea of institutional racism (Dummett, 1973: 131–53), occurs when practices which are nominally equivalent to their effects upon different groups of people create conditions or requirements which can be less easily satisfied by a certain group, as a consequence of which members of that group suffer a detriment (Lustgarten, 1980: 43–64; McCrudden, 1982a). The practices concerned must not, for indirect discrimination to be proved, be justifiable on the grounds of business necessity. Examples of practices which have fallen foul of the law in this respect are inappropriate English language requirements, 'word of mouth' recruitment (in certain settings) and dress regulations (such as those requiring female shop assistants to wear uniform skirts – an obstacle for Muslim women).

The introduction of the notion of indirect discrimination into English law was an attempt to tackle routine (and frequently thoughtless) ethnocentrism and the everyday practices, incrementally formed during the historical establishment of custom and practice, which serve to produce and maintain ethnic inequalities. It was also a recognition of the inherent difficulties in attempting to prove intentionality in discrimination. As such, it has had only a limited success, due to weaknesses in the definitions of 'justifiability' and 'condition or requirement' (Commission for Racial Equality, 1983: 11–12; Jenkins, 1986: 249–52), the inability of English common law to accommodate the kind of social scientific or statistical evidence upon which the American law relies (McCrudden, 1983: 66–7) and the pro-management bias of Industrial Tribunals (Hepple, 1983: 83).

Analytically speaking, the distinction between indirect and direct discrimination, while it focuses our attention upon the subtleties of ethnic disadvantage, is of only limited and imprecise utility. It is, in fact, more an aspect of the situation being studied than an analytical tool of any exactitude. The next important aspect of that situation to be discussed here is the relationship between ethnic disadvantage in employment and educational achievement.

■ Education, skill and disadvantage

The relationship between educational attainment and labour market outcomes has been the object of much research, both at the macro level of statistics and surveys (Bowles and Gintis, 1976; Goldthorpe, 1980; Jencks, 1973; Sewell and Hauser, 1975) and the micro level of ethnography and participant observation (Coffield et al., 1986; Griffin, 1985; Jenkins, 1983; Willis, 1977). The topic has also engendered a considerable amount of more or less heated argument, both political and academic (Hurn, 1978: 85–107; Karabel and Halsey, 1977: 307–65; Oxenham, 1984). The flavour of some of this discussion is accurately captured in phrases such as 'the great training robbery' (Berg, 1970) and 'the diploma disease' (Dore, 1976). The debate within labour-market economics about 'human capital' remains lively and of relevance (Siebert, 1985). Regardless of which view is adopted, it seems safe to conclude that whatever the relationship between education and labour-market outcomes might be, it is neither straight-forward nor self-evident.

To look at the situation of black young people, the great majority of whom have received all their education in Britain, it may be summarized thus: while most British-born Asian children (Bengali speakers apart) do well in school, their Afro-Caribbean peers achieve less, in formal educational terms, than white children (Jeffcoate, 1984; Parekh, 1983). The reasons for this state of affairs are controversial and there is not space to discuss them here (see Rampton, 1981; Stone, 1981; Swann, 1985). What, however, are its implications for labour-market outcomes?

The nature and extent of the labour-market disadvantage of black workers in Britain has already been outlined. Young black workers are particularly disadvantaged. To what degree is their labour-market position related to their levels of formal educational achievement? Lee and Wrench, in their study of apprenticeships (1983), found that although the Asian, West Indian and white youngsters they studied had similar aspirations and levels of educational achievement, the white sample was more successful in obtaining apprenticeships. The gulf between career goals and outcomes was most marked for the black samples.

Other research has produced similar findings. The Afro-Caribbean youngsters in one study were markedly less successful than their white equivalents in obtaining the kind of jobs they wanted. This difference could not be explained by the educational differences between the two groups (Commission for Racial Equality, 1978). Subsequent research has confirmed this pattern (Anwar, 1982). Further, while most young Asians achieve *at least* as much as young white people with respect to formal educational qualifications, this does not appear to translate into comparable employment outcomes. Although Asian young people suffer from unemployment to a lesser extent than Afro-Caribbean youth, they are consistently and significantly more likely to be unemployed than young white people (Brown, 1984: 190).

Longitudinal studies of a cohort of white and West Indian school leavers in the 1970s point in the same direction (Dex, 1982; Sillitoe and Meltzer, 1986). Black youngsters, both male and female, are more likely to fail in pursuing their goals, and their employment careers are more subject to interruption by 'involuntary events' (dismissal, redundancy or personal circumstances external to the workplace). As a result, they are more vulnerable to unemployment. These contrasting employment profiles cannot be related to educational differences. This research, and that of others (Brown, 1984: 135–6; Roberts et al., 1981), also demonstrates that black young people are more interested, and have higher participation rates, in further education, than the white population.

To emphasize the point further, Cross's analysis of the accessibility of vocational training for black young people in Britain demonstrates that the unemployed black youngster is typically better qualified than his or her white equivalent (1982a). He has also shown that the *ratio* of black to white unemployment is higher for young people in non-manual or skilled manual occupations requiring formal educational qualifications, even though the unskilled suffer higher *levels* of unemployment (Cross, 1982b: 47–8). What is more, despite the fact that black young people are, for the purposes of this particular comparison, similarly qualified to white people, they have been disproportionately placed on state employment schemes 'with a tenous or non-existent connection with the labour market' (Cross, 1987: 86). Finally, although formal qualifications are for white people a buffer, to some extent, against unemployment, the same does not appear to be the case for black people (Smith, 1981: 16–17).

Research in Northern Ireland has shown that much of the long-standing educational differences between the Catholic and Protestant populations had been eroded by the late 1970s. There was, however, still an appreciable underrepresentation of Catholics in the group of school-children obtaining five or more O-levels or A-levels (Osborne and Murray, 1978). The gap between the two populations has continued to decrease, but more slowly. Important factors influencing this process are social class, the experience of unemployment and the provision of grammar school places (the Northern Ireland secondary education system remains selective and is, effectively, ethnically segregated). Nor is it simply a matter of level of qualifications: there remains a tendency for Catholic pupils to be overrepresented in arts and humanities subjects by comparison with mathematics and the sciences (Osborne, 1985). A similar concentration is apparent in higher education, where the expansion of Catholic participation has largely taken place towards the low end of the spectrum (Osborne *et al.*, 1983).

What is, however, clear is that the major employment differentials between the two populations are not attributable to educational differences: 'protestant and catholic pupils with the same level of academic attainment do not have the same success in obtaining employment' (Department of Economic Development, 1986: 10). Nor are these differentials easily attributable to ethnic differences with respect to 'attitudes to work' (Miller, 1978). These conclusions are supported by research concerned with the post-school transition of working-class youth in Belfast and Derry (Cormack and Osborne, 1983; Murray and Darby, 1983).

There is a clear conclusion to be drawn from the evidence summarized above: while there are differences between blacks and whites or Catholics and Protestants as collectivities, with respect to educational achievement, these are only in very small part, if at all, the 'cause' of the current employment differentials which exist between them. Nor is this causal relationship, such as it may be, immediately obvious or straightforward. This is not to say, however, that education is irrelevant to labour-market outcomes. Rather, the suggestion is that educational attainment is influential in the context of other factors, having a different 'trade-in' or market value for members of different ethnic groups.

Formal educational qualifications are one aspect of suitability, as discussed in the previous section on the nature of discrimination. Another important facet of suitability is formally recognized or accredited skill. It has already been demonstrated that British black people and Northern Irish Catholics are disproportionately represented in unskilled and semi-skilled jobs. Bearing in mind the socially constructed and situationally defined nature of 'skill' (Lee, 1981), it is reasonable to ask how this situation has developed.

Looking at black workers, there are a number of factors to take into account. In the first place, the original wave of post-war migrants were specifically recruited to fill jobs at the bottom end of the market. Most of them have remained there, trapped by a combination of stigmatization, language barriers (for some) and their own eventual acquiescence. Secondly, the skills possessed by many migrants were rejected by British employers and trade unions. For many, the move to Britain resulted in de-skilling and occupational downgrading (Daniel, 1968: 57–82; Phizacklea and Miles, 1980: 78–89; Ratcliffe, 1980: 19–21). Thirdly, for subsequent generations of British-born black people access to skill training such as apprenticeships has been systematically frustrated by a combination of direct and indirect discrimination (Lee and Wrench, 1983). There is a wide body of research which demonstrates that black people, regardless of educational suitability, find it more difficult to obtain training, particularly at higher levels or in vocationally relevant areas (Cross, 1987; Lee, 1987). Finally, with respect to those dimensions of skill which are informally constituted in experience, the acquisition of such experience depends on 'getting in' in the first place. This is likely to be more difficult for black workers than for white workers.

The situation for Catholics in Northern Ireland is, in some respects, broadly comparable. Historically speaking, Catholics were incorporated into the labour market in Northern Ireland as ex-agricultural workers regarded as, at best, semi-skilled. This process was dependent upon their systematic and organized exclusion from skilled work by an alliance of organized (Protestant) labour and Unionist employers. Patterns of recruitment into training and skilled positions were set up which, combined with the sectarian geography of residence and employment in places like Belfast and violent intimidation during times of tension, ensured the virtual monopoly of skilled work by Protestants. The pattern persists to this day: such evidence as is available suggests that Protestant school leavers are more likely to obtain 'proper' apprenticeships, for example, than their Catholic counterparts who end up, at best, in government Training Centres, with less expectation of a job at the end of their training (Cormack and Osborne, 1983; Murray and Darby, 1983). Finally, as in the case of British black workers, higher levels of unemployment among Catholics, and their concentration in certain kinds of employment, renders them disproportionately less likely to have access to the important informal dimensions of skill acquisition.

Skill requirements, and even the definition of 'skill', change with economic circumstances. In the last fifteen years a number of important changes have occurred in Britain and Northern Ireland, which are relevant to this discussion. There has been a massive increase in unemployment, a shift away from employer-based training towards government training schemes, a decline in manufacturing and an expansion of service-sector employment, an expansion of part-time employment (often taken by women) and a revolution in information technology. In theory, this might present an opportunity for ethnically disadvantaged men – and women – to improve their relative labour-market position. Inasmuch as the attributes which are likely to be required of workers in the future are *generic capacities* rather than *specific skills*, their exclusion from skill training may be less of a disadvantage.

This does not, however, appear to be the case, as the material on ethnic disadvantage testifies. The continued importance of criteria of acceptability, combined with trends in industrial location away from inner-city areas (where the majority of black people live) and heightened competition for the scarce resources of employment, seems likely to ensure that any changes with respect to relative ethnic disadvantage in employment are likely to be for the worse, not for the better. This issue will be discussed in greater detail in the next section.

The arguments advanced in this section concerning the relationship between educational qualifications and labour-market outcomes should not be interpreted as suggesting that the pursuit of more and better education by ethnic minorities is futile. This is emphatically not the case (Troyna and Smith, 1983). What is important, however, is that education should not be held out as offering, in and of itself, social mobility or enhanced labour-market position.

■ Towards greater equality

In interpreting the facts of ethnic disadvantage in employment in the United Kingdom, a number of factors have been highlighted as contributing to the situation: prejudice or ethnic antipathy, more subtle forms of discrimination (both intentional and otherwise), the – possibly unintended – consequences of informal recruitment procedures, the history of any specific group's incorporation into the occupational and industrial structure, demographic factors, geographical location and – something about which more will be said below – the recession. Although first-generation migrants may have been educationally and, for some at least, linguistically at a disadvantage, these factors are not a convincing explanation for the labour-market experience of their children.

As Marx said, having interpreted the world in various ways, the point is to change it. It is possible to distinguish four strategies for, or approaches to, the amelioration of ethnic disadvantage: the legal, the administrative, the voluntaristic and that associated with struggle or community action. Before discussing each of these, it is necessary to clarify what the goals of such strategies might be.

Essentially, there are two different kinds of goal: 'fair shares' and 'equality of opportunity' (Mayhew, 1968). The first is the more radical, depending upon mechanisms of reverse or positive discrimination to redistribute resources more equitably within society. This is a collectivist social philosophy of group entitlements. The second, resting upon an individualistic philosophy with its roots in the freedom of the market, aims to remove discriminatory barriers on the demand side and encourage thereby the participation of members of disadvantaged groups in the 'normal' processes of social mobility. Equal opportunity is the less controversial objective; positive discrimination – and the manner in which it has been pursued in the USA – has generated at least as much heat as light in academic and political debate.[4] As the law and state policy presently stand in the United Kingdom, the emphasis is almost exclusively on equality of opportunity. This is the main focus therefore, of the discussion which follows.

The law is one of the main mechanisms which has been used to try to improve the lot of black Britons and Northern Irish Catholics with respect to employment. The 1968 Race Relations Act expanded the scope of the 1965 Act to prohibit discrimination in employment. The 1976 Race Relations Act drew the novel distinction between direct and indirect discrimination, in the process broadening the theoretical reach of the law considerably, established the Commission for Racial Equality (CRE) by the amalgamation of the Race Relations Board and the Community Relations Commission, permitted direct access for complainants to the Industrial and Employment Appeal Tribunals and defined certain narrow conditions under which 'positive action' – not, it should be noted, 'positive discrimination' – is permissible (Lustgarten, 1980; McCrudden, 1981).

Despite these legal provisions, there is a consensus that the actual impact of the 1976 Act has, at best, been minimal (Lustgarten, 1987: 14–15; Sanders, 1983: 75). The evidence summarized earlier in this chapter is clear in this respect. There are a number of reasons for this unhappy situation, some of which have already been touched upon: the nature of British common law, the increasing complexity of the discrimination case law, specific weaknesses in the framing of the 1976 Act, lack of political support for the principles informing the Act and resistance on the part of employers to state or legal intervention in their affairs (Jenkins and Solomos, 1987: 210–12).

In Northern Ireland, following the van Straubenzee report, the 1976 Fair Employment Act (Northern Ireland) prohibited discrimination on the grounds of political or religious affiliation. It established the Fair Employment Agency (FEA), with the twin duties of eliminating discrimination and promoting equality of opportunity. In the first of these objectives the Act and the Agency have not been particularly successful (McCrudden, 1981, 1982b; Rolston, 1983). The reasons for this failure include caution and lack of enforcement experience within the FEA, lack of confidence in the Agency's ability to effect change on the part of the Catholic community, the inadequacies of the Act – particularly the absence of any explicit concept of indirect discrimination – confusion about the Agency's semi-autonomous role within the Northern Ireland state and resistance by Protestant employers and workers. In addition, the Act suffers some of the same problems with the common law as the 1976 Race Relations Act in Britain.

Many of these criticisms are summarized in the Standing Advisory Commission on Human Rights report (1987) on discrimination in Northern Ireland. This document was accompanied by a comprehensive – and locally controversial – three-volume research report (Smith and Chambers, 1987). Among the proposals announced in February 1988 by the Northern Ireland Department of Economic Development (DED) in the wake of these reports are the prohibition of indirect discrimination, the introduction of statutory requirements that all firms with more than twenty-five employees monitor their work-forces and that *all* employers provide equality of opportunity, and the replacement of the FEA by a newer, more powerful, organization. All these will be enshrined in new legislation.

Moving on to the administrative approach, as advocated by Lustgarten (1987), this suggests that the state, using its power as an employer, contractor and consumer, should intervene directly to ameliorate ethnic disadvantage, changing its own employment practices and those of the organizations with which it does business. Since 1982 the Northern Ireland government has, for example, refused to accept contract tenders from firms not holding an Equal Opportunity Certificate issued (and removable) by the FEA. As yet, however, there is little evidence of this power being used to any great effect. The DED's proposals of February 1988 include a strengthening of this sanction.

If one accepts Miller's analysis of the resistance of government in Northern Ireland to the investigation of its own employment policies and procedures by the FEA (1986: 227–30), then the prospects seem less than bright. Where such, admittedly external, administrative pressure has been felt, however – from the United States Air Force in its dealings with Short Brothers and Harland – some changes have resulted (Darby, 1987: 68–9). There is, what is more, some evidence, in the shape of the Northern Ireland Civil Service's Equal Opportunities Unit, that government is beginning to take the issue of putting its own house in order more seriously than it has done in the past (Cormack and Osborne, 1987). The Secretary of State has also increasingly been publicly supporting the pursuit of equal opportunity. External political influences – in the shape of Dublin and the Anglo-Irish agreement – are also important here.

In Britain, there is less enthusiasm on the part of central government for an administrative approach, in large part at least because of the political tenor of the post-1979 Conservative administrations with respect to 'race', equal opportunity and state intervention (Solomos, 1987). Some local authorities, both as employers and – in pursuit of their perceived duties to promote equal opportunity under Section 71 of the Race Relations Act – with respect to 'contract compliance' (the insistence that contractors for authority business are equal opportunity employers), have enthusiastically adopted such an orientation. During 1987 these contract compliance approaches were threatened by the new Local Government Bill, which aimed to outlaw the use of non-financial criteria in local authority contractual decision-making. In the light of its conflict with Section 71 of the 1976 Act, this clause in the Bill was, however, modified. State intervention with respect to inner-city programmes and training also fall within the administrative approach. In the area of training, for both young people and adults, there is evidence that black people are systematically disadvantaged (Cross, 1987; Lancashire Industrial Language Training Unit, 1983). With respect to the inner city, in the absence of any attempt either to reverse industrial locational shifts (Fothergill and Gudgin, 1982; Massey and Meegan, 1982) or take seriously the 'racial' dimension of the inner-city problem (Rex, 1981), little seems likely to change. The contrast between the Conservative government's different positions in Belfast and at Westminster with respect to equality of opportunity is an instructive example of the expedient contextuality of policy-making.

Administrative pressure and the threat of legal sanctions are, of course, designed to evoke 'voluntary' responses from employers. The promotional work of the CRE (Ollerearnshaw, 1983) and the FEA (Darby, 1987) is also directly aimed at this goal. The major voluntarist response is the organizationally specific equal opportunity policy, a package of employment policies and procedures designed to ensure equality of opportunity within an organization. Such a package might include ethnic monitoring, more formal recruitment procedures, compensatory training and changes to the organization's channels of recruitment. The changes which have been introduced by Short Brothers and Harland in Belfast, as mentioned above, are an example of such a policy, as is the approach adopted by the Ford Motor Company (House of Commons, 1981: 850–73). Reviewing the recent literature (Hitner et al., 1982; Jenkins, 1986: 189–219; 1987; Jewson and Mason, 1986b, 1987; Torrington et al., 1982; Young, 1987; Young and Connelly, 1981), there are a number of broad conclusions which may be offered concerning the limitations of equal opportunity policies.

First, the introduction of such policies is subject to all the general constraints, to do with things such as habit, inertia, communication problems and personnel performance, which are attendant upon any process of change or innovation within bureaucratic organizations. Secondly, and more specifically, considerable resistance may be encountered from white, male work-forces – from management to shopfloor – to the notion of equal opportunity. The employment procedures of the organization, thirdly, may require considerable modification in order to improve accountability and allow for a monitored recruitment and promotion process. Without systematic monitoring, it is impossible to enforce an equal opportunity policy. Fourthly, there is a considerable amount of confusion about what 'equal opportunity' actually means, and how it relates to notions such as 'positive discrimination' and 'positive action'. The lack of clear guidance from the law and other authoritative policy sources in certain areas is a problem. Fifthly, the weakness of the personnel function within many organizations serves to limit the effectiveness of employment policies for which they are responsible. Equal opportunity is generally an issue which is handled by personnel (Jenkins and Parker, 1987). Finally, the importance of training as an integral part of equal opportunity initiatives, in terms of equalizing access to all training opportunities, specific training for equal opportunity and the provision of compensatory training, is often overlooked (Lee, 1987). Taken as a whole, these must be considered major barriers to the effectiveness of equal opportunity policies. They are not, however, insuperable and progress is being made in places to overcome them.

Finally, there is the role of struggle or community action in ameliorating labour-market disadvantage. In the USA, for example, black political pressure, both constitutional and 'on the streets', has been a major factor producing change (Burstein, 1985). The scope for such action in Britain seems limited, however, largely because, given the numerical size of the black vote and the continued significance of popular racism,[5] there is little or no political mileage to be had, on either the left or the right, from such an issue. Central government, despite the importance of the 'inner cities' issue in the period following the 1987 General Election, has yet to recognize the role of the unemployment of young black people in the 'riots' of the early 1980s. In municipal local government, where the black vote may be more important, there has been more enthusiasm for the promotion of equal opportunity (Ben-Tovim et al., 1986). In the light of central government's limitation of the powers and responsibilities of local authorities in Great Britain, however, the future of such initiatives seems to be in doubt.

With respect to Northern Ireland, there can be little disagreement that the political violence of the last eighteen years or so has had an enormous impact upon the economy: employment has been lost and inward investment deterred. It is difficult to imagine any sense in which the minority population can have benefited *economically* from such a situation. The gap between the two populations remains, although employment profiles for Catholics employed in the public sector are improving (Osborne, 1987: 274–7). It is, of course, true that the struggle in which the Catholic community, or sections of it, is involved is a *political* struggle. The removal of discrimination or the promotion of greater equality are pursued only as secondary consequences of the overall goal, the unification of Ireland.

Community action of another kind includes self-help. One form of self-help which has frequently been proposed as an avenue of escape from disadvantage for minorities is self-employment and business (Sowell, 1981). For a number of ethnic communities in the USA this has, indeed, proved to be the case (Bonacich and Modell, 1980; Light, 1972), as too for the Jewish community in Britain (Aris, 1970; Pollins, 1982). In Britain the field of 'ethnic business' has been a growing area of research activity (Waldinger et al., 1985; Ward, 1987; Ward and Jenkins, 1984). One of the clearest conclusions to be drawn from this research is that, in the present situation, business activity offers ethnic minorities in Britain only the most limited mobility opportunities, and this for only some minorities. Nor is ethnic business likely to be able to fill the role in inner-city regeneration which some politicians have claimed for it, if only because of the small numbers of entrepreneurs involved and the precarious marginality of their enterprises (Aldrich *et al.*, 1984; Auster and Aldrich, 1984). This is not, of course, to suggest that ethnic business activity is undesirable. It is simply that one should be sceptical of claims that self-employment and entre-preneurship are solutions to ethnic disadvantage in the labour market. The number of black people to whom such solutions are open is likely to be small.

In both Britain and Northern Ireland, the strongest barrier to greater equality of opportunity is neither legal, administrative, organiza-tional nor political. The deteriorating United Kingdom economic situation since the early 1970s – the recession – is probably the single most important obstacle, although it is inextricably bound up with the four factors mentioned above (O'Dowd, 1986; Rhodes and Braham, 1987). There are a number of reasons why this is so, some of which have already been discussed.

The historical pattern of labour-force participation of black people and Catholics has rendered them vulnerable to unemployment, in a situation where 'traditional' unskilled and semi-skilled manual work and manufacturing employment are in decline. Similarly, particularly in Britain, the migration of industry away from the inner city has left many ethnic minority communities marooned in terms of employment. In Northern Ireland, although some attempt has been made to use govern-ment-assisted employment policies to rectify the situation (Bradley *et al.*, 1986), the bulk of employment has always been sited in Protestant areas, and there is evidence that the differential in this respect is widening (Doherty, 1982; Hoare, 1982). The demographic profile of the two minority communities, weighted towards the younger end of the spectrum in each case, further renders them more vulnerable to youth unemployment.

At the time of increased competition for the scarce resource of employment, it is likely that, for a variety of reasons, exclusionary strategies will be employed by majority workers. Ethnic sentiment is unlikely to decrease in salience – and it must be recognized that the 'troubles' in Northern Ireland further exacerbate the situation – and greater labour-market closure may be a result. If it is the case that employers are, for a variety of 'non-ethnic' reasons, increasingly likely to turn to informal recruitment channels (and, it should be remembered, there is conflicting research evidence in this respect), processes of labour-market closure and segmentation are given further momentum. Black workers and Catholics are likely to be even more firmly shut out of employment.[6] For employers, having to manage and survive in an economically hostile environment, equal opportunity is likely to be regarded as a low priority, particularly given, in the absence of strong legal or administrative pressure, the low cost of ignoring the issue. Finally, in a labour market which has become a buyer's market, and an associated political climate which stresses market freedom and minimum regulation or state intervention with respect to capital, many employers are likely to be impatient with attempts to promote or enforce equal opportunity.

Looked at in the light of the above, the most pressing question, perhaps, is not what can be done to improve the labour-market position of minority workers? It is, rather, how can their position be prevented from deteriorating further? It is a question for which there appear to be few likely answers.

■ Conclusions

To sum up this review of ethnic disadvantage in employment in the United Kingdom there are a number of points which require emphasis. First, in looking at the situation of black workers in Britain and Catholics in Northern Ireland, it is necessary to recognize the historical importance of colonialism in creating the present state of affairs. It is precisely in the contrasts between the two cases in this respect – in the nature of the original colonial situations, subsequent economic developments, patterns of migration and the contemporary state and political contexts – that their major lines of differentiation lie. In Northern Ireland, the primary principle of social cleavage, for the purposes of our discussion, is political ethnicity; in Britain, it is a case of racism and economic exploitation.

Beyond this, however, there are many similarities: in the nature of labour-market disadvantage, processes of discrimination, the role of education, strategies for the pursuit of greater equality of opportunity and the gloomy prospects for the reduction of ethnic differentials in employment. Little has so far been done, however, with respect to systematic comparative research into ethnic disadvantage in employment in Great Britain and Northern Ireland. This chapter has done little more than scratch the surface of the problem. Therein lies a worthwhile avenue for further investigation.

Acknowledgements

Bob Cormack, Duncan Gallie, Bob Osborne and John Wrench all made useful comments on an earlier draft of this chapter. I did not always choose to incorporate their suggestions, however, and the responsibility for any imperfections is all my own.

Notes

1. Contributions to this debate other than those cited in the text include those of Hewitt (1983, 1985, 1987), Kovalchek (1987), O'Hearn (1983, 1985, 1987) and Simpson (1983: 100–7).
2. Other important studies of 'word of mouth' recruitment are by Granovetter (1974), Grierco (1987), Manwaring and Wood (1984), Manwaring (1984), Wood (1986), Rees (1966), Sheppard and Belitsky (1966) and Windolf (1986).
3. In fact, it is a little less clear than this. The Commission for Racial Equality has argued (1983: 11) that, as legally defined, direct discrimination need not be intentional. It is, however, difficult to imagine how treating someone unfavourably on racial grounds, to paraphrase section 1(i)(a) of the 1976 Race Relations Act, can be anything other than intentional.
4. The debate on positive discrimination has generated a large literature: see e.g. the contributions by Banton (1984, 1985), Cohen *et al.* (1977), Eastland and Bennett (1979), Edwards (1987), Liebman (1983), Lustgarten (1980), McCrudden (1983), McKean (1983) and Young (1987). This is only a very small selection.
5. On the continued vitality of popular racism, see the evidence provided by Cashmore (1987), Jenkins (1986: 80–115), Jowell and Airey (1984: 122–30), and Jowell *et al.* (1986: 149–50).
6. Such a conclusion could seem to imply an increasing degree of dualism in the UK labour market. Writing in the early 1970s, Bosanquet and Doeringer (1973) suggested that the dual labour-market model (Doeringer and Piore, 1971) might apply to the UK, a view that was subsequently strongly criticized by, among others, Blackburn and Mann (1979: 23). The dualist model, albeit in developed forms, has continued to be applied to the USA (Edwards, 1979; Gordon *et al.*, 1982; Piore, 1979) and Europe (Berger and Piore, 1980). Without wishing to advocate the use of the dual labour-market model as such, it may be time to reconsider whether, in fact, the situation has changed at all since Blackburn and Mann's critique, and, if so, in what ways.

References

Akinnaso, F. N. and Seabrook Ajirotutu, C. 1982. 'Performance and ethnic style in job interviews'. *Language and Social Identity*, ed. Gumperz, J. J. Cambridge University Press.

Aldrich, H., Jones, T. P. and McEvoy, D. 1984. 'Ethnic advantage and minority business development'. *Ethnic Communities in Business*, eds Ward, R. and Jenkins, R. Cambridge: Cambridge University Press.

Anwar, M. 1982. *Young People and the Job Market – A Survey*. London: Commission for Racial Equality.

Aris, S. 1970. *The Jews in Business*. London: Cape.

Ashton, D. N., Maguire, M. J. and Garland, V. 1982. 'Youth in the labour-market'. Research Paper no. 34. London: Department of Employment.

Aunger, E. A. 1983. 'Religion and class: an analysis of 1971 census data'. *Religion, Education and Employment*, eds Cormack, R. J. and Osborne, R. D. Belfast: Appletree Press.

Auster, E. and Aldrich, H. 1984. 'Small business vulnerability, ethnic enclaves and ethnic enterprise'. *Ethnic Communities in Business*, eds Ward, R. and Jenkins, R. Cambridge: Cambridge University Press.

Banton, M. 1983. *Racial and Ethnic Competition*. Cambridge: Cambridge University Press.

—— 1984. 'Transatlantic perspectives on public policy concerning racial disadvantage'. *New Community*, 11 (Spring), 325–36.

—— 1985. *Promoting Racial Harmony*. Cambridge: Cambridge University Press.

Barker, M. 1981. *The New Racism: Conservatives and the Ideology of the Tribe*. London: Junction Books.

Barritt, D. P. and Carter, C. F. 1972. *The Northern Ireland Problem: A Study in Group Relations*. London: Oxford University Press.

Barth, F. (ed.) 1969. *Ethnic Groups and Boundaries*. Bergen: Universitetsforlaget.

Becker, G. S. 1971. *The Economics of Discrimination*, second edition. Chicago: University of Chicago Press.

Berg, I. 1970. *Education and Jobs: The Great Training Robbery*. Harmondsworth: Penguin.

Berger, J. and Mohr, J. 1975. *A Seventh Man*. Harmondsworth: Pelican.

Berger, S. and Piore, M. J. 1980. *Duality and Discontinuity in Industrial Societies*. Cambridge: Cambridge University Press.

Ben-Tovim, G., Gabriel, J., Law, I. and Stredder, K. 1986. *The Local Politics of Race*. London: Macmillan.

Benyon, J. and Solomos, J. (eds) 1987. *The Roots of Urban Unrest*. Oxford: Pergamon.

Black, B., Ditch, J., Morrisey, M. and Steele, R. 1980. *Low Pay in Northern Ireland*. London: Low Pay Unit.

Blackburn, R. M. and Mann, M. 1979. *The Working Class in the Labour Market*. London: Macmillan.

Boal, F. W. and Douglas, J. N. H. (eds) 1982. *Integration and Division: Geographical Perspectives on the Northern Ireland Problem*. London: Academic Press.

Bonacich, E. and Modell, J. 1980. *The Economic Basis of Ethnic Solidarity: Small Business in the Japanese American Community*. Berkeley: University of California Press.

Bosanquet, N. and Doeringer, P. B. 1973. 'Is there a dual labour market in Great Britain?'. *Economic Journal*, 83 (June), 421–35.

Bourne, J. and Sivanandan, A. 1980. 'Cheerleaders and ombudsmen: the sociology of race relations in Britain'. *Race and Class*, 21 (Spring), 331–52.

Bowles, S. and Gintis, H. 1976. *Schooling in Capitalist America*. London: Routledge & Kegan Paul.

Bradley, J. F., Hewitt, V. N. and Jefferson, C. W. 1986. 'Industrial location policy and equality of opportunity in assisted employment in Northern Ireland 1949–1981'. Research Paper 10. Belfast: Fair Employment Agency.

Brooks, D. and Singh, K. 1979. 'Pivots and presents: Asian brokers in British foundries'. *Ethnicity at Work*, ed. Wallman, S. London: Macmillan.

Brown, C. 1984. *Black and White Britain: The Third PSI Survey*. London: Heinemann.

—— and Gay, P. 1985. *Racial Discrimination: 17 Years After the Act*. London: Policy Studies Institute.

Burstein, P. 1985. *Discrimination, Jobs and Politics: The Struggle for Equal Employment Opportunity in the United States since the New Deal*. Chicago: University of Chicago Press.

Cashmore, E. E. 1987. *The Logic of Racism*. London: Allen & Unwin.

—— and Troyna, B. (eds) 1982. *Black Youth in Crisis*. London: Allen & Unwin.

Castles, S., Booth, H. and Wallace, T. 1984. *Here for Good: Western Europe's New Ethnic Minorities*. London: Pluto.

—— and Kosack, G. 1985. *Immigrant Workers and Class Structure in Western Europe*, second edition. Oxford: Oxford University Press.

Coffield, F., Borrill, C. and Marshall, S. 1986. *Growing Up at the Margins*. Milton Keynes: Open University Press.

Cohen, M., Nagel, T. and Scanlon, T. (eds) 1977. *Equality and Preferential Treatment*. Princeton: Princeton University Press.

Cohen, R. 1978. 'Ethnicity: problem and focus in anthropology'. *Annual Review of Anthropology*, 7, 379–403.

Commission for Racial Equality, 1978. *Looking for Work: Black and White School Leavers in Lewisham*. London: CRE.

—— 1981. *BL Cars Ltd . . . Report of a Formal Investigation*. London: CRE.

—— 1982. *Massey Ferguson Perkins Ltd . . . Report of a Formal Investigation*. London: CRE.

—— 1983. *A Consultative Paper. The Race Relations Act 1976 – Time for a Change?*. London: CRE.

Compton, P. A. 1982. 'The demographic dimension of integration and division in Northern Ireland'. *Integration and Division*, eds Boal, F. W. and Douglas, J. N. H. London: Academic Press.

—— 1986. *Demographic Trends in Northern Ireland*. Report 57. Belfast: Northern Ireland Economic Council.

Cormack, R. J. and Osborne, R. D. 1983. 'The Belfast study: into work in Belfast'. *Religion, Education and Employment*, eds Cormack, R. J. and Osborne, R. D. Belfast: Appletree Press.

—— and Osborne, R. D. 1987. 'Fair shares, fair employment: Northern Ireland today'. *Studies* (Autumn), 273–85.

Cross, M. 1982a. *Transformation Through Training?* Berlin: CEDEFOP.

—— 1982b. 'The manufacture of marginality'. *Black Youth in Crisis*, eds Cashmore, E. and Troyna, B. London: Allen & Unwin.

—— 1987. ' "Equality of opportunity" and inequality of outcome: the MSC, ethnic minorities and training policy'. *Racism and Equal Opportunity Policies in the 1980s*, eds Jenkins, R. and Solomos, J. Cambridge: Cambridge University Press.

—— and Smith, D. I. (eds) 1987. *Black Youth and YTS: Opportunity or Inequality?* Leicester: National Youth Bureau.

Curran, M. M. 1985. *Stereotypes and Selection: Gender and Family in the Recruitment Process*. London: HMSO.

Daniel, W. W. 1968. *Racial Discrimination in England*. Harmondsworth: Pelican.

Darby, J. (ed.) 1983. *Northern Ireland: The Background to the Conflict*. Belfast: Appletree Press.

—— 1987. 'Religious discrimination and differentiation in Northern Ireland: the case of the Fair Employment Agency'. *Racism and Equal Opportunity Policies in the 1980s*, eds Jenkins, R. and Solomos, J. Cambridge: Cambridge University Press.

Deakin, N. 1970. *Colour, Citizenship and British Society*. London: Panther.

Department of Economic Development, 1986. *Equality of Opportunity in Employment in Northern Ireland. Future Strategy Options. A consultative Paper*. Belfast: HMSO.

Department of Employment, 1987. 'Ethnic origins and economic status'. *Employment Gazette*, 95 (January), 18–29.

Department of Finance and Personnel, 1985. *Continuous Household Survey: Religion*. PPRU Monitor no. 2/85. Belfast: Department of Finance and Personnel.

Dex, S. 1982. 'Black and white school-leavers: the first five years of work'. Research Paper no. 33. London: Department of Employment.

Doeringer, P. B. and Piore, M. J. 1971. *Internal Labor Markets and Manpower Analysis*. Lexington, Mass.: D. C. Heath.

Doherty, P. 1982. 'The geography of unemployment'. *Integration and Division*, eds Boal, F. W. and Douglas, J. N. H. London: Academic Press.

Dore, R. P. 1976. *The Diploma Disease*. London: Allen & Unwin.

Duffield, M. 1985. 'Rationalisation and the politics of segregation: Indian workers in Britain's foundry industry, 1945–62'. *Race and Labour in Twentieth Century Britain*, ed. Lunn, K. London: Frank Cass.

—— 1988. *Black Radicalism and the Politics of De-Industrialisation: The Hidden History of Indian Foundry Workers*. Aldershot: Avebury.

Dummett, A. 1973. *A Portrait of English Racism*. Harmondsworth: Pelican.

Eastland, T. and Bennett, W. J. 1979. *Counting by Race*. New York: Basic Books.

Edwards, J. 1987. *Positive Discrimination, Social Justice and Social Policy: Moral Scrutiny of a Policy Practice*. London: Tavistock.

Edwards, R. 1979. *Contested Terrain: The Transformation of the Workplace in the Twentieth Century*. New York: Basic Books.

Edye, D. 1987. *Immigrant Labour and Government Policy*. Aldershot: Gower.

Evason, E. 1985. *On the Edge: A Study of Poverty and Long-term Unemployment in Northern Ireland*. London: Child Poverty Action Group.

Fair Employment Agency, 1983a. *Report on Employment Patterns in the Londonderry Area*. Belfast: FEA.

—— 1983b. *Report of an Investigation by the Fair Employment Agency ... Into the Northern Ireland Civil Service*. Belfast: FEA.

—— 1984. *Report of an Investigation by the Fair Employment Agency ... Into the Fire Authority for Northern Ireland*. Belfast: FEA.

Fevre, R. 1984. *Cheap Labour and Racial Discrimination*. Aldershot: Gower.

Ford, J., Keil, T., Jenkins, R., Bryman, A. and Beardsworth, A. 1984. 'Internal labour market processes'. *Industrial Relations Journal*, 15 (Summer), 41–50.

—— Bryman, A., Beardsworth, A. D., Bresnen, M., Keil, E. T. and Jenkins, T. 1986. 'Changing patterns of labour recruitment'. *Personnel Review*, 15: 2, 14–18.

Fothergill, S. and Gudgin, G. 1982. *Unequal Growth: Urban and Regional Employment Change in the UK*. London: Heinemann.

Fryer, P. 1984. *Staying Power: The History of Black People in Britain*. London: Pluto.

Goldthorpe, J. H. 1980. *Social Mobility and Class Structure in Modern Britain*. Oxford: Clarendon Press.

Gordon, D. M., Edwards, R. and Reich, M. 1982. *Segmented Work, Divided Workers*. Cambridge: Cambridge University Press.

Granovetter, M. S. 1974. *Getting A Job: A Study of Contracts and Careers*. Cambridge, Mass.: Harvard University Press.

Grieco, M. 1987. 'Family networks and the closure of employment'. *The Manufacture of Disadvantage*, eds Lee, G. and Loveridge, R. Milton Keynes: Open University Press.

Griffin, C. 1985. *Typical Girls? – Young Women from School to the Job Market*. London: Routledge & Kegan Paul.

Gumperz, J. J. 1982. *Discourse Strategies*. Cambridge: Cambridge University Press.

Hepburn, A. C. 1983. 'Employment and religion in Belfast, 1901–1951'. *Religion, Education and Employment*, eds Cormack, R. J. and Osborne, R. D. Belfast: Appletree Press.

Hepple, B. A. 1983. 'Judging equal rights'. *Current Legal Problems*, 36, 71–90.

Hewitt, C. 1981. 'Catholic grievances, Catholic nationalism and violence in Northern Ireland during the civil rights period'. *British Journal of Sociology*, 32 (September), 362–80.

—— 1983. 'Discrimination in Northern Ireland: a rejoinder'. *British Journal of Sociology*, 34 (September), 446–51.

—— 1985. 'Catholic grievances and violence in Northern Ireland'. *British Journal of Sociology*, 38 (March), 102–5.

—— 1987. 'Explaining violence in Northern Ireland'. *British Journal of Sociology*, 38 (March), 88–93.

Hitner, T., Knights, D., Green, E. and Torrington, D. 1982. 'Racial minority employment: equal opportunity policy and practice'. Research Paper no. 35. London: Department of Employment.

Hoare, A. G. 1982. 'Problem region and regional problem'. *Integration and Division*, eds Boal, F. W. and Douglas, J. N. H. London: Academic Press.

House of Commons, 1981. *Fifth Report from the Home Affairs Committee. Session 1980–1981. Racial Disadvantage*, 4 vols. HC424-i to HC424-iv. London: HMSO.

Hubbuck, J. and Carter, S. 1980. *Half a Chance? A Report on Job Discrimination against Young Blacks in Nottingham*. London: Commission for Racial Equality.

Hurn, C. J. 1978. *The Limits and Possibilities of Schooling*. Boston: Allyn and Bacon.

Jeffcoate, R. 1984. *Ethnic Minorities and Education*. London: Harper & Row.

Jencks, C. 1973. *Inequality: A Reassessment of the Effect of Family and Schooling in America*. Harmondsworth: Peregrine.

Jenkins, R. 1983. *Lads, Citizens and Ordinary Kids: Working-class Youth Life-styles in Belfast*. London: Routledge & Kegan Paul.

—— 1984. 'Black workers in the labour market: the price of recession'. *New Approaches to Economic Life*, eds Roberts, B., Finnegan, R. and Gallie, D. Manchester: Manchester University Press.

—— 1986. *Racism and Recruitment: Managers, Organisations and Equal Opportunity in the Labour Market*. Cambridge: Cambridge University Press.

—— 1987. 'Equal opportunity in the private sector: the limits of voluntarism'. *Racism and Equal Opportunity Policies in the 1980s*, eds Jenkins, R. and Solomos, J. Cambridge: Cambridge University Press.

—— Bryman, A., Ford, J., Keil, E. T. and Beardsworth, A. 1983. 'Information in the labour market: the impact of recession'. *Sociology*, 17 (May), 260–7.

—— and Parker, G. 1987. 'Organisational politics and the recruitment of black workers'. *The Manufacture of Disadvantage*, eds Lee, G. and Loveridge, R. Milton Keynes: Open University Press.

—— and Solomos, J. 1987. 'Equal opportunity and the limits of the law: some themes'. *Racism and Equal Opportunity Policies in the 1980s*, eds Jenkins, R. and Solomos, J. Cambridge: Cambridge University Press.

Jewson, N. and Mason, D. 1986a. 'Modes of discrimination in the recruitment process: formalisation, fairness and efficiency'. *Sociology*, 20 (February), 43–63.

—— and Mason, D. 1986b. 'The theory and practice of equal opportunities policies: liberal and radical approaches'. *Sociological Review*, 34 (May), 307–34.

—— and Mason, D. 1987. 'Monitoring equal opportunities policies: principles and practice'. *Racism and Equal Opportunity Policies in the 1980s*, eds Jenkins, R. and Solomos, J. Cambridge: Cambridge University Press.

Joll, C., McKenna, C., McNabb, R. and Shorey, J. 1983. *Developments in Labour Market Analysis*. London: Allen & Unwin.

Jones, K. and Smith, A. D. 1970. *The Economic Impact of Commonwealth Immigration*. Cambridge: Cambridge University Press.

Jowell, R. and Airey, C. (eds) 1984. *British Social Attitudes: The 1984 Report*. Aldershot: Gower.

—— Witherspoon, S. and Brook, L. (eds) 1986. *British Social Attitudes: The 1986 Report*. Aldershot: Gower.

Karabel, J. and Halsey, A. H. (eds) 1977. *Power and Ideology in Education*. New York: Oxford University Press.

Kelley, J. and McAllister, I. 1984. 'The genesis of conflict: religion and status attainment in Ulster, 1968'. *Sociology*, 18 (May), 171–90.

Kennedy, R. E. 1973. 'Minority group status and fertility: the Irish'. *American Sociological Review*, 38 (February), 85–96.

Kovalcheck, K. A. 1987. 'Catholic grievances in Northern Ireland: appraisal and judgement'. *British Journal of Sociology*, 38 (March), 77–87.

Kreckel, R. 1980. 'Unequal opportunity structure and labour market segmentation'. *Sociology*, 14 (November), 525–50.

Lancashire Industrial Language Training Unit, 1983. *In Search of Employment and Training*. London: Commission for Racial Equality.

Lee, D. J. 1981. 'Skill, craft and class: a theoretical critique and a critical case'. *Sociology*, 15 (February), 56–78.

Lee, G. 1987. 'Training and organisational change: the target racism'. *Racism and Equal Opportunity Policies in the 1980s*, eds Jenkins, R. and Solomos, J. Cambridge: Cambridge University Press.

—— and Wrench, J. 1983. *Skill Seekers – Black Youth, Apprenticeships and Disadvantage*. Leicester: National Youth Bureau.

—— and Wrench, J. 1987. 'Race and gender dimensions of the youth labour market: from apprenticeship to YTS'. *The Manufacture of Disadvantage*, eds Lee, G. and Loveridge, R. Milton Keynes: Open University Press.

Liebman, L. 1983. 'Anti-discrimination law: groups and the modern state'. *Ethnic Pluralism and Public Policy*, eds Glazer, N. and Young, K. London: Heinemann.

Light, I. 1972. *Ethnic Enterprise in America: Business and Welfare among Chinese, Japanese and Blacks*. Berkeley: University of California Press.

Lustgarten, L. 1980. *Legal Control of Racial Discrimination*. London: Macmillan.

—— 1987. 'Racial inequality and the limits of law'. *Racism and Equal Opportunity Policies in the 1980s*, eds Jenkins, R. and Solomos, J. Cambridge: Cambridge University Press.

McCrudden, C. 1981. 'Legal remedies for discrimination in employment'. *Current Legal Problems*, 34, 211–33.

—— 1982a. 'Institutional discrimination'. *Oxford Journal of Legal Studies*, 2 (Winter), 303–67.

—— 1982b. 'Law enforcement by regulatory agency: the case of employment discrimination in Northern Ireland'. *Modern Law Review*, 45: 6, 617–36.

—— 1983. 'Anti-discrimination goals and the legal process'. *Ethnic Pluralism and Public Policy*, eds Glazer, N. and Young, K. London: Heinemann.

McKean, W. 1983. *Equality and Discrimination under International Law*. Oxford: Clarendon Press.

Maguire, M. 1986. 'Recruitment as a means of control'. *The Changing Experience of Employment*, eds Purcell, K., Wood, S., Waton, A. and Allen, S. London: Macmillan.

Manwaring, T. 1984. 'The extended internal labour market'. *Cambridge Journal of Economics*, 8 (June), 161–87.

—— and Wood, S. 1984. 'Recruitment and the recession'. *International Journal of Social Economics*, 11: 7, 49–63.

Massey, D. and Meegan, R. 1982. *The Anatomy of Job Loss*. London: Methuen.

Mayhew, L. 1968. *Law and Equal Opportunity*. Cambridge, Mass.: Harvard University Press.

Miller, R. 1978. 'Attitudes to work in Northern Ireland'. Research Paper 2. Belfast: Fair Employment Agency.

—— 1983. 'Religion and occupational mobility'. *Religion, Education and Employment*, eds Cormack, R. J. and Osborne, R. D. Belfast: Appletree Press.

—— 1986. 'Social stratification and mobility'. *Ireland: A Sociological Profile*, eds Clancy, P., Drudy, S., Lynch, K. and O'Dowd, L. Dublin: Institute of Public Administration.

—— and Osborne, R. D. 1983. 'Religion and unemployment: evidence from a cohort survey'. *Religion, Education and Employment*, eds Cormack, R. J. and Osborne, R. D. Belfast: Appletree Press.

Moore, R. 1972. 'Race relations in the six counties: colonialism, industrialisation and stratification in Ireland'. *Race*, 14 (July), 21–42.

Murray, R. and Darby, J. 1983. 'The Londonderry and Strabane study: out and down in Derry and Strabane'. *Religion, Education and Employment*, eds Cormack, R. J. and Osborne, R. D. Belfast: Appletree Press.

Nelson, S. 1975. 'Protestant "ideology" reconsidered: the case of "discrimination"'. *British Political Sociology Yearbook*, 2, 155–87.

O'Donnell, E. E. 1977. *Northern Irish Stereotypes*. Dublin: College of Industrial Relations.

O'Dowd, L. 1986. 'Beyond industrial society'. *Ireland: A Sociological Profile*, eds Clancy, P., Drudy, S., Lynch, K. and O'Dowd, L. Dublin: Institute of Public Administration.

O'Hearn, D. 1983. 'Catholic grievances, Catholic nationalism: a comment'. *British Journal of Sociology*, 34 (September), 438–45.

—— 1985. 'Again on discrimination in the North of Ireland: a reply to the rejoinder'. *British Journal of Sociology*, 36 (March), 94–101.

—— 1987. 'Catholic grievances: comments'. *British Journal of Sociology*, 38 (March), 94–100.

Ollerearnshaw, S. 1983. 'The promotion of employment equality in Britain'. *Ethnic Pluralism and Public Policy*, eds Glazer, N. and Young, K. London: Heinemann.

Osborne, R. D. 1982. 'Fair employment in Cookstown? A note on anti-discrimination policy in Northern Ireland'. *Journal of Social Policy*, 11 (October), 519–30.

—— 1985. 'Religion and educational qualifications in Northern Ireland'. Research Paper 8. Belfast: Fair Employment Agency.

—— 1987. 'Religion and employment'. *Province, City and People: Belfast and its Region*, eds Buchanan, R. H. and Walker, B. M. Antrim: Greystone Books/British Association for the Advancement of Science.

—— and Murray, R. C. 1978. 'Educational qualifications and religious affiliation in Northern Ireland'. Research Paper 3. Belfast: Fair Employment Agency.

—— and Cormack, R. J. 1986. 'Unemployment and religion in Northern Ireland'. *Economic and Social Review*, 17 (April), 215–225.

—— and Cormack, R. J. 1987. 'Religion, occupations and employment, 1971–1981'. Research Paper 11. Belfast: Fair Employment Agency.

—— Cormack, R. J., Reid, N. G. and Williamson, A. P. 1983. 'Political arithmetic, higher education and religion in Northern Ireland'. *Religion, Education and Employment*, eds Cormack, R. J. and Osborne, R. D. Belfast: Appletree Press.

Oxenham, J. (ed.) 1984. *Education Versus Qualifications?* London: Allen & Unwin.

Paine, S. 1974. *Exporting Workers: The Turkish Case*. Cambridge: Cambridge University Press.

Parekh, B. 1983. 'Educational opportunity in multi-ethnic Britain'. *Ethnic Pluralism and Public Policy*, eds Glazer, N. and Young, K. London: Heinemann.

Peach, C. 1968. *West Indian Migration to Britain*. London: Oxford University Press.

Phizacklea, A. and Miles, R. 1980. *Labour and Racism*. London: Routledge & Kegan Paul.

—— and Miles, R. 1987. 'The British trade union movement and racism'. *The Manufacture of Disadvantage*, eds Lee, G. and Loveridge, R. Milton Keynes: Open University Press.

Piore, M. J. 1979. *Birds of Passage: Migrant Labour and Industrial Societies*. Cambridge: Cambridge University Press.

Pollert, A. 1985. *Unequal Opportunities: Racial Discrimination and the Youth Training Scheme*. Birmingham: Trade Union Resource Centre.

Pollins, H. 1982. *Economic History of the Jews in England*. Toronto: Associated University Press.

Ramdin, R. 1986. *The Making of the Black Working Class in Britain*. Aldershot: Gower.

Rampton, A. 1981. *West Indian Children in our Schools*. Cmnd. 8273. London: HMSO.

Ratcliffe, P. 1980. *Race Relations at Work: An Investigation into the Extent and Sources of Inequality in the Treatment of Ethnic and Racial Minorities*. Leamington Spa: Warwick District Community Relations Council.

Rees, A. 1966. 'Information networks in labour markets'. *American Economic Review*, 56 (May), 559–66.

Rex, J. 1973. *Race, Colonialism and the City*. London: Routledge & Kegan Paul.

—— 1981. 'Urban segregation and inner city policy in Great Britain'. *Ethnic Segregation in Cities*, eds Peach, C., Robinson, V. and Smith, S. London: Croom Helm.

—— 1986. *Race and Ethnicity*. Milton Keynes: Open University Press.

Rhodes, E. and Braham, P. 1987. 'Equal opportunity in the context of high levels of unemployment'. *Racism and Equal Opportunity Policies in the 1980s*, eds Jenkins, R. and Solomos, J. Cambridge: Cambridge University Press.

Roberts, K., Duggan, J. and Noble, N. 1981. 'Unregistered youth unemployment and outreach careers work. Final report, part one: nonregistration'. Research Report no. 31. London: Department of Employment.

Rolston, B. 1980. 'The limits of trade unionism'. *Northern Ireland Between Civil Rights and Civil War*, eds O'Dowd, L., Rolston, B. and Tomlinson, M. London: CSE Books.

—— 1983. 'Reformism and sectarianism: the state of the union after civil rights'. *Northern Ireland: The Background to the Conflict*, ed. Darby, J. Belfast: Appletree Press.

Sanders, P. 1983. 'Anti-discrimination law enforcement in Great Britain'. *Ethnic Pluralism and Public Policy*, eds Glazer, N. and Young, K. London: Heinemann.

Sewell, W. and Hauser, R. 1975. *Education, Occupation and Earnings*. New York: Academic Press.

Sheppard, H. L. and Belitsky, A. H. 1966. *The Job Hunt*. Baltimore: Johns Hopkins University Press.

Siebert, W. S. 1985. 'Developments in the economics of human capital'. *Labour Economics*, eds Carline, D., Pissarides, C. A., Siebert, W. S. and Sloane, P. J. London: Longman.

Sillitoe, K. and Meltzer, H. 1986. *The West Indian School-Leaver*. London: HMSO.

Silverman, D. and Jones, J. 1976. *Organisational Work: The Language of Grading/ The Grading of Language*. London: Collier-Macmillan.

Simpson, J. 1983. 'Economic development: cause or effect in the Northern Ireland conflict'. *Northern Ireland: The Background to the Conflict*, ed. Darby, J. Belfast: Appletree Press.

Sloane, P. J. 1985. 'Discrimination in the labour market'. *Labour Economics*, eds Carline, D., Pissarides, C. A., Siebert, W. S. and Sloane, P. J. London: Longman.

Smith, D. J. 1974. *Racial Disadvantage in Employment*. London: Political and Economic Planning.

—— 1977. *Racial Disadvantage in Britain*. Harmondsworth: Pelican.

—— 1981. *Unemployment and Racial Minorities*. London: Policy Studies Institute.

—— and Chambers, G. 1987. *Equality and Inequality in Northern Ireland*. London: Policy Studies Institute.

Solomos, J. 1985. 'Problems but whose problems: the social construction of black youth unemployment and state policies'. *Journal of Social Policy*, 14 (October), 527–54.

—— 1986. 'Political language and violent protest: ideological and policy responses to the 1981 and 1985 riots'. *Youth and Policy*, 18 (Autumn), 12–24.

—— 1987. 'The politics of anti-discrimination legislation: planned social reform or symbolic politics?'. *Racism and Equal Opportunity Policies in the 1980s*, eds Jenkins, R. and Solomos, J. Cambridge: Cambridge University Press.

Sowell, T. 1981. *Markets and Minorities*. Oxford: Basil Blackwell.

Standing Advisory Commission on Human Rights, 1987. *Religious and Political Discrimination in Northern Ireland: Report on Fair Employment*. Cmnd 237. Belfast: HMSO.

Stone, J. 1985. *Racial Conflict in Contemporary Society*. London: Fontana.

Stone, M. 1981. *The Education of the Black Child in Britain*. London: Fontana.

Swann, 1985. *Education for All*. Cmnd. 9453. London: HMSO.

Torrington, D., Hitner, T. and Knights, D. 1982. *Management and the Multi-Racial Work Force*. Aldershot: Gower.

Troyna, B. and Smith, D. I. (eds) 1983. *Racism, School and the Labour Market*. Leicester: National Youth Bureau.

Visram, R. 1985. *Ayahs, Lascars and Princes: The Story of Indians in Britain 1700– 1947*. London: Pluto.

Waldinger, R., Ward, R. and Aldrich, H. 1985. 'Ethnic business and occupational mobility in advanced societies'. *Sociology*, 19 (November), 586–97.

Wallman, S. (ed.) 1979. *Ethnicity at Work*. London: Macmillan.

Walvin, J. 1984. *Passage to Britain*. Harmondsworth: Pelican.

Ward, R. 1987. 'Resistance, accommodation and advantage: strategic development in ethnic business'. *The Manufacture of Disadvantage*, eds Lee, G. and Loveridge, R. Milton Keynes: Open University Press.

—— and Jenkins, R. (eds) 1984. *Ethnic Communities in Business: Strategies for Economic Survival*. Cambridge: Cambridge University Press.

Watson, J. L. 1977. 'Introduction: immigration, ethnicity, and class in Britain'. *Between Two Cultures*, ed. Watson, J. L. Oxford: Basil Blackwell.

Weber, M. 1978. *Economy and Society*. Berkeley: University of California Press.

Whyte, J. 1983. 'How much discrimination was there under the Unionist regime, 1921–68?' *Contemporary Irish Studies*, eds Connell, J. and Gallagher, T. Manchester: Manchester University Press.

Willis, P. 1977. *Learning to Labour*. Farnborough: Saxon House.

Windolf, P. 1986. 'Recruitment, selection and internal labour markets in Britain and Germany'. *Organization Studies*, 7: 3, 235–54.

Wood, S. 1986. 'Recruitment systems and the recession'. *British Journal of Industrial Relations*, 24 (March), 103–20.

Wrench, J. 1987. 'Unequal comrades: trade unions, equal opportunity and racism'. *Racism and Equal Opportunity Policies in the 1980s*, eds Jenkins, R. and Solomos, J. Cambridge: Cambridge University Press.

Young, K. 1987. 'The space between words: local authorities and the concept of equal opportunities'. *Racism and Equal Opportunity Policies in the 1980s*, eds Jenkins, R. and Solomos, J. Cambridge: Cambridge University Press.

—— and Connelly, N. 1981. *Policy and Practice in the Multi-Racial City*. London: Policy Studies Institute.

Chapter 9

The Assessment: Education, Training and Economic Performance

E. Keep and K. Mayhew

■ Introduction

In Britain, during the last decade, debate about every aspect of the education and training system has become particularly intense. Its inadequacies are thought to be a major contributor to a poor international trading performance and to an inability to cope successfully with economic change. Suggested cures abound, but diagnosis of the ailment is confused. [...] This assessment first describes the historical background, and goes on to consider the links between vocational education and training (VET) and economic performance. It then attempts a diagnosis of Britain's failings, briefly evaluates the current stance of Government, and ends with some policy implications.

■ The historical dimension

Contemporary debate about the failings of British vocational education and training is usually conducted with reference to the demands imposed by rapid change, increasing competition in world markets, and burgeoning

Source: © Oxford University Press and OREP 1988. Reprinted from the *Oxford Review of Economic Policy* vol. 4, no. 3 (1988) by permission of Oxford University Press.

new technologies. This has sometimes obscured the historical picture. In fact, public concern about Britain's VET performance, relative to that of other countries, goes back well over a century.

As early as 1852, Lyon Playfair, in a lecture on 'Industrial Instruction on the Continent', was warning that improvements in technical education were urgently required if Britain's manufacturers were to maintain their lead over foreign competitors. In the years that followed, two royal commissions and various departmental inquiries delved into the inadequacies of the country's education and training provision. No one who reads these early investigations can escape a strong sense of *déjà vu*, for they identified a number of features which have persistently echoed through subsequent discussion. For example, as Sanderson (1988, p. 39) indicated, British failings in the realm of science education were a major Victorian preoccupation, and one that remains highly topical. Thus the Devonshire Commission (1872–75), investigating scientific and technological education within the universities, concluded that the output of graduate scientists and engineers was inadequate, that 'the Present State of Scientific Instruction in our Schools is Extremely Unsatisfactory', and that this situation was likely to have serious consequences for 'the Material Interests of the Country' (Devonshire Report, 1875, p. 10).

Perhaps the most important of these nineteenth-century investigations was the Royal Commission on Technical Instruction (the Samuelson Commission), which operated between 1882 and 1884. Its remit drew an explicit link between economic performance and the operation of the education system, and the Commission's extensive programme of research attempted a systematic comparison between Britain and its major overseas competitors (Perry, 1976, p. 30). The Commission concluded that the other industrialized nations were adapting better to technological and structural change, and that in Britain, part of the problem lay in the relatively low importance afforded education and training by the state. The Commission also drew attention to the fact that while much of Britain's industrial training was of a high quality, the volume being undertaken was insufficient. The Samuelson Commission was followed, in 1886, by the Royal Commission on the Depression in Trade and Industry. Its final report ascribed the severe depression to eight principal causes (Perry, 1976, p. 32), of which one was the general inferiority of the technical instruction received by the British workforce.

In the early twentieth century concern about technical and scientific education resurfaced, and with it came growing doubts about the effectiveness of the training being provided by British employers compared with that offered by overseas competitors (Sheldrake and Vickerstaff, 1987, pp. 6–7). These worries focused on the fact that, left to their own devices, some employers tended to provide little training and were free-riding on the efforts of those who did, thereby producing an under-supply of qualified manpower at the aggregate level. Simultaneously, concern was being expressed about the problems caused by the heritage of the British craft apprenticeship system, with which, for most UK manufacturers, training had been almost entirely equated. Its distinctive features included limits on the age at which apprentices could be recruited and exclusivity in terms of the narrow range of skills being imparted. The duration of apprenticeships was also fixed, no matter at what pace the trainee acquired the required skills and knowledge, and there were usually no tests of competence; it was enough that the trainee had 'served his time'.

The origin of these features, which were not to be found in most apprenticeship arrangements overseas, can be traced to the attitudes of both the craft unions and the employers. It had been the latter who, in the first half of the nineteenth century, had helped to introduce inflexible models of handicraft trade apprenticeships into new industries and who then continued to accept them, not merely out of conservatism, but also because lack of standardization in British product markets made the replacement of the craft system with mass-production techniques unattractive (More, 1980, p. 157). Craft unions, for their part, developed their hold over apprenticeships as a means of controlling the supply of skilled labour and therefore skilled wage rates.

The First World War presented both problems and opportunities for education and training. The demands imposed by mass conscription and war production forced the state to abandon its reliance on voluntarism and to intervene in the provision of industrial training on a massive scale. In 1918, however, the Government returned to the pre-war status quo and once more left employers to their own devices, its training efforts being concentrated on providing opportunities for disabled ex-servicemen. With the sharp downturn in the economy in the inter-war years, the focus of training policy shifted towards 'the creation of schemes calculated to mitigate the worst effects of mass unemployment' (Sheldrake and Vickerstaff, 1987, pp. 10–11). These included the use of Government Training Centres to offer the unemployed instruction in a skilled trade, programmes to train unemployed women for domestic service, and the development of Junior Instructional Centres to help ease the problems of youth joblessness.

The drive for rearmament in the late 1930s reduced the problems of unemployment, and the onset of war meant that the Ministry of Labour once more found itself in a position to exercise leadership over the provision of training. This it did, as in the First World War, through an array of special programmes, though the responsibility for the majority of training continued to rest with employers. What is important to note is that, partly as the price for trade union support for special temporary measures, there was no attempt at any radical reform of the apprenticeship system (Sheldrake and Vickerstaff, 1987, pp. 24–5). As after the First War, the end of hostilities led to a rapid dismantlement of state supervision of training.

In the years after the Second War some employers and commentators were beginning seriously to question the entrenched traditions of the craft apprenticeship system, but reform required the solution of complex industrial relations problems which neither the majority of employers nor unions were keen to tackle. At the same time, full employment removed from the agenda the issue of training to meet unemployment.

It was only in the late 1950s and early 1960s that long-standing concerns about the volume of training being undertaken by British employers came to a head. The onset of a major bulge in the number of school leavers entering the labour market during these years triggered worries about the provision of adequate training opportunities for young people (Lindley, 1983, p. 343). Initially, the Goverment set its face against legislation to enforce a statutory duty to train upon employers, its preferred solution being for voluntary action on the part of individual companies to improve their provision. Official disenchantment rapidly set in as industry failed to respond in any very concrete fashion to government exhortations, and this disillusionment with the fruits of the voluntarist tradition ultimately found expression in the passage of the 1964 Industrial Training Act (Perry, 1976).

The Act led to the establishment of Industrial Training Boards (ITBs) with the statutory authority to operate a levy/grant system on employers. Under this system a levy or payroll tax was imposed on all employers within an industry and grants were then disbursed to those companies which attained acceptable volumes and levels of training. By 1972, 27 ITBs had been established, covering about 12 million workers and raising total levies of £203 million in the year 1970–71. In 1973, following criticism from some small employers (Sheldrake and Vickerstaff, 1987, pp. 37–8) and a number of economists (see Lees and Chiplin, 1970), the Employment and Training Act altered the levy/grant system, so that ITBs were now empowered to give exemptions from levy arrangements to those employers who were deemed to be training to satisfactory levels. In the wake of the 1973 reform, the Government, the Confederation of British Industry (CBI) and the Trades Union Congress (TUC) eventually agreed upon the need for some form of national training agency to coordinate and oversee training activity and to act as a central clearing house for manpower forecasting and information. The result was the creation of the tripartite Manpower Services Commission (MSC). In the years that followed, the MSC acted as the conduit through which an increasing volume of state funding was directed in an attempt to stem various skill shortages and tackle the growing problem of unemployment.

In summary, the history of vocational education and training in Britain is one of recurring cycles of concern, usually prompted by worries about British competitiveness. In education, fears about the low levels of educational attainment among the general workforce, and concern about technical and scientific competence, reappeared with monotonous regularity. In the area of training, the failure of the voluntary efforts of employers, allied with Britain's worsening economic performance, meant that the role of the state in training provision increased from the mid-1960s onwards. Although there are obviously strong threads running through the years of debate, the emphasis has varied over time. For example, present concern appears to be directed more closely towards the need for a commitment to the creation of a system of continuing education and training for adult workers, than has been the case in the past. This historical context may be of more than background interest. The fact that many of the problems which current policies aim to tackle have periodically been identified during the last hundred years and yet remain unresolved, suggests that the causes which underlie Britain's poor record in VET are deep-seated.

■ VET and economic performance

As Finegold and Soskice (1988), and White (1988) demonstrate, contemporary complaints have been directed at virtually every major part of our VET system. These include the quality and non-vocational direction of our schools, the small numbers of pupils staying on in full-time education after the age of 16, the content and direction of our university courses, the amount and standards of youth training, the absence of continued training for those at work, and the lack of adult retraining provision. Recurrent skill shortages have provided clear reminders that something is wrong. Yet it is disturbing that, despite the long-standing conviction that inadequacies in VET have hampered the UK's economic performance, evidence on the *precise* linkages is somewhat scanty.

Work at the National Institute has gone further than most in this respect. For example, using matched samples of British and West German manufacturing plants in furniture and metalworking, the National Institute researchers found that a number of technological and organizational differences explained superior German productivity and their higher quality products. Though manufacturers in the two countries had 'access to the same machinery' on world markets, the German workforce was more qualified. 'It was with the help of a thoroughly qualified workforce that advanced machinery and advanced production methods were introduced, put into smooth operation and fully exploited' (Steedman and Wagner, 1987).

Studies of this detailed micro variety are rare. Other researchers have attempted to correlate the success of individual firms with their training policies. The IFF, for example, conducted two surveys for the MSC which tried to do this with respect to adult training (IFF Research

Ltd., 1985, 1986). In their small firms survey, for instance, the indicators of 'success' included: whether the number of employees and output had increased over the previous five years, whether new products or services had been introduced, whether there was a significant increase in the need for high-tech skills, and whether the firm was profitable. By such criteria firms were classified as high-, medium- or low-performers. The IFF claimed to find a strong correlation between a firm's classification and its propensity to train. This type of approach is of dubious use. Even if one could be certain that the direction of causation ran from training to success rather than in the opposite direction, the surveys have nothing to say about the precise mechanisms involved.

Despite the paucity of hard, detailed evidence of direct causal links, much of present VET policy in the UK is founded on the presumption that these links exist. Such a presumption is reasonable, but insufficient account may have been taken of the many other factors that intervene in the relationship between investment in education and training and the resultant return in the form of increased performance. Comparative research undertaken by a group of French social scientists based at the University of Aix-en-Provence (Maurice, Sorge and Warner, 1980; Maurice, Sellier and Silvestre, 1986) suggests that distinctive national structures of educational provision, methods of work organization, and the style and institutional arrangements of industrial relations combine to influence the ways in which skills are defined and provided for, and that the conjunctions of these factors vary dramatically from one country to another. The research approach adopted by the Aix group, whereby investigation focuses on the influence of national societal and cultural factors on the operation of economic institutions (Rose, 1985), is one that holds promise in helping to add direction to the present debate about the design of a national VET system that will best fit British circumstances. It suggests that training provision is part of a complex of factors. Because of this, careless empirical research might either overlook, or in contrast, over-emphasize, lack of training as against other explanations of poor economic performance. For example, inferior product quality and design are often mentioned as important components of the UK's lack of non-price competitiveness. Such failings could be part of the low-quality/low-skill equilibrium stressed by Finegold and Soskice (1988), of which poor training is but a part. But to break into the explanatory circle by picking out just one variable for consideration will yield misleading results. For the same reason, to construct a policy which attends to just one variable is likely to be ineffective. None of the above is meant to suggest that the search for linkages should not be pursued, but rather is a plea for a sophisticated multivariate analysis or, in terms of learning from other countries, for a comparative systems approach. Better training may not be a sufficient condition for economic success, but it is certainly a necessary one.

■ VET and economic analysis

Although the empirical linkages have not been thoroughly explored, economists have had a great deal to say, in a theoretic and prescriptive sense, about specific aspects of our VET system. Other academic disciplines as well as practical interest groups have had an influence, but the views of economists have been particularly influential with policy makers. For example, Lees and Chiplin (1970) put forward a market-based argument which had a major influence on the reform of the ITB's in 1973. Economic thinking can be divided into a number of strands. One school of thought stresses the virtues of the market. The market gives, so it is argued, an accurate indication of demand, provides better and more effective incentives, and gives a more rapid response both to changes in demand and to other changes than would a non-market system. The Great Education Reform Bill (GERBIL) provides an example of this type of emphasis (see White, 1988). Other economists, by contrast, emphasize market failure – the inability of the market to deliver socially optimal results. Without slavery, it is asserted, the individual firm will probably provide too little training. The private returns are likely to be less than the social simply because the firm cannot totally bind an employee to itself. Related to this is the danger that some firms may decide to free-ride on the training investments of other employers. Similarly, if training is left to the individual, a socially suboptimal amount will be provided – partly because of poor information and partly because of inadequate capital markets. Important in this tradition is the distinction between specific and general skills. The former are usable only in the firm in which they are acquired; the latter are more generally applicable. The distinction is relevant for the question of who bears the cost of training. Jones (1988) considers the issue of whether the right pay signals are produced by the labour market – specifically whether skill differentials are sufficiently large to induce individuals to undergo training and whether the earnings of younger workers are so relatively high as to deter employers from investing in their training. This school of thought stresses the need for government intervention to correct such market failures. Intervention might be in the form of direct provision, but could also be indirect – for example, tax incentives for training, or a loan system for higher education funding. The aim of most economists would be to reconcile the two approaches by capturing the virtues of the market whilst taking steps to deal with its failures. The disagreement comes in judgement about just how extensive market failure is, and in how best to cope with it. There is more general agreement about the role of manpower planning. This no longer enjoys the vogue it once had, largely because people have come to realize the massive difficulties of forecasting demand for particular occupations.

A third strand of economic thought is to be found in the rates of return literature. Stemming from the work of Becker (1975) and others on human capital analysis, an early obsession was with the calculation of the return to investment in education. Though this obsession continued, added to it was subsequent analysis of the precise mechanism by which education influenced earnings. In particular this revolved around whether education augmented human capital and thereby productivity and earnings, or whether education acted as a screening device, whereby, for example, those who were already more productive got to university and survived there. This fact is what influences employers to hire them rather than the fact that university *per se* has increased their productivity. Worse than screening is credentialism, where university provides a passport into good jobs, without even accurately signalling higher productivity. Perlman (1988) uses distinctions such as these in his discussion of American education. The same distinctions have also informed much of the debate about the extent, type, and funding of tertiary education in Britain. There are those, for instance, who believe that university education involves a large element of screening as opposed to human capital augmentation. Because of this, they contend that the social returns are significantly less than the private returns, and are thus predisposed to question the extent of public investment.

The insights into Britain's VET problem offered by conventional economic analysis, while undoubtedly useful in illuminating certain aspects of the subject, can be too unidimensional to offer an overall understanding of this complex area. This is partly a matter of measurement. For example, as far as the business or the individual is concerned, it may be that the true returns to training are hard to calculate. The extra ability of a worker to help his company meet unknown challenges in a changing world may be easily overlooked by the corporate planner, just as the individual worker may under-value the indirect future returns to extra training in the form of enhanced promotion prospects and the like. But, more important than such lacunae in the conventional literature, is that the concept of market failure employed is often too narrow. Whilst we may identify and correct one such failure, this may make little contribution towards improving our provision of VET. In particular, as we have seen from our earlier discussion of the Aix approach, both the demand and supply sides are affected by a whole network of institutional factors. [...]

■ Why is Britain's VET performance so poor?

A good starting-point is Britain's distinctive heritage of craft apprenticeships. As has been emphasized above, the craft system was virtually synonymous with training, and its effects in structuring managerial attitudes towards the value of training have therefore been considerable.

Unfortunately, the traditional craft system offered a model in which employers gained relatively little from their investment. The skills that individual craft workers could utilize were closely circumscribed by job demarcations in the workplace. Moreover, the ethos of the apprenticeship was in many respects as much about offering an indoctrination in the ideology of the craft and its union, as it was about the acquisition of skills.

Job demarcations imposed by the craft tradition also had implications for employers' attitudes towards the training of other sections of the workforce, in that there was often very limited scope to promote semi- and unskilled workers into areas that had been defined as skilled work. The promotion of non-craft workers to supervisory and managerial positions was also problematic because of the unwillingness of craft workers to operate under the charge of those who had not completed an apprenticeship in the same trade. These barriers to the mobility of labour within the firm effectively reduced the incentive for employers to offer non-craft workers training above and beyond what was needed to perform the immediate task (MSC, 1977, p. 11).

To the ingrained problems caused by the craft tradition should be added the wider legacy of the British system of industrial relations, which has not encouraged a strong emphasis on the value of training. It has been a system in which the best that managers could generally hope for was that their subordinates would act as the passive recipients of instructions passed down through a hierarchical and authoritarian management structure. The traditional aim of British industrial relations, put simply, was to extract compliance from the workforce, rather than attempting to seek their active commitment to shared goals. This mode of operation has been in marked contrast to the industrial relations systems of many overseas competitors, such as West Germany and Sweden, where the concepts of management/worker co-determination and social partnership have proved important, particularly with respect to the provision of vocational training (Maclure 1985; Swedish Ministry of Labour, 1988).

The result has been that British managers, compared with those in many other countries, have only latterly begun to recognize the motivational benefits of training as part of a more people-centred business strategy (Brown and Read, 1984; National Economic Development Office/ MSC, 1984, pp. 87–8). Moreover, the notion that the non-managerial workforce represented a reservoir of skills, knowledge, and ideas that could be harnessed to improve business performance has been alien to most British managements. With the exception of a handful of companies, such as IBM and Marks and Spencer, it is only in recent years, and mostly among large firms, that the spread of the concept of human resource management (HRM) has alerted managers in this country to the need to acknowledge the workforce's potentially crucial contribution to business performance.

Another aspect of the UK's industrial relations heritage has been that in the absence of structured systems of co-determination, craft-imposed job demarcations have meant that training has not traditionally figured as an important issue in collective bargaining, except for craft unions. Pressure for improved training opportunities from the workforce at large have therefore been muted. There are at least signs that this is beginning to change. The TUC has indicated that it wishes its members to make training a major bargaining point, and some trade unions have already begun to take action, for example the Electrical, Electronic, Telecommunication, and Plumbing Union (EETPU) who have established their own training schools and the newly created Manufacturing Science Finance Union (MSF) who have pioneered the negotiation of training agreements with employers (MSF, 1988).

A second factor that constrains the UK's VET performance is the small size of the UK's post-compulsory education system relative to those possessed by nearly every other developed nation. The numbers remaining in full-time education after the age of 16 are lower in the UK than in the USA, Japan, or most European countries, and the proportion of the relevant age group in Britain going on to higher education is also much lower. As one Japanese manager suggested, in a subsequently much quoted letter to a group of visiting American managers:

> '... the intelligence of a handful of technocrats, however brilliant ... is no longer enough. Only by drawing on the brainpower of all its employees can a firm face up to the turbulence and constraints of today's environment; this is why our large companies ... demand from the education system increasing numbers of graduates as well as bright and well-educated generalists.' (NEDO/MSC, 1984, p. 51).

The problem, for Britain, is that reliance on the talents of a well-educated few has been one of the underlying premises upon which both the public and private systems of education have been based. This has been reflected [...] by an educational ethos dominated by the demands of higher education, as expressed through the public examination system, and geared, through early specialization, towards producing a small, academic élite. The results have been that practical, technical, and vocational skills have tended to be undervalued, and the needs of the relative few going on to higher education have often been met at the expense of those of average or below-average academic ability (Young, 1984, p. 453).

The costs imposed by having retained until very recently an education model that eschewed mass post-compulsory education are considerable. One of the most important is the lack of a crucial mass of more highly qualified people among the working population. As Finegold and Soskice (1988) argue, this means that there is an inadequate foundation of broad-based skills and qualifications among the population upon which training programmes can build. Jones (1988) also notes how the future of the Youth Training Scheme (YTS) might be prejudiced by the lack of suitably educated entrants. Secondly, low levels of education among the workforce at large and the relatively limited supply of scientists, engineers, and technologists that results from a small higher education sector renders innovation and technological change more difficult to introduce and sustain. Thirdly, the fact that the majority of young people do not carry on in education after 16 means that 'young people in the UK are not as accustomed to, nor as well prepared for, the continuing education and training which must be an increasingly important feature of modern economics' (Holland, 1985, p. 15). Moreover, the lack of a large body of people holding higher level qualifications has implications for the success of subsequent efforts to expand the education system, in that teacher shortages, especially in science and technology, are already becoming a major problem and one that will worsen as competition from other employers of graduates increases in the 1990s. [. . .]

One further consequence of this rapidly-tapering pyramid of educational attainment is to be found within the management population. Comparative research indicates that one of the most distinctive features of British companies is the low level of education and training with which their managerial workforce are equipped (Swords-Isherwood, 1980; Mangham and Silvers, 1986; Handy, 1985; Constable and McCormick, 1987). For example, a comparison of top managers indicates that whereas only 24 per cent of senior British managers possess a degree, the figure for the American managers is 85 per cent, for West Germany 62 per cent, France 65 per cent, and Japan 85 per cent (Handy, p. 2). A further exacerbating factor is a lack of management training and development, with more than half of all UK companies apparently making no formal provision for the training of their managers (Mangham and Silvers, p. 1).

Given the paucity of training opportunities available to many managers, it may be that they do not perceive a lack of training among other employees as a particularly acute problem (Crockett and Elias, 1984, p. 42). As Finegold and Soskice (1988) emphasize, many British managers believe that the tasks undertaken by their subordinates require only minimal skills and hence little in the way of training. This attitude stands in marked contrast to that adopted by their West German managerial counterparts, who see a three-year period of structured training as an essential foundation for the vast majority of their workers (Steedman and Wagner, 1986, pp. 91–2; Pointing, 1986). Furthermore, in the light of Britain's legacy of hierarchical, non-participatory management, it is open to question how far managers, who are themselves relatively poorly educated and trained, will welcome the challenge presented by the prospect of a better educated and trained workforce.

A third institutional source of obstruction to improvement in the UK's training performance stems from the relationship between finance and industrial capital. Despite recent attempts by the CBI to vindicate the

City's attitude towards the financing of industry, the current balance of evidence suggests that this country's failure to evolve the type of stable, long-term relationship that exists in Japan and West Germany between companies, stockholders and banks, has made it more difficult for UK management to adopt a long-term view of the relationship between investment and profit (Dore, 1985). To this can be added the pressures generated by the stockmarket's concentration on short-term performance and the threat of hostile takeover bids. The result has been to make it more difficult for industry to invest, at the expense of short-term profit, in areas, such as training, and research and development, which by their very nature do not produce quick returns (Dore, 1985; Walker, 1985; Fifield, 1987).

External financial pressures to maximize short-term profit are in turn re-enforced by internal developments in the organizational structures of many large British companies. To those elements mentioned by Finegold and Soskice (1988), two others can be added – the growth of diversified or conglomerate companies, and the associated rise of internal cost-control systems. Companies that have followed a strategy of growth through takeover, with subsequent divestment of units that no longer match the approved product mix, or that are not achieving adequate short-term returns, are unlikely to sustain a relationship with their subsidiaries that favours a long-term investment in training. The increasing use of profit and cost-control systems as a means of managing large, diversified companies causes similar problems (Allen, 1985; Kaplan, 1985; Benjamin and Benson, 1986; Fox, 1988).

The final institutional element to be discussed here is Britain's inability to evolve and maintain a coherent national VET system. [...] Despite the multiplicity of VET initiatives taken in the UK over the last decade, we are still lacking such a system. In this respect, the absence of statutory backing for training appears to be particularly important. Our current rejection of a legislative framework within which the rights and duties of those involved in vocational training are spelt out, stands in marked contrast to the situation in many European countries. [...]

It should be apparent that these [institutional] factors may tend to form a matrix of mutually reinforcing pressures. Thus the perceived benefits gained by management who invest in the training of their workforce have been limited by a distinctive industrial relations system, and by management's own lack of training. Financial pressures and cost-control systems make investment in training problematic. At the same time an inadequate educational foundation among the broad mass of the working population renders training more difficult, and more likely to be remedial in character, as well as hindering any attempt to expand the provision of VET. These factors operate against a backcloth of systems for delivering VET that are incoherent and subject to constant change. When the economists' notions of market failure and the problems posed by free-riders are added to this picture, it becomes apparent that there exists a tightly woven nexus of forces within British society that have acted to impede progress in VET. It is this 'interlocking network of societal institutions', as Finegold and Soskice (1988) term it, that poses such considerable difficulties for analysis and policy formulation in this area.

■ Present policy

Having discussed the often deep-seated causes of Britain's VET problem, we now turn to examine the policies that have, in recent years, been advanced as offering a solution. It would be no overstatement to suggest that VET in Britain has undergone a revolution in the last decade. Its importance in terms of national political priorities has risen dramatically. The main political parties, the NEDO, the CBI and the TUC are all agreed that major improvements in the structure and performance of Britain's VET system are a vital prerequisite for economic success.

As we have seen, concern about Britain's failings in the area of vocational education and training is nothing new. Why then should the issue of VET have acquired renewed priority in the last decade? The answer is two-fold. First, the great emphasis given to supply-side policies generally. Second, the rapid growth of unemployment, particularly youth unemployment.

The starting-point of this current round of the debate has normally been identified as James Callaghan's Ruskin College speech in 1976, though arguably its real genesis came somewhat earlier, in the late 1960s and early 1970s, with the 'black papers' on education and the associated controversy about the comprehensivization of secondary state schooling and allegation of a general fall in academic standards (Beck, 1983, pp. 221–3; St. John-Brooks, 1985, p. 12).

As White (1988) demonstrates, the Government has been engaged in a reconstruction of educational provision which is probably the most far-reaching since the 1944 Educational Act. White gives a detailed appraisal of the myriad developments that have occurred in the last few years, the main thrust of which has been a series of measures aimed at promoting greater central influence and control over a traditionally semi-autonomous system of educational institutions and authorities. Allied to this have been attempts to foster an increasing emphasis upon vocational and pre-vocational training.

At secondary school level, one of the most important developments has been the introduction, by the MSC, of the Technical and Vocational Education Initiative (TVEI). This has the dual objective of introducing a technically and vocationally-oriented curriculum, and of increasing the number of pupils staying on in full-time education after compulsory schooling-leaving age.

The Department of Education and Science (DES) has introduced in parallel a number of its own initiatives, such as the Certificate of Pre-Vocational Education (CPVE), which have the aim of increasing the importance of pre-vocational elements within the secondary school system. More controversial has been the decision to establish a number of City Technology Colleges (CTCs), which are to be privately sponsored by industrial and commercial organizations. In addition, the influence of employers within the education system is being increased by measures to boost their representation on the governing bodies of educational institutions at all levels. Other measures have included the establishment of a National Council for Vocational Qualifications (NCVQ), which is charged with the task of rationalizing and simplifying the current profusion of vocational courses and qualifications. Within higher education there has been the promotion of a limited 'switch' in resources and student places away from the humanities towards science and technological subjects. Finally, a number of initiatives are under way, sponsored by the MSC and the Department of Trade and Industry, that aim to help create an ethos within the education system that fosters an entrepreneurial spirit and supports an enterprise culture.

The changes affect not only examinations and curriculum content and style, but also the ways in which the educational workforce is managed and deployed, and the manner in which education itself is governed and delivered. Taken together, these changes mark a radical break with tradition, and have taken place against an overall background of expenditure constraint.

At the same time as these reforms have been taking place in the education system, equally dramatic changes have occurred within vocational training. Finegold and Soskice (1988) offer a detailed assessment of these changes, and only a few of the more important developments will be touched upon here.

A major strand running through the history of training since 1964 had been a gradual increase in the degree to which the state assumed responsibility. The election of the Conservative Government in 1979 signalled a reversal of this policy, for, in 1981 the existing structure of Industrial Training Boards (ITBs), with statutory powers to impose a training levy on all employers, was swept away by the Government, to be replaced by voluntary Non-Statutory Training Organizations (NSTOs). The aim of this fundamental shift in policy was to give expression to the Government's basic contention that responsibility for training primarily rests with individual firms, and that the free play of market forces is the most efficient means of regulating the volume and quality of training provision.

More or less simultaneous with this change in the structure of training provision came a major MSC-sponsored exercise in strategic planning, under the title of the New Training Initiative (NTI) (MSC,

1981). After extensive consultations among employers, trade unions, educationalists, and training providers, the NTI established a national agenda for reform on three broad fronts: the reform of the apprenticeship system, improved vocational training provision for the young employed and unemployed, and the widening of training opportunities for adults. Much of the subsequent activity in the field of British training policy has been directed at attempting to meet these three objectives.

In the case of craft apprenticeships, reform had long been mooted, but, by the time the MSC finally spurred employers and trade unions into action in the early 1980s, the craft training system was already in a state of virtual collapse, from which it has yet to recover to any appreciable extent. Some indication of the scale of this decline can be gauged from the fact that whereas there were 240 000 apprentices in British manufacturing industry in 1964, by 1979 this had fallen to 155 000, and by 1986 it had dropped to only 63 700 (*New Society*, 8 August 1986). Against this background of precipitate decline, reform of those apprenticeship schemes that have survived has proceeded fairly successfully, if more slowly than originally envisaged, with employers and trade unions negotiating an end to restrictions on the age of entry to apprenticeships and to the fixed duration of apprenticeships, and agreeing the introduction of competence testing.

In the area of vocational training for the young, the Government and MSC's efforts have been concentrated on the YTS. Originally introduced as a one-year traineeship which included elements of planned work experience combined with a minimum of 13 weeks off the job or a period in further education, the duration of the traineeships was extended to two years with effect from September 1986. The MSC believed that YTS, besides bringing British provision of vocational training more into line with overseas practice, would also have a major role to play in acting as a catalyst to promote changes in companies' attitudes towards the general value of training for all sections of their employees (MSC, 1983, p. 15).

In adult training the main focus of government efforts and funding has been directed at schemes, such as the Community Programme, to aid the long-term unemployed. These various schemes are now being replaced by a single unified Job Training Scheme. Training for the adult employed is identified by the Government as the joint responsibility of the employer and the individual worker. Government and MSC efforts have therefore largely been limited to exhortation, pump-priming grants for training innovation, support for training in certain narrow areas where skill shortages are critical, and the provision of start-up funding for 'open' or 'distance' learning ventures, such as the Open Tech and Open College. At present education ministers are placing pressure on the Treasury to introduce tax incentives for employees who finance their own training or retraining (*Transition*, June 1988).

The latest structural change in the training system came with the

Government's decision to transfer the MSC's responsibility for Jobcentres and various other services to the unemployed back to the Department of Employment, to increase employer representation on the MSC, and to alter its name to the Training Commission, in line with its new, more specialized role. Officials have suggested that the Commission's future priorities will lie in improving communication between industry and education, and in promoting the need for increased levels of adult training.

■ Policy implications

[...] One of the most important problems facing attempts to evaluate current British efforts in the field of VET is the lack of reliable, up-to-date information, particularly in the area of vocational training. Since the abolition of the ITBs in 1981, the collection of training statistics has lapsed in many parts of industry. As a result it is impossible to state with any degree of certainty how much training is currently taking place within a particular sector. This absence of accurate data is one of the distinctive features of British VET, and stands in contrast to the 'transparency' of many overseas VET systems wherein the flow of detailed information on VET outputs and costs are seen as important to the overall success of the system (NEDO/MSC, 1984). The provision of adequate information is arguably an important prerequisite for any sensible planning and policy making, and an area where progress urgently needs to be made. In this respect, it is hoped that the results of a recent large-scale study, sponsored by the Training Commission, of the training costs of British employers will be published this autumn. These should provide the first detailed recent overview of employers' provision of training in the UK.

A second development that would help to clarify British policy making, would be greater efforts to 'demythologize' foreign VET systems via more detailed comparative research of the type conducted by the Aix group. The basis of current British VET policy is a belief that our overseas competitors have somehow developed more effective systems, and from this belief have stemmed attempts at change and reform. [...]

Besides a need to acquire a better overall understanding of other national VET systems, there are specific institutional arrangements that might profitably be examined. Within Europe, the training systems of France and West Germany have frequently been cited as potentially useful models. Our understanding of several salient features of their approaches still requires development. In Germany the important role played by the chambers of commerce, to which all employers by law must belong, in supporting the 'dual system' of apprenticeships deserves greater attention

(Willat, 1982; Lawler, 1985). Within the French VET system there are at least two areas of direct potential interest to British policy makers (Occhslin, 1987). First, there is the role of employers' associations in the collective provision of training, via a network of regional, multi-industry, and occupational training associations. Second, there is the issue of statutory backing to training in the form of employee rights to paid educational leave and the operation of a national remissible training tax. [...]

The provision of adequate information on the current British training effort, and a more comprehensive understanding of how overseas VET systems operate, are important elements in arriving at more effective long-term policy prescriptions. A third factor is the need for a more coherent style of policy formulation. To date, attempts to create a national VET system have been characterized by a series of fragmented and narrowly focused incremental changes, with little or no attempt being made to view the education and training system as a single entity, or to undertake a complete restructuring from first principles (Kushner, 1985, p. 9). The results of this *ad hoc* style of reform has been the promotion of a jumble of uncoordinated, overlapping schemes sponsored by rival bodies. Rather than a single, over-arching focus for policy making, there are instead a multitude of competing agencies and government departments – the Training Commission, the NEDO, the DTI, the DES and, holding the purse strings, the Treasury.

The confusion and incoherence that has resulted from this situation is detailed by both White (1988) and Finegold and Soskice (1988). It arises not only within the individual fields of education and training, but also at the point where government is attempting to coordinate the two. The contrast between centralist trends and strengthened state control of education, and the Government's reliance in training on the enlightened self-interest of individual firms, is one that is not easily reconciled within the context of an overall objective of establishing a unified VET system (Keep, 1987).

In the light of [this] discussion [...] of the interlocking of forces that have underlain Britain's weak performance in VET, it would seem apparent that policies aimed at reform need to be based on an adequate analysis of these causal inter-relationships. Only then would it be possible to formulate the institutional restructuring required to create a set of countervailing incentives and penalties that would encourage and sustain a greater quantity and quality of VET activity. Moreover, the complexity of this nexus of forces, and their tendency together to create a vicious rather than a virtuous circle, renders a piecemeal, *ad hoc* approach to reform unlikely to prove successful. As a result, there is a requirement to formulate some form of coherent strategic overview of VET policy, both in terms of the nature of the national VET system that is being sought, and also in terms of the measures necessary to realize this overall objective.

Evidence from overseas VET systems indicates a need to secure a reasonable degree of national consensus for these strategic goals from all those who will be involved in their delivery. In Britain there is presently broad agreement that VET is a problem, but little in the way of consensus about objectives or solutions. Without some clear national framework of rights and duties, agreed between all parties concerned with VET – government, employers, trade unions, educationalists, and the population at large – progress will at best be difficult.

The discussion of current British VET policy [...] implicitly raises the question of the importance the government actually attaches to achieving a sustained improvement in Britain's VET performance. It is possible to argue that high levels of activity have helped to disguise a certain lack of clarity as to the final objective. The precise degree to which the government sees an upgrading in the education and training of the nation's workforce as being vital to the overall success of British economy is uncertain. Examination of VET systems in Japan, France and Sweden indicates that in these countries education and training operate in the context of a wider system of economic planning and social partnership, notions which have never fully taken root in Britain [...]. Certainly education, training and skills are not part of the Treasury's economic model, except insofar as skill shortages tend to underlie symptoms of 'overheating' in the economy.

What is clear is that appropriate VET policies require a high degree of coordination in decision making, if optimal results are to be obtained. Otherwise, the multitude of mutually reinforcing factors that underlie our relative failure in this area will continue to create forces that limit the incentives available to the individual decision takers. Such coordination involves many layers – within companies and within sectors, as well as between them. Government has a key role to play in encouraging and ensuring coordination, as well as in achieving consistency in those areas for which it has direct responsibility. There is an uneasy tension between the need to achieve this and the desire to obtain, wherever possible, the benefits of the market. The solution, as with many aspects of modern economics, lies in the careful marriage of analysis with knowledge of detail and of institutions. It is this that makes VET provision a particularly difficult element of supply-side policy. That it is important for the health of our economy is evident. It is also important for the sort of society in which we live. If, for example, our schools produce young people who, at the low achievement end, are unable to benefit significantly from subsequent training, as both Jones (1988) and White (1988) suggest, then not only does this have implications for the quality of our labour force, it also has considerable distributional consequences, since such people are con-demned to the lower margins of economic activity for the rest of their lives. In a world which has to encounter frequent change, and where particular skills acquired in one's youth subsequently become redundant, a society which recognizes and values the merits of continued education and training will cope – in social as well as economic terms – far more successfully than otherwise.

The need to improve the quality and flexibility of our labour force gives a critical role to VET policy. It is often easy to see what is wrong. The challenge is to find something better.

Acknowledgement

The authors would like to thank Chris Allsopp and Tim Jenkinson for helpful comments.

References

Allen, D. (1985), 'Strategic management accounting', *Management Accounting*, March, 25–27.

Beck, J. (1983), 'Accountability, industry and education', in J. Ahier and M. Flude (eds), *Contemporary Education Policy*, London, Croom Helm.

Becker, G. S. (1975), *Human Capital*, 2nd edition, New York, Columbia University Press.

Benjamin, A. and Benson, N. (1986), 'Why ignore the value of people?', *Accountancy*, February, 81–4.

Bevan, S. and Hutt, R. (1985), *Company Perspectives on the Youth Training Scheme*, Institute of Manpower Studies, Sussex University, report no. 104.

Brown, G. F. and Read, A. R. (1984), 'Personnel and training policies – some lessons for Western companies', *Long Range Planning*, 17 (2), 48–57.

Constable, J. and McCormick, R. (1987), *The Making of British Managers*, London, British Institute of Management.

Crockett, G. and Elias, P. (1984), 'British managers: a study of their education, training, mobility and earnings', *British Journal of Industrial Relations*, 22, 34–46.

Daly, A., Hitchens, D. M. W. N. and Wagner, K. (1985), 'Productivity, machinery and skills in a sample of British and German manufacturing plants', *National Institute Economic Review*, February, 48–65.

Devonshire Report (1875), *Report of the Royal Commission on Scientific Instruction and the Advancement of Science 1872–5, Sixth Report*, London, HMSO.

Dore, R. P. (1985), 'Financial structures and the long-term view', *Policy Studies*, 6 (part I), 10–29.

Fifield, D. M. (1987), 'The implications and expectations of ownership', *Business Graduate Journal*, 17, 44–50.

Finegold, D. and Soskice, D. (1988), 'The failure of training in Britain: analysis and prescription', *Oxford Review of Economic Policy*, 4 (3), 21–53.

Fox, J. (1988), 'Norsk Hydro's new approach takes root', *Personnel Management*, January, 37–41.

Handy, C. (1985), *The Making of Managers: A Report on Management Education, Training and Development in the United States, West Germany, France, Japan and the UK*, London, National Economic Development Office.

Holland, G. (1985), 'An MSC perspective', in A. G. Watts (ed.), *Education and Training 14–18: Policy and Practice*, Cambridge, Careers Research and Advisory Centre.

IFF Research Ltd. (1985), *Adult Training in Britain*, Sheffield, MSC.

IFF Research Ltd. (1986), *Small Firms Survey*, Sheffield, MSC.

Jones, I. (1988), 'An evaluation of YTS', *Oxford Review of Economic Policy*, 4 (3), 54–71.

Kaplan, R. S. (1985), 'Yesterday's accounting undermines production'. *The McKinsey Quarterly*, Summer, 31–42.

Keep, E. (1987), *Britain's Attempts to Create a National Vocational and Training System: A Review of Progress*, Warwick Papers in Industrial Relations, no. 16, Industrial Relations Research Unit, University of Warwick.

Kushner, S. (1985), 'Vocational "chic": an historical and curriculum context to the field of transition in England', in R. Fiddy (ed.), *Youth Unemployment and Training: A Collection of National Perspectives*, Brighton, Falmer Press.

Lawler, G. (1985), 'Land of youth opportunity', *Times Higher Education Supplement*, 14 January.

Lees, D. and Chiplin, B. (1970), 'The economics of industrial training', *Lloyds Bank Review*, 94, 29–41.

Lindley, R. (1983), 'Active manpower policy', in G. S. Bain (ed.), *Industrial Relations in Britain*, Oxford, Basil Blackwell.

Maclure, S. (1985), 'An industrial education lesson for UK?', *Times Educational Supplement*, 1 February.

Mangham, I. L. and Silvers, M. S. (1986), *Management Training – Context and Practice*, Claverdon, School of Management, University of Bath.

Manpower Services Commission (1977), *Training for Skills: A Programme for Action*, London, MSC.

—— (1981), *A New Training Initiative – A Consultative Document*, London, MSC.

—— (1983), *MSC Corporate Plan 1983/87*, Sheffield, MSC.

Manufacturing Science Finance Union (1988), *Training for a Future: Can Britain Compete?*, London, MSF.

Maurice, M. A., Sorge, A., and Warner, M. (1980), 'Societal differences in organizing manufacturing units: a comparison of France, West Germany and Britain'. *Organisation Studies*, 1, 59–86.

Maurice, M., Sellier, F., and Silvestre, J-J. (1986), *The Social Foundations of Industrial Power*, London, The MIT Press.

More, C. (1980), *Skills and the English Working Class, 1870–1914*, London, Croom Helm.

National Economic Development Office/Manpower Services Commission (1984), *Competence and Competition*, London, NEDO.

Occhslin, J. J. (1987), 'Training and the business world: the French experience', *International Labour Review*, 126, 653–67.

Perlman, R. (1988). 'Education and training: an American perspective', *Oxford Review of Economic Policy*, 4 (3), 82–93.

Perry, P. J. C. (1976), *The Evolution of British Manpower Policy*, London, British Association of Commercial and Industrial Education.

Pointing, D. (1986), 'Retail training in West Germany', *MSC Youth Training News*, April, 2–3.

Roberts, K. *et al.* (1986), 'Firms' uses of the Youth Training Scheme', *Policy Studies*, 6 (part 3), 37–53.

Rose, M. (1985), 'Universalism, culturalism and the Aix group: promise and problems of a societal approach to economic institutions', *European Sociological Review*, 1, 65–83.

Sako, M. and Dore, R. (1986), 'How the Youth Training Scheme helps employers', *Department of Employment Gazette*, June, 195–204.

Sanderson, M. (1988), 'Education and economic decline, 1880–1980s', *Oxford Review of Economic Policy*, 4 (1), 38–50.

Sheldrake, J. and Vickerstaff, S. (1987), *The History of Industrial Training in Britain*, Aldershot, Gower Publishing Co.

Steedman, H. and Wagner, K. (1987), 'A second look at productivity, machinery and skills in Britain and Germany', *National Institute Economic Review*, November, 84–95.

St. John-Brooks, C. (1985), *Who Controls Training? – The Rise of the MSC*, Fabian Tract 506.

Swedish Ministry of Labour (1988), *Swedish Labour Market Policy*, London, Campaign for Work.

Swords-Isherwood, N. (1980), 'British management compared', in K. Pavitt (ed.), *Technical Innovation and British Economic Performance*, London, Macmillan, 88–99.

Walker, D. A. (1985), 'Capital markets and industry', *Bank of England Quarterly Bulletin*, December, 570–5.

White, A. (1988), 'Education policy and economic goals', *Oxford Review of Economic Policy*, 4 (3), 1–20.

Willatt, N. (1982), 'Germany's industrious apprentices', *Management Today*, March, 62–5.

Young, D. (1984), 'Coping with change: the New Training Initiative', *Royal Society of the Arts Journal*, 132 (5335), 449–59.

Chapter 10

The Failure of Training in Britain: Analysis and Prescription

D. Finegold and D. Soskice

■ Introduction

In the last decade, education and training (ET) reform has become a major issue in many of the world's industrial powers. One theme which runs throughout these reform initiatives is the need to adapt ET systems to the changing economic environment. These changes include: the increasing integration of world markets, the shift in mass manufacturing towards newly developed nations and the rapid development of new technologies, most notably information technologies. Education and training are seen to play a crucial role in restoring or maintaining international competitiveness, both on the macro-level by easing the transition of the workforce into new industries, and at the micro-level, where firms producing high quality, specialized goods and services require a well-qualified workforce capable of rapid adjustment in the work process and continual product innovation [. . .].

This paper will highlight the need for policy-makers and academics to take account of the two-way nature of the relationship between ET and the economy. We will argue that Britain's failure to educate and train its workforce to the same levels as its international competitors has been both a product and a cause of the nation's poor relative economic performance: a product, because the ET system evolved to meet the needs of the world's

Source: © Oxford University Press and OREP 1988. Reprinted from the *Oxford Review of Economic Policy* vol. 4, no. 3 (1988) by permission of Oxford University Press.

first industrialized economy, whose large, mass-production manufacturing sector required only a small number of skilled workers and university graduates; and a cause, because the absence of a well-educated and trained workforce has made it difficult for industry to respond to new economic conditions.

The best way to visualize this argument is to see Britain as trapped in a low-skills equilibrium, in which the majority of enterprises staffed by poorly trained managers and workers produce low-quality goods and services.[1] The term 'equilibrium' is used to connote a self-reinforcing network of societal and state institutions which interact to stifle the demand for improvements in skill levels. This set of political–economic institutions will be shown to include: the organization of industry, firms and the work process, the industrial relations system, financial markets, the state and political structure, as well as the operation of the ET system. A change in any one of these factors without corresponding shifts in the other institutional variables may result in only small long-term shifts in the equilibrium position. For example, a company which decides to recruit better-educated workers and then invest more funds in training them will not realize the full potential of that investment if it does not make parallel changes in style and quality of management, work design, promotion structures and the way it implements new technologies.[2] The same logic applies on a national scale to a state which invests in improving its ET system, while ignoring the surrounding industrial structure.

The argument is organized as follows: the second section uses international statistical comparisons to show that Britain's ET system turns out less-qualified individuals than its major competitors and that this relative ET failure has contributed to Britain's poor economic record. The third section explores the historical reasons for Britain's ET problem and analyses the institutional constraints which have prevented the state from reforming ET. The fourth section argues that the economic crisis of the 1970s and early-1980s and the centralization of ET power undertaken by the Thatcher Administration have increased the possibility of restructuring ET, but that the Conservative Government's ET reforms (both the major changes already implemented and the Bill which has just passed through Parliament) will not significantly improve Britain's relative ET and economic performance. The fifth section proposes an alternative set of ET and related policies which could help Britain to break out of the low-skill equilibrium.

■ International comparisons

☐ Britain's failure to train

Comparative education and training statistics are even less reliable than cross-national studies in economics; there are few generally agreed statistical categories, wide variations in the quality of ET provision and qualifications and a notable lack of data on training within companies. Despite these caveats, there is a consensus in the growing body of comparative ET research that Britain provides significantly poorer ET for its workforce than its major international competitors. Our focus will be on differences in ET provision for the majority of the population, concentrating in particular on the normal ET routes for skilled and semi-skilled workers. This need not be technical courses, but may – as in Japan or the US – constitute a long course of general education followed by company-based training.

The baseline comparison for ET effectiveness begins with how students in different countries perform during compulsory schooling. Prais and Wagner (1983) compared mathematics test results of West German and English secondary schools and found that the level of attainment of the lower half of German pupils was higher than the average level of attainment in England, while Lynn (1988, p. 6) reviewed thirteen-year-olds' scores on international mathematics achievement tests from the early 1980s and found that 'approximately 79 per cent of Japanese children obtained a higher score than the average English child'. The results are equally disturbing in the sciences, where English fourteen year-olds scored lower than their peers in all seventeen countries in a recent study (Postlethwaite, 1988).

This education shortfall is compounded by the fact that England is the only one of the world's major industrial nations in which a majority of students leave full-time education or training at the age of sixteen. The contrast is particularly striking with the US, Canada, Sweden and Japan, where more than 85 per cent of sixteen-year-olds remain in full-time education. In Germany, Austria and Switzerland, similar proportions are either in full-time education or in highly structured three or four-year apprenticeships. Britain has done little to improve its relative position. It was, for example, the only member of the OECD to experience a decline in the participation rate of the sixteen-to-nineteen age group in the latter half of the 1970s (OECD, 1985, p. 17). Although staying-on rates have improved in the 1980s – due to falling rolls and falling job prospects – Britain's relative position in the OECD rankings has not.

The combination of poor performance during the compulsory schooling years and a high percentage of students leaving school at sixteen has meant that the average English worker enters employment with a relatively low level of qualifications.

Workers' lack of initial qualifications is not compensated for by increased employer-based training; on the contrary, British firms offer a lower quality and quantity of training than their counterparts on the Continent. A joint MSC/NEDO study (National Economic Development Office, 1984, p. 90) found that employers in Germany were spending approximately three times more on training than their British rivals, while

Steedman's analysis (1986) of comparable construction firms in France and Britain revealed that French workers' training was more extensive and less firm-specific. Overall, British firms have been estimated to be devoting 0.15 per cent of turnover to training compared with 1–2 per cent in Japan, France and West Germany (Anderson, 1987, p. 69). And, as we will show in the fourth section, neither individuals nor the Government have compensated for employers' lack of investment in adult training.

☐   **Why train? The link between ET and economic performance**

Britain's relative failure to educate and train its workforce has contributed to its poor economic growth record in the postwar period. While it is difficult to demonstrate this relationship empirically, given the numerous other factors which affect labour productivity, no one is likely to dispute the claim that ET provision can improve economic performance in extreme cases, e.g. a certified engineer will be more productive working with a complex piece of industrial machinery than an unskilled employee. Our concern, however, is whether marginal differences in the quality and quantity of ET are related to performance. We will divide the evidence on this relationship in two parts: first, that the short-term expansion of British industry has been hindered by the failure of the ET system to produce sufficient quantities of skilled labour; and second, that the ability of the British economy and individual firms to adapt to the longer-term shifts in international competition has been impeded by the dearth of qualified manpower.

A survey of the literature reveals that skill shortages in key sectors such as engineering and information technology have been a recurring problem for UK industry, even during times of high unemployment. The Donovan Commission (1968, p. 92) maintained that 'lack of skilled labour has constantly applied a brake to our economic expansion since the war'; a decade later, a NEDO study (1978, p. 2) found that 68 per cent of mechanical engineering companies reported that output was restricted by an absence of qualified workers. The problem remains acute, as the Manpower Services Commission's first *Skills Monitoring Report* (May 1986, p. 1) stated: 'Shortages of professional engineers have continued to grow and there are indications that such shortages will remain for some time, particularly of engineers with electronics and other IT skills.'

The shortages are not confined to manufacturing. Public sector professions, i.e. teaching, nursing and social work, which rely heavily on recruiting from the limited group of young people with at least five O-levels, are facing a skilled (wo)manpower crisis as the number of school-leavers declines by 25 per cent between 1985 and 1995. In the case of maths and science teachers, the shortages tend to be self-perpetuating, as the absence of qualified specialists makes it harder to attract the next generation of students into these fields (Gow, 1988a; Keep, 1987, p. 12).

The main argument of this paper, however, is that the evidence of skill shortages both understates and oversimplifies the consequences Britain's ET failure has on its economic performance. Skill shortages reflect the unsatisfied demand for trained individuals within the limits of existing industrial organization, but they say nothing about the negative effect poor ET may have on how efficiently enterprises organize work or their ability to restructure. Indeed, there is a growing recognition among industry leaders and the major accounting firms that their traditional method of calculating firms' costs, particularly labour costs, fails to quantify the less tangible benefits of training, such as better product quality and increased customer satisfaction (*Business Week*, 6 June 1988, p. 49).

There are, however, a number of recent studies which show the strong positive correlation between industry productivity and skill levels. Daly (1984, pp. 41–2) compared several US and UK manufacturing industries and found that a shift of 1 per cent of the labour force from the unskilled to the skilled category raised productivity by about 2 per cent, concluding that British firms suffered because 'they lacked a large intermediate group with either educational or vocational qualifications'. The specific ways in which training can harm firm performance were spelled out in a comparison of West German and British manufacturing plants (Worswick, 1985, p. 91):

> 'Because of their relative deficiency in shop-floor skills, equivalent British plants had to carry more overhead labour in the form of quality controllers, production planners ... the comparative shortage of maintenance skills in British plants might be associated with longer equipment downtime and hence lower capital productivity.'

Likewise, employee productivity levels in the French construction industry were found to be one-third higher than in Britain and the main explanation was the greater breadth and quality of French training provision (Steedman, 1986).

While these studies have all centred on relatively comparable companies producing similar goods and services, a high level of ET is also a crucial element in enabling firms to reorganize the work process in pursuit of new product markets, what Reich has called 'flexible-system' production strategies (1983, pp. 135–6). 'Flexible-system' companies are geared to respond rapidly to change, with non-hierarchical management structures, few job demarcations and an emphasis on teamwork and maintaining product quality. They can be located in new industries, i.e. biotechnology, fibre optics, or market niches within old industries, such as speciality steels and custom machine tools.

A number of recent studies have highlighted the role of training in 'flexible-system' production: in Japanese firms, Shirai found that employees in 'small, relatively independent work groups ... grasped the total production process, thus making them more adaptable when jobs have to be redesigned'. Streeck (1985) took the analysis one step further in his study of the European car industry, arguing that the high-quality training pro-grammes of German automakers have acted as a driving force behind product innovation, as firms have developed more sophisticated models to better utilize the talents of their employees. Even in relatively low-tech industries, such as kitchen manufacturing, German companies are, accord-ing to Steedman and Wagner (1987), able to offer their customers more customized, better-quality units than their British competitors because of the greater flexibility of their production process – a flexibility that is contingent on workers with a broad skill base.

■ Why has Britain failed to train?

Economists' normal diagnosis of the undersupply of training is that it is a public good or free ride problem: firms do not invest in sufficient training because it is cheaper for them to hire already-skilled workers than to train their own and risk them being poached by other companies. While the public good explanation may account for the general tendency to underinvest in training, it does not explain the significant variations between countries' levels of training nor does it address the key public policy question: given the market's inability to provide enough skilled workers, why hasn't the British Government taken corrective action? To answer this question we will look first at why political parties were long reluctant to intervene in the ET field, and then, at the two major obstacles which policy-makers faced when they did push for ET change: a state apparatus ill-equipped for centrally-led reform and a complex web of institutional constraints which kept Britain in a low-skills equilibrium.

□ Political parties

Through most of the postwar period, the use of ET to improve economic performance failed to emerge on the political agenda, as a consensus formed among the two major parties on the merits of gradually expanding educational provision and leaving training to industry. Underlying this consensus was an economy producing full employment and sustained growth, which covered any deficiencies in the ET system. The broad consensus, however, masked significant differences in the reasons for the parties' positions. For Labour, vocational and technical education was seen as incompatible with the drive for comprehensive schooling, while the party's heavy dependence on trade unions for financial and electoral support prevented any attempts to infringe on unions' control over training within industry (Hall, 1986, p. 85). In the case of the Conservatives, preserving the grammar school track was the main educational priority, while intervening in the training sphere would have violated their belief in the free market (Wiener, 1981, p. 110). An exception to the principle of non-intervention came during the war, when the Coalition Government responded to the manpower crisis by erecting makeshift centres that trained more than 500 000 people. When the war ended, however, these training centres were dismantled.

☐   The state structure

One of the main factors which hindered politicians from taking a more active ET role was the weakness of the central bureaucracy in both the education and training fields. On the training side, it was not until the creation of the MSC in 1973 (discussed in the fourth section) that the state developed the capacity for implementing an active labour market policy. The staff of the primary economic policy-making body, the Treasury, 'had virtually no familiarity with, or direct concern for, the progress of British industry' (Hall, 1986, p. 62) and none of the other departments (Environment, Trade and Industry, Employment, or Education and Science) assumed clear responsibility for overseeing training. There was, for example, a dearth of accurate labour market statistics, which made projections of future skill requirements a virtual impossibility (Reid, 1980, p. 30). Even if the state had come up with the bureaucratic capability to develop a coherent training policy, it lacked the capacity to implement it. Wilensky and Turner (1987, pp. 62–3) compared the state structure and corporatist bargaining arrangements of eight major industrialized nations and ranked the UK last in its ability to execute manpower policy.

While responsibility over education policy in the central state was more clearly defined, resting with the Department of Education and Science (DES), the historical decentralization of power within the educational world made it impossible for the DES to exercise effective control (Howell, 1980; OECD, 1975). Those groups responsible for delivering education, the local authorities (Jennings, 1977) and teachers (Dale, 1983a), were able to block reforms they opposed, such as vocationalism. The lack of central control was particularly apparent in the further education sector, an area accorded low priority by the DES until the 1970s (Salter and Tapper, 1981).

The main obstacle to ET reform, however, was not the weakness of the central state, which could be remedied given the right external circumstances and sufficient political will, but the interlocking network of societal institutions which will be explored in the following sections, beginning with the structure, or lack of it, for technical and vocational education and entry-level training.

☐ The ET system

Technical and work-related subjects have long suffered from a second-class status in relation to academic courses in the British education system (Wiener, 1981). The Norwood Report of 1943 recommended a tripartite system of secondary education, with technical schools to channel the second quarter of the ability range into skilled jobs; but while the grammar schools and secondary moderns flourished, the technical track never accommodated more than 4 per cent of the student population. In the mid-1960s two programmes, the Schools Council's 'Project Technology' and the Association for Science Education's 'Applied Science and the Schools', attempted to build an 'alternative road' of engineering and practical courses to rival pure sciences in the secondary curriculum (McCulloch *et al.*, 1985, pp. 139–55). These pilot experiments were short-lived, owing to:

1. Conflicts between and within the relevant interest groups,
2. Minimal coordination of the initiatives,
3. The absence of clearly defined objectives and strategies for implementing them (ibid., pp. 209–12).

The efforts to boost technical education were marginal to the main educational transformations of the postwar period: the gradual shift from division at eleven-plus to comprehensives and the raising of the school-leaving age to fifteen, and eventually to sixteen in 1972. The education establishment, however, was slow to come up with a relevant curriculum for the more than 85 per cent of each age cohort who were now staying longer in school, but could not qualify for a place in higher education. Success for the new comprehensives continued to be defined by students' performance in academic examinations (O- and A-levels), which were designed for only the top 20 per cent of the ability range (Fenwick, 1976) and allowed many students to drop subjects such as mathematics and science at the age of fourteen. The academic/university bias of the secondary system was reinforced by the powerful influence of the public schools which, while catering for less than 6 per cent of students, produced 73 per cent of the directors of industrial corporations (Giddens, 1979), as well as a majority of Oxbridge graduates, MPs and top education officials; thus, a large percentage of those charged with formulating ET policy, both for government and firms, had no personal experience of state education, much less of technical or vocational courses.

The responsibility for vocational education and training (VET) fell by default to the further education (FE) sector. The 1944 Education Act attempted to provide a statutory basis for this provision, declaring that county colleges should be set up in each LEA to offer compulsory day-release schemes for fifteen-to-eighteen year-olds in employment. The money was never provided to build these colleges, however, with the result that 'a jungle' of different FE institutions, courses and qualifications developed. There were three main paths through this 'jungle': the academic sixth form, the technical courses certified by independent bodies, such as City and Guilds, BTEC or the RSA, and 'the new sixth form' or 'young stayers on', who remain in full-time education without committing to an A-level or specific training course (MacFarlane Report, 1980). A host of factors curtailed the numbers pursuing the intermediate route: the relatively few careers requiring these qualifications, the lack of maintenance support for FE students and the high status of the academic sixth, which was reinforced by the almost total exclusion of technical students from higher education.

The majority of individuals left education for jobs which offered no formal training. Those who did receive training were almost exclusively in apprenticeships. The shortcomings of many of these old-style training programmes, which trained 240 000 school-leavers in 1964, were well known: age and gender barriers to entry, qualifications based on time served (up to seven years) rather than a national standard of proficiency and no guarantee of off-the-job training (Page, 1967). The equation of apprenticeships with training also had the effect of stifling training for positions below skilled level and for older employees whose skills had become redundant or needed updating.

In the early 1960s the combination of declining industrial competitiveness, a dramatic expansion in the number of school-leavers and growing evidence of skill shortages and 'poaching' prompted the Government to attempt to reform apprenticeships and other forms of training (Perry, 1976). The route the state chose was one of corporatist compromise and minimal intervention, erecting a network of Industrial Training Boards (ITBs) in the major industries staffed by union, employer and government representatives (Industrial Training Act, 1964). The ITBs' main means of overcoming the free-rider problem was the levy/grant system, which placed a training tax on all the companies within an industry and then distributed the funds to those firms that were training to an acceptable standard, defined by each board (Page, 1967).

The boards created a fairer apportionment of training costs and raised awareness of skill shortages, but they failed to raise substantially the overall training level because they did not challenge the short-term perspective of most companies. The state contributed no new funds to training and each board assessed only its industry's training needs, taking as given the existing firm organization, industrial relations system and management practices and thus perpetuating the low-skill equilibrium. Despite the Engineering ITB's pioneering work in developing new, more flexible training courses, craft apprenticeships remained the main supply of skilled labour until Mrs Thatcher came to power in 1979.

☐ Industrial/firm structure

Industry type. One of the main reasons that British industry has failed to update its training programmes is the concentration of the country's firms in those product markets which have the lowest skill requirements, goods manufactured with continuous, rather than batch or unit production processes (Reich, 1983). An analysis of international trade in the 1970s by NEDO found that the UK performed better than average in 'standardized, price-sensitive products' and below average in 'the skill and innovation-intensive products' (Greenhalgh, 1988, p. 15). New and Myers' (1986) study of 240 large export-oriented plants confirmed that only a minority of these firms had experimented with the most advanced technologies and that managements' future plans were focused on traditional, mass-production market segments.

Training has also been adversely affected by the long-term shift in British employment from manufacturing to low-skill, low-quality services. Manufacturing now accounts for less than one-third of British employment and its share of the labour market has been declining. The largest growth in employment is in the part-time service sector, where jobs typically require and offer little or no training. The concentration of British service providers on the low-skill end of the labour market was highlighted in a recent study of the tourist industry (Gapper, 1988).

While the type of goods or services which a company produces sets limits on the skills required, it does not determine the necessary level of training. Recent international comparisons of firms in similar product markets (e.g. Maurice *et al.*, 1986; Streeck, 1985) have revealed significant variations in training provision depending on how a company is organized and the way in which this organizational structure shapes the implementation of new technologies. In the retail trade, for instance, 75 per cent of German employees have at least an apprenticeship qualification compared with just 2 per cent in the UK. The brief sections which follow will outline how, in the British case, the many, integrally-related components of firms' organizational structures and practices have combined to discourage training.

Recruitment. British firms have traditionally provided two routes of entry for young workers: the majority are hired at the end of compulsory schooling, either to begin an apprenticeship or to start a semi- or unskilled job, while a select few are recruited from higher education (HE) for management posts (Crowther Report, 1959). (Nursing is one of the rare careers which has sought students leaving FE at the age of 18.) As a result, there is little incentive for those unlikely to gain admittance to HE to stay on in school or FE. Indeed, Raffe (1984, ch. 9) found that Scottish males who opted for post-compulsory education actually had a harder time finding work than their peers who left school at sixteen. Vocational education is perceived as a low-status route because it provides little opportunity for career advancement and because managers, who themselves typically enter employment without practical experience or technical training, focus on academic examinations as the best means of assessing the potential of trainees.

Job design and scope.   After joining a company, employees' training will depend upon the array of tasks they are asked to perform. Tipton's study (1982, p. 33) of the British labour market found that 'the bulk of existing jobs are of a routine, undemanding variety' requiring little or no training. The failure to broaden individuals' jobs and skill base, e.g. through job rotation and work teams, has historically been linked to craft unions' insistence on rigid demarcations between jobs, but there is some evidence that these restrictive practices have diminished in the last decade. The decline in union resistance, however, has been counterbalanced by two negative trends for training: subcontracting out skilled maintenance work (Brady, 1984) and using new technologies to de-skill work (Streeck, 1985). The latter practice is particularly well documented in the automobile industry, where British firms, unlike their Swedish, Japanese and German rivals, have structured new automated factories to minimize the skill content of production jobs, instead of utilizing the new technology to increase flexibility and expand job definitions (Scarbrough, 1986). Tipton concludes (p. 27): 'the key to improving the quality of training is the design of work and a much needed spur to the movement for the redesign of work ... may lie in training policies and practice'.

Authority structure.   In the previous section we used job design to refer to the range of tasks within one level of a firm's job hierarchy (horizontal scope); how that hierarchy is structured – number of levels, location of decision-making power, forms of control – will also affect training provision (vertical scope). Coopers and Lybrand (1985, pp. 4–5) discovered that in a majority of the firms surveyed, line managers, rather than top executives, are generally responsible for training decisions, thereby hindering long-term manpower planning. British firms also lack structures, like German work councils, which enable employees to exercise control over their own training.

Career/wage structure.   A company's reward system, how wages and promotion are determined, shapes employees' incentives to pursue training. While education levels are crucial in deciding where an employee enters a firm's job structure, these incentives are low after workers have taken a job because pay and career advancement are determined by seniority, not skill levels (George and Shorey, 1985). This disincentive is particularly strong for the growing number of workers trapped in the periphery sector of the labour market (Mayhew, 1986), which features part-time or temporary work, low wages and little or no chance for promotion.

Management. Linking all of the preceding elements of firm organization is the role of management in determining training levels. The poor preparation of British managers, resulting from a dearth of technical HE or management schools and a focus on accounting rather than production, is often cited as a reason for the lack of priority attached to training in Britain. A recent survey of over 2500 British firms found that less than half made any provision at all for management training (Anderson, 1987, p. 68). In those firms which do train, managers tend to treat training as an operating expense to be pared during economic downturns and fail to incorporate manpower planning into the firm's overall competitive strategy. For managers interested in career advancement, the training department is generally seen as a low-status option (Coopers and Lybrand, 1985, pp. 4–5). And for poorly qualified line managers, training may be perceived as a threat to their authority rather than a means of improving productivity. It is important, however, to distinguish between bad managers and able ones who are forced into decisions by the institutional structure in which they are operating. We will explore two of the major forces impacting on their decisions, industrial relations and financial markets, in the following sections.

☐ **Financial markets**

The short-term perspective of most British managers is reinforced by the pressure to maximize immediate profits and shareholder value. The historical separation of financial and industrial capital (Hall, 1986, p. 59) has made it harder for British firms to invest in training, with its deferred benefits, than their West German or Japanese competitors, particularly since the City has neglected training in its analysis of companies' performance (Coopers and Lybrand, 1985). Without access to large industry-oriented investment banks, British firms have been forced to finance more investment from retained profits than companies in the other G5 nations (Mayer, 1987).

☐ **Industrial relations**

Just as the operation of financial markets has discouraged training efforts, so too the structure, traditions, and common practices of British industrial relations have undermined attempts to improve the skills of the work force. The problem must be analysed at two levels: the inability of the central union and employer organizations to combine with government to form a coordinated national training policy, and the historical neglect of training in the collective bargaining process.

Employer organizations. The strength of the Confederation of British Industry (CBI) derives from its virtual monopoly status – its members employ a majority of Britain's workers and there is no competing national federation. But while this membership base has given the CBI a role in national training policy formulation, the CBI lacks the sanctions necessary to ensure that employers implement the agreements which it negotiates with the Government. The power lies not in the central federation, nor in industry-wide employers' associations, but in individual firms. The CBI's views on training reflect its lack of control, as Keep, a former member of the CBI's Education, Training and Technology Directorate, observes (1986, p. 8): 'The CBI's stance on training policy ... was strongly anti-interventionist and centred on a voluntary, market-based approach. Legislation to compel changes in training policy ... was perceived as constituting an intolerable financial burden on industry.'

This free-market approach, combined with the absence of strong local employer groups, like the West German Chambers of Commerce, has left British industry without an effective mechanism for overcoming the 'poaching' problem. Among the worst offenders are the small and medium-sized firms, poorly represented in the CBI, which lack the resources to provide broad-based training.

Trade unions. There are four key, closely connected variables which determine the effectiveness of a central union federation in the training field (Woodall, 1985, p. 26): degree of centralization, financial membership and organization resources, degree of youth organization and structure and practice of collective bargaining. Woodall compared the Trades Union Congress (TUC) with European central union federations and found it weak along all of these axes. Like the CBI, it could exert a limited influence on government policy, but it lacked the means to enforce centrally negotiated initiatives on its members.

The TUC has had to deal with 'the most complex trade union structure in the world', (Clegg, 1972, p. 57) while having little control over its affiliated unions. And whereas the German central union federation, the DGB, claims 12 per cent of its member unions' total receipts, the TUC has received less than 2 per cent and devotes only a small fraction of these resources to training. This inattention to education and training is reflected in unions' lack of involvement in the transition from school to work. Britain's major youth organizations, the National Union of Students and Youthaid, grew outside the formal union structure and have often criticized the labour movement for failing to address the needs of the nation's school-leavers, particularly the unemployed. The uncoordinated nature of British collective bargaining, with agreements varying from coverage of whole industries to small portions of a particular factory, and the lack of central input in the negotiations further hinder TUC efforts to improve training provision. The combination of these factors prompted Taylor (1980, p. 91) to observe that 'by the standards of other Western industrialised nations, Britain provides the worst education services of any trade union movement.'

Although we have broken down this analysis into separate sections for conceptual clarity, it is essential to view each element as part of a historically evolved institutional structure which has limited British ET. In the next section we will examine how the economic crisis of the 1970s destabilized this structure, creating the opportunity for the Thatcher Government's ET reforms.

■ Mrs Thatcher's education and training policies

During the 1970s a confluence of events brought an end to the reluctance of central government to take the lead in ET policy-making. The prolonged recession which followed the 1973 oil shock forced the Labour Government to cut public expenditure, necessitating a re-examination of educational priorities. This reassessment came at a time when the education system was drawing mounting criticism in the popular press and the far Right's 'Black Papers' for allegedly falling standards and unchecked teacher progressivism (Centre for Contemporary Cultural Studies, 1981). The response of the then Prime Minister, James Callaghan, was to launch the 'Great Debate' on education in a now famous speech at Ruskin College, Oxford in October 1976, where he called on the ET sector to make a greater contribution towards the nation's economic performance (Callaghan, 1976).

The increase in bipartisan political support for vocational and technical education was matched by a strengthening of the central state's capacity to formulate ET policy. MSC, a tripartite quango funded by the Department of Employment, was established in 1973 to provide the strong central organization needed to coordinate training across industrial sectors which was missing from the Industrial Training Board structure. In practice, however, the ITBs were left to themselves, while the MSC concentrated on the immediate problem of growing youth unemployment. The Commission supervised the first substantial injection of government funds into training, beginning with TOPS (Training Opportunities Scheme) and later through YOP (Youth Opportunities Programme). The

Table 10.1 Mrs Thatcher's education and training policies.

Phase/date	Characteristics	Programmes		
		Education	Youth training	Adult training
I. Preparation 1979–81	Market orientation; weaken resistance; lack overall strategy	Budget cuts	Apprenticeship collapse	Dismantle ITBs
II. NTI 1982–86	Focus on 14–18s; concern with youth unemployment; enterprise economy; increase central control	TVEI; pilot to national programme in 4 years	YTS/ITeCs NCVQ YOP; 1 year YTS; 2 year YTS; YTS apprentice route	TOPS/JTS/CP TOPS-new JTS Focus on adult unemployment
III. Expansion 1987–	Education – new priorities; adults – first attempt at coherence	GERBIL/ CTCs; TVEI extension or extinction?	Weaken MSC; compulsory YTS; NCVQ finish in 1991	Weaken MSC; training for employment; 600 000 places; no new money

rapid increase in government spending (the MSC budget rose from £125 million in 1974–75 to £641 million in 1978–79) did little to improve skills, however, since the funds were concentrated on temporary employment, work experience and short-course training measures and the demands for quick action precluded any long-term manpower planning.

Spurred on by its new rival, the MSC, the DES set up the Further Education Unit (FEU) in 1978, which produced a steady stream of reports that helped shift educational opinion in favour of the 'new vocationalism' (e.g. *A Basis for Choice*, 1979). The Department teamed up with the MSC for the first time in 1976 to launch the Unified Vocational Preparation (UVP) scheme for school-leavers entering jobs which previously offered no training. Although this initiative never advanced beyond the early pilot phase, it set a precedent for subsequent reform efforts.

The state structure was in place for the new Thatcher Government to transform the ET system. The first half of this section will outline three distinct phases in the Conservatives' ET reform efforts (see Table 10.1), examining how the Government has avoided many of the pitfalls which plagued past efforts at change, while the latter portion will argue that these reforms, while leading to significant shifts in control over ET, will not raise Britain's relative ET performance.

☐ Phase I: preparation

It is only in retrospect that the first few years of the Thatcher Administration can be seen as an effective continuation of the movement towards greater centralization of ET power. At the time, Government economic policy was dominated by the belief that controlling the money supply and public expenditure were the keys to reducing inflation and restoring competitiveness. Education and training accounted for approximately 15 per cent of the budget and thus needed to be cut if spending was to be curtailed. The cuts included: across-the-board reductions in education funding, a drop in state subsidies for apprenticeships and the abolition of 17 of the 24 training boards (one new one was created), despite the opposition of the MSC. The financial rationale for the cuts was underpinned by the then strongly held view of the Government that training decisions were better left to market forces.

The net effect of these cuts, coming at the start of a severe recession in which industry was already cutting back on training, was the collapse of the apprenticeship system. The number of engineering craft and technician trainees, for example, declined from 21 000 to 12 000 between 1979 and 1981, while construction apprentice recruitment fell by 53 per cent during the same period (from Engineering Industry Training Board and Construction Industry Training Board in *TUC Annual Report 1981*, pp. 434–5). The destruction of old-style apprenticeships, combined with the Government's attacks on trade unions' restrictive practices through industrial relations legislation, meant that when the state eventually chose to reform initial training within companies, there was only minimal resistance from organized labour and employers.

☐   Phase II: the New Training Initiative

By 1981 the deepening recession and the dramatic rise in youth unemployment which it caused compelled the Government to reassess its non-interventionist training stance. While the Conservatives' neo-liberal economic philosophy offered no immediate cure for mass unemployment, it was politically essential to make some effort to combat a problem which the polls consistently showed to be the voters' primary concern (Moon and Richardson, 1985, p. 61). This electoral need was highlighted in a Downing Street Policy Unit paper from early 1981:

> 'We all know that there is no prospect of getting unemployment down to acceptable levels within the next few years. (Consequently) we must show that we have some political imagination, that we are willing to salvage something – albeit second-best – from the sheer waste involved.' (Riddell, 1983, p. 50.)

What this 'political imagination' produced was the New Training Initiative (NTI) (MSC, 1981), whose centrepiece, the Youth Training Scheme (YTS), was the first permanent national training programme for Britain's school-leavers. YTS replaced YOP, which had begun as a temporary scheme in 1978 to offer a year's work experience and training to the young unemployed. In just four years, however, YOP had swelled to more than 550 000 places, and as the numbers grew so did the criticism of the programme for its falling job-placement rates and poor-quality training. YTS attempted to improve YOP's image by upgrading the training content, 'guaranteeing' a year's placement with at least thirteen weeks off-the-job training to every minimum-age school-leaver and most un-employed seventeen-year-olds and more than doubling the programme's annual budget, from £400 to £1000 million.

Despite these improvements, the scheme got off to a difficult start, with a national surplus of close to 100 000 places, as school-leavers proved reluctant to enter the new programme. In response, the MSC implemented a constant stream of YTS reforms: the scheme was lengthened from one to two years, with off-the-job training extended to twenty weeks; all sixteen and seventeen-year-olds, not just the unemployed, were made eligible; some form of qualification was to be made available to each trainee; and monitoring and evaluation were increased by requiring all training providers to attain Approved Training Organization (ATO) status. While the majority of YTS places continue to offer trainees a broad sampling of basic skills ('foundation training') and socialization into a work environ-ment, some industries, such as construction, engineering and hairdressing, have used the scheme to finance the first two years of modernized apprenticeships.

The other major ET reform originating in this period was the Technical and Vocational Education Initiative (TVEI), launched by the Prime Minister in November 1982. TVEI marked the Thatcher Ad-ministration's first attempt to increase the industrial relevance of what is taught in secondary schools, through the development of new forms of teacher training, curriculum organization and assessment for the fourteen-to-eighteen age group. Under the direction of the MSC's Chairman David (now Lord) Young, the Initiative grew extremely rapidly, from fourteen local authority pilot projects in 1983 to the start of a nationwide, £1 billion extension just four years later. Lord Young conceived TVEI as a means of fostering Britain's 'enterprise economy', by motivating the vast majority of students who were not progressing to higher education: 'The curriculum in English schools is too academic and leads towards the universities. What I am trying to show is that there is another line of development that is equally respectable and desirable which leads to vocational qualifications ...' (*Education*, 19 November 1982, p. 386).

This line of development was extended into the FE sector in 1985 with the introduction of the Certificate of Pre-Vocational Education (CPVE), a one-year programme of broad, work-related subjects for students who wished to stay on in full-time education, but were not prepared for A-levels or a specific career path.

In 1985 the Government set up a working group to review Britain's increasingly diverse array of vocational qualifications. The De Ville

Committee's report (1986) led to the establishment of the National Council for Vocational Qualifications (NCVQ) which has the task of rationalizing all of the country's training qualifications into five levels, ranging from YTS to engineering professionals, with clear paths of progression between stages and national standards of proficiency. The Council, which is scheduled to complete its review in 1991, will be defining broad guidelines for training qualifications into which the courses of the independent certification bodies (e.g. RSA, BTEC, City and Guilds) can be slotted.

Taken together, these initiatives represent a dramatic reversal in the Government's approach to ET. The scope and pace of reform was made possible by the centralization of power in the hands of the MSC, an institution which has proved adept at securing the cooperation required to implement these controversial changes. In the case of YTS, the MSC has thus far retained trade union support, despite protests from over one-third of the TUC's membership that the schemes lead to job substitution and poor-quality training (*TUC Annual Report*, 1983–86), because the TUC leadership has refused to give up one of its last remaining channels for input into national policy-making.

The MSC has also become a major power in the educational world because it offered the Conservatives a means of bypassing the cumbersome DES bureaucracy (Dale, 1985, p. 50). The Commission was able to convince teachers and local authorities, who had in the past resisted central government's efforts to reform the curriculum, to go along with TVEI through the enticement of generous funding during a period of fiscal austerity and the use of techniques normally associated with the private sector, such as competitive bidding and contractual relationships (Harland, 1987). Its influence over education increased still further in 1985, when it was given control of over 25 per cent of non-advanced further education (NAFE) funding, previously controlled by the LEAs. This change has, in effect, meant that the MSC has the power to review all NAFE provision.

☐   Phase III: expanding the focus

The constantly changing nature of ET policy under Mrs Thatcher makes it hazardous to predict future developments, but early indications are that education and training reform will continue to accelerate in her third term. The combination of a successful economy (low inflation, high growth and falling unemployment) and a solid electoral majority has enabled the Conservatives to turn their focus toward fundamental social reform. As a result, the narrow concentration of ET policy on the fourteen-to-eighteen age group appears to be broadening to include both general education – the Great Education Reform Bill (GERBIL, 1987) – and adult training – *Training for Employment* (1988).

The 1987 Conservative Election Manifesto signalled the emergence of education reform as a major political issue. While GERBIL is primarily an attempt to raise standards by increasing competition and the accountability of the educational establishment, a number of its provisions will impact on the vocational education and training area: the National Curriculum, which will ensure that all students take mathematics and science until they reach sixteen; City Technical Colleges, which may signal the beginning of an alternative secondary school track, funded directly by the DES with substantial contributions from industry; the removal of the larger Colleges of Further Education (CFEs) and polytechnics from LEA control, freeing them to compete for students and strengthening their ties with employers; and increased industry representation on the new governing body for universities, the UFC (University Funding Council).

At the same time, the Government has begun restructuring adult training provision. Over the previous eight years, the MSC concentrated on reducing youth unemployment, while financing a succession of short-duration training and work experience programmes for the long-term unemployed; TOPS (Training Opportunities Scheme – short courses normally based in CFEs), JTS, and new-JTS (Job Training Scheme – work placement with minimal off-the-job training for 18-to-24s), and the CP (Community Programme – state-funded public work projects). In February 1988 the Government's White Paper, *Training for Employment*, introduced a plan to combine all of these adult initiatives into a new £1.5 billion programme that will provide 600 000 training places, with initial preference given to the 18-to-24 age group. To attract the long-run unemployed into the scheme the Government is using both carrot and stick: a training allowance at least £10 above the benefit level, along with increases in claimant advisors and fraud investigators to ensure that all those receiving benefit are actively pursuing work.

The new scheme will be administered by the Training Commission, the heir to the MSC. The Employment Secretary surprised both critics and supporters when he announced that the Government's most effective quango would come to an end in 1988. The new Training Commission lacks the MSC's employment functions, which have been transferred to the Department of Employment, and its governing board structure has been altered to give industry representatives, some now appointed directly rather than by the CBI, effective control. The changes seem to indicate that the Thatcher Government no longer feels the need to consult trade unions and wants to play down the role of the CBI in order to push forward its training reforms.

The Government has also started to devote a limited amount of resources to broadening access to ET for those already in employment. The DES is expanding its Professional, Industrial and Commercial Updating Programme (PICKUP), which is now spending £12.5 million a year to help colleges, polytechnics and universities tailor their courses more closely to employers' needs. And in 1987, the MSC provided start-up money for the Open College, which along with Open Tech uses open-learning techniques to offer individuals and employers the chance to acquire new skills or update old ones.

☐   Problems with Mrs Thatcher's ET policies

While Mrs Thatcher has brought about more radical and rapid changes in the ET system than any British leader in the postwar period, there are a number of reasons to doubt whether her reforms will succeed in closing the skills gap which has grown between Britain and its major competitors. Rather than detail the shortcomings of specific programmes, we will focus on two major flaws in her Government's ET policy: the lack of coherence and weakness in the many initiatives designed to change the transition from school to FE or employment (reforms for the fourteen-to-eighteen age group) and the absence of an adult training strategy and sufficient funding to facilitate industrial restructuring.

The transition from school to work.   Oxford's local education authority has coined a new term, 'GONOT'. GONOT is the name of a committee set up to coordinate GCSE, OES, NLI, OCEA and TVEI,[3] just some of the reforms introduced by the Government since 1981 for the fourteen-to-eighteen age group. The need to create abbreviations for abbreviations is symptomatic of the strains which the Conservatives' scattershot approach to ET policy has placed on those charged with implementing the reforms. The case of TVEI provides a clear illustration of the difficulties created by this incoherence.

When TVEI was first announced, one of its primary objectives was to improve staying-on rates. This goal has since been de-emphasized, however, because TVEI's sixteen-to-eighteen phase comes into direct conflict with YTS. Students have a dual incentive to opt for the narrower training option: first, because YTS offers an allowance, while TVEI does not, and second, because access to skilled jobs is increasingly limited to YTS apprenticeships. The failure of the MSC to coordinate these programmes is evident at all organizational levels, from the national, where the headquarters are based in different cities, to the local, where the coordinators of the two initiatives rarely, if ever, come into contact.

The success of individual TVEI pilot schemes is also threatened by recent national developments. Local TVEI consortia, for example, have built closer ties between schools and the FE sector to rationalize provision at sixteen-plus, a crucial need during a period of falling student numbers. But these consortia are in jeopardy due to GERBIL's proposals for opting out, open enrolment and the removal of the larger Colleges of Further Education from LEA control, which would foster competition rather than cooperation among institutions. Likewise, TVEI's efforts to bridge traditional subject boundaries and the divide between academic and vocational subjects are in danger of being undermined by the proposed National Curriculum with its individual subject testing and the failure to include academic examinations (GCSE and A-level) in the National Review of Vocational Qualifications (DeVille Report, 1986, p. 4).

These contradictions stem from divisions within the Conservative Party itself. Dale (1983b) identifies five separate factions – industrial trainers, populists, privatizers, old-style Tories and moral educationalists – all exercising an influence on Thatcher's ET policies. Do the Conservatives, for instance, want to spread technical and vocational subjects across the comprehensive curriculum (the TVEI strategy) or resurrect the old tripartite system's technical school track (the City Technical College route)? Another conflict has emerged in the examination sphere, where modular forms of assessment pioneered under TVEI and GCSE, which are already improving student motivation and practical skills, have been stifled by Conservative traditionalists, such as the Minister of State at the DES, Angela Rumbold, insisting on preserving the narrow, exclusively academic focus of A-levels and university admissions (Gow, 1988b, p. 1). The splits within the party were highlighted in a leaked letter from the Prime Minister's secretary to Kenneth Baker's secretary, indicating Mrs Thatcher's reservations concerning the forms of assessment proposed by the Black Committee to accompany the National Curriculum.

Emerging from this uncoordinated series of reforms appears to be a three-tiered, post-compulsory ET system (Ranson, 1985, p. 63) which will not significantly raise the qualifications of those entering the workforce. At the top, higher education will continue to be confined to an academic élite, as the White Paper *Higher Education – Meeting the Challenge* (1987) projects no additional funds for HE in the next decade, despite growing evidence of graduate shortages; the middle rung of technical and vocational courses in full-time FE seems equally unlikely to expand, given that the Government refuses to consider educational maintenance allowances (EMAs) and that the extension funding for TVEI appears inadequate to sustain its early successes; the basic training route, then, will remain YTS, a low-cost option which has not succeeded in solving the skills problem (Deakin and Pratten, 1987; Jones, 1988). As of May 1987, more than half of all YTS providers had failed to meet the quality standards laid down by the MSC (Leadbeater, 1987). And though the quality of training may since have improved, organizations are finding it increasingly difficult to attract school-leavers on to the scheme, as falling rolls lead to increased competition among employers for sixteen-year-olds to fill low-skill jobs (Jackson, 1988).

Restructuring/adult training. As we have shown (in the second section), the capacity for continuously updating the skills of the workforce is a key factor in the process of industrial restructuring, at either firm or national level. But in the rush to develop new ET initiatives for the fourteen-to-eighteen sector, the Conservatives have neglected the largest potential pool of trainees: adults in employment. The Government has not secured sufficient extra resources from any of the three basic sources of funding for post-compulsory ET – the state, individuals or companies – to finance a major improvement in British ET performance.

The largest increase in expenditure has come in the state sector, but it is crucial to examine where the money was spent. Although the MSC's budget tripled (to £2.3 billion) during the Conservatives' first two terms, only just over 10 per cent of these funds were spent on adult training, the vast majority on the long-term unemployed. Those courses, like TOPS, which did offer high-quality training geared to the local labour market, have been phased out in favour of the much-criticized JTS and new-JTS, which offer less costly, lower-skill training. This emphasis on quantity over quality was continued in the new 'Training for Employment' package, which proposes to expand the number of training places still further without allocating any new resources. Mrs Thatcher's efforts to improve training within companies have been largely confined to a public relations exercise designed to increase 'national awareness' of training needs (*Training for Jobs*, 1984). Former MSC Chairman Bryan Nicholson (1986) made the Government's position clear: 'The state is responsible for education until an individual reaches sixteen. From sixteen to eighteen, education and training are the joint responsibility of industry and government. But from eighteen on, training should be up to the individual and his employer.'

The Conservatives, however, have had little success in convincing the private sector to assume its share of responsibility for training. While the MSC has been gradually placing a greater portion of YTS funding on employers, the bulk of the cost is still met by the state. In fact, a National Association of Humanities Education study (1987) revealed that private training organizations were making a profit off the MSC's training grants. The Government may be regretting its decision to do away with the one legislative means of increasing employers' funding for training, as this remark made by Nicholson indicates: 'Those industries who have made little effort to keep the grand promises they made when the majority of ITBs were abolished should not be allowed to shirk forever' (Clement, 1986).

Mrs Thatcher has made somewhat more progress in her attempts to shift the ET burden on to individuals, who can fund their own ET either through direct payments (course fees, living expenses) or by accepting a lower wage in exchange for training. The state has compelled more school-leavers to pay for training by removing sixteen and seveteen-year-olds from eligibility for benefits and then setting the trainee allowance at a level well below the old apprenticeship wage. It has also forced individuals staying on in full-time education to make a greater financial contribution to their own maintenance costs through the reduction of student grants, a policy which seems certain to accelerate with the introduction of student loans.

These measures, however, are not matched by policies to encourage adults to invest their time and money towards intermediate or higher-level qualifications. This failure can be traced to three sources: lack of opportunity, capital and motivation. The state's assumption of the full costs of higher education, among the most expensive per pupil in the world, has resulted in a strictly limited supply of places. Those individuals who wish to finance courses below HE level suffer both from limited access to capital and a tax system which, unlike most European countries, offers employees no deductions for training costs (DES, 1988). But the main reason for workers' reluctance to invest in their own training is that the Government has done nothing to alter the basic operation of British firms which, as we saw above, are not structured to reward improvements in skill levels.

This underinvestment in ET raises the question: if it is true that training is critical to economic restructuring and that Mrs Thatcher has failed to improve Britain's poor ET record, why has the UK grown faster than all the major industrial nations, except Japan, over the last eight years? Part of the answer lies in the Conservatives' success in creating a more efficient low-cost production and services economy. A series of supply-side measures, weakening Wage Councils and employment security legislation, subsidizing the creation of low-wage jobs (the Young Workers Scheme) and attacking trade unions, have improved labour mobility and company profitability. Training programmes, like YTS, have played a pivotal role in this process, providing employers with a cheap means of screening large numbers of low-skilled, but well-socialized young workers (Chapman and Tooze, 1987). The liberalization of financial markets, with the resultant pressure on firms to maximize short-term profits, and the explosion of accountancy-based management consultancy (*Business Week*, June 1988) have further reinforced industry's cost-cutting approach. The irony is that while Britain is striving to compete more effectively with low-cost producers such as South Korea and Singapore, these nations are investing heavily in general education and training to enable their industries to move into flexible, high technology production.

■ Policies for the future

This section suggests in broad terms what policies could remedy the insufficiencies of the British system of education and training. It covers both those in the sixteen-to-twenty age group and the (far larger) adult labour force. We take the quantitative goal to be the broad level which the

Japanese, Germans and Swedes have achieved, namely where about 90 per cent of young people are in full-time highly-structured education and training until nineteen or twenty. And, less precisely, that major improvements take place in the training of those already in the workforce, both by the employer and externally. Training of managers, in particular of supervisers, is treated in relation to these goals.

What type of education and training? There is broad agreement about the need to raise ET standards and levels, but less about its content. This reflects the failure of the (opposed) ET methodologies of the postwar decades: manpower planning, on the one hand, and human capital theory, on the other. Manpower planning has proved too inflexible in a world in which long-run predictions about occupational needs can seldom be made. And the rate of return calculations underlying human capital approaches to optimal training provision have foundered on the difference between social and market valuations. While both approaches have a role to play when used sensibly, few practitioners would see either as sufficient to determine the content of ET.

Reform of education and training is seen in this section as part of the process of 'managing change'. This context argues for three general criteria as determining the content of education and training.

First, the uncertainty of occupational needs in the future requires *adaptability*. Many people in the labour force will have to make significant career changes in their working lives, which will require retraining. There is some agreement that successful retraining depends on a high level of general education and also on previous vocational training. Moreover, as much training for new occupations covers skills already acquired in previous ET (e.g. computing skills), a modular approach to training is efficient.

Second, ET needs to equip workers with the skills required for *innovation in products and processes* and the *production of high-quality goods and services*. One implication is that participation in higher education will have to steadily increase. And there is a more radical implication, as Hayes and others have stressed: effective innovation and quality production requires participation; that means that workers and managers should acquire not just technical competence, but also the social and managerial skills involved in working together. We may need increasingly to blur the distinction between management ET and worker ET. The implications are various: a high level of general education, sufficiently broad that young people are both technically competent and educated in the humanities and arts; strong emphasis on projects, working together and interdisciplinary work; vocational education and training which provides management skills as well as technical understanding. More generally, ET should be designed to reduce class barriers, not only as a good in itself, but also because of the requirements of innovation and high-quality production.

Third, ET must be *recognizable* and *useful*, so that employers want to employ the graduates of the ET system and young people and adults want to undertake ET. There is a potential tension here with the previous paragraph. For the abilities stressed are at present only demanded by a minority of companies. Vocational education is thus a compromise between the characteristics needed in the longer term and the skills and knowledge which companies can see as immediately useful to them. A second implication of the need for recognition and usefulness is that there be a widely agreed and understood system of certification, based on acceptable assessment.

Much policy discussion, sensibly, concerns potential improvements within the broad context of the existing framework of ET provision within the UK. As a result less thought has been given to the wider transformations which we believe the management of change and the move to a high-skills equilibrium imply. The discussion of this section thus takes a longer-term perspective.

There are five interdependent parts to these recommendations for reform: reforming ET provision for the sixteen-to-twenty age group; training by companies; individual access to training; the external infrastructure of ET; and the macro-economic implications of a major ET expansion.

☐   The education and training of sixteen to twenty-year-olds

The focus of this section is on how incentives, attitudes, institutions and options can be changed so that young people will choose to remain in full-time education and training until the age of nineteen or twenty, rather than entering the labour market or YTS at age sixteen.

For two reasons, the next decade offers a window for reform which was not previously open. First, the demographic decline in the sixteen-plus age cohort will mean a drop of nearly a third over the next ten years in the numbers of young people aged between sixteen and nineteen. It will therefore be an ideal period for bringing our system into line with that of other advanced countries, for the resource cost, although considerable, of a substantial increase in the ET participation ratio of sixteen to nineteen-year-olds will be significantly less than in the past decade.

The second reason was spelt out in the fourth section. The institutional constraints against change are in two ways significantly weaker now than a decade or two decades ago. Unions at national level, far from seeking to frustrate change, would support it in this area; they would see it as a means of regaining membership, rather than a threat to the bargaining position of existing skilled workers. The education system (teachers, LEAs, educationalists and teachers' unions) no longer sees itself as having the right to determine education policy alone; central government has far stronger control over it than in the past, and this will increase over the next decade as opting out develops; the larger CFEs will no longer be run by LEAs; teachers' unions are moving away from the belief that they can successfully oppose government to the view that they need to cultivate wider alliances, including industry, and educationalists today are far more aware of the role which schools can play in helping children to get employment. In addition, political parties are no longer constrained as they were (say) two decades ago in formulating policy in these areas.

What basic requirements are implied for a sixteen-to-twenty ET system by the discussion in the introduction above? Five should be stressed:

- Good general education, covering both technical subjects and the humanities.
- This should be designed to encourage interaction (project, etc.) and reduce social class differences.
- Rising percentage over time of those going on to HE, and ease of switching between more vocational and more academic routes.
- Structured vocational training for those not going on to HE, with acquisition of broad skills, including communications and decision-making competences.
- Modularization and certification.

Despite the 'window of opportunity', how feasible is the sort of major change envisaged? Apart from the question of financing, formidable problems will need to be resolved:

- Young people have the option at sixteen to remain in full-time education. About 65 per cent choose not to. Raising the legal minimum school-leaving age to eighteen is politically not a possibility, and in any case it is desirable that young people should choose to stay on. How are incentives to be structured and attitudes changed to raise the staying-on rate to above 80 per cent?
- Relatively few businesses are currently capable of providing high-quality training. And, while employer organizations are becoming more committed to involvement in ET, effective action on their part will require a coordinating capacity which is beyond their present power or resources.
- In comparison with other countries with well-developed vocational training systems, the UK lacks an effective administrative structure and a major research and development capacity.

Of these constraints the first must be overcome. It will be argued in this section that the involvement of employers and their organizations and a proper state infrastructure will be needed to achieve both this and the ET desiderata set out above. To see why this is the case, we look first at why sixteen-year-olds choose to leave education and training, and with this in mind, examine the experience of sixteen-to-twenty ET in other countries.

Why do such a large proportion of young people choose to join the labour market or YTS at sixteen? There are two main reasons. The first is financial. On YTS or social security young people get a small income. If they remain in full-time education they receive nothing (their parents receive child benefit). There are therefore strong inducements to leave full-time education at sixteen. The demographic shrinking of the sixteen-plus age group (while it will make reform easier) will, in the absence of reform, strengthen the incentive to leave; this is because employers are accustomed to recruiting from this age group, directly or nowadays through YTS, since it provides relatively cheap and pliable labour, so that relative earnings at sixteen-plus may be expected to rise.

In the second place, staying on in full-time ET has not been seen as a bridge to stable employment. The best route to employment for most sixteen-year-olds today is via YTS, which is used by many employers as a screening device for the choice of permanent employees. YTS trainees who show themselves to be cooperative have a high probability of securing permanent employment, and that probability will rise as the demographic decline in the sixteen-plus age cohort sets in.

Foreign experience can give an idea of different possible systems of sixteen-to-twenty ET, as well as alerting to some of the problems:

- One country often cited as an exemplar is the US. About 75 per cent of the relevant age group graduates from high school by age eighteen after a broadly based course, more academically geared for those going on to HE, more vocational for those going directly into the labour market. Over 40 per cent go on to two-year junior colleges or university, producing a remarkably educated population. But there are problems with the education and training of those who do not go on to HE. In many areas, lack of coordinated employer involvement has meant there is no clear bridge between education and employment. The 'Boston compact', under which a group of companies guaranteed training and employment against good high school performance, acknowledged this need. And lack of involvement by companies in sixteen-to-twenty ET has limited firms' provision of training for manual workers and low-level white-collar workers.

- France has a more highly structured system of initial vocational training. Less-able children can go to vocational schools from fourteen to eighteen, and end with craft-level qualifications. More emphasis in the future is being placed on the various higher-level vocational *baccalauréat* courses, from sixteen to nineteen, which turn out technician engineers with managerial skills. Compared with the UK, both routes are impressive, especially the second. But, as in the US, there is limited employer involvement. One consequence is staying-on rates at sixteen-plus well below the Northern European and Japanese, and a higher rate of youth unemployment. A second is limited training for manual workers in companies.

- In the Germanic (Germany, Austria, Switzerland) system, those going on to higher education spend two years from sixteen to eighteen in a high school before taking the *abitur*. Those working for vocational qualifications become apprenticed at sixteen for three or four years and follow a highly structured, carefully monitored system of on-the-job and off-the-job training and education, with external exams on both practical and theoretical subjects.

- In the Scandinavian (Norway, Sweden) system, young people remain in the same college between sixteen and eighteen, specializing in vocational or academic areas; vocational education is then completed in vocational centres post-eighteen.

- Denmark has been actively experimenting with post-sixteen ET in the last two decades. The Danes have been moving towards a system in which all young people remain within the same educational institution between sixteen and eighteen, more or less a tertiary college. If they choose the vocational route, they move into a two-year apprenticeship at eighteen, for which much work will have already been covered in the college.

Both the Germanic and Scandinavian systems succeed in attaining very high participation rates for the sixteen-to-eighteen age group, and in delivering high-quality vocational training as well as good general education. There are, however, arguments against both Germanic and Scandinavian systems as the optimal model for the UK, despite the fact that both systems are greatly superior to Britain's. The main argument against applying the Scandinavian system to the British context is that Britain lacks the infrastructure to make it work: the close involvement of employer organizations with the public system of vocational education. Moreover, there is powerful union and state pressure on companies to maintain training standards.

The Germanic system also has disadvantages, in part because it would be based too strongly on employers if transplanted to the UK. There are four reasons why we should be wary of advocating a German-type division at sixteen between academic education and an employer-based three or four-year apprenticeship:

- The greater the employer involvement (unless restrained by powerful employer organizations and unions as in Germany), the more the apprenticeship will reflect the short-term needs of the employer. This is illustrated by the otherwise excellent EITB engineering apprenticeship scheme in the UK: broken into modules, employers select those modules most relevant to their own needs, rather than to the longer-term needs of the trainee.

- Few UK employers are in a position to run quality three or four-year apprenticeships; but these would be needed across the board in public and private sectors, and in industry and services.

- If young people were to move into employer-based apprenticeships at sixteen, it would *de facto* close them off from higher education.

- Equally, by dividing the population at sixteen, the opportunity to reduce class distinctions would not be taken.

How, then, should sixteen-to-twenty ET evolve in the future? We believe a system very roughly along Danish lines is the most feasible model to aim for, given the current UK position.

1. *A common educational institution from sixteen to eighteen.* Apart from the Germanic countries, the US and Scandinavia, as well as Japan (more or less), have a common institution from sixteen to eighteen. France and Denmark have both been moving towards it as a matter of conscious choice. It is an obvious vehicle for encouraging a rising percentage of young people to go on to higher education at eighteen. Equally, it has a necessary part to play in reducing class differences.

2. *Accelerated apprenticeships post-eighteen: the bridge to employ-ment.* The Germanic and Scandinavian systems, and Japan and South Korea, provide at least four years of ET post-sixteen. This could be done in the UK by short, highly structured apprenticeships, which would at the same time build clear bridges to employment. If further training was carried out mainly in vocational schools post-eighteen, this bridging perception would be less clear; of course, vocational schools would be important post-eighteen, since UK companies would require considerable help if they were to provide high-quality training. The next section discusses how companies could develop high-quality training capacities: it is evident that if they can the benefits would go beyond sixteen-to-twenty ET; the need for companies in both public and private sectors to develop effective training capacities is central to the management of change.

3. *Linking post-eighteen apprenticeships with pre-eighteen ET.* In

order for two-year apprenticeships to be of high quality, considerable preparatory work towards them will need to have been completed pre-eighteen. It is also important to make clear to students the link between what is expected from them in the sixteen-to-eighteen period and their subsequent training opportunities. Preparatory work covers both general and vocational education. The role of a good general education, covering technical subjects and the humanities, has already been stressed, as has the parallel need for vocational education to include the acquisition of broad skills including communications and decision-making competences, with emphasis on developing individual initiative and team-work through projects. Vocational education will also be focused in part on the chosen apprenticeship area. Thus, for those who choose it at sixteen, there will be a 'vocational' route, with specific and general requirements for particular apprenticeship areas.

4. *Modules and certification*. Vocational qualifications would be awarded and HE entrance requirements satisfied by successfully completed modules. In the case of HE the modules would all be taken in the common institution; it would be natural to think of AS-levels as module-based (the original intention), and that the major part of the most common route to satisfying HE entrance requirements would consist in completing the modules needed to gain so many AS-levels. To gain a vocational qualification, and to fulfil the condition for entry to an apprenticeship, a substantial proportion of the necessary modules could and should be completed pre-eighteen. A modular system in a single institution provides considerable flexibility. Most students would choose early on a vocational or an HE route; but if some proportion of AS modules were allowed for vocational qualification purposes and some proportion of vocational modules for entry into HE, those students who wished to do so could keep their options open for longer. Modules could also be used to broaden HE entry requirements, and to increase the general education component in vocational qualification. There might in addition be a case for a college graduation diploma, as in many countries, based on successful completion of modules.

5. *Employer coordination and involvement*. A high degree of employer coordination and involvement will be needed to make this system work. That is the positive lesson of Northern Europe. Local coordination is necessary to link 'training' employers with educational institutions and with students. At a regional and national level, employer involvement is needed to help develop curricula, monitoring of 'trainers', assessment procedures, and so on. This will

require more powerful employer organizations, nationally, sec-
torally and locally than the UK has now. How this might be achieved
is further discussed below.

6. *Role of unions.* Many 'training' employers, especially in the public
   sector, are unionized, so that union cooperation will be needed.
   Union involvement in curriculum developments and the like will
   also be important in balancing the power of employer organizations.
   This again is a lesson from the experience of Sweden and Germany.

7. *Local and national government.* Government has played a key
   role in providing a coherent framework for the sixteen-to-twenty ET
   system at local, regional and national level in each of the countries
   discussed, with the exception of the US. The UK lacks institutional
   coherence in this area, and has only a limited research and policy-
   making capacity.

8. *Education maintenance allowance and financial incentives.* A
   central purpose of the reform strategy suggested above has been to
   construct a clear bridge from education to employment so that
   young people stay within a well-structured ET system from the age
   of sixteen to nineteen or twenty. This is in line with the instrumental
   view of education taken by most young people who leave at sixteen
   (Brown, 1973). But to be successful in raising the sixteen-plus
   participation rate, it is also necessary to ensure that leaving at
   sixteen is less attractive than staying on. This will require, first, an
   education maintenance allowance for those who stay on, at least
   equal to state payments for those who leave. More fundamentally, it
   raises the question of reducing employer incentives to hire sixteen-
   year-olds, and convincing them to stop seeing the sixteen-plus age
   group as its main recruiting ground for unskilled and semi-skilled
   labour (Ashton and Maguire, 1988). This is discussed in the next
   section.

☐   **Developing the training capacity of employers**

International comparisons suggest that UK employers devote a smaller
share of value added to training expenditures than any other major
advanced country. For radical reform to be successful, the attitude of
employers will have to change, as has been seen in the discussion in the last
section of post-sixteen ET and restructuring: specifically, the development
by employers of a training capacity is necessary for a system of accelerated

apprenticeships. In addition to sixteen-to-twenty ET, a training capacity is needed for restructuring within organizations for training and retraining existing employees.

In looking at restructuring, it is useful to distinguish between retraining by the existing employer, which will be referred to as internal retraining, and retraining elsewhere, primarily in state/union/employer-organization or private vocational training centres. This will be referred to as external retraining and will be discussed below. Roughly, the internal/external retraining distinction corresponds to that between internal (e.g. changing product composition within a company) and external (e.g. closures/running down an industry) restructuring.

With internal restructuring, companies meet declining demand by product innovation. In countries where product innovation strategies are emphasized they are associated with reliable sources of long-term finance, and long-term relations with suppliers, which the company does not wish to disrupt. More important, they are associated with internal training capacities in companies, a retrainable workforce with on-the-job flexibility and a high perceived cost to making workers redundant (Streeck *et al.*, 1985; Sorge and Streeck, 1988; Hotz-Hart, 1988). The high perceived cost may arise from legal requirements, as in Germany, or collective bargaining power, as in Sweden, or from a basic communitarian view of the enterprise, as in Japan (Dore, 1987). Cost reduction strategies under these circumstances will tend to focus on reducing capital or material or financing costs, rather than labour saving changes. Again, retraining capacities are critical.

In the UK much more use has been made of external restructuring. This reflects the lack of the characteristics described in the last paragraph as associated with internal restructuring in countries such as Germany, Japan and Sweden. Instead, the UK is characterized by:

- The organization of production around relatively standardized goods and services, with low skill requirements and cost-cutting rather than technically competent management; aggravated by
  - the public goods problem, and
  - the pressure of financial institutions and, in the public sector, cash limits against long-term investment activity.
- The lack of pressure from employees to maintain training; and the ease with which companies can make workers redundant without being required to consider product innovation and retraining as alternative ways of maintaining employment.
- The lack of an effective infrastructure. Few sectors of the economy have well developed training structures, with worked out systems of certification, training schools, and information and counselling for companies. Employer organizations are weak, and unions are

seldom equipped to provide good training services to their members.

The difficulties involved in increasing company expenditure on training and ensuring it is of the right quality are thus substantial. In a longish-term perspective, two general points may be made:

- The increase in the educational level of young people entering the labour force and a different attitude to adult education and training will make it easier for companies to move to a higher skills equilibrium.

- Policies to change company behaviour on training should be one part of a coordinated strategy to help companies focus on marketing, product innovation, new technology, high-quality production, and provision of long-term finance. Education and training policies should be closely linked to industrial and regional policies; but to trace out these links would be beyond the scope of this paper. Four main policy directions are set out here: how they might be financed, where not implicit, is discussed below.

1. *Financial incentives.*   There is little question that companies in both public and private sectors need financial incentives (positive or negative) if they are significantly to increase their training activities. This is because, for the foreseeable future, there will be a divergence between private and public returns because of the public-good problem and the low-skills equilibrium. (The general strategy advocated in this paper is designed to reduce the divergence over time, but specific incentives will be necessary until then.)

   The form of the incentives is critical. A minimum legal requirement is unlikely to be productive, at least by itself. It might take one of two forms: a requirement to spend a certain minimum percentage of value added or payroll on training, and/or a requirement to carry out certain types of training, e.g. to take so many apprentices, with a significant enough penalty to gain compliance. One problem with both approaches is that some companies may be better placed to carry out effective training than others. In addition, the minimum percentage approach (by itself) says nothing about who gets trained: in France this approach led to senior managers being sent to expensive hotels in the French Pacific to learn English. And the 'minimum number of apprentices' approach poses formidable quality problems.

   A sensible approach, at least to start with, is to give financial incentives to companies (private and public) who are prepared to train and undergo the monitoring and other conditions necessary to

ensure both quality and coverage (i.e. that training covers apprenticeships and semi-skilled workers as well as managers, etc.). The
further conditions are discussed in the next paragraph. These
incentives would not need to be uniform across industries, regions or
types of training.

2. *Meisters and certification.* How are we to ensure that companies
   train to the right quality and over the desired coverage? In Japan,
   Germany and similar countries, the role of the supervisor in both
   industry and services is different to the UK supervisor (see e.g. Prais
   and Wagner, 1988). In those countries, supervisors (in German,
   meister) are technically skilled as well as playing a management
   role; moreover they have major responsibility for training. In the
   German system, they have themselves to pass a rigorous training
   after having gained a technician or craft-level qualification. The
   above suggests ideas along the following lines:

   • A distinction should be drawn between certified skills and
     non-certified skills. This would be similar to the distinction
     between marketable and firm-specific skills. In practical terms
     it would reflect those that the NCVQ included as certifiable.

   • Companies wishing to participate in the training of employees
     for certified skills would be required to employ certified
     'training supervisors', i.e. similar to German *meisters*.

   • The Government could then negotiate with employer or-
     ganizations tariffs for different certified skills, and use this as
     one means of influencing the size and distribution of training.
     Those companies would then get automatic payments for
     certified training, subject to periodic inspections and subject
     to satisfactory results of trainees in external assessment.

   In summary, financial incentives should be used, not just to produce
   a desired amount of training, but also to ensure that companies
   acquire a training capacity and supervisory staff with a professional
   commitment to training.

3. *Changing the age structure of hiring.* Specific disincentives will be
   needed to dissuade businesses from hiring sixteen-to-eighteen year
   olds over the next decade.

4. *Employee representation.* Again, as in Northern Europe, it is
   sensible to give employees a role in decision-making on training
   within companies. They have an interest in the acquisition of

certified skills. For this role to be effective, decisions on training would need to be codetermined between management and employees. In addition, continental experience suggests that employee representatives need union expertise if they are to challenge low-spending management with any chance of success.

In particular, it is important to enable employees to challenge management decisions on redundancies. In the German model, management is required to reach an agreement with the works council on how redundancies are to be dealt with. The cost to management of not reaching an agreement means that managers emphasize innovation and retraining in their long-term planning.

5. *External infrastructure.* Both (2) and (3) impose strong demands on an external infrastructure. Companies will in practice rely heavily on the advice of employer organizations, whom they can trust at least to give advice in the interest of the sector they represent, if not in the interest of the individual company. Employees need the advice of unions if they are to challenge company decisions on training and redundancies. Public or tripartite bodies will be required to provide research and development on training technology and labour market developments (e.g. skill shortages); to run a system of certification; and to provide training where it is needed to complement company training. How this can be done is discussed on page 251.

☐   A culture of lifetime education and training

There is an apparent lack of interest by adults in the UK in continuing education and training. In countries with good training systems, a strong belief by individuals in the benefits of ET reinforces the system: parents can see the value of education and training for their children; employees put pressure on laggardly employers to provide training; the public-good problem which companies face is reduced by individuals paying for the acquisition of marketable skills. Yet in the UK little adult training takes place which is not paid for by the employer; this is in particular the case for unskilled and semi-skilled employees and for the unemployed. Why is human capital theory wrong in asserting that individuals will be prepared to pay for the acquisition of marketable skills? Why, especially, is this the case when vacancies for skilled jobs coexist with high unemployment and insecure semi-skilled employment?

In the first place, individuals seldom have access to financial resources sufficient to finance any extended period of vocational training:

- Borrowing: financial institutions are reticent about lending without security for training, except for a few cases where returns from the training are high. This is not particular to UK financial institutions. Banks in most countries will not lend for ET purposes to individuals, unless the loans are guaranteed or subsidized or unless the bank has close connections and knowledge of a community. This probably reflects both moral hazard and adverse selection problems.

- There is limited access to state subsidy for most adult vocational training, particularly for maintenance, but also for tuition. Individual expenditure on training is in general not tax deductible. The unemployed likewise have limited access to funds: their retraining possibilities seldom relate to those areas in which there are vacancies.

- Major reductions in income are seldom feasible for those who are employed, *a fortiori* for those who are unemployed.

Secondly, the individual return from much vocational training is not high. There are several reasons for this:

- The low-skills equilibrium organization of work means that the marginal productivity of skills for individual workers is below what it would be in an economy where a large enough proportion of the workforce was skilled to permit a high-skills pattern of work organization.

- For a large proportion of the workforce (manual and low-level white-collar) there reflects the organization of work discussed. Second, differentials for skilled workers were heavily compressed in the 1970s, and though they have widened since, they are still not high in comparison to high-skill countries.

- A large proportion of the workforce does not have the basic education required to proceed to craft-level vocational training; so a major prior investment is necessary.

- The existing system of certification is unhelpful, as the NCVQ has emphasized. Apart from being confusing, it fails to give employers real guarantees in many areas as to the competences of the certified employee, because of the lack of proper assessment procedures. In addition, and more important, portability is limited. In the modern economy, skills obsolesce. The acquisition of new skills should not involve returning to square one, as it frequently does today.

- Finally, for those who are currently employed, and wish independently to take leave to pursue education or training, there is seldom a guarantee that they will be able to keep their job.

This means that major self-financed training or retraining is not seen as a realistic possibility, if it is considered at all, by most unskilled or semi-skilled workers or those who are unemployed. Moreover, with the exceptions of a few unions who provide good counselling services, little advice is available.

1. *A comprehensive external training system.* Those who seek, or might be persuaded to seek, external training fall into two categories with some overlapping: people with clear goals and courses in mind, adequate previous education and training, but held back by unavailability of finance or employment insecurity; and the un-skilled, semi-skilled and unemployed with little belief in the possibility of effective retraining. For both groups adequate financing is necessary. There is a strong case for formalizing a system of education credits for adults. These credits would be intended for training not covered by companies. The general question of financing is considered below, but it should be noted here that if individuals had their own 'training accounts', into which education credits were put, these credits could be added to by saving, perhaps topped-up by public funding. For most people in the second group, additional financing will be necessary, since it will not be reasonable to expect them to save enough. It is of great importance that those threatened by redundancy or made redundant are given sufficient resources for long periods of ET. Along Swedish lines, a reasonable income might be conditioned on what is in effect a contract to train for a given range of skills in which there are vacancies or in which employment is likely.

   For this group, much more is required than financing. Also needed are counselling, an information system covering vacancies and future areas of demand, structured basic education if necessary, training and retraining facilities (though they might be in the private sector and hired by the state), and a support system to facilitate mobility if needed. How an external retraining system might be set up is discussed in the next section.

2. *Returns to skills.* This is an important problem to which there are few easy solutions. We argued above for policies to encourage the development of a supervisory grade with technical qualifications: if successful, that would help the concept of a career ladder based on skills. It is harder for the government to intervene in the process of wage determination, and widen skill differentials even if there is a case for doing so. In our view, the more sensible approach is to give incentives to employers to increase training, on the one hand, and to develop an external training policy to help redundant and poten-tially redundant workers, who have less need of incentives to acquire skills, on the other.

□   Institutional infrastructure

Radical reform of ET requires a more effective institutional infrastructure than presently exists. Our view is that radical reform is not a simple political option, but one requiring major institutional changes which will be difficult to bring about in the UK, at least if reform is to realize its full potential. This returns the argument to those economic historians who maintain that our basic economic problems lie in our institutions.

It was argued above that the old constraining infrastructure has broken down; and that the Government has substituted increased centralized control via the MSC (as was) and the DES, combined with the use of contracts with training agencies. The centralization of policy-making has not been accompanied by a significant expansion of the very limited research and information-gathering capacities of the MSC and the DES. A parallel can be drawn between this system and large conglomerates controlled by a small financially-oriented headquarters. The new system will become more pronounced as:

1. Local education authorities have a diminished role in post-sixteen ET, with the removal of polytechnics and the larger CFEs from their control, with the decline in importance of TVEI, and with the possible opting out of secondary schools;

2. The wide variety of course development, assessment and accreditation bodies are encouraged to behave more competitively;

3. The NCVQ becomes more a body carrying out government instructions, especially in relation to certification of YTS trainees, than a forum in which different points of view, of the business community, of unions and of educationalists and trainers can be expressed.

The new system is hardly adequate for dealing with YTS and ATS (Adult Training Strategy); it has major drawbacks if it is to carry through radical reform. We will argue that a different system needs to be developed in which employers' organizations, unions, educationalists and the regions should all ideally play a more important part; and in which the role of government should be more concerned with the provision of information, research and development, and coordination, than with unilateral policy-making.

1. *The need for better information, R & D, and coordination.* The reforms discussed above involve major course developments: for sixteen-to-eighteen year olds; for accelerated apprenticeships; for those at work; for *meisters*; for those undertaking external retraining; together with development of assessment procedures, certification and accreditation of examining bodies. It will be

necessary to coordinate academic examining boards with vocational training institutions such as BTEC (Business Technician Education Council); and to coordinate the activities of the vocational institutions themselves. Also, it is important to allow experimentation and thus course development by individual teachers or trainers, and a mechanism is needed to permit the diffusion of best-practice innovations. All this demands a much greater role of government in the R & D and coordination process. This might perhaps be on the lines of the regional labour market and regional education boards in Sweden.

For two broad reasons, a more effective ET system also requires involvement by the social partners (employers' organizations and unions) as well as educational institutions and the Government. The first is to ensure that policy-making is conducted in a balanced way, (2) below). The second is to bring about the participation of companies (3), and employees (4).

2. *Multilateral participation in ET governance.* Running a complex ET system is a principal–agent problem. However clear the ideas of the Government (the principal) and however effective its own research and development activities, the cooperation of teachers and trainers as agents is essential to efficient course development, assessment, etc. But educators will have their own interests. (Japan is a case in point, where educationalists dominate the development of sixteen-to-eighteen education, business has no influence, and where rote learning still plays a major role.) A tempting solution is for governments to use expert civil servants as additional agents; of course, it is important that government experts should be involved, but there is a danger: if detailed policy-making is left to government experts and educationalists, the former may assimilate over time the goals of the latter, particularly if governments change.

A more effective solution is to balance the interests of educators against the interests of employers and those of employees. Hence the case for involving their representatives as additional agents, to bring about more balanced objectives. If this is to be successful, both employers' organizations and unions need expertise; here again Northern European experience, where the social partners have their own research institutions, in some cases financed by the state, is suggestive. Moreover, as employers' organizations and unions acquire expertise, so a common culture of understanding and agreement on a range of training issues gets built up by professionals on all sides. Thus the agents, with their different interests but shared culture, become players in a cooperative game over time in which compromise and flexibility are available to meet changing conditions. (For a broader use of this type of approach, see the insightful Lange, 1987.)

A similar case can be made for involving representatives of regions in addition to central government. For individual regions will have their own economic goals, and more political stability than central government. Again, effective involvement requires expertise. This reinforces the argument for regional labour market and regional education boards.

3. *Employers' organizations and the participation of companies.* Most companies see no gain in participating in training in marketable skills and associated activities to a socially optimal degree. This is both because of the standard prisoner's dilemma problem and the low-skills equilibrium. As a partial solution to both problems we suggested the use of financial incentives to encourage the building up of a training capacity within companies. Important though that is by itself, its effectiveness can be greatly enhanced through employers' organizations. First, getting companies to train in the right way is difficult for government, because of an asymmetry of information: the company knows much more about how good its training is than the Government. Companies are often loath to be monitored by, or give detailed information to, government, because they distrust the use to which the information will be put. Employers' organizations are in a better position to engage the cooperation of companies, because they are seen to be on the side of companies as a whole. Secondly, powerful employers' organizations, as in Germany, can sanction free-riders more cheaply than the Government. This is the case where employers' organizations distribute a range of valued services to companies, not necessarily just in the training area, and have a degree of discretion over their distribution. One of these services may be training advice; others might be in, say, export marketing. This gives the organization potential sanctions, which might enable it, for instance, to organize local coordination of companies with respect to the bridge between education and employment; or to prod companies into increasing training activities.

4. *Employees and unions.* Unions have several important roles to play in an effective ET system, as mentioned above. Here we want to stress the role of unions in promoting employee involvement in training decision-making. Such involvement is a critical component of high-skill economies. If it is to be effective, employees must be properly backed up by union advice and expertise.

Much of the argument of this sub-section is influenced by the study of why the Scandinavian and Germanic ET systems have been successful. There is an important research agenda here for the UK. We do not want to suggest that the type of powerful employers' organizations or union confederations as in those countries, or regional government as in Germany is transplantable; it is not. But there is a strong case for giving muscle to employers' organizations and unions, and to regions and perhaps metropolitan areas, in the training field. Unions are moving in the UK (some much faster than others) to consider training as a core area of their interests. Business organizations are moving less fast, but in the right direction. Radical reform of ET will need a push by government. One possibility, for a radical reforming government, is to give the social partners the resources to develop major expertise in training. A second is to consider whether chambers of commerce can play a more significant role at local level, so as to enable them to develop local employer networks. Third, to consider the possibilities of regional labour market and regional education boards as quadripartite institutions, with educationalists and regional representatives as well as the social partners.

☐   **Macroeconomic and financing implications**

The preceding four sub-sections have looked at the micro aspects of policies needed for transforming the post-sixteen education and training system. They have suggested how to change incentives facing individuals and organizations; how coordinating and providing institutions could be built up; and how training policies should be seen as part of a broader microeconomic strategy directed at changing ways in which companies operate. If successful, these changes carry great benefits in terms of macro-economic performance. But to be successful they require a major injection of resources.

In a steady state, the benefits can be assumed to outweigh the resource cost. But in the process of transforming the system, resource costs would be likely to precede the benefits of additional resources. There is not the space in this article to discuss in detail the financing of this gap. But we want to make some brief points to indicate why we believe that increased expenditures in this area can be more easily managed than in many others.

The increased resources devoted to ET can be met in one or more of three ways:

- an increase in GDP;
- a reduction in other expenditures;
- an increase in imports.

There are two reasons why some part of the resource cost can be met by reduction in other expenditures. First, specific forms of taxation or quasi-taxation can be exploited with minimal economic damage.

- A training levy on companies who do not undertake certified training. It will be difficult for these companies to pass on the levy in the form of higher prices if some competitors are undertaking certified training and hence not paying the levy. And since most of the non-training companies are likely to be in the sheltered sector of the economy, any reduction in their activity levels as a result of the levy will have the beneficial effect of transferring business to training competitors.

- Individual training accounts. If individuals choose to contribute to an individual training account, it will come from a voluntary reduction in consumers' expenditure.

Second, other government expenditures will be reduced:

- Reduction in government expenditures on YTS and other MSC-related activities which would be phased out as a new system of sixteen-to-twenty ET developed.

- Reduction in government expenditures on education and training post-sixteen as a result of demographic decline.

Thus some part of the necessary resources can be met from reduced expenditure elsewhere but without relying on an increase in general taxation. The damage caused by the latter is not only political, but also, via its inflationary potential, economic. But there are limits beyond which it may be unwise or impossible to push these reductions.

This means that the resources to finance a training programme will have to come in part from increased GDP and increased imports. The point to be made here is that the standard problems associated with an expansionary policy can be more easily handled within the context of a training programme than in other cases.

The first problem is that of inflation caused by the increased bargaining power of employees as employment rises. Appropriate increases in the skilled workforce can reduce inflationary pressures in two ways. Directly, it reduces skilled labour bottlenecks and the power of 'insiders' relative to outsiders. Indirectly, it facilitates wage restraint, especially if unions are involved in the training institutions.

The second problem is financing the external deficit and the public sector deficit, at least without a fall in the exchange rate or a rise in the interest rate. Avoiding these consequences requires that inflation does not increase; and that the increase in the Public Sector Borrowing Requirement (PSBR) and the external deficit are seen as eventually self-correcting. The last paragraph was concerned with inflation. A training programme can, more easily than most programmes involving increased government expenditure, be credibly seen as self-correcting in its effect on the PSBR and the external deficit.

■ Concluding remarks

The UK has long suffered from a low-skills equilibrium in which the ET system has delivered badly educated and minimally trained sixteen-year-old school-leavers to an economy which has been geared to operate – albeit today more efficiently – with a relatively unskilled labour force. Some companies have broken out of this equilibrium with the aid of strategic managers, to see training and innovation as core activities. Most have not.

Despite the much-vaunted reforms of the ET system of the last few years, major improvements are unlikely to be brought about:

- The majority of children will still leave school at sixteen, and will gain a low-level training in YTS; referring to the certification of YTS by the NCVQ, Jarvis and Prais argued that it would lead to 'a certificated semi-literate under-class – a section of the workforce inhibited in job-flexibility, and inhibited in the possibility of progression' (1988).

- There are no substantive policies to remedy the vacuum in training in most companies.

- There are no measures to undertake the depth education and training frequently needed in a rapidly restructuring world economy to enable those made redundant to acquire relevant skills.

We have argued the case in the last section for: full-time education to eighteen, with 'accelerated' apprenticeships thereafter, for those not going on to higher education; building up training capacities within companies; and an external retraining system to deal with restructuring between companies and industries.

Instead of summarizing these proposals, we want to underline certain points which have not always been adequately brought out in discussions of reform:

- It is important to think in terms of the incentives which face individuals, rather than make the mistake of some educators of just talking about institutions or educational innovations. But equally the economist's mistake, of treating of incentives as only financial, must be avoided. We lay stress on the idea of enabling individuals to see career progressions: thus importance is attached to the bridge from education to employment for sixteen to twenty-year-olds.

- Companies should be seen not as profit-maximizing black boxes, but as coalitions of interests, particularly among managers. We argue that, rather than incentives being used to increase the amount of training as such, they can more effectively be used if they increase a company's training capacity, by giving companies an incentive to train or hire *meisters*, or training supervisors. This produces a stake in training as a company activity.

- Along similar lines, employees should be given a role in training decision-making within the company. Here, there are lessons to be learned from industrial democracy procedures in Germany and Sweden. This reinforces the idea of groups within the company with a stake in training.

- More generally, the problem of moving companies from a low-skill to a high-skill equilibrium involves much more than training and education. It requires changes in management style, R & D, financing, marketing, etc., so training policy should be seen as part of a wider industrial strategy.

- Countries with successful ET systems devote substantial resources to research on education and training and labour-market developments. In the UK today policy-making has become highly centralized but based on limited information and research.

- Successful countries also place great reliance on employers' organizations and unions. In the UK their role in the governance of training has been progressively reduced. If radical reform is to be successful, it will be important to build up the expertise and involvement of the social partners.

To conclude, the UK is becoming isolated among advanced industrialized countries. They have either attained or are targeting a far higher level of generalized education and training than is being considered here. This should be worrying enough in itself. What makes it more so, is the progress made by other countries with substantially lower labour costs: South Korea currently has 85 per cent in full-time education to the age of seventeen or eighteen, and over 30 per cent in higher education (*Financial Times*, 30 June 1988).

Acknowledgements

The authors would like to thank Kay Andrews, Geoffrey Garrett, Ken Mayhew, Derek Morris, John Muellbauer and Len Schoppa for helpful comments; and to acknowledge intellectual indebtedness to Chris Hayes and Professor S. Prais.

Research on comparative aspects of training was financed in part by a grant to D. Soskice from the ESRC Corporatist and Accountability Research Programme.

Notes

1.   'Equilibrium' is not meant to imply that all British firms produce low-quality products or services, or that all individuals are poorly educated and trained. A number of companies (often foreign-owned multinational corporations) have succeeded in recruiting the educational élite and offering good training programmes.
2.   An excellent discussion of the differences in each of these dimensions between British and German companies is contained in Lane (1988).
3.   These initials stand for: General Certificate of Secondary Education (GCSE), Oxford Examination Syndicate (OES), the New Learning Initiative (NLI) – part of the Low-Attaining Pupils Programme (LAP) – Oxford Certificate of Educational Achievement (OECA) – part of the Record of Achievement Initiative – and, of course, Technical and Vocational Education Initiative (TVEI).

References

Anderson, A. (1987), 'Adult training: private industry and the Nicholson letter', in *Education and Training UK 1987*, Harrison, A. and Gretton, J. (eds), *Policy Journals*, pp. 67–73.
Ashton, D. N. and Maguire, M. J. (1988). 'Local labour markets and the impact on the life chances of youths' in Coles, R. (ed) *Young Careers*, Milton Keynes, Open University Press.
Brady, T. (1984), *New Technology and Skills in British Industry*, Science Policy Research Unit.
Brown, P. (1987). 'Schooling for inequality: ordinary kids in school and the labour market' in Brown, P. and Ashton, D. N. (eds) *Education, Unemployment and Labour Markets*, London, Falmer.
Business Week (1988), 'How the new math of productivity adds up', pp. 49–55, June 6.
Callaghan, J. (1976), Ruskin College Speech, *Times Educational Supplement*, 22 October, p. 72.
Centre for Contemporary Cultural Studies (1981), *Unpopular Education*, London, Hutchinson.
Chapman, P. and Tooze, M. (1987), *The Youth Training Scheme in the UK*, Aldershot, Avebury.
Clegg, H. (1972), *The System of Industrial Relations in Great Britain*, Oxford, Basil Blackwell.
Clement, B. (1986), 'Industry threatened over training lapses', *Independent*, p. 3, 29 November.

Coopers and Lybrand Associates (1985), *A Challenge to Complacency: Changing Attitudes to Training*, MSC/NEDO, Moorfoot, Sheffield.

Crowther Commission (1959), *15 to 18, Report to the DES*, HMSO.

Dale, R. (1983a), 'The politics of education in England 1970–1983: state, capital and civil society', Open University, unpublished.

—— (1983b), 'Thatcherism and education', in Ahier, J. and Flude, M. (eds), *Contemporary Education Policy*, London, Croom Helm.

—— (1985), 'The background and inception of TVEI', in Dale, R. (ed.), *Education, Training and Employment*, Milton Keynes, Open University.

—— (forthcoming), TVEI: From National Guidelines to Local Practice.

Daly, A. (1984), 'Education, training and productivity in the US and Great Britain', *NIESR*, no. 63, London.

Deakin, B. M. and Pratten, C. F. (1987), 'Economic effects of YTS', *Department of Employment Gazette*, 95, 491–7.

Department of Education and Science (1987), Education Reform Bill, 20 November.

—— (1988), *Tax Concessions for Training*, HMSO, May.

Department of Employment (1984), *Training for Employment*, HMSO, February.

Department of Education and Department of Education and Science, *Training for Jobs*, HMSO, January.

De Ville, H. G. *et al.* (1986), *Review of Vocational Qualifications in England and Wales*, report to MSC and DES, April.

Donovan, Lord (1968), *Royal Commission on Trade Unions and Employers' Associations 1965–1968*, HMSO, London.

Dore, R. (1987), *Taking Japan Seriously*, London, Athlone Press.

Fenwick, I. G. K. (1976), *The Comprehensive School 1944–1970*, London, Methuen.

Gapper, J. (1988), '£500,000 scheme to boost training in tourist sector', *Financial Times*, 17 March.

George, K. D. and Shorey, J. (1985), 'Manual workers, good jobs and structured internal labour markets', *British Journal of Industrial Relations*, 23:3, pp. 425–47, November.

Giddens, A. (1979), 'An anatomy of the British ruling class', *New Society*, 4 October, pp. 8–10.

Gow, D. (1988a), 'Teaching Shortage Catastrophe Feared', *Guardian*, p. 4, 16 June.

—— (1988b), 'Fury at A-Level Rejection', *Guardian*, p. 1, 8 June.

—— and Travis, A. (1988), 'Leak exposes Thatcher rift with Baker', *Guardian*, p. 1, 10 March.

Greenhalgh, C. (1988), *Employment and Structural Change: Trends and Policy Options*, mimeo, Oxford.

Hall, P. (1986), *Governing the Economy*, Oxford, Polity Press.

Harland, J. (1987), 'The TVEI experience', in Gleeson, D. (ed.), *TVEI and Secondary Education*, Milton Keynes, Open University.

Hotz-Hart, B. (1988), 'Comparative research and new technology: modernisation in three industrial relations systems', in Hyman, R. and Streeck, W. (eds), *New Technology and Industrial Relations*, Oxford, Blackwells.

Howell, D. A. (1980), 'The Department of Education and Science: its critics and defenders', *Educational Administration*, 9, pp. 108–33.

Independent (1986), 'Managers "a Decade Out of Date" ', 11 December.

Jackson, M. (1988), 'More leavers shun youth training scheme', *Times Educational Supplement*, 19 February, p. 13.

Jennings, R. E. (1977), *Education and Politics: Policy-Making in Local Education Authorities*, London, Batsford.

Jones, I. (1988), 'An evaluation of YTS', *Oxford Review of Economic Policy*, 4 (3), 54–71.

Keep, E. (1986), *Designing the Stable Door: A Study of how the Youth Training Scheme was Planned*, Warwick Papers in Industrial Relations no. 8, Coventry.

—— (1987), *Britain's Attempts to Create a National Vocational Educational and Training System: A Review of Progress*, Warwick Papers in Industrial Relations no. 16, Coventry.

Lane, C. (1988), 'Industrial change in Europe: the pursuit of flexible specialisation', *Work, Employment and Society*, 2, 2, 141–68.

Lange, P. (1987), *The Institutionalisation of Concertation, International Political Economy*, WP no. 26, Duke University.

Leadbeater, C. (1987), 'MSC criticises standard of youth training', *Financial Times*, 13 May, p. 1.

Lynn, R. (1988), *Educational Achievement in Japan*, Basingstoke, Macmillan.

MSC (1981), *A New Training Initiative, a Consultative Document*, HMSO, May.

—— (1986), *Skills Monitoring Report*, MSC Evaluation and Research Unit, Sheffield.

Maurice, M., Sellier, F. and Silvestre, J. J. (1986), *The Social Foundations of Industrial Power: A Comparison of France and West Germany*, Cambridge, MIT Press.

Mayer, C. (1987), 'The assessment: financial systems and corporate investment', *Oxford Review of Economic Policy*, Winter.

Mayhew, K. (1986), 'Reforming the labour market', *Oxford Review of Economic Policy*, Summer.

McArthur, A. and McGregor, A. (1986), 'Training and economic development: national versus local perspectives', *Political Quarterly*, 57: 3, July–September, pp. 246–55.

McCulloch, G. *et al.* (1985), *Technological Revolution? The Politics of School Science and Technology in England and Wales since 1945*, London, Falmer.

Macfarlane, N. (1980), 'Education for 16–19 year olds', report to the DES and Local Authority Associations, HMSO, December.

Moon, J. and Richardson, J. (1985), *Unemployment in the UK*, Aldershot, Gower.

Morton, K. (1980), *The Education Services of the TGWU*, Oxford University, Ruskin College Project Report.

—— (1978), *Engineering Craftsmen: Shortages and Related Problems*, London, NEDO.

National Economic Development Office (1984), *Competence and Competition: Training in the Federal Republic of Germany, the United States and Japan*, London, NEDO/MSC.

New, C. and Myers, A. (1986), *Managing Manufacturing Operations in the UK, 1975–85*, Institute of Manpower Studies.

Nicholson, B. (1986), press conference at People and Technology Conference, London, November.

OECD (1975), *Educational Development Strategy in England and Wales*, Paris.

—— (1985), *Education and Training After Basic Schooling*, Paris.

Page, G. (1967), *The Industrial Training Act and After*, London, Andre Deutsch.

Perry, P. J. C. (1976), *The Evolution of British Manpower Policy*, London, BACIE.

Postlethwaite, N. (1988). 'English last in science', *Guardian*, 1 March.

Prais, S. J. and Wagner, K. (1983), 'Schooling standards in Britain and Germany', London, NIESR Discussion Paper no. 60.

Raffe, D. (1984), *Fourteen to Eighteen*, Aberdeen University Press.

Rajan, A. and Pearson, R. (eds) (1986), *UK Occupational and Employment Trends*, IMS, London, Butterworths.

Ranson, S. (1985), 'Contradictions in the government of educational change', *Political Studies*, 33: 1, pp. 56–72.

Reich, R. (1983), *The Next American Frontier*, Middlesex, Penguin.

Reid, G. L. (1980), 'The research needs of British policy-makers', in McIntosh, A. (ed.), *Employment Policy in the UK and the US*, London, John Martin.

Riddell, P. (1983), *The Thatcher Government*, Oxford, Martin Robertson.

Salter, B. and Tapper, T. (1981), *Education, Politics and the State*, London, Grant McIntyre.

Scarbrough, H. (1986), 'The politics of technological change at BL', in Jacobi, O. *et al.* (eds), *Economic Crisis, Trade Unions and the State*, London, Croom Helm.

Sorge, A. and Streeck, W. (1988), 'Industrial relations and technological change', in Hyman, R. and Streeck, W. (eds), *New Technology and Industrial Relations*, Oxford, Blackwells.

Steedman, H. (1986), 'Vocational training in France and Britain: the construction industry', *NI Economic Review*, May.

—— and Wagner, K. (1987), 'A second look at productivity, machinery and skills in Britain and Germany', *NI Economic Review*, November.

Streeck, W. (1985), 'Industrial change and industrial relations in the motor industry: An international overview', Lecture at University of Warwick, 23 October.

—— *et al.* (1985), 'Industrial relations and technical change in the British, Italian and German automobile industry', IIM discussion paper 85–5, Berlin.

Taylor, R. (1980), *The Fifth Estate*, London, Pan.

Tipton, B. (1982), 'The quality of training and the design of work', *Industrial Relations Journal*, pp. 27–42, Spring.

Wiener, M. (1981), *English Culture and the Decline of the Industrial Spirit*, Cambridge, Cambridge University Press.

Wilensky, H. and Turner, L. (1987), *Democratic Corporatism and Policy Linkages*, Berkeley, Institute of International Studies.

Woodall, J. (1985), 'European trade unions and youth unemployment', Kingston Polytechnic mimeograph, London, unpublished.

Worswick, G. D. (1985), *Education and Economic Performance*, Aldershot, Gower.

Chapter 11

The Education–Industry Mismatch

K. Corfield

■ Mismatch: unemployment yet skill shortages

There are over 3 million unemployed people in Britain today and nearly half are under the age of 25. Yet, paradoxically and tragically, many British companies are constrained in their growth by skill shortages. Studies of the manpower requirements of several industrial sectors carried out in the past five years by the National Economic Development Office and several academic bodies, as well as government, characterize the trend of skill shortages. They are especially severe in the electronics industry for professional grades, including a wide range of electronics engineers, test technicians, systems analysts, technical authors, design, development and sales engineers.

These skill shortages have both immediate and long-term impacts: for example, shortages of manpower such as systems analysts and designers amongst computer users are limiting the rate of diffusion and innovation in the application of the technology; a constraint on current (and also future) growth is thus a shortage of skilled personnel. Similarly, shortages of electronics engineers can lead to diversion from research and development effort and thus a decline in a company's long-term ability to compete through its technological edge.

Whilst, however, the studies and the statistics throw up the global problem, industrial companies experience the shortages as very specific and very immediate problems. The shortage of perhaps two or three key

Source: K. Corfield (1984) 'The education–industry mismatch', in *Trespassing? Businessmen's Views on the Education System*, D. Anderson (ed.), Social Affairs Unit, London, pp. 50–55.

engineers with specialized skills inhibits project development and leads to lost contracts. The specific nature of those skills is lost in the broad statistics and, in parallel, by the time the education system has picked up the dimensions of the problem, business has moved on. It is this mismatch between supply and demand which the education system has to overcome. The problem has been long recognized; what has not been found, however, are the practical solutions which could establish self-regulating mechanisms so that supply matches demand.

■ Specifying the educational requirements of industry

Educationists have long complained that industrialists do not specify what they expect of the education system and industrialists have equally long complained that the education system does not meet their needs. This is a further manifestation of the cultural divide in Britain, in which the mute cannot talk to the deaf, and vice versa. In the face of rapidly changing markets and technologies, industrialists cannot actually specify 'skill requirements' as, for example, they might products. Nor would they want to: industry depends upon the flexibility and creativity and spontaneity of its people. There are, however, characteristics in people which are valuable to industry and to which skill-training can be applied so as to refine and build on them.

The pace of change is demanding, at all levels in companies, the ability of employees to acquire new skills more rapidly and to be able to relate one acquired skill with another. Thus there is a need, especially in fast-growing and high-technology companies, for general extension of education and a general raising of basic standards so that new skills can be more readily acquired. On the shop floor the introduction of new machine tools, integrated manufacturing processes and new production techniques is much easier when those operating them understand what they are about: this has industrial relations implications insofar as those involved are less resistant to change, but also real productivity implications in that the operators are better skilled in their use of new equipment. On modern shop floors today there are highly qualified technicians with hardware and software skills at their fingertips. In other parts of companies, there is a need for people with technical and managerial skills complemented, for example, with languages and knowledge of government affairs because of the increasing influence throughout the world of governments on markets. This latter group may broadly be termed 'strategic managers', on whose breadth of vision as much as on their organizational and leadership capability the future of international companies increasingly depends. They have special educational requirements, but for the majority of workers today, the more extended the general level of education, the greater the flexibility of the individual.

Yet the percentage of the UK's student population which enjoys tertiary education compares poorly with that of other industrial countries. In the UK this figure is 4.5%, having risen to this level in the late 1970s from 3.3% in the mid-1960s. The figures for the European Community as a whole are 8.1% and 4.8% respectively. Those economies at the present time in which there are the lowest levels of unemployment and the fastest rates of growth are those which have invested most in their education systems and set the highest national standards. If young people are to be employable in their lifetimes, they need to be numerate, literate and naturally curious and creative, and on these bases industry can build. The existing system scarcely responds to this, not only because it is rooted in nineteenth-century concepts and values but because it continues to differentiate between education and training, physically and mentally dividing two complementary activities.

■   The divided educational response: 'education' and 'training'

Training, manifested institutionally by the Manpower Services Commission (MSC), continued to be perceived and associated with the development of a narrow range of skills to be applied to a particular job from sixteen onwards: education, manifested in the Department of Education and Science (DES) is something broader and available after the age of sixteen to a relatively small number of people. Whilst industry requires longer-term and better educated people, they are all too readily 'streamed' by the age of sixteen.

The situation is made worse because the least able, indeed anyone not aspiring to become a graduate, enter an uncharted morass in which it is difficult to identify opportunities and follow a clear-cut progression. The least able are least protected as they wallow amidst a plethora of schemes which give limited experience, maximum hope and little opportunity. By contrast, although the most able, the potential graduates, have a clear-cut route, at the end of it they are over-specialized. In particular the engineers have insufficient broadening relative to the demands which are going to be made of them. Getting this top level of graduates right is going to be as important as other reforms on the system, for it is on their leadership that the successful international development of industry will depend.

The seriousness of the situation is best illustrated by looking at our counterparts. In France, for example, those who aspire to senior management will have first to get into one of the *grandes écoles*. Entry involves a tough competitive examination which may have to be taken two or three times before students are admitted after completion of the *baccalauréate*. They will then have a minimum of three, and more likely five, years of education and training, not just in management or engineering but in diverse activities which are likely to demand experience in the public sector and overseas. Their horizons are widened whilst their experience and knowledge are deepened. It is these managers who are the measure of our own, for it is in international markets that our companies compete and we have to replicate in our own way these experiences if we are to succeed. Similarly, throughout the system, higher general levels of education are expected, and general skill levels are more systematically developed and applied. *Might we not recognize the need to fuse training, work and education by integrating the Departments of Education and Employment?*

■ More influence for industry on education

Even if the 'system' were more reflective of industrial requirements, it would still be inappropriate because it is predominantly influenced by the academic standards set by the universities. This single standard will have to be replaced with a system which demands of the individual excellence in what he or she is able to do, but is not a single universal measure. It is right that the standards demanded for university entrance should be of the highest, just as it is right that the standards required for entry into a company should be of the highest. But they are different and, whilst excellence needs to be maintained, the criteria need to be different.

Only the State can intervene decisively to correct the inefficient system the State has created. And the State, in Britain, is inhibited from intervention in the education system by traditional notions of the infringement of academic, that is teachers' and lecturers', freedom. The objectives of any intervention will be twofold. First, the State is responsible for ensuring that the standards of education are of the right level to meet both the economic and cultural aspirations of the country: the one cannot be ignored in favour of the other, for they are both concerned with the quality of life. The second objective will be to establish mechanisms which bring the education system (the 'supplier') into a one-to-one contact with those who can provide jobs (the 'users'); *this means creating an efficient market mechanism in the education system, in the place of the existing cumbersome bureaucracy*. Simplification of the education and training system in a unified form, and reform of the standards established to measure performance, would be two bold steps towards greater responsiveness to business requirements within the education system. Further reform includes changing the funding of education.

■ Multi-source funding for education

The funding system remains complex and often incomprehensible, especially for polytechnics, colleges of further education and schools. Without radical reform of this element of the system, such that the State pays for the running of schools and provides core funds for the tertiary sector on which colleges have a right to *build* by selling their services in response to 'demand', they will remain ossified and tied to a system which is essentially unresponsive. These reforms should be based on the concept of *multi-sourced funding*, such that there are a number of banks of money available to the education system, for which faculties and departments 'bid'. Providing these 'banks' cover all aspects of education, some concerned with support for fundamental research and the arts, others with more practical subjects (although they might be resourced by the State as well as the private sector), then the balance between different types of education will be struck.

Second, the education system itself is becoming circular as teachers are increasingly those who have left school, gone on to further education and then returned to the schools. Just as business expects its entrants to have broader and deeper experience, so mechanisms may have to be introduced which will delay the re-entry of trained teachers into the education system until they have reached a point in their own development where they can offer more than they have done in the past. At the root of any changes lies the capacity and willingness of individuals to respond to opportunities, and to do this requires several interconnected changes. Greater experience provides hooks on which to hang ever-broadening learning, but also a deeper sense of personal security so that an individual *knows* how to react. But even if the individual is prepared to take such risks, there are institutional barriers to be overcome. Some of the more obvious are concerned with employment conditions (such as pension schemes) and apply throughout Britain; they are open to change through new legislative approaches, for example. Others are the product of an attitude of mind – that people doing one kind of job cannot do another. How often is it assumed that an industrialist could not make a good academic (and vice versa), a teacher a good civil servant (and vice versa)?

■ Conclusion

Many minor attempts, and a large number of them successful, have been made in the past few years to bring industry and the education system closer together. These initiatives have created the groundswell on which we can now build. But because these many initiatives together are not making sufficient progress for the UK to become a competitive economy, I am calling for radical reform.

Chapter 12

The Business of Education

W. Goldsmith

■ Introduction

All employers recognize that a good system of basic education which produces literate and numerate school-leavers is a prerequisite for industrial success. Yet for nearly two decades large parts of the state system have been subject to mismanagement, general lack of clarity of purpose and the plummeting of standards in pursuit of the chimera of 'equality'. There has not been a generally noticeable improvement since 1979, but with a second term of Conservative government, and perceptible changes in public attitudes, there is no reason why drastic changes should not be attempted.

■ Schools suitable for the abilities of the pupils?

The last twenty years have seen the progressive disintegration of a system of secondary education which, although it had faults, nevertheless had reasonably clear aims of where it was going and what it was supposed to be doing. Thus the 1944 Education Act provided that within a tripartite system of grammar, secondary modern and technical schools, each type of education should equip its pupils for the type of work suitable to each; and that the three systems should enjoy 'parity of esteem'.

But scarcely were the foundations of a workable education system laid than a self-appointed educational anti-elite, consisting of teachers' unions, educational bureaucrats and dons decreed that a child had no right

Source: W. Goldsmith (1984) 'The business of education', in *Trespassing: Businessmen's Views on the Education System*, D. Anderson (ed.), Social Affairs Unit, London, pp. 24–32.

to an education suited to his abilities and aptitudes, but rather an equal right to a uniform type of education. This inefficient egalitarian device ensures unmitigated boredom for all those subjected to it: the bright child is denied a sound academic education, while the 'bottom 40%' leave school in many instances illiterate, innumerate, and without the technical competence that their parents had acquired. The alarming increase in truancy can be directly correlated with the failure of schools to provide a suitable education.

The process has advanced remorselessly – first comprehensive schooling, then mixed-ability teaching, with concomitant 'permissive' teaching styles. None of this has achieved the results hoped for; in particular it has not helped to boost the standing of technical and vocational education which now needs to be seen as separate from, but equal in status and esteem to, academic education.

The time has come for selection to be restored as a pre-eminent principle in education. Selection need not be divisive – that is a very negative way of looking at it – dividing those that 'can' from those who 'cannot'. Rather it is a recognition of the fact that different abilities require different types of education and different approaches to talent-stimulation. The readoption of selection would restore a principle of rationality and goal-directedness to the education system. Indeed, one can hope to go further than the 1944 scheme. Even the Soviet Union has recognized the need for 'specialist subject' high schools, centres of excellence in the arts, sciences and music, which enable the abilities of those gifted in those areas to be stretched to the full. One might note that if the Soviet Union fosters excellence in education, in such dramatic contrast to the proletarianizing tendencies of its admirers in the West, that furnishes strong evidence of economic and cultural benefit! (Similar establishments are to be found in West Germany and in other countries of the free world.)

This is not a reactionary plea to 'put back the clock' but rather a recognition that the future of the whole nation depends on full use of people's abilities. Thus the recent National Council for Educational Standards' study of *Standards in English Schools* found that pupils at secondary modern and grammar schools obtained more O level passes than pupils at comprehensives both nationally and within the same social class groups – between 30% and 40% more O level passes per pupil nationally and nearly 50% more in areas for which the social class mix was near the national average. Secondary modern schools did particularly well.

■ Technical education: MSC propping up DES?

With respect to technical education also, the Department of Education and Science has been found wanting and it has been left to the Manpower

Services Commission to pick up the pieces. The MSC as far as training is concerned has become effectively a second Ministry of Education. It should not escape notice that its costs are *additional*, not alternative, to those of the DES. While it was gratifying to see DES/Department of Employment cooperation over the production of the White Paper *Training for Jobs*, this does not obscure the fact that two ministries doing what one should be doing is wasteful and indicative of ineffectiveness on the part of the one that has to be 'propped up'.

Featured in the White Paper was the new Technical and Vocational Education Initiative. This was announced by the Prime Minister in November 1982, with the aim of stimulating technical and vocational education for 14–18 year-olds across the ability range within the education system. As it is a pilot scheme, it is at present open only to those young people in schools and colleges involved by the 14 local education authorities (LEAs) that have been selected to operate pilot projects; although the number of projects will be greatly increased this year. Negotiations are currently in progress between the MSC and 50 other local authorities. If each of these takes up its quota of 250 places, the scheme will provide 125 000 places in the school year 1984–85.

Owing to the experimental nature of the scheme, the projects advanced by LEAs adopt differing approaches within the national criteria and guidelines. But certain aspects are common to all. The course lasts four years and provides full-time general, technical and vocational education, including appropriate work experience; all of which leads to nationally-recognized qualifications. The student is prepared for particular aspects of employment and for adult life in a society liable to rapid change. The courses, which began in September 1983 and have places for up to 10 000 pupils are optional; young people are helped in their choice by all the guidance and education available in the schools and colleges concerned.

■ TVEI in Bedfordshire: an example

As an example of implementation of the TVEI, we may look at what Bedfordshire County Council is doing. Bedfordshire is a heterogeneous area, having a very high incidence of ethnic minorities (over 30% in Bedford and 20% in Luton), an industrial conurbation in the south and a rural north, and two different forms of school organization. Just over 50 pupils in each of the five participating schools have started on the project; these pupils reflect the full ability range and an almost equal male/female ratio. There are a range of courses in the five schools that have an element of vocational preparation, including Business Studies, Technology and Information Technology, Food Industries and Agricultural Technology.

About 20% of the timetable is spent on an area linked to one or more of the 11 Occupational Training Families identified by the MSC. Within the framework of an integrated course, attention will be given to a core curriculum: maths, English, games, social and general education, careers, a science option, a humanities option and usually a practical option are all followed by everyone. In every case the development of vocational skills will involve appropriate periods of work experience. Considerable emphasis will be placed upon relating curriculum to the technologies and likely manpower needs of the 1980s and 1990s, building upon the strengths of existing initiatives in Bedfordshire and the unique position of the county in its stage of development in respect of technology, vocational training, economic awareness and work experience.

Provision in the pilot institutions will be supported and enhanced through a Technical and Vocational Resources Unit based upon the existing County Technology Unit, which will also form the administrative, organizational and staff development base for the Project Team. From September 1984 there will be 150 pupils per school starting on TVEI and the range of available courses will be extended. It is greatly to be hoped that monitoring of the pilot scheme will attest to its success and that TVEI will expand to cover the needs of all those presently denied a suitable secondary education.

Also welcome is the projected 17+ Certificate of Pre-Vocational Education. This is to start in 1984–85 and is expected to attract 80 000 pupils. It is aimed at those pupils who stay on in school after being unsuccessful at CSE or GCE examinations. Although a pilot form of the course is now in operation in schools under which existing vocational courses are followed, it is intended that as from 1985 a curriculum which draws on the best aspects of the vocational courses should be pursued. This curriculum will combine core subjects – literacy, numeracy, business appreciation – with periods of work experience.

■ The views of Institute of Directors members

Such is the importance of vocational education and training that groups of Institute members have recently met to discuss these issues. Papers sent from these branches demonstrate three main strands in their thinking:

- Recognition of the good work done within some schools;
- Underlying anxiety about young people's ability to make the transfer from school to work smoothly;
- A continuing need for further voluntary efforts to improve liaison between the world of business and that of education.

Most branches felt that up to the age of 16, education should be general and not specifically oriented towards vocational activity. A sound 'general' education would be highly relevant to the world of work. Most branches thought that schools were deficient in educating young people in the 'three Rs'. This is amply borne out by the findings of the National Children's Bureau survey, a longitudinal survey on the age cohort born in 1958 who reached the age of 23 in 1981, which revealed on an extrapolation from the sample that 10% of the adult population, or 2–3.5 million adults, were functionally illiterate (i.e. had the reading age of an average 9-year-old).

To a greater or lesser degree, literacy appears to be a problem at all levels. Thus the *Daily Telegraph* of 28 July 1983 carried a letter from the head of a school of librarianship which quoted an application from a graduate with a IIi degree in English who was interested in 'persuing a course in librarianship and would be grateful for information'. A similarly qualified graduate wrote to 'The Principle' and an applicant with three A levels asked for information on 'causes in librarianship'. It is currently the case that North American universities have to run remedial courses in literacy for their students! The waste to the country that such deficiencies imply is impossible to quantify. Inadequate literacy can be a factor in operational problems – e.g. when a manager has to waste time in rewriting reports by juniors; it can disqualify otherwise suitably qualified applicants for a post; and it may necessitate the provision of training by employers.

One Institute of Directors branch discussion concluded in suggesting that schools should also concentrate on education in the 'three Cs': communication, comprehension and computation. Whereas branches unanimously rejected the suggestion that preparation for work should be a legislative requirement for all school curricula, some considered that schools should concentrate on young people's attitudes to work, focusing on their ability to act as leaders. Some branches suggested that there should be more formal and informal meetings between business people and careers teachers; one branch suggested that a coordinating group be established, comprised of business associations and representatives of the educational establishment. It was also considered that greater emphasis should be given to providing relevant education for those who are not academically able but who have the capacity for skilled work.

Compared with Germany, British standards of vocational education are appallingly low. A recent NIESR study has shown that:

> 'The very much larger proportion of the German workforce attaining vocational qualifications has done so at standards which are generally as high as, and on the whole a little higher than, those attained by the smaller proportion in Britain' (S.J. Prais and K. Wagner, 'Some practical aspects of human capital investment: training standards in five occupations in Britain and Germany', *National Institute Economic Review*, August 1983).

The numbers qualifying each year as mechanical fitters, electricians and building craftsmen in Britain are between a half and a third of corresponding numbers in Germany; in clerical work, at the level of the broadly competent office worker familiar with both basic book-keeping and basic correspondence, the rate is still less favourable in Britain, at about a fifth; and in the training of shop-workers and others engaged in distributive activities, the amount of formal qualification in Britain is negligible in comparison with Germany. The vocational education initiatives referred to above, coupled with the commencement of the Youth Training Scheme, ought to repair some of the damage done to our education system over the past two decades, and to lay the foundation for a more prosperous, technologically-oriented society.

■ Renewable teacher contracts: more freedom to manage

It is well known that the motivations of those who work for bureaucracies in time come to be solely concerned with the preservation of their own positions. It is high time that the education system be run in a more business-like manner and less like a social service for the benefit of its employees.

Welcome moves in the direction of efficiency have recently been made. Before 1983, HMIs could make recommendations to LEAs about schools, but there was no obligation on the authority to say what it had done in the way of implementation. LEAs are now obliged to state what steps they have taken following an Inspector's report. Indeed, it would be desirable for the activities of HMIs to be monitored, to see whether they are all worthwhile. Also encouraging is the wish of the current Secretary of State to end the 'job-for-life' attitude which prevents the dismissal of incompetent teachers. The principle should, however, be taken further: teachers and head teachers should be offered five-year contracts, and parents should have a far greater say in cases of dismissal, otherwise the incompetent are likely to be shielded by their colleagues. Also important for efficiency is that the privatization of school cleaning and meals services proceeds apace.

Given the vast amount of money which schools consume, it is little short of amazing that few education authorities have yet engaged the services of management consultants to help them identify inefficiencies. In this regard Cambridgeshire is a notable exception. There a pilot scheme which started in 1978 in two secondary schools looked at performance management. The output of teaching jobs was defined, together with a means of assessing whether targets were being achieved, and meetings between teachers and headteachers were initiated for the participants to discuss how things were going. The scheme is still in operation. Eight other County Councils have employed management consultants to some extent. To hasten what is clearly a beneficial process the DES ought to engage a team of independent management consultants, and send them to other selected areas. Statute should provide that their recommendations are available for the purposes of public debate, and that they are given due consideration on decision-making. Even more important is the implementation of a proper management structure. Common to both health and education services is a lack of management and accountability. Applicants for the post of headteacher are not required to show any evidence of management abilities or experience. On appointment they are not sent on management courses. Indeed, it is often complained that it is the best teachers who are lured into the upper levels of administration, thus depriving their school of their teaching gifts but bringing with them no management competence in compensation.

Nor is there a proper management structure in schools. The head of a school cannot be compared with a managing director. He is not responsible for the building or the budget of his school, although it is encouraging that at least one LEA, Cambridgeshire, is experimenting with more school financial autonomy. Neither can the Director of Education exercise the function of a managing director; the sheer number of schools in his area makes this an impossibility.

■ Vouchers and performance-related funding

What is needed is accountability at the level of provision of the service. Although the education voucher scheme has been rejected by the DES, it would have had the very substantial merit of necessitating management changes as a result of changes in financing. Thus the boards of governors would play a role analogous to that of boards of directors, actively overseeing the broad strategy of the school, with discretion over day-to-day management being delegated to the headteacher. They would be accountable to the 'shareholders' (i.e. the parents), who would supply finance through the voucher scheme. Removal of incompetent headteachers and teachers would be helped by improved accountability and the more immediate nature of the pressure from parents. Yet although 'vouchers' are dead, the idea of demand-led accountability is still alive in Britain, thus giving rise to the possibility of new forms of its expression.

Individual teachers must be encouraged to realize that they are preparing the majority of their pupils for the world of work. In this connection it should be stated that teacher knowledge of the world of commerce and industry is virtually non-existent. This is not the fault of the teachers themselves, but of institutional factors (such as different conditions of employment and non-portable pensions) and of an educational system which, because it has persistently devalued the world of commerce and industry, has never considered knowledge of this area of life to be an essential part of a teacher's corpus of skills. Initial teacher-training courses should contain a compulsory module on 'understanding industry': preferably as much time should be spent immersed in an industrial environment as is currently spent on teaching practice in schools. This suggestion was strongly urged by our branches. This need not lengthen the courses in question. The courses, as structured at present, are by general consensus too long and insufficiently concentrated. Once qualified, teachers should combine industrial/commercial experience with in-service training.

If the education system is to be considered in this new light, then the notion of requiring some state expenditure on education to be performance-related does not seem to be misplaced; schools should become more accountable for their performance. Performance assessors should include representatives of private-sector business, who will be specifically concerned to judge whether the school is getting the best value out of its resources. Since resources can broadly be construed to include 'pupils', the assessment would, of course, have to take account of social class and catchment areas of pupils. Such performance assessments would provide a useful continuation of the work initially carried out by management consultants as suggested above.

■ Conclusion: two revolutions

We are now on the threshold of two exciting revolutions. Firstly, a technological revolution which necessitates a high level of technical education if Britain is not to lose out to her competitors. Secondly, a social revolution which requires that existing methods of provision are subjected to critical scrutiny in order that the most efficient ways of doing things can be found. The two revolutions are to some extent interdependent – if we are not efficient, we will not be able to give our technological endeavours the impetus they require; if we do not enjoy excellence in technology, we will be back to the days of mediocre achievement of the 1960s and 1970s, during which our social structures ossified. It is up to all of us to work to turn our dream into a reality.

Chapter 13

Education, Employment and Recruitment

R. Moore

This chapter will consider the way in which educational qualifications are *actually* used in the labour market in the recruitment of young workers. In general, recent studies have found that the use of qualifications varies significantly between different sectors of the labour market and is subject to considerable regional variation. Non-educational criteria almost invariably have priority in recruitment over educational ones and employers tend to have only the vaguest notions as to what particular qualifications entail or imply.

These factors are differentiated by sex and race and also work to reproduce gender and racial differentiation in employment (and unemployment). The findings to be considered here (and the broader body of research of which they are typical) suggest that the link between education and occupation is much more tenuous than is often supposed and call into question many of the assumptions currently held about employers' attitudes to young workers and to educational standards. This is particularly significant given the place of these assumptions within the occupational rhetoric of the present assault upon education and liberal education in particular.

■ Qualifications and recruitment

A number of illuminating pieces of research have been published recently which look in detail at the way in which qualifications are used by

Source: Moore, R. (1988) 'Education, employment and recruitment', in *Frameworks for Teaching*, R. Dale, R. Ferguson and A. Robinson (eds), Hodder and Stoughton, London, pp. 206–22.

employers in the process of the recruitment of young workers. Cumin, for instance, traces a group of school-leavers from school, through the labour market and into employment. He notes a sharp contrast between the expectations of pupils, parents and teachers about the importance of qualifications and their real significance (Cumin, 1983). A study by Jones (Jones, 1983) provides detailed evidence on the almost complete lack of communication between examination boards and employers and on the uninformed and arbitrary way in which employers use qualifications. Ashton *et al.* (1983, 1986), in an extremely thorough investigation of the relative positions of young workers in contrasting local labour markets, define a number of different recruitment strategies in which qualifications vary in significance, are used in different ways and are almost invariably of secondary importance relative to other factors. It is precisely the subordinate role of qualifications which is the striking feature of this type of detailed work.

□   **Expectations and practice**

The study by Cumin follows a group of school-leavers from their college in Leicestershire out into 'the world of work'. The purpose was to discover precisely how important qualifications were in determining their occupational chances. The study begins by noting the high expectations that the pupils, their parents and their teachers had in this regard. 57 per cent of pupils and 62 per cent of parents thought that qualifications would be *very important*, and 98 per cent and 96 per cent respectively thought they would be either *very* or *fairly* important. After examining what happened in practice, Cumin concludes that these expectations were not 'based upon actuality' (p. 58).

The study found that 56 per cent of the jobs taken by the young people in fact had no formal educational requirements attached to them. In the end, only 15 per cent of the school-leavers considered that their qualifications had been essential to their getting jobs. Cumin makes the significant point that employers appoint school-leavers to posts *before* examination results are known in any case. It is very rare for young people recruited on that basis to be sacked if they subsequently fail to pass the exam or gain a certain grade. Obviously the simple non-availability of the result must severely limit the significance the employers can place on exam passing *per se*.

However, the limitations upon examinations in shaping recruitment practices are not restricted to the effects of this particular practical exigency. Employers in the main seem to see little direct relevance of education to specific job requirements. This would seem to be the general conclusion of research in this area, and Cumin's conclusion that:

'In terms of the overall needs employers had of young people, it was clear that non-academic criteria, attitudes to work and personal characteristics, and basic skills, essentially those of reading, writing and arithmetic, were far more important to employers than academic qualifications' (Cumin, 1983, p. 57).

is one widely echoed elsewhere.

☐   Employers and qualifications

The study by Jones (1983) provides information on the use of qualifications by employers in three English regions (London and the South East, the West Midlands, and Yorkshire and Humberside) and also includes some comparisons with other European countries. 1500 establishments were surveyed, ranging in size from employing less than 25 to more than 500 and spanning 10 sectors of the Revised Standard Classification of Industry. Five categories of workers were defined: professional and managerial, technician, clerical and sales, skilled manual, and operatives. These categories were represented to varying degrees in the various sectors. Employers were found to use five main selection devices: application forms, academic qualifications, school references, performance in aptitude tests, and interviews.

The relative importance of academic qualifications varied between categories, being more significant for non-manual than for manual workers. In all cases the interview was the most important device, with qualifications coming second for non-manuals. The level of qualifications varied according to the level of employment. There was particular emphasis upon English and maths. Jones concludes her detailed investigation by saying that:

'These figures suggest that employers, at least with the present education system, largely feel that basic knowledge in a few subjects is all that they find useful for their purpose. Case study experience further suggests that even this use is questionable. Observation ... suggest(s) that employers' expectations of the subject content and skills are often very wide of the mark. This appears especially true of Maths, Physics and English, the most frequently required subjects.' (Jones, 1983, p. 22.)

The report shows that employers tend to have only extremely vague notions as to what examinations in particular subjects actually involve. There was virtually *no* direct communication between employers and examination boards. Out of 22 GCE and CSE examination boards, only eight (all CSE) gave out information specific to employers and only nine (eight CSE and one GCE) actively disseminated information to employers.

At the same time, only 11 boards (eight CSE and three GCE) reported ever having received requests for information *from* employers. Only three boards (one CSE and two GCE) had an interest in researching employers' views.

Given this, it is probably not surprising that even where qualifications were stipulated, the requirement was not rigidly enforced. Jones (1983) found that although a reasonably high number of employers thought that qualifications were desirable, less than half thought them to be essential. Even where they did, there was a fair degree of flexibility. Interestingly, 'very few' employers saw examinations as essential for specific jobs (p. 23). Rather, they were demanded most rigorously where *further training* involved FE or professional courses where the educational qualification was an entry requirement. In other words, the educational qualification was related to further *educational* needs. not to the needs of jobs as such. Jones concludes that 'these results support the ... assertion that desirability of certain qualifications is not closely related to actual job performance' (p. 23).

☐ Recruitment strategies

The findings of Jones's work are very much in line with those of Ashton *et al.* (1983). Only half of the employers interviewed in Leicester, Sunderland and St Albans thought that qualifications were useful as 'yardsticks of a candidate's ability' (p. 55). 23 per cent of them thought that 'they could possibly be of some use with certain reservations' and 27 per cent considered them to be of no use at all. 45 per cent of the first group (i.e. 45 per cent of 50 per cent) thought them to be a true measure of ability and a third saw them as useful indicators of attitude. In the second group, 69 per cent thought that other factors were more important than qualifications and in the third, 75 per cent ignored them altogether or considered them meaningless.

Ashton *et al.* found that employers adopt a range of *recruitment strategies* in which educational qualifications are combined with other attributes to varying degrees. The most common approach was that where 'the balance between academic and non-academic criteria shifts in favour of the non-academic' (p. 52). It is important to note that the educational qualifications are not being treated as an *index* of non-educational attributes (e.g. docility). The other factors which employers take into account (self-presentation, attitude to work, interest in the job, family background) are seen as *independent* from education.

The authors define *five* recruitment strategies, which can be summarized as follows:

1. Educational qualifications perform a *determinative* function. Here

the qualification is the most important criterion in recruitment, although other factors might be considered in the interview stage, though in a subordinate role.

2. Educational qualifications perform a *screening* function. Qualifications are used to pre-select the sample of candidates. A minimum level is set and those at or above that level are then selected by *non-academic* criteria. Qualifications above the minimum bestow no advantage.

3. Educational qualifications perform a *focusing* function. They will be waived if a candidate possesses the appropriate non-academic criteria. This is the point at which non-academic come to take precedence over academic criteria.

4. Educational qualifications are *functionless*. Recruitment is based on personality or physical attributes which are seen as having *nothing* to do with education.

5. Educational qualifications have a *negative* function. Qualifications *disqualify* the person from being considered (e.g. on the grounds that they will become easily bored or might become a trouble maker). It is, of course, being assumed here that there is some kind of relationship between the qualification level and the nature of the work.

In this study it was the *third* strategy which was most commonly used (53 per cent), followed by the fourth (39 per cent). Hence non-academic criteria have a clear priority over the academic.

The use of strategies varied according to the occupational category: at the *professional and managerial* level, 82 per cent of employers used strategy 2, and at the *technician* level it was used by 74 per cent. Strategy 3 was that most used for *clerical and sales* (57 per cent) and for *skilled manual* (60 per cent). At the *operative* level, strategy 4 is most common (see Ashton *et al.*, 1983, Table 49).

The use of different strategies relates to the size of the firm. In general, larger firms tended to make more use of qualifications (possibly reflecting the existence of a trained personnel staff who themselves owe their position to qualifications). More reliance was placed upon O than A-levels. The study found that 72 per cent of employers in the top size band saw qualifications as useful as against only 30 per cent in the smallest, where 49 per cent saw them as not useful compared with only 12 per cent in the largest (see Ashton *et al.*, 1983, Tables 46, 48 and 50).

The size of the establishment could reasonably be expected to affect the number of young people being exposed to the different recruitment strategies (although the relative numbers of small employers would also have to be borne in mind). However, it was found that many large companies took on very few young people: 20 per cent of those employing above 1000 recruited fewer than ten per year (Ashton *et al.*, 1983, p. 47). Hence, 'the relationship between the size of the employing unit and the number of young people recruited each year was not as close as might have been expected' (p. 47).

Ashton *et al.*'s extremely detailed studies indicate the dangers of generalizing about the education/production relationship. Their more recent work emphasizes the very considerable regional variations which reflect relative unemployment rates. The complex variations and interactions between factors such as recruitment strategies, size of firm, sector, area and local industry mix introduce a wide range of contingencies into the situation which are further complicated by gender and race.

■ Employers, educational standards and young workers

A central plank of the current attack upon education and the teaching profession (and one which has grown since Callaghan's Great Debate speech) is that of employers' dissatisfaction with educational standards and with the quality of young workers. This alleged 'failure' on the part of teachers is a main feature of the rhetoric which legitimizes the changes which are being imposed. Consequently it is important critically to examine its basis in reality.

The type of detailed empirical research reviewed above suggests that scepticism is to be strongly recommended. Employers, in fact, appear to be not only ill-informed about education but relatively arbitrary in the uses to which they put it. Given the crucial role that the Manpower Services Commission has played in the undermining of education and the construction of its current occupationalist surrogate, its contribution to this debate deserves close scrutiny. It is ironic that the MSC's Holland Report was published in the same year (1977) as Shirley Williams' Green Paper on education which followed on from 'The Great Debate'. The Holland Report looked explicitly at the issue of employers' dissatisfaction with young workers and presented its information in such a way as to support the idea of education's failure in this area. I have suggested elsewhere[1] that their presentation of their evidence benefits from closer examination.

The Report (Holland, 1977) discusses employers' evaluations of young workers relative to older ones in terms of 13 'essential' attributes. In the case of unskilled/semi-skilled young workers (i.e. the Youth Opportunities Programme/Youth Training Scheme target group), 81 per cent of the employers listed 'willingness/attitude to work' as the most important attribute (Table 13.1). The second most popular one was 'good level of

Table 13.1   Employers' evaluations of young workers on 'essential attributes' compared to adults. (Source: Holland Report.)

Attribute	% of employers agreeing 'essential'	% of employers saying that young people are:				Rating (B − W)
		Different		Better	Worse	
		No	Yes			
1 Willingness/attitude to work	81	46	54	11	43	−32
2 Good level of general fitness	47	70	30	24	6	+18
3 Appearance/tidiness	39	60	40	6	34	−28
4 Specific physical attributes	36	72	28	22	6	+16
5 Basic 3Rs	21	46	54	10	44	−34
6 Mature/stable	20	40	60	5	55	−50
7 Ability to communicate	18	53	47	11	36	−25
8 Willingness to join union	16	89	11	8	3	+5
9 Good level of numeracy	13	50	50	8	42	−34
10 Past experience	7	39	61	2	59	−57
11 Good written English/literate	6	40	60	9	51	−42
12 Existing union membership	4	85	15	4	11	−7
13 Specific educational qualifications	2	49	51	28	23	+5

general fitness', mentioned by 47 per cent, followed by 'appearance/ tidiness' (39 per cent) and 'specific physical attributes' (36 per cent). The first specifically educational attribute ('basic 3Rs') appears fifth, being mentioned by only 21 per cent of employers (Table 13.2). The rest of the 13 essential attributes range between a mention by 20 per cent for 'mature/ stable' down to a mere 2 per cent for 'specific educational qualifications'(!).

The discussion which follows in the Report for young people in general is based mainly on a rating which is established by subtracting the number of employers who think that young people are worse than older workers from those who think that they are better on each of these attributes. On this basis they come out very badly, with negative marks on nine out of the 13 attributes. However, inspection shows that there are in fact three employer positions: (1) young people are no different/non-comparable, or, if they are different, are (2) better or (3) worse. The *rating* on which young people do so badly is derived only from that fraction of employers who say they are different.

It is a simple arithmetical exercise to reconstitute the original

Table 13.2 Position of educational 'essential attributes'. (Source: constructed from The Holland Report, Tables 7:1 and 7:2.)

Attribute	Position out of 13	Essential %	Worse %
Basic 3Rs	5	21	24
Good level of numeracy	9	13	21
Good written English/literate	11	6	51
Specific educational qualifications	13	2	12

figures. When this is done, a rather different picture emerges. In fact, young people come out worse overall on only three out of the 13 attributes relative to older workers. Two of these are directly age related – 'past experience' (worse: 59 per cent), and 'mature/stable' (worse, 55 per cent). The third is 'good written English/literate' (worse: 51 per cent).

Ironically, the attribute on which young people do best relative to older workers is specific educational qualifications which actually comes *bottom* of the employers' list of essential attributes, being mentioned by only 2 per cent of employers! In fact, employers give *all* the educational attributes a low priority.

The data corresponds precisely to the situation described by Ashton *et al.*'s recruitment strategies, with non-educational criteria taking priority over educational ones. The top four attributes are each of this type. If we take the attribute which employers most often saw as 'essential', willingness/attitude to work (mentioned by 81 per cent), we see that the MSC's poor rating of −32 in fact reflects a negative judgement by less than half of employers (54 per cent said that young workers are different in this respect and 43 per cent said they were worse). In fact, this represents the precise opposite of the MSC position – the majority of employers *think that* young workers are either no different or better! Interestingly this figure is consistent with that most often encountered in the literature in this area where usually between 70 per cent to 80 per cent of employers are favourable to young workers. Ashton *et al.*, for instance, say that:

> 'Despite the many grumbles and adverse comments, 70 per cent of all employers interviewed claimed to have been satisfied with the standard of work of young people taken on by them in the previous two years, and only 14 per cent expressed dissatisfaction. Indeed, of the respondents in the 60 establishments employing over 5000 workers, all but one expressed satisfaction.' (Ashton *et al.*, 1983, p. 56.)

The probable significance of all this is that it is mistaken to attempt to generalize about employers' attitude to young workers. Clearly many are dissatisfied and feel that they can point to declining standards (e.g. in the numeracy of engineering apprentices), but this situation is more likely to reflect changing social patterns of recruitment rather than a real decline in 'educational standards'. Paradoxically it could result from an actual general improvement in standards combined with expanding opportunities in further and higher education. The 'type of lad' who once became an apprentice now goes on to take an engineering degree and is replaced at that qualification level by a different category of young person. In earlier times the former had been underachieving educationally whereas the latter are now near the peak of their attainment level. If these complex changes over time in the relationship between general improvements in attainment, social bases of recruitment and expanded further educational opportunities are not taken into account, the general improvement can appear from the fixed position of an employer as a decline in standards.

□   Work experience

As the examination of the Holland Report data indicates, the problem which young people have in the labour market reflects the age-related issue of lack of experience. It is this rather than defective education that disadvantages them. An examination by Richards (1982) of the factors employed in the recruitment of apprentices in the East Midlands illustrates some of the problems in this area, especially in relation to the current occupationalist assertion that young people will benefit from a more 'vocational' education in order to counteract the lack of experience.

Richards asked employers about the factors they took into account when recruiting apprentices. The percentages of employers mentioning the following were: evening classes (92 per cent), holiday jobs (85 per cent), Saturday jobs (84 per cent), hobbies and interests (77 per cent), paper rounds (73 per cent), membership of clubs and social societies (68 per cent), school work experience schemes (52 per cent) (Richards, 1982, Table B, p. 7).

The poor showing of school work experience is striking. The reasons for this are illuminating. The contrast between work experience schemes and informal work experience lies in the fact that the latter are taken by employers as evidence of initiative, an interest in earning money and the ability to sustain regular work discipline (getting up early, etc.). Paper rounds in particular were seen as significant in these respects. Work experience, on the other hand, was seen by employers as part of the school's discipline and as giving little information about the pupil as an individual. Richards says that:

'The feature that impressed these employers about the spare/part-time jobs of young people applying for apprenticeship in their firms were mainly elements which were absent in WE [work experience] schemes. WE schemes did not involve the 'initiative' involved in going out and finding your own part-time job. This was all done by the school following DES and LEA guidelines. The element of 'reliability' (getting up early consistently for a substantial period of time, etc.) was also absent.' (Richards, 1982, p. 9.)

Where employers did see value in work experience schemes, it had to do with information about career choices. They felt that such schemes allowed young people to have direct experience of engineering rather than relying purely upon second-hand information (from teachers or the media). If they then still chose to seek engineering jobs, this could be seen as evidence of *commitment*. This is a central feature of the employers' view.

Richards found a preoccupation among employers with the image of engineering. They were very concerned that pupils, and the 'bright' ones in particular, should be given a positive view of the industry and be attracted to it. This was the main value they attributed to school work experience rather than seeing it in any direct sense as preparation for engineering work. Richard's conclusion is that:

'According to these employers it was teachers who needed WE more than pupils, so that they could get a picture of what engineering was really like (as opposed to media misrepresentations – strikes, redundancies, etc.) and so put across a "good image" of engineering, hopefully attracting the "brighter pupils" into the industry.' (Richards, 1982, p. 11.)

As far as the actual content of the education was concerned, the employers wanted no more than a solid, old fashioned grounding in 'the basics' and that 'bright pupils' should be positively encouraged to seek jobs in the industrial sector rather than in the academic world or public services. The major problem was seen to be the hostility of teachers towards industrial and commercial values and the way in which this deflected 'bright', traditionally educated pupils away from industry. It was not direct preparation for production that the schools should be providing, but image building. Furthermore, this exercise should be aimed at the 'bright' pupils. Richards says that:

'Some writers went on to argue that attracting high ability youngsters into manufacturing industry was one of the conditions for a regeneration of the British economy. Employers making these connections between the 'ignorance' of 'our brightest children', WE, the entry of these youngsters into manufacturing industry and the rejuvenation of British capitalism were clearly *not interested in the notion that WE was essentially concerned with ROSLA or the "average and below average ability ranges"*.' (Richards, 1982, p. 16, my emphasis.)

We can say that the problem being defined here is not so much that the pupils are getting the wrong education (though they might be getting the wrong teachers) as that industry is getting the wrong pupils! The 'high-fliers' go elsewhere. This reflects the antipathy towards industry and commerce from traditionally educated, liberal-humanist teachers. It is *they* who need to be changed.

Richards argues that employers' attitudes imply a dual system of work experience – image building for the high-fliers and realism for the rest. In the case of the former, it is a traditional rather than a vocational education which is required, and as to the latter, the evidence suggests that employers are really indifferent to *their* education.

Given that so much of the occupationalist initiative in education and outside (YTS, etc.) is aimed at the lower academic ability bands, it is useful to emphasize certain points:

1.   The evidence strongly indicates that employers are not especially concerned with the educational attainment of young workers in those sectors of the labour market in which such individuals tend to seek employment. Non-educational criteria have a clear priority in recruitment strategies.

2.   In part this reflects the fact that occupational skill levels are of such a low order that they present no real requirement for educational preparation. Indeed, even training is problematical – as the Further Education Unit, for instance, has conceded.[2] Where extended education or training is provided (e.g. in response to youth unemployment) it tends, consequently, to stress so-called social and life skills or personal effectiveness rather than technical skills. This has the important implication of presenting these young people as personally and socially deficient and incompetent.

3.   Significantly, pupils of this type tend to have acquired significant degrees of work experience through part-time and spare-time work and also to possess the social skills of network membership which facilitate grapevine recruitment (of course, both of these things are affected by local unemployment levels). These issues will be looked at in more detail below. It is important to stress that (a) this type of work experience is precisely that welcomed by employers, and (b) such young people are socially competent members of labour market social networks.

☐   **Recruitment and the problems of youth**

If young people are not deficient in the ways that current rhetoric suggests, then what is the explanation for the high levels of youth unemployment?

The view that they lack work experience is contradicted by a substantial body of evidence. A study by Finn (1987), for instance, illustrates the tendency for non-academic young people to have comparatively more such informal work experience.[3] Lack of conventional school success cannot be seen, in any straightforward way, as indicative of problems in coping with working life. I have suggested elsewhere that difficult behaviour at school can, in fact, reflect a readiness for work and the resentment at having that ambition frustrated (Moore, 1984). Clarke, in a review of the literature on the transition to work, says that it tends to support the view that the 'majority of early leavers adjust fairly painlessly to working life' (Clarke, 1980, p. 10). She concludes a section on young people 'at risk' with the statement that:

> 'This suggests, rather unpalatably, that apart from bright children who do well at both school and work, it is those children who are apathetic about, or even alienated from, school who adjust best to work.' (Clarke, 1980, p. 11.)

The major problem that young people suffer is simply that they are *young*. The re-presented Holland Report data showed how young people are judged to be 'worse' by employers on age-related attributes. Obviously, however much informal work experience young people may have acquired, it cannot compete with that of older workers. However, there is a more significant factor. The Holland Report stated that:

> 'Whilst a little over a third of employers thought there was no difference, those employers who did state a preference were, in almost all cases, more likely to prefer other recruits to young people. This was especially true when young people were compared to up-graded existing employees, those recruited from other firms or women returning to work.' (Holland, 1977, p. 41.)

Employers' preference for various categories of older workers reflects, in part, the importance of on-the-job training and experience over that of formal education (especially in relation to recruitment within the firm's internal labour market). But it also reflects the fact that older workers are, by virtue of their life situation, more reliable. The significance of attitude to work has been highlighted by numerous studies. It is important to note that this is not simply to do with naturalistic notions of 'emotional maturity'. Blackburn and Mann, on the basis of their extensive study of the labour market for semi and unskilled labour in Peterborough, say that:

> 'The ideal worker is male, around thirty, married with small children, related to other employees and with a stable educational and work history. He is not necessarily cleverer than other workers, but his commitments are less likely to make him jeopardise his job.' (Blackburn and Mann, 1979, p. 13.)

What is significant about the 'ideal worker' has nothing to do with his (the female 'ideal' is usually somewhat different) education *per se*. It is simply that he *is* a married man, around 30, with wife and children, a car, a mortgage (?), etc. Employers' preferences refer not to personality characteristics developed by a specialized, occupational socializing agency – the school – but to life-cycle characteristics. The difference between the young and the adult worker reflects their different positions on the trajectories of (common) social career paths. It is not 'the dull compulsion of the labour market' which disciplines the worker through the brute necessities of basic subsistence, but the more developed range of needs and commitments which trap them in, what Blackburn and Mann call, 'the life-cycle squeeze' (p. 108). The ideal model helps to differentiate the workforce (by age, sex and colour) according to how far different groups approximate to the model and can be seen as representing its exemplary qualities of commitment and reliability.

This kind of division in the labour market between youth and adults' jobs was also investigated by Ashton *et al.* (1986). In a similar fashion, changes in opportunities reflect the development of the social career:

> 'Age barriers also served to structure that young adults' experience of the labour market. This was particularly true of the unemployed. They were too old for most of the jobs which provided training and which only recruit school or college leavers, and too young for many of the adult jobs which required recruits to be over 21, and where employers *preferred those who were married, with a family and a large mortgage*.' (Ashton *et al.*, 1986, p. 104, my emphasis.)

Equally it is the case that the lack of opportunity to participate in employment blocks the development of the social career. Occupational and social careers are mutually facilitating in this respect. Unemployment does not only deny an adequate income, it can create deep crises of social identity.

■ Recruitment and the matching process

Investigation of recruitment strategies indicates that the role of education in occupational allocation is much more contingent than is often allowed. The relationship between qualifications and jobs is attenuated by the complexities of labour market segmentation and this itself is subject to local diversification. The importance of labour market segmentation is emphasized in Ashton *et al.*'s most recent study (1986). This work stresses the fact that there is no simple hierarchy of jobs (matched by a corresponding hierarchy of educational qualifications). The segmentation of the occupational system effectively creates discrete spheres of employment which exhibit radical discontinuities in terms of their structures, processes and possibilities. These in turn are associated with distinctive entry requirements, varying uses of qualifications in recruitment and career development (where career development occurs at all), differing pre- and post-entry orientations to work by young workers and differential effects by age, sex and 'race'.

Ashton *et al.* also stress the importance of *local* labour markets and argue that their variations can have more significant effects than social class differences. They conceptualize these differences in terms of 'separate local labour market cultures' (p. 104). A particularly significant feature of these 'cultures' in respect of occupational recruitment is that of social network or grapevine recruitment. This informal method was found to become increasingly important as individuals moved into second and subsequent jobs. This reflects, the authors argue, an 'increasing awareness of the ways in which employers recruit' (p. 84). Job search, on this basis, is seen as 'more efficient, in that it is more closely aligned to employers' recruitment methods' (p. 84). At the third-job level, between 25 per and and 60 per cent of recruits found their position through 'word of mouth'.

Granovetter (a pioneer of the study of this dimension of recruitment) has argued that sociologists and economists have seriously neglected this aspect of 'the matching process', i.e. the *actual* process whereby individuals come to get the jobs they do (Granovetter, 1975). He stresses the rationality and efficiency of network recruitment for both employers and prospective employees. It is a cheaper and more reliable way of getting information about jobs or workers.

> 'Furthermore, my empirical work suggests that the signal chosen in the usual models – education – is not actually the main conveyor of information in labour markets. It is true that most jobs have clear cut educational requirements, such that employers assume workers lacking them to be ipso facto unqualified. This is however, a crude sort of screen indeed, and if used alone would leave the employer still with a large and unmanageable information problem. On paper, there are few jobs for which large numbers of people are not qualified; in practice, employers use a more refined and differentiated signal than educational qualifications: they use the recommendations of people personally known to them and prospective employees. Similarly, prospective employees know better than to rely on landscaping or other signals put out by employers and attempt, instead, to find out the inside story from their contacts.' (Granovetter, 1981, p. 25.)

He points out that processes of this type are difficult to accommodate within orthodox economics because they are not amenable to 'costing' in the standard economic sense. Because of this, and despite their obviousness to common-sense experience, they have been excluded from formal analysis.

Granovetter's original sample of professional, technical and managerial workers in the Boston, Massachusetts area indicates that these processes are not restricted to either élite 'old boy networks' or to tight-knit working class communities such as dockers or printers. The basic rationality principle of their greater efficiency holds across the occupational system. There is, however, a further dimension to network recruitment which goes beyond the basic exchange of information. This has to do with the way in which network membership involves possession of the social skills and reciprocal relationships which that membership entails.

Grieco (1984), in a fascinating and detailed series of ethnographic studies of working-class networks in Britain has pointed to a number of advantages which workers and employers gain from 'the network':

> 'Firstly, employee referrals provide the cheapest method of obtaining labour. Secondly, employee referrals provide an efficient screening mechanism. Thirdly, recruitment through employees acts as a form of control since responsibilities and obligations hold between workers so recruited: for if the sponsored antagonises the employer, the reputation of the sponsor himself will be damaged; thus, the new worker is constrained by the interests and reputation of his sponsor.' (Grieco, 1984, p. 30.)

A number of significant points emerge from these studies:

1. Network membership supplies not only information, but also the tacit skills which enable individuals to become competent and accepted members of occupational groups.

2. Membership provides a means of social control in the workplace both because those recruited have an obligation to preserve the reputation of their sponsors and also because, in some cases, family authority principles can be transferred from the home to the job, e.g. as with a 'dads' lads' recruitment system.

3. Membership also provides a source of social support in the workplace while a newcomer learns the ropes and the tricks of the trade, e.g. network members will make up shortfalls in production while the newcomer settles in. People without access to these support mechanisms can be severely disadvantaged.

4. Grieco's work has also pointed to the wider social importance of women in maintaining and enforcing the system of network reciprocity, even when not themselves in work. She also stresses the strategic, collective role of the network in maintaining employment opportunities, *and* a 'family' income. This has important implications for current trends in thinking about the role of the family (and the extended family) in the occupational system of advanced societies and for certain feminist approaches to the issues of women in the

labour market which tend to operate from an essentially middle-class paradigm of the *individualized* career and salary and the consequent marginalization of women in the domestic context.[4]

Although it is possible to see networks as a mechanism through which workers exercise some degree of control over their labour market, it is important to acknowledge the extent to which they are, by definition, *discriminatory*. Lack of access to network membership can be a major limitation upon employment opportunities and, consequently, a major source of labour market differentiation. As Jenkins and Troyna (and other contributors) have pointed out (in Troyna and Smith, 1983), this has a particular impact upon ethnic minority groups.

> 'First, in an organisation with an all white or largely white workforce, network recruitment will help to ensure that this stays the case, particularly at a time when large numbers of white workers are unemployed and prepared to re-enter the comparatively poorly paid and less pleasant jobs they deserted in the past few years. At best, this will help to ensure that black workers remain in those employment sectors they entered in the boom years of the 50's and 60's. Secondly and the reasons for this are unclear, there is good reason to suggest that West Indian workers are more likely to use formal or official job-search channels than are white or Asians, who use informal channels to a comparatively greater extent.' (Troyna and Smith, 1983, pp. 14–15.)

This indicates a powerful way in which labour market factors can effectively negate educational advances, e.g. in changing the pattern of 'racial' or gender inequalities in attainment. It is striking how even when certain minority groups tend to achieve mean levels of attainment above those of the white majority, they still remain heavily disadvantaged in employment terms.

A similar point about the way in which labour market structures and processes limit educational reform can be made in relation to gender. Crompton and Jones (1984) have highlighted the significance of the relationship between pre-entry academic qualifications and post-entry professional qualifications in shaping the gender inequalities in white collar employment which emerge as occupational careers develop. In their study, young men and women were very similar in their academic qualifications at O and A-level at the point of entry into work. As a result of the bi-modal pattern of female involvement in paid employment (reflecting the demands of child rearing), women tend to be absent from work during the period in which men tend to acquire the post-entry professional qualifications which are required for promotion.

This points to the importance of the relationship of education to the articulation between social and occupational career paths and to specific labour market structures such as internal labour markets. It also suggests that educational reforms will be of limited success unless complemented by policies such as contract compliance which act directly upon demand-side institutions. A general implication of the material considered throughout has been the limitation of supply-side analysis.

■ Conclusion

The material reviewed in this chapter indicates that the manner in which educational qualifications are used in employment is both highly variable and subject to a wide range of contingent factors located in labour market structures and processes. Specifically, the following points can be made:

1. Employers have tended to be extremely ill-informed about the content of educational courses and the significance of qualifications.

2. Little direct relationship is seen to exist between specific qualifications and actual job requirements.

3. Qualifications are invariably used alongside other criteria and these usually take priority in recruitment.

4. Employers tend to use a range of recruitment strategies employing a number of devices. Their use and the relative significance and the role of education varies according to sector, size of firm, level of recruitment and local conditions.

5. Given employers' lack of knowledge about qualifications and the relatively arbitrary way in which they use them, it is difficult to give credence to the widespread notion that they are dissatisfied with the educational levels of young workers. The evidence suggests that they are often indifferent to their educational attainment and are interested in only a narrow range of basic skills or in traditional education for the 'high-fliers'. In general, employers seem to be satisfied with those young workers they employ.

6. This is consistent with the findings which indicate that young people tend to adjust relatively easily to working life and that the less academic tend to do so more than others.

7. Young workers are disadvantaged in the labour market mainly by age itself and the view that, because of their lack of family commitments, they will be unreliable. Evidence suggests that jobs are often distributed according to age life-cycle criteria.

The material considered emphasizes the importance of labour market structures and processes in mediating the relationship between education and production and between qualifications and work. It also suggests that they create radical discontinuities between the educational and occupational systems which are a major limitation upon the effectiveness of educational reforms. This both attenuates the force of the current occupationalist attack upon the liberal education tradition and suggests that occupationalist objectives will do little more than merely dilute the quality of the education which pupils might otherwise have received.

It also suggests that teachers should oppose their critics on educational grounds rather than being forced continually onto the sterile terrain of vocationalism. More generally, it can be suggested that the social reforms which have been pursued through educational reform in the post-war period, prior to the collapse of the liberal consensus and its political constituency, need to be approached through a direct assault upon the structural sources of inequality in demand-side institutions.

Notes

1. From Moore, 1983.
2. See *Vocational Preparation* (Further Education Unit, 1981), in which it is argued that vocational preparation students present a problem for FE colleges because they are neither academic enough to follow a traditional educational course nor destined for jobs of sufficient skill level for a craft type course. The answer is to turn to 'personal development' based in social and life skills. This is underpinned by a psychological maturation theory which presents these young people as immature and, so, actually requiring this type of approach.
3. See Finn, 1987. This book is an excellent and strongly argued study of the issues relating to the current education and training situation which places their development in an historical perspective.
4. See Grieco and Whipp, 1984.

References

Ashton, D. N., Maguire, M. J. and Garland, G. (1983) *Youth in the Labour Market*, Research Paper no. 34. London: Department of Employment, HMSO.

Ashton, D. N. and Maguire, M. J. (1986) *Young Adults in the Labour Market*, Research Paper no. 55. London: Department of Employment, HMSO.

Blackburn, R. and Mann, M. (1979) *The Working Class and the Labour Market*. Basingstoke: Macmillan.

Clarke, L. (1980) *The Transition from School to Work*. London: Department of Employment, HMSO.

Crompton, R. and Jones, G. (1984) *White Collar Proletariat.* Basingstoke: Macmillan.

Cumin, D. (1983) *School-Leavers, Qualifications and Employment*, mimeo. Nottingham.

Further Education Unit (1981) *Vocational Preparation.* London: HMSO.

Finn, D. (1987) *Training Without Jobs.* Basingstoke: Macmillan.

Granovetter, M. (1975) *Getting a Job.* Cambridge, Mass.: Harvard University Press.

Granovetter, M. (1981). 'Towards a sociological theory of income difference' in Berg, I. (ed.) *Sociological Perspectives on Labour Markets.* New York: Academic Press.

Grieco, M. (1984) *Using the Network* .... Paper given to Development Studies Association Annual Conference, University of Bath.

Grieco, M. and Whipp, R. (1984) *Women and the Workplace.* Work Organisation Research Centre, University of Ashton.

Holland, G. (1977) *Young People and Work: Report on the feasibility of a new programme of opportunities for unemployed young people* (The Holland Report), Manpower Services Commission.

Jones, J. (1983) *Interim Report*, British Petroleum. London.

Moore, R. (1983) 'Further education, pedagogy and production' in Gleeson, D. (ed.) *Youth Training and the Search for Work.* London: Routledge & Kegan Paul.

Moore, R. (1984) 'Schooling and the world of work', in Bates, I. *et al.*, *Schooling for the Dole?* Basingstoke: Macmillan.

Richards, G. (1982) *Work Experience Schemes for School Children: the shape of things to come?* mimeo. University of Warwick.

Troyna, B. and Smith, D. L. (eds) (1983) *Racism, School and the Labour Market.* Leicester: National Youth Bureau.

Chapter 14

Two Nations of Shopkeepers: Training for Retailing in France and Britain

V. Jarvis and S. J. Prais

■ Wider issues

A comparison between Britain and France of training for the retail trades brings to the fore some very basic questions, the answers to which are probably relevant to many other trades and to wider issues of training policy. First, how much training is really essential for most employees in this kind of industry for their immediate employment – which may require much common sense, but few complex technical skills? Secondly, is more than a bare minimum of training perhaps justified on broader grounds; for example, because training to higher vocational standards leads to higher general educational standards, with direct benefits to the individuals concerned, and benefits for the economy in improving flexibility between trades? Thirdly, changes in technology have – as is familiar – reduced skill requirements in some occupations and increased them in others; in retailing we have to ask what are the effects on training requirements not only of the recent electronic advances affecting the work of the cashier, but also of the continuing trend towards self-service and the additional skill-flexibility required from a reduced labour force.

As we shall see, Britain and France rely on very different schemes of training for retailing; both countries have encountered serious problems in their training, and in both countries considerable changes are in progress

Source: V. Jarvis and S. J. Prais (1989) 'Two nations of shopkeepers: training for retailing in France and Britain', *National Institute Economic Review*, May 1989, pp. 58–74.

or being planned. Our task here is to evaluate the gaps between the two countries to see what may be learnt from French experience that may be of wider benefit.

In both countries the retailing industry is a substantial employer, accounting for 1.4 million full-time employees and self-employed in Britain and 1.3 million in France; in addition there are 0.9 million part-time employees in Britain, mostly women often working for very few hours a week, and 0.3 million in France.[1] Altogether nearly a tenth of the total (full-time equivalent) workforce in each country is engaged in retailing. The industry accounts for a yet higher proportion of all young female entrants to the workforce – about one in five of all employed women under 20 in both countries – and a proper resolution of training issues is of particular importance to them.[2]

A particularly serious difficulty in organizing retail training is that labour turnover in these occupations is extremely high. The rate of turnover varies according to age and location: perhaps half of employees of all ages leave within a year; at younger ages labour turnover is undoubtedly very much greater. In large cities with plentiful employment opportunities, labour turnover rates of '100 or 200 per cent a year' were frequently mentioned; but this is no more than an approximate manner of speaking. Employers who are much affected by this problem speak in terms of 'survival rates' within the first year: for example, half of all young new employees have left within three months of recruitment, and 80 per cent within six months (the position in large stores in London's West End). With such very high rates of labour turnover, employers obviously do not find it worth investing very much in the way of training; for part-time employees the difficulties of organizing training are greater, even if labour turnover for certain categories (for example, Saturday-only employees) is often lower than for full-time employees.[3]

Pressures to reduce costs of distribution have increased – not simply as a result of increased competition amongst the many types of local retailers (supermarkets, chain stores, small independent shopkeepers) – but as a result of fundamental underlying economic forces: retailing has become expensive in relation to the costs incurred at the manufacturing stages. This is because retailers sell individual items to individual customers, whereas manufacturing costs continue to fall as mass production and automation continue to advance. The time that a sales assistant spends with a customer has consequently had to be reduced to economize in staff-time per unit sale, by adopting self-service in varying degrees. There are ever fewer assistants to advise on varieties or sizes; product information tends to be limited to that shown on the wrapper or label; in some shops the customer sees only the cashier. It is not that old-fashioned service has disappeared, but rather that a smaller section of the buying public is prepared to pay for it, and then only in special lines.[4]

The required mix of retailing skills consequently continues to change. Some may be employed as little more than 'mechanical shelf-fillers' in large supermarkets; others need to be capable of carrying out a wider range of routine functions; and some must be able to absorb new information, deal courteously with customers' requests for information, deal with complaints and returned goods, take remedial action, and exercise their initiative in advancing the cause of their business.

As explained in our previous comparisons with France of training for other occupations (construction workers, office workers, mechanics and electricians), the French system of vocational training relies heavily on *full*-time vocational schools for 14–18-year-olds;[5] these provide a substantially greater supply of vocationally-qualified personnel in these occupations than the British system and, as will be seen, this applies also to retailing occupations.

An initial word on the German system of training for retailing will help in understanding the French approach. As described in a previous National Institute study,[6] training for retail distribution in Germany is very widely undertaken, mainly on two-year or three-year *part*-time courses under their system of obligatory day-release at college for virtually all who have left full-time schooling and are under the age of 18. Some 100 000 candidates a year in Germany pass vocational tests in distributive occupations at the end of such courses, usually at ages 18–20; they account for about one in five of all female school-leavers, and about one in three of all females passing vocational tests in all occupations together. These numbers are immensely greater than for Britain. The final three to four years of compulsory secondary schooling for most pupils in Germany (at ages 12 to 15–16) contain increasing elements of vocational instruction, and prepare the transition from general full-time schooling to vocational part-time schooling; knowledge of common retail products, such as textiles and their care, and an introduction to statistics in commercial applications (up to the calculation of a correlation), are included in such courses at secondary schools.[7]

Our next task, in the section below, is to outline the main recognized qualifications in retailing in France and Britain and to compare the number of candidates attaining them. Important differences in the subjects covered in the training courses for the main retailing qualifications in each country are described in the third section. This is followed by a brief account of other levels of qualifications. The fifth section is concerned with important developments in the past decade. The sixth section provides a summary, and discusses the implications of our comparisons.[8]

■ Numbers obtaining vocational qualifications

The French system of full-time vocational schools (*lycées professionels*, abbreviated LP[9]) for 14–16-year-olds includes schools with courses for those wishing to prepare for work in retailing. These schools usually also include courses on office work for those intending to qualify as secretaries, book-keepers, etc; courses on typing and the elements of book-keeping are obligatory for those following a course in distribution. For many pupils these courses include the last two years of their compulsory schooling, and at least one additional year. These French commercial LPs typically have about 500 pupils, often almost all girls; larger LPs have both technical and commercial departments. They are similar to the technical or central[10] schools that formed part of the publicly-funded secondary schooling system in larger towns in Britain until comprehensive schooling became the dominant policy a generation ago.

Apart from those attending full-time courses at secondary vocational schools in France, other school-leavers (including some from the general comprehensive schools – the *collèges* – who finish school at 16) go on to take an apprenticeship with a retailing employer and attend part-time courses at apprenticeship centres for two years (usually a day or two each week, or one week in four; for some apprentices it may amount to twice that).[11] Employers taking on apprentices are required to have a qualified master craftsman (*maître d'apprentis*) under whose supervision the apprentice follows an approved programme of tasks. Apprentices' wages are deductible from the training levy of ½ per cent of the annual wage bill, to which all employers are subject irrespective of whether they have apprentices or not. The part-time apprenticeship route has become somewhat less important in retailing since the early 1980s and now accounts for 45 per cent of those passing; both routes lead to the same nationally-recognized vocational qualifications.

In total some 14 500 candidates passed their final examinations in France in 1986 as sales-persons at the end of such two- and three-year courses; the majority (11 000) passed at the basic level known as the *certificat d'aptitude professionnelle* (CAP), and the remainder (3500) at the higher level known as the *brevet d'enseignement professionnel* (BEP).

Courses in Britain leading to the status of a qualified sales-person are available at Colleges of Further Education for those over 16, that is, after the completion of compulsory schooling; the courses last between one year part-time and two years full-time. As described in section 3 below, standards comparable to those in France (the CAP and the BEP) lie somewhere between the General level and the National Diploma level of the Business and Technician Education Council (BTEC) with specialization in distribution.[12] A number of other bodies in Britain also examine at this level, and some are highly specialized (such as the Drapers' Chamber of Trade and the Institute of Grocery Distribution; further details are given in Table 14.1, footnotes (p) and (u)).[13] The number passing all these courses at this standard in Britain in 1986 totalled some 1650.

Table 14.1 Numbers gaining vocational qualifications in distribution in France and Britain, 1986. (Sources: Britain: Annual statistical summaries from the bodies mentioned. France: Ministère de l'Education Nationale, *Statistique des Diplômes de l'Enseignement Technique: Session 1986* (doc. nos. 5649–50), Paris, 1987.)

France		Britain[h]	
Qualification	Number qualifying	Qualification	Number qualifying
Qualified salesperson			
BEP			
Retail distribution[a]	3700	BETC National[k]	150
CAP			
Sales person (general)[b]	7800	BETC General Diploma	400
Grocery[c]	900	BTEC General Certificate[m]	400
Florist[d]	700	Pitman's Level II[n]	400
Prepared meats[e]	600	Others[p]	300
Others[f]	900		———
	10800		1500
	Total 14500		1650
Pre-vocational courses for junior sales assistant			
Comprehensive school:			
retailing courses[g]	3000	C&G foundation courses[q]	3000
	———	CPVE retailing modules[r]	1200
		RSA Vocational Preparation[s]	1500
		Pitman's Level I[t]	600
		Others[u]	300
	3000		6600

(a) *BEP Commerce: 1ère option aux employés des services de vente* (course 3315).
(b) *Vendeur* (course 3304). Many who study for the BEP take the CAP at the same time: to avoid double-counting, the published CAP figure has here been reduced by 82 per cent of the BEP total (as suggested in a personal communication from the French Ministry of Education, consistent with the general overlap noted in the *Annuaire Statistique*, 1986, p. 295).
(c) *Commis épicier* (course 3307).
(d) *Fleuriste (fleurs naturelles)* (course 3309).
(e) *Commis vendeur en charcuterie* (course 3311).
(f) *Commis vendeur en librairie* (course 3305); *commis poissonnier* (3306); *commis vendeur en quincaillerie* (3312); *agent de commercialisation; pièces de rechange et accessoires-automobiles* (3313); *agent de magasinage et de messagerie* (3330).

(g) No recognized vocational qualification in France at this level: based on numbers (unpublished estimate kindly provided by French Ministry of Education) attending courses for 15–16-year-olds at French full-time comprehensive schools (*option technologique economique* at the *collèges*) which include retail distribution. These courses appear close in standard to the British courses listed at this level in this table.

(h) Coverage of the constituent countries varies slightly (for example, City and Guilds excludes N Ireland; figures for BTEC exclude Scotvec).

(k) Certificates and Diplomas (the latter is probably of a higher standard than the BEP: see text).

(m) The scope of the BTEC General Certificate is much narrower than the French CAP; since the standard of the courses taken for the BTEC General Certificate are the same as for the Diploma, the numbers have been included here. No deduction has been made for those continuing to National level.

(n) Pitman's Retail and Distribution Course, Level II.

(p) Drapers' Chamber of Trade, Buying and Merchandizing Course, and Retail Selling Course; National Institute of Hardware Commodity Certificate; National Association of Retail Furnishers, National Certificate and Diploma; National Institute of Fresh Produce, Trade Knowledge Certificate.

(q) City and Guilds Retail Distribution Skills (course 9441) and Foundation Certificate in Distribution (course 692, now phased out and replaced by 9441).

(r) Not externally examined: based on numbers *attending* CPVE classes in retail distribution (at the 'exploratory' level) at secondary schools and awarded a final 'profile' by the teacher (*Statistics for CPVE Students and Schemes*, DES, September 1987).

(s) Not externally examined: based on number of candidates assessed by employers, colleges, or YTS managing agents, as having satisfactorily completed a range of tasks (now replaced by the Vocational Certificate and Diploma in Retail Distribution, assessed in the same way).

(t) Pitman's Retail and Distribution Course, Level I.

(u) National Institute of Hardware Introductory Certificates; Institute of Grocery Distribution Commodity Knowledge Certificate; National Institute of Fresh Produce, Retail Assistant course; Wines and Spirits Educational Trust, Off-licence Retail Personnel; City and Guilds Delicatessen and Provisions course: these figures have been reduced to avoid double counting of those who continue to a higher level.

Taken together, it seems that about nine times as many now reach this standard each year in France as in Britain. France is far from training as many as Germany in these occupations, but is still well ahead of Britain.

This disparity between the current flows of persons qualifying each year in France and Britain is broadly confirmed by population surveys in the two countries which cast light on the 'stock' of those employed as sales persons who have a vocational qualification (see Table 14.2). In France in 1982 some 24 per cent of those employed as sales-persons had vocational qualifications at the level of a CAP or a BEP.[14] In Britain in 1984 about 3 per cent of those employed as sales-persons or sales assistants had a

Table 14.2 Stock of qualified employees in retailing occupations in France, 1982, and Britain, 1984 (as percentages of all employed). (Sources: Britain: *Labour Force Survey 1984*, special tabulations kindly provided by Department of Employment Statistical Division. The figures quoted here relate to Occupation 055.1 (salesmen and sales assistants). France: *Recensement général 1982: Formation*, INSEE, table 07 (p. 111); occupation category 55 (*'employés de commerce'*).)

	France	Britain	
Qualifications above A-level			
University degree, BTS, etc.[a]	1	University degree, BTEC Higher, etc.[b]	1
Intermediate vocational qualifications			
CAP, BEP[c]	24	BTEC National, City and Guilds, etc[d]	3
		Trade apprenticeships	2
Intermediate general educational qualifications			
Baccalauréat	5	A level[e]	4
General first-level educational qualifications			
CAP, BEPC, none	70	O-level, CSE, none	90
Total	100		100

(a) Includes all qualifications of at least two years post-Baccalauréat study.
(b) University/CNAA degree. Member of Professional Institution, BTEC Higher National Certificate and Diploma, teaching qualification.
(c) CAP, BEP, BP, BEI, BEC, BEA, *Bac Technologique.*
(d) BTEC National Certificate and Diploma, City and Guilds.
(e) The original source unfortunately includes BTEC General in this category; for our purposes, it should be included with intermediate vocational qualifications.

corresponding qualification (BTEC National Certificate or Diploma, or a City and Guilds Certificate); if we include those declaring they had served a trade apprenticeship, without having received a formal qualification, the total rises to 5 per cent. For females alone – who form the great majority of employees in this trade – the proportions were virtually the same as just quoted; for males they were slightly higher in both countries (27 per cent qualified in France, and 8 per cent in Britain for those qualified or having served an apprenticeship). In both countries the range of qualified specializations encompassed at this level in these surveys is broader than retailing, and includes others working as retailing assistants who have formally qualified – say, as butchers or office workers – at the same levels (for example, CAP in France, or BTEC in Britain).

The differences between British and French employees in distribution can perhaps be put in this way: in Britain, a qualified employee in distribution is a rarity – with only one in about 30 having a formal qualification; in France the majority of shop employees are also unqualified, but there is a significant proportion – about one in four – who have acquired examination vocational qualifications. They set the standard which helps the shop to be run in a more 'professional' way, and provide a larger qualified 'seedbed' for managerial levels.

The deficiencies in Britain at the main 'craft' level of qualification are partly compensated by training to lower levels.[15] As part of the current Youth Training Scheme some attend day-release classes or receive equivalent training on employers' premises; others receive short spells of instruction in their shops during, for example, the first half-hour on a Thursday morning (the practice in many of the larger stores in London's West End). YTS courses may lead to a variety of qualifications, almost all hitherto – that is, under the one-year YTS arrangements – below anything that would be recognized in France or Germany as a 'vocational qualification' (further details are in the fourth section and below). Together, the total number reaching this initial standard amounted to some 7000 in 1986.[16] These courses should be welcomed for what they are, namely, foundation or pre-vocational courses which raise standards to a limited extent, and may subsequently lead some candidates to higher levels – though so far that has not been evident.

At secondary schools in Britain, encouraged by the Government's recent Technical and Vocational Education Initiative, experimental pre-vocational courses have been promoted for 14–18-year-olds in the last few years, some of which lead to a Certificate of Pre-Vocational Education in retailing for the over 16s. At present, this is the nearest arrangement in Britain which might, if developed, approach the French full-time vocational schools. Standards aimed at are variable (we have seen a very good course at one school); but, in general, only an introductory level is aimed at, and candidates are not externally examined. Some 1200 completed such courses in retailing in 1986.[17] The French general secondary comprehensive schools (the *collèges*, not the LP with which we have been concerned above) also have introductory pre-vocational courses which were taken by some 3000 pupils aged 15–16 in commercial subjects with specialization in retailing.

Whilst our concern in this study is with the main vocational qualifications acquired by the broad cross-section of school-leavers who go on to work in shops, a few words relating to higher levels of qualification may be offered here for the sake of perspective. The highest British qualification shown in Table 14.1, the BTEC National Certificate or Diploma in distribution, is intended for those who leave school with the equivalent of O-level qualifications and aspire to middle-management positions in retailing, and eventually to top management. There were some 150 such National awards in Britain in 1986. The nearest French equivalent (not shown in Table 14.1 because of the wider scope of the course) is probably the *Baccalauréat Technologique G3, Techniques Commerciales* (till 1987, *Baccalauréat de Technicien*) taken as three-year full-time courses at ages 16–19 at their *lycées (section d'enseignement technologique)*;[18] this course covers business studies in a broad sense with an emphasis on retail and wholesale distribution. Entry to the course requires that the candidate has previously passed examinations equivalent to our O-levels. Over 12 000 passed their *Bac* in this field in 1986.[19]

■ What should a shop assistant know?

The scope and depth of knowledge required by a 'shelf-filler' in order to do his work well in a supermarket obviously differs from that required by someone in a personal-service shop who advises customers on, for example, the quality of an item of clothing (appearance, washability), and can measure how much a sleeve may need shortening; or advise on the various makes of vacuum cleaners (durability, power, length of guarantee period and conditions); or is involved in re-ordering supplies. Education, training and certification clearly depend on the *mix* of ultimate objectives: it is necessary to decide, for example, whether most trainees should be given an understanding of some speciality, together with training in wider aspects of retailing with the aim of flexibility amongst the various tasks in a shop; or, on the other hand, whether it is satisfactory that most are instructed barely beyond the immediate tasks on which they are to be employed.

Differences on this kind in general objectives are to be detected in the instruction given to distributive trainees in France and Britain. Briefly, French courses are broader and deeper and, in particular, place more emphasis on:

1. Knowledge of products,
2. Practical selling techniques,
3. Commercial documentation,
4. Mathematical skills,
5. The study of general 'academic' subjects, including a foreign language.

The paragraphs below explain these differences in more detail with the help of illustrations from the qualification taken most frequently in France, the *certificat d'aptitude professionnelle* (CAP), and the most widely available nearest British equivalents, the BTEC General Diploma and General Certificate. But something needs first to be said on the scope and balance of the curriculum and of the final examinations.

□   Curriculum

The British BTEC General Diploma and the BTEC General Certificate each cover a common 'core' of three subjects:

	Length of test
People and communications	2 hours
Business calculations	2 hours
Elements of distribution	2 hours

In addition, the Certificate (based on part-time study) requires one optional subject; and the Diploma (based on full-time study) requires five optional subjects. These are chosen from a range, dependent on the particular college, and include subjects such as: Consumer Legislation, World of Work, Health and Safety, Merchandise Display, Elements of Data Processing.[20]

The scope of the French CAP courses is the same whether studying full-time in the LPs or part-time under apprenticeship. Half the study-time is spent on general educational subjects: French, applied mathematics, a foreign language, social studies, etc.; and half on vocational aspects, including: commercial documentation, organization of distribution, product knowledge, typing, and practical selling skills. All studying full-time at the LPs are required to obtain work experience (*stages*) for a minimum of 12 weeks during the second and third years of their course; an employer's report on that experience is endorsed on their official record book (*carnet de stages*).

The final CAP examination involves some 12 hours of written, practical and oral tests, as follows:

	Length of test
Industrial knowledge and commercial correspondence	2 hours
Product knowledge	1
Selling (practical examination)	1
French	2
Business calculations	1½

Organization of distribution	1
General legal and socio-economic knowledge (oral)	¾
Modern foreign language (oral)	¼
Display and window dressing	1
Typing	½
Specialized complementary skills (practical examination)[21]	1

In order to pass the examination as a whole – and receive his certificate – the candidate has to attain a pass-mark in each of the first three subjects, and an average pass-mark in the next four; the final four subjects have to be taken by all candidates, but a pass-mark in these is not essential in order to pass the examination as a whole (for each such subject passed, there is an endorsement on the final CAP certificate). A grade – equivalent to distinction, credit or bar pass – is awarded in relation to the whole examination (no partial certificates are issued; if only one or two subjects are failed they may be re-taken, otherwise the whole year has to be repeated). In assessing that grade, the test on practical selling receives as much as a quarter of the total marks: this indicates the importance attached in France to instruction in practical selling methods (as discussed further below). Also noteworthy is the French requirement of objective external assessment by examiners who do not know the candidates; in contrast to the current British trend, assessment by the candidate's teacher or employer is not considered adequate in France.

The scope of the British BTEC General *Certificate* is clearly narrower than the French CAP; the BTEC General *Diploma* with its broader coverage of optional subjects is closer to the French course, though some important gaps still exist – particularly product knowledge and practical selling skills. Since candidates in Britain have to choose from the particular range of options that are available at each college, not all of which are related to distribution, there is no necessary correspondence with the broad background relevant to retailing expected of all French candidates.[22]

Roughly the same proportions of candidates pass the French and British examinations at this level (60–62 per cent for CAP and BEP, 64 per cent for the BTEC General award in distribution). For lower-level courses in Britain (such as City and Guilds 9441), hardly a candidate fails;[23] and for some courses (such as CPVE), certificates are issued based on attendance, and not on final tests.

☐   **Product knowledge**

The CAP can be taken both as a course for the general sales-person and for those in specialized shops (see Table 15.1); the general course – *CAP*

Vendeur – is the most popular and is taken by all studying full-time in the LPs, while the specialized courses are taken mainly by those in apprenticeship.[24] Even those on the general course are required to study a specialist product area (for example, domestic electrical appliances) based on their spell of work experience. They are required to produce a *dossier* (coursework file) of product-specific information covering, for example, quality of materials, weight, country of origin, care, uses, selling points, disadvantages, substitutes, accessories.

The final written examination includes related questions, such as:

> 'Should a shop exchange an electric iron under guarantee if the sole plate became rough? The user had scrubbed it with an abrasive powder to remove cloth which had stuck to it (the examinee is provided with a copy of the guarantee, which refers to misuse).'[25]

The essential point of this part of the course is that the pupil looks for the different properties and qualities of competing varieties of a product; he learns that a higher price does not simply mean a greater profit margin, but may reflect many aspects of a product which may not be obvious; and he learns that these 'analytical techniques' can be applied to other products – apart from those studied – so that he develops professionalism, pride and justified confidence in relation to his work.[26]

In Britain the major nearest equivalent courses for sales assistants (the BTEC Certificate and Diploma) do not include a systematic approach to product knowledge as an obligatory component. Optional subjects in this area are available in some colleges but are taken only by a minority of pupils. The specialized trade bodies (for example Drapers' Chamber of Trade), however, regard commodity knowledge as an integral part of their courses.[27]

□   Practical selling

The *dossier* prepared by the pupil on a particular range of products, as described above, is used again in the final French practical selling examination. An examining panel consistuting of a shopkeeper and a teacher – both of whom must be *unknown* to the candidate – question him on the products on which he has acquired a deeper practical knowledge. The candidate goes through a selling demonstration of a particular item to a member of the panel; marks are awarded separately on: receiving the customer courteously, ascertaining his requirements, presentation of the product, knowledge of associated products, communication skills, basic mental arithmetic, handling of cash, etc. He is also questioned on broader aspects of retailing, such as the legal obligation of the shop to the customer. The standard of presentation of the *dossier* and the candidate's employment record book (*carnet de stages*) are taken into account in awarding the final mark.

☐ Commercial documentation

Candidates at CAP level are expected to be competent in basic administrative tasks and prepare related documents, such as delivery notes, invoices, statements, calculations of customer discounts, re-ordering stock, and the use of computer keyboards. This extends, for example, to asking a candidate, as part of the final test, to revise current filing methods with a view to introducing a computer: he is given a specimen list of seven customers and required to construct a five-digit code incorporating the client's name, county (*département*), year of first order and method of payment.[28]

In Britain, though the BTEC General qualification is at a fairly basic level, the course seems to aim for a greater degree of responsibility; the candidate has to deal with things that have gone wrong – but more in a cosmetic than a fundamental way. For example, he has to be able to write a letter to a customer apologizing for an error, or a memo to the stockroom manager for an assurance that stock would not in future be 'wrongly labelled and wrongly priced' and not 'damaged by careless handling' (but without being expected to diagnose and remedy the source of these errors).[29] These is a surprising lack of gradation in responsibilities, probably reflecting the paucity of candidates with formal qualifications.

☐ Mathematical skills

In both countries the final tests include question papers on business calculations. In Britain the BTEC paper examines basic arithmetic. (If a van sets out at 13.45 on a 3½ hour journey, when is it due to arrive? What is the total cost of two items at £18.85 each plus six items at £5.50 each? What is the price of an item discounted by 35 per cent? Questions on rates of interest on hire-purchase transactions were included in the BTEC test in 1980, but no longer in 1985).[30] Calculators are expected to be used in Britain in such tests, partly because they would be used in practice, and partly because such questions are considered by BTEC to be otherwise made unnecessarily difficult for most candidates. The standard corresponds to that expected in England of those who have not attempted a school-leaving qualification in mathematics, or attained only low-level grades at CSE; it recognizes the need for remedial education in mathematics (making good what has not been learnt at secondary school), though many candidates on BTEC General courses would be capable of a higher level.[31]

The French mathematics test aims a little higher. At the simplest level an invoice has to be completed in which values have to be calculated from given prices and quantities (and other combinations involving long divisions); a discount has to be allowed from the total, and VAT added. These calculations have to be done by pencil-and-paper methods, *not* with a calculator. A more difficult calculation involves choosing between foreign exchange rates available in the home and destination countries. Occasionally an acquaintance with algebra is called for, if only at an elementary level: the candidate has to express the interest payable (y) as a 'function of the number of months (m)' for which the capital is deposited, draw a graph of the function, and read from that graph the number of months when the interest reaches a certain sum.[32] The veneer of algebra is not, of course, essential for questions of this sort in practice; it is a mark of the higher academic aspiration in France that pupils for these occupations are expected to reach this higher mathematical level despite the fact that many (if not most) previously had low general attainments in their secondary schools.

Standards in mathematics at CAP for specialized retail trades (for example, ironmonger, automobile spares) and for technical courses, such as motor mechanic, are substantially higher than for the general retailing course.[33]

☐   General subjects

The French educational ideal of making *culture générale* available to every pupil leads to readings in classical French literature being included as part of the classwork for those on retailing courses. The final examination in French thus includes, for example, passages from the nineteenth-century writer Emile Zola, and requires the pupil to explain phrases that a modern-day teenager might not find straightforward. A dictation is also included and may also be from such a classical literary source.[34]

The nearest comparable BTEC test of literacy, labelled *People and Communications*, is pitched at a more prosaic level; it requires candidates, for example, to prepare notes for a telephone call telling X to deputize for Y at an appointment next week; or to draft a memorandum banning staff from smoking in a new showroom.[35] The British approach is obviously more narrowly oriented to work-tasks; even so, such tasks are a source of complaint amongst retailing employers in Britain since sales-persons do not usually need to write memoranda of this type. Colleges in Britain have not found it easy to settle on the right balance; the French explicit objective of raising *general* education standards as part of *vocational* training makes it easier for them to choose an acceptable syllabus.

The French candidate is also required to study a foreign language; in practice this is usually English (the pass-mark corresponds roughly to a CSE grade 4). It is of obvious practical value in dealing with tourists; it also keeps the door open for those who may wish at a later stage to proceed to higher education (for which competence in a foreign language is a pre-requisite in France).

Taken as a whole, the above details clearly express the fundamental French view that vocational education at those ages should be acquired hand-in-hand with additional general education. For very many pupils proposing to work in retailing, instruction in such vocational topics is seen – by parents and teachers – as providing an important means for simultaneously advancing their standards of general education;[36] for some, it also opens the door to higher education.

■ Vocational qualifications at other levels

So far we have been concerned with the main level of qualification in retailing in France and its nearest British equivalent. This section describes briefly two other levels of qualification: one which is lower, and of growing importance in Britain; and one which is higher, and of growing importance in France.

A very basic qualification in Retail Distribution Skills (City and Guilds course no. 9441) was obtained by some 2300 persons in Britain in 1986. The intention of this qualification was to meet employers' needs for a reliable certificate confirming that an applicant for employment already has an acquaintance with basic sales skills. It is usually attained by a new entrant in nine months on the basis of brief part-time instruction on practical skills while at work (for example, during half-hour sessions on Thursday mornings plus one full day's off-the-job instruction[37]); no attendance at college is required – which is seen as an advantage for those not wishing to be 'sent back to school'.

The candidate has to carry out ten specified basic practical tasks, such as: using the telephone, restocking shelves, handling payments (including cheques and credit cards), and 'handling complaints'.[38] The aim is similar to part of the practical selling tests in the French CAP examination described above; but no commodity knowledge is called for, and no written work (comparable to the *dossier*) has to be produced. The completion of these tasks is signed for by someone accredited by the employer's designated training supervisor – a person not required to hold any formal qualifications – whose assessment techniques may, or may not, be 'moderated' by City and Guilds.[39]

There is also a final written test of an hour's duration, externally set by City and Guilds, with 50 multiple-choice questions in which one of four alternatives has to be ticked, such as:

- When goods are stolen from a store, they become part of the store's (a) loss leaders, (b) perishables, (c) shrinkage, (d) consumer durables.

- If interrupted by a customer when changing displays, the sales-person should (a) ask the customer to wait a minute, (b) leave the display to serve the customer, (c) ask the customer to shout when he/she needs some help, (d) call for someone to serve the customer.[40]

These multiple-choice questions are also marked by the training supervisor; if the candidate attends a college, a teacher may do the marking.[41]

The absence of an external examiner for the practical tasks led some employers to remark to us that the system is 'open to abuse', and that they would not engage anyone solely on the basis of this certificate. The Royal Society of Arts provides a qualification at more or less the same level; certification is also based on employers' or instructors' assessment, and not on external examinations. There has been a very rapid growth in Britain in the number of youngsters taking these basic courses: in 1983–86 there was a rise from 600 to 2300 in those passing the City and Guilds course 9441, and other certifying bodies have had similar rises. This is clearly related to the MSC's recognition of qualifications at that level as adequate to attract the subsidy for the one-year Youth Training Scheme (discussed in the next section).

The main vocational qualification in retailing in France, the CAP, was attained by some 11 000 pupils in 1986 (see Table 14.1); as mentioned above, a slightly higher qualification – the *brevet d'études professionelles* (BEP[42]) – was passed by almost 4000 pupils after a two-year full-time course starting usually at age 16. It was originally intended for pupils of somewhat higher academic ability aspiring to supervisory positions in retailing (head of department in a large store, assistant manager in a small shop); and it provides access to higher-level baccalaureate courses. The BEP has a broader scope than the CAP and a somewhat greater level of difficulty (until 1987 it did not require a practical selling test, but since then the same practical selling test as for the CAP is required). Twelve weeks' work experience is now required (as for the CAP), together with the production of a *dossier* on a particular range of products. The greater level of difficulty of the written examination may be illustrated from the mathematics tests which include, for example, calculations of payments by instalment at given rates of interest, and statistical calculations of quartiles from grouped frequency distributions.

As from September 1987 the content of the main CAP course has been amalgamated with the higher-level BEP course;[43] both levels of qualification continue, but a greater proportion of pupils are now expected to attain the higher level.

■ Recent developments

The growth of self-service, of longer shop-opening hours, and of electronic cash registers, have all had important influences in the past decade on retailers' *demand* for labour, both in quantity and quality; similarly, the tendency to stay on at full-time schooling to higher ages, and the introduction of new training schemes, have affected the *supply* of labour to this industry. The industry's actual mix of skills inevitably can adjust only over a period of years to such developments and, while doing so, recruitment of particular types of labour may almost cease. Such short-term imbalances need to be distinguished from desirable long-term objectives.

The long-term trend towards self-service is now so familiar that it is easy to overlook its continuing growth in commodity coverage, and the consequential continuing pressures on traditional smaller retailers. Over the years the variety of lines offered by supermarkets has broadened from their original concentration on foodstuffs ('groceries') to include clothing, toys, chemists' sundries, do-it-yourself household items, etc.; with increased ownership of cars, out-of-town hypermarkets are being es-tablished where larger quantities can be bought at less frequent intervals at lower costs. The goods are almost all pre-packed, or packed and weighed by the customer – no need for the shopkeeper or his trainee assistant to weigh out a pound of pearl barley, and no need for anyone to explain differences between varieties, since everything is printed on the package. The trends towards pre-packaging and self-service continues in both Britain and France; while it now seems clear from both US and European experience that there is a residual demand for smaller shops (growing in certain lines – the 'boutiques') and for specialist service-sections within supermarkets to offer more service, expertise and customer guidance, the net tendency has undoubtedly been for small shops to decline in number. There has consequently been a fall in demand for personnel trained in the broad mix of skills traditionally required in a small shop.[44]

This has been very apparent in France, where a large proportion of those qualifying in the past decade with a CAP or BEP in retailing have been very slow in securing employment. Of those in the final year of their CAP courses in 1985 in all subjects, a special survey showed 25 per cent were still seeking employment nine months after qualification; 34 per cent continued in full-time education in the following year, so that, of those who left school after their CAP, 54 per cent were unemployed. Amongst females who had been on a CAP course in distribution and had sought work, unemployment was higher still, at 67 per cent.[45] These figures cast *prima facie* doubt on the efficacy of French vocational education; they need however to be seen in the perspective that amongst *all* school-leavers (not simply amongst those with CAP qualifications) unemployment has risen to 37 per cent (for girls, 47 per cent) when calculated according to the same methods.

Changes in general education have exacerbated France's problem of the initial employment of those leaving vocational courses. An increasing proportion of pupils now stay on to higher ages in full-time French secondary schools (up from 44 per cent of all 18-year-olds in 1968 to 67 per cent in 1982[46]), and the kind of pupil who moves to vocational schools to take retailing courses has changed from, say, being somewhere near the middle of the ability range to somewhere nearer the bottom quarter: these are the kind of pupils who, having had difficulty at school, subsequently also have difficulty in finding and retaining employment. Even if they attain a vocational qualification, as many do as a result of hard work and perseverance, they find it difficult to compete with those of higher ability who have taken more advanced general or vocational qualifications (at *Bac* level).[47]

Despite these difficulties – and, indeed, adding to them at this time – the numbers qualifying each year with a CAP or BEP in retailing have tripled during the past decade, from some 5000 in 1975 to nearly 15 000 in 1986; the rate of increase has been slightly greater at the higher level of qualification (BEP).

In Britain during the same decade the numbers attaining the BTEC *General* Certificate and Diploma rose from 300 to 800, but this was almost entirely offset by a decline at the higher level – the BTEC *National* Certificate and Diploma – which fell from 500 to 150.

☐   **Extended shopping hours**

One of the most prominent recent changes in labour requirements has resulted from extended shopping hours and more weekend shopping, in response to consumers' demands reflected in changes in legislation. With the help of part-timers, employers can match the availability of staff more closely to the needs of customers. The increase in the employment of part-timers has been particularly marked in Britain: in 1987 some 61 per cent of all women in retailing in Britain were part-timers (three-quarters of whom were married), and 25 per cent in France.[48] Employers prefer the responsibility and maturity of the married woman to the inexperienced younster, and married women find such part-time work fits in well with their domestic responsibilities. Shopping hours in Britain are at present more flexible than in France, and there is also a tax advantage in Britain in employing part-timers; these seem to be important reasons why part-time employment has become more important in Britain than in France.[49]

☐ New technology

Electronic cash registers, with central recording of sales and stock changes, have contributed to greater efficiency at checkouts, in stock recording and in re-ordering; perhaps more important for the success of the retailer, especially in fashion items, is that electronic recording has speeded up the rate of adaption of a shop's range to changes in fashion and to unexpected changes in weather: speed of restocking is the essence of success in such shops. Nevertheless, these technical developments have not greatly affected the work of the great majority of retailing employees. Retraining of checkout operators to use electronic point-of-sale equipment seems to require between half a day and three days, and much of that training seems to be concerned with what to do when the operator makes a mistake or equipment goes wrong![50] On some electronic systems the work of checkout operators initially became more complex since they were required to enter more numerical information than previously; the use of bar-coding, and associated devices for the automatic recognition and pricing of items at the cash desk, is now considerably easing and speeding their tasks. Much of the saving of direct costs with such systems arises not at the checkout, but at an earlier stage, in that individual price-ticketing of products in supermarkets – a labour-intensive process hitherto required to speed the work of the checkout operator – can now be dispensed with: a single label on the relevant shelf-edge is now adequate for the customer, and the electronic till finds the latest price from its memory after reading the bar-code.

The net effect of these factors requires a distinction to be drawn between small shops, larger department stores, and supermarkets. For smaller, more specialized shops, a greater economy today in the use of labour favours the employment of those with the capability to adapt quickly and responsibly to a variety of tasks. Smaller retailers in France with whom we discussed the problem of the unemployment of CAP and BEP pupils fully endorsed the continuing value of the education and training provided by these courses, especially in product knowledge and approach to the customer; they continue to regard these qualifications as the *minimum* for their staff.[51] But they have not recently been recruiting additional staff for expansion, presumably because of growing competition from department stores and supermarkets, and because of increased efficiency in labour and store layout.

Among larger department stores (*grands magasins*) there is little doubt in both France and Britain that the prime characteristics required today for the great majority of those employed as sales assistants are a welcoming manner (while maintaining a 'proper distance'), the ability to listen and answer, good *rapport* and communication, and arithmetical competence; someone with a good general education (to *baccalauréat*) level is at present often preferred to someone with vocational qualifications and of lower general ability. In supermarkets, shelf-filling can be done with hardly any training; and at the checkout, the main requirement appears to be the ability to work under pressure and to withstand tedium. Most retailing employees thus no longer require a high level of specialized vocational preparation, extending over several years, in the way that those working in, say, engineering today find beneficial or even essential. These may seem well-worn truths; they nevertheless need re-stating here in view of the problems currently experienced by qualified retailing trainees in France.

☐   Comparison with Germany

France's experience of training for retailing stands in remarkable contrast with Germany's. Nearly 100 000 young persons, almost seven times as many as in France, qualified in Germany in 1986 as retail assistants; and the number qualifying in Germany has increased by about a third in the past decade. The German trainees benefit in many ways from their system of day release (obligatory for all school-leavers under 18 wishing to take employment); those benefits extend well outside the skills required for retailing, and have to be assessed in terms of increased responsiveness to technical change, increased workforce flexibility between trades, and raised general standards of education.[52] The German unemployment rate, six months after the completion of a two-year retailing course, was only 8 per cent (the latest statistics for this occupation relate to 1985; the present position is similar according to informed opinion).[53]

The most apparent difference between the French and German systems of vocational training is that the German system is almost entirely work-based, while the French rely – for just over half their retailing trainees – on a school-based system. In other words: in Germany a youngster seeks his training place with an employer *before* arranging his vocational schooling; if he cannot find a place in retailing, he will seek a place in another branch of activity, and will be trained in that other branch.[54] But in France – for those at full-time vocational schools – the search for employment is postponed till after the trainee has completed his course. French sample surveys of those entering the labour market confirm that those who had followed the apprenticeship route had a better employment experience (28 per cent unemployed nine months later) than those who had followed the full-time schooling route (46 per cent unemployment); even so, unemployment amongst the apprenticeship-trained seems very high.[55]

It is clear that radical changes are in progress in French schooling and training. The greater numbers now educated to higher levels in France have not yet found their optimal path into employment; at present they are prepared to take work in retailing, so displacing those who have been specifically trained for that occupation. All this may change in the coming years. At the beginning of the 1980s an OECD report concluded that there was a need in France to 'reconcile a school-leaver's uninformed or ill-formed perceptions of what he or she wants to learn or become, with his or her capacities and the realities of the labour market'.[56] There seems also to be a greater lag in the responsiveness of the French vocational schooling system to the changing requirements of the labour market; in Germany, the vocational schooling system inevitably becomes aware more rapidly of changes in employers' openings for apprenticeships. Though it is often suggested in Germany that the content of many vocational courses needs to be updated more frequently, the present course in retailing seem to be regarded as highly satisfactory.[57]

The French response so far to the problems faced by youngsters training for retailing, and to employers' demands for better qualified personnel, has been to encourage higher standards of qualification through the full-time schooling route and to introduce or increase the work experience required on new or existing courses. They have done this by:

1. Amalgamating the CAP and BEP courses so that a greater proportion of pupils may reach the (higher) BEP level;
2. Treating the BEP as a preparation for yet higher-level vocational courses (the technical or vocational *baccalauréats*) to which about a third now proceed;[58]
3. Encouraging more pupils with higher levels of *general* education to proceed to full-time *vocational* education at higher levels.

In effect, the French seem increasingly to regard extended vocational education with specialization in retailing as the route leading eventually to positions of responsibility in the trade; while for a surprisingly high proportion of other jobs in retailing, the employment of someone with a *baccalauréat* – whether in general or technical subjects – has bcome increasingly usual (for example, for shop assistants in larger stores in Paris, and even supermarket cashiers). There is, however, considerable flux, and there is also much self-questioning as to whether more needs to be learnt from the employment-led German system.[59]

☐ Development of training in Britain

In Britain fundamental changes have been brought about in this industry by the Youth Training Scheme, originally introduced in response to general youth unemployment and later developed to help meet the need for a better trained workforce. Since 1984 a subsidy has been paid to those taking on school-leavers (whether in the status of 'trainees' or 'employees') and providing them with 'approved' training: the current (April 1989) subsidy is nearly £40 a week for each 16 or 17-year-old trainee, and is payable for two years (for only one year under the original arrangements that applied till April 1986). The training requirements amount to an average of one day a week of approved 'off-the-job' training, together with the 'opportunity' to gain any of the great variety of 'recognized vocational qualifications', but without distinction as to the level of qualification. In this industry, under the original one-year YTS arrangements, these requirements were not too strictly applied, reflecting the novelty of the scheme and a lack of clarity in the details of what is properly required by way of further education and training. 'Off-the-job' training was usually carried out within the store, but sometimes involved working with other employers – not necessarily retailers – for a few weeks. Attendance at college was not favoured because – so employers told us – much of the college-course was not related to the specific work of the trainee (in clear contrast to the French and German approaches, which require progress in general educational subjects), and because of lack of effective means of ensuring attendance at college. Requirements relating to vocational qualifications were introduced as part of two-year YTS in April 1986, together with clearer requirements for off-the-job training (job rotation is no longer adequate for this purpose). In 1986–88 (according to preliminary returns) only about a quarter of those leaving YTS in retailing had attained additional vocational or educational qualifications, mostly well below the French CAP level.

Of those who had been on YTS in retailing in 1986, 30 per cent were unemployed nine months after leaving the scheme: this is a worryingly high proportion but, if anything, perhaps lower than shown by the French surveys mentioned above (low response rates to these surveys in both countries prevent a more precise judgement).

About 30–40 000 have been taken on as trainees each year in retailing under the YTS since 1984 (now includes 4000 in their second year). This is some four times as many as attained vocational qualifications at any level in retailing in 1986 (as shown in Table 15.1); retailing has become one of the largest sectors benefiting from YTS (8 per cent of all YTS trainees starting in 1986). Some improvements in workforce skills must be expected as a result of all this, even if only a small proportion of trainees attain examined vocational qualifications at the levels considered in earlier sections of this paper. In practice the scheme is still evolving, with unemployment pressures changing from year to year, and new training procedures becoming more established and clearer. YTS has provided employers in this trade with better possibilities of choosing, on the basis of practical experience, from amongst those who might join their permanent staff. The vocational standards attained by the majority of trainees are, however, so modest – so very much below the standards of France and Germany – that it is difficult to see why the YTS subsidy in this trade need extend to a second year (nor, to press the point further, is it entirely clear that the amount of training received in Britain at present in the first year justifies a subsidy for the *whole* of the first year).[60]

That judgement would be changed in two circumstances. First, looked at solely from the point of view of the efficiency of retailing, a second year's subsidy might be justified if it was intended for those aiming to progress to a higher qualification (for example, a BTEC National award), and made conditional on attaining a lower-level examined qualification at the end of the first year. Secondly, from the broader point of view of raising general educational standards and of increased flexibility in careers, if it came to be accepted in Britain – as it is in France and Germany – that all youngsters under 18 who are at work need to pursue both vocational and general education, then a coherent programme of studies could be developed to cover a two-year period, and might justify a continued subsidy.

Important steps are being taken towards bringing the great variety of vocational qualifications available in Britain into a more coherent hierarchical framework comparable, in principle, to the French system of three broad, and widely understood, vocational levels applicable to all occupations;[61] this is part of the task of the National Council for Vocational Qualifications established in 1986. By making British vocational qualifications more understandable, both to employers and trainees, it was hoped that they would become more popular.

The retailing industry's initial difficulties in deciding which elements of training were desirable in modern conditions led to delays in NCVQ accrediting qualifications for the retail sector.[62] At the beginning of 1988 one of the larger employers' associations representing mainly supermarkets and departmental stores, a voluntary organization called the National Retail Training Council, proposed a new introductory qualification – the Retail Certificate – to be taken at two levels corresponding to National Vocational Qualifications Levels 1 and 2 respectively. These require no more than a list of basic practical tasks to be 'assessed' wholly in the workplace by the trainee's supervisor. For example, at Level 1 the candidate has to handle payments (cash, cheques, credit cards), and replenish stock; at Level 2 the candidate has to set up and dismantle a sales display, and receive and make telephone calls.[63] Selling and product presentation are optional extras, rather than essential elements as in France. This scheme was approved by NCVQ in September 1988, and these 'qualifications' are required as a condition for the receipt of the YTS subsidy from April 1989. The expressed hope was that this will lead to a ten-fold increase in the numbers receiving qualifications.[64]

Taking into account the limited tradition of training in retailing in

Britain, these signs of progress may seem admirable; but it has to be emphasized here that the scope and level of such proposed initial qualifications are far below those current in France (described earlier in this paper), and below those taken by even larger numbers in Germany.[65] The MSC in its general requirements for vocational qualifications seems to have fixed its mind (too largely, in our view) on the performance of specified tasks in the workplace, assessed by someone there, rather than on a judicious combination of practice and courses on general principles taught in colleges, in which written tests and external examinations have a large part.[66] There is a need for further and fuller consideration: are Britain's policies in these matters right in being so different from those of France and Germany? The danger is that an administrative apparatus is being set up which will have the effect of enshrining low standards as acceptable 'qualifications'. A policy of this sort is likely to inhibit the progress of many individual trainees who will be inadequately stretched, and insufficiently prepared to train to higher levels; it will also inhibit the transferability of skills and, in turn, the future efficiency of the economy as a whole.[67]

■ Summary and conclusions

Retailing is a diverse and rapidly changing industry, with consequent diverse and changing requirements for manpower training. From our comparisons of France and Britain, the following are the main points that have emerged; they relate to standards of training, numbers trained, standards of general education in relation to vocational qualifications, changes in the labour market, and justification for the second year of the Youth Training Scheme subsidy.

1. France and Britain differ much more in the standards of qualification required for sales-persons than for technical occupations (such as mechanics, electricians or building craftsmen) where – as previous studies in this series have shown – broadly similar standards prevail in the two countries. The typical qualified French sales-person is trained in specialized product knowledge, has been examined in practical selling, and progressed further in general educational subjects (native language, mathematics, a foreign language) as part of his vocational course. Expectations in Britain are lower: little is required for the main corresponding retail training qualifications by way of product knowledge, and general educational subjects are rarely pursued.

To put it in practical terms: the reason British shop assistants so often know hardly anything about what they are selling is that no one has ever taught them; and those responsible for the main British courses in retailing continue to regard such knowledge as less than essential. The comprehensiveness of the French courses and qualifying tests means that someone with a CAP or BEP diploma – even from a full-time vocational school – is closer to being fully 'operational' from the first day of employment. It may not be necessary for all working in supermarkets to have as broad a training as is available in France; with an understanding and commitment to a career with prospects of advancement, there is much to be said in favour of the French system of instructing all qualified sales-persons in the acquisition of product knowledge, and how to draw upon it when helping a customer.

2. The numbers attaining qualifications each year as sales-persons in France after their two to three-year full-time courses at commercial secondary schools have doubled in the past decade and are now about nine times greater than the numbers reaching the nearest equivalent standard here. There has recently been considerable unemployment in France amongst those qualifying in these occupations at this level, and the current trend there is towards vocational qualifications at yet higher levels. In Britain the Youth Training Scheme has increased greatly the numbers undergoing some form of basic training in retailing; but the numbers attaining 'recognized' vocational qualifications here have increased only at lower levels of qualification, mainly based on short part-time courses – at what the French would regard as the *pre*-vocational level.

3. The work of the National Council for Vocational Qualifications is intended to help towards a clearer ladder of qualifications; progress in systematizing retailing qualifications has focused on standards that are low in comparison to both France and Germany. Their proposed lower levels of qualification for these trades are narrowly job-specific ('competence based'); their exclusion of externally-marked written tests of technical knowledge and of general educational subjects will, we fear, lead to a certificated semi-literate under-class – a section of the workforce inhibited in job flexibility, and inhibited in the possibilities of progression. (Matthew Arnold's remark may be recalled: 'Philistinism! We have not the expression in English. Perhaps we have not the word because we have so much of the thing'.) It will not encourage, and perhaps ultimately discourage, the raising of basic school-leaving standards amongst low-attaining pupils.

Our comparisons suggest the need for reconsideration of the NCVQ's heavy concentration on practical skills assessed in the workplace, as against written and practical tests which are externally marked – and which in France and Germany form a large part of the essential basis of qualification. Wide issues of social policy are involved, and a public enquiry into these matters may now be appropriate.

4. The preparation for work provided by French retailing courses shows – as for Germany – that high standards in vocational courses are appropriate even for youngsters who have had difficulties in other school

subjects. Clear policy conclusions for Britain cannot however at present be drawn without hesitation from French training practices in this industry. This is because the doubling of retailing places in full-time vocational schools in France in the past decade coincided with a rise in youth unemployment at virtually all educational levels. The impact has been particularly serious for those qualifying in retailing. The numbers of school-leavers with higher educational attainments corresponding to our A-levels (their *baccalauréat*) increased considerably in this period, and many failed to find the type of employment they hoped for; instead they increasingly took jobs that might otherwise have been available to those with basic vocational qualifications.

It seems likely that some years have yet to elapse before something approaching equilibrium is reached in France in the flows of teenagers of different aptitudes through the education and training systems; till then it will be difficult to obtain a clear view of the correct balance of high- and low-level skills required in retailing as a result of the continuing trend towards self-service. The German vocational training system – which provides retailing qualifications for even greater numbers than the French – has not experienced such serious problems of adjustment to changing demand as the French system; the reason probably is that the German trainee is required to secure a place with an employer before he begins his training (as under our YTS), rather than after completing it as under the French full-time system.

5. The subsidy provided by the Youth Training Scheme for the first years of employment after leaving school has increased considerably the numbers receiving introductory training in this industry in Britain. From the point of view of the British retailing employer, one year of training may seem more than adequate for his employees; from the point of view of the employee, and of the economy as a whole, the advantages of job flexibility and long-term adaptability might justify the longer period of training usual in France and Germany. However, justification of a subsidy for a second year of training requires a clearer and broader ladder of progression in vocational standards than has so far been developed here; a second year's subsidy should be made dependent on the acquisition of a recognized vocational qualification at the end of the first year, and perhaps should also require higher general educational standards for those in the YTS age range.

Notes

1. Based on returns from employers (*Employment Gazette*, January 1987, pp. 38, 44; and *Annuaire Statistique*, 1986, p. 716). The great number of casual and part-time employees in this industry, and of family members

attached formally or informally to smaller shops, makes it difficult to speak with precision of the total numbers employed. Some part-timers may work in a number of shops and are duplicated in these statistics. Under-counting of casual employees is more than likely in both countries. Estimates of numbers employed in this industry are sensitive to the statistical definitions used, and should be treated with caution.

2. From the population censuses of Britain in 1981 and of France in 1982.

3. Despite its obvious importance for the economics of training, no statistical survey seems to have been carried out in Britain to establish rates of leaving or new employees in this industry. Some pointers to the current position are given in a recent report by NEDO, *Part-time working in the Distributive Trades* (vol. 1, *Training Practices and Career Opportunities*, vol. 2, *Evidnece from Company Case Studies and Employee Attitude Survey*, NEDO, 1988–9). The analytic approach based on 'survival curves' was explored in articles some thirty years ago (and still worth reading) by H. Silcock in *J. Roy. Stat. Soc.*, 1954, p. 429; K. F. Lane and J. E. Andrews, *ibid.*, 1955, p. 296; and by D. J. Bartholemew, *ibid.*, 1959, p. 232. See also A. Gregory, 'The growth of part-time work in grocery in Britain and France', *Retail and Distribution Management*, September 1987.

4. The prohibition of resale price maintenance agreements in the UK at the end of the 1950s permitted price-competition between different kinds of shops, in place of the previous attenuated competition in accompanying service at fixed prices. Following the abolition of RPM, consumers were able to express their choice in the market as between a lower price combined with less service, on the one hand, and a higher price with more service on the other; they clearly preferred more of the former. The continued trend in that direction – thirty years after the change in legislation – must however be attributed to costs and other factors as suggested above.

5. *National Institute Economic Review*, May 1986, May 1987, and National Institute Discussion Paper no. 130.

6. *National Institute Economic Review*, August 1983, pp. 61–3.

7. See, for example, the books for *Arbeitslehre* courses on textiles and statistics produced by teachers in Berlin for their comprehensive school pupils (available from the Pedagogisches Zentrum, Berlin 31).

8. The present study is based mainly on comparisons of qualifications in the two countries (in distinction from the more resource-intensive studies of matched plants carried out for our associated comparisons with Germany). Discussions were held in 1987–88 with 11 vocational colleges and schools, and with representatives of the ministries, training organizations and examining bodies in the two countries. In addition, we visited 19 employers (mostly large and middle-sized shops with a particular interest in training). Detailed comparisons of the qualifying examinations in the two countries were made with the help of teachers in vocational colleges. For a previous, very brief, comparison of the systems of retail training in France and Britain, see Tony Parkinson Associates, *Review of Distributive Industry Education and Training Needs* (Further Education Unit, RP245, 1985), Appendix 4, pp. 28–29; it also summarized the main vocational provisions for this sector in the Netherlands, US, New Zealand and Japan. Recent useful studies of British training for retailing are to be found in two reports

prepared for the Distributive Trades EDC, *Youth Training and the Distributive Trades* (NEDO, 1986) and C. Trinder, *Young People's Employment in Retailing* (NEDO, 1986); also relevant are *Retailing and NVQ: A study of the application of the four-level structure to the retail industry* (Further Education Unit, 1987), and *Education and Training at Sainsbury's: A report by HMI* (HMSO, 1987). The current French situation is described in the CEREQ Dossier, *Formation et Emploi – Les emplois du commerce et de la vente* (Collection des Etudes no. 22, April 1986).

9.   Till 1986 known as *lycées d'enseignement professionnel* (LEP).

10. See, for example, Board of Education, Report of the Consultative Committee, *The Education of the Adolescent* (HMSO, 1926), especially pp. 31–2.

11. See M.-C. Combes, *L'Apprentissage en France* (CEREQ, Paris, 1987); and J. Biret, M.-C. Combes, P. Lechaux, *Centres de Formation d'Apprentis et Formes d'Apprentissage* (CEREQ, Collection d'études, no. 9, Paris, 1984).

12. The position described here relates to mid-1986; since then the BTEC 'General' courses have been replaced by the Certificate of Pre-Vocational Education and BTEC 'First' courses. The latter are still in the process of change and development, and it seems too early to attempt an assessment here. There is also the complication that the previous nationwide externally-set and externally-marked examinations for core subjects under BTEC General have been replaced by tests and coursework set and marked by each local college. The consequent lack of uniformity amongst colleges in content and standards has been a worry to employers and teachers – though BTEC remains confident of the correctness of its approach (see, for example, the letters in *The Times Educational Supplement* for 3 June 1988 under the heading 'BTEC students let down by amateur moderation system'; and complaints from the universities originating in the lack of 'external moderation' of marking, which have reached an 'impasse' in discussions with BTEC, reported in *The Times Higher Education Supplement*, 10 June 1988). Perhaps the time has come for an independent inquiry into the principles governing the development of BTEC courses and testing (as part of the inquiry suggested in the fifth section).

13. A comprehensive enumeration of all specialized trade bodies has not proved possible here, but we believe that the numerically most important have been covered. For further qualifying bodies, see the study by the Further Education Unit, *Retailing and NVQ* (1987), pp. 29–30 and 53–4. The total of 1552 successful students in 1985–86 reported there (p. 20) is higher than our total of 600 in Table 14.1 mainly because they have included some 800 who have qualified at the Institute of Meat (the French had 5000 qualifying at this level in that year): the latter have been excluded here because the retailing elements of these courses are subsidiary to craft aspects.

14. The tabulations that are available in both countries relate to employees (that is, exclude the self-employed); note that Table 14.2 is based on the *occupation* of the respondent, not his *industry*, since we are here concerned particularly with the training of the great majority of those entering the industry as sales assistants. Alternative statistical analyses by industry of employment were available to us on a comparable basis only for retailing and wholesaling combined; they show similar results except for the top

educational categories (which rise to 6 per cent in France, and 5 in Britain), and the lowest category (which falls to 59 per cent in France, and 87 in Britain).

15. In addition in both countries there is much informal training – difficult to measure – and learning by experience ('the university of life'); all this lies outside the scope of the present study, the concern of which is with training which provides the youngsters with a recognized standard of competence and transferable skills.

16. Some duplication is possible with those mentioned above as qualifying at higher levels.

17. This relates to the number completing the main intermediate phase of these courses, known as the 'exploratory module'; about double that number took an 'introductory module', which seems to require attendance at only two or three lessons; and under half that number completed a more specialized 'preparatory module' (for example, in display). These developments seem to be guided by the best of intentions and are still in an early developmental phase; the published material produced for the guidance of teachers is unfortunately marred by the curiosities of fashionable educational theorizing in Britain, and is often too general to be useful (the reader with a taste for humour of this kind may wish to look at *CPVE Assessment – Core Competence Statements* with the exaggerated and vague requirements for these young, mostly non-academic, pupils to 'recognize the impact of science/technology on society', and to 'suggest appropriate solutions to technical/scientific problems').

18. The nearest corresponding institutions in Britain are probably those 'tertiary colleges' offering both A-level courses and vocational qualifications such as BTEC National.

19. Pupils on associated *Bac* courses – the G1 which specializes in business administration, and the G2 which specializes in business and finance – to some extent compete on the labour market with the G3 pupils mentioned above. It is therefore worth noticing that the number qualifying in these three specializations in France in 1986 totalled some 51 000. The comparable score in Britain is probably given by those passing BTEC National Certificates and Diplomas in Business Studies; the number passing totalled some 19 000 in that year.

20. Under the revised arrangements for BTEC 'First Courses', the equivalent of two weeks of work experience is now also required for those taking full-time courses (compared with 12 weeks in France, as mentioned below).

21. Based on work experience. A candidate working in a clothing retailers, for example, may be asked to advise on what can and cannot be altered on a coat, and take measurements for shortening a sleeve. From our recent case book: only one in half a dozen assistants in the clothing department of a leading department store in London's West End knew how to measure for a sleeve alteration (and even that required four visits, because he was not yet in, got it wrong first-time, etc.).

22. Though it is not possible to survey the variety of the courses available in Britain, it deserves to be mentioned that the Pitman Diploma in Retailing and Distribution (level II) is closer to the French examinations in the scope of subjects covered and levels of competence demanded.

23.   For example, 2168 passed out of an entry of 2172 in 1986 in the City and Guilds course just mentioned.

24.   The account given here reflects the situation till the summer of 1986; since then there have been modifications as noted in the fifth section.

25.   Académie d'Orléans-Tours, CAP 1983, *Vendeur: Travail sur Fiche Analytique de Produit*, question 2a.

26.   Another example from our recent case book: modern fluorescent lamps are of the 'quick start' variety, and a shop assistant should be able to inform the customer who returns a lamp purchased there – because it turned out to be of the old-fashioned slow-starting (thunder and lightning) type – that it was of the older type containing cheaper circuitry; the assistant should not simply offer the customer a replacement subject to the same limitations (in fact, neither the assistant nor her immediate superior in this leading West End store – not the one in note 21 – had any idea of the difference between the two types of lamps).

27.   The Pitman Retailing and Distribution course requires candidates to demonstrate familiarity with specific products through coursework assessed by their teachers, but it is not externally examined; an ability to describe verbally a chosen product in terms of colour, size and selling points is all that is usually demanded (see the notes given to centres offering Pitman's courses in their handbook, *Retailing and Distribution Course Assessment and Examination Regulations*, January 1984, pp. 15–16).

28.   CAP *Vendeur: Connaissance de l'entreprise et documents commerciaux*, Toulouse, 1986.

29.   BTEC General, *Elements of Distribution* (paper H200), June 1981.

30.   BTEC General, *Business Calculations*, October 1985. The paper for 1980 – but not for 1985 – included a question on compound interest. It appears that there has been a lowering of 'expectations' in relation to this group of candidates.

31.   Some of the larger retailing employers in London whom we interviewed have become sufficiently dissatisfied with shop assistants having only a CSE pass grade in mathematics that they now often look for an O-level or equivalent pass (the standard for the top third of school-leavers) when recruiting shop assistants; the expected rapidly declining numbers of school-leavers from 1988 to 1993 may well make it more difficult for retailers to recruit youngsters of this calibre. Decreasing emphasis in the past generation on basic numerical skills in English school-mathematics syllabuses must carry a large part of the blame.

32.   CAP *Vendeur: Calculs commerciaux*, Strasbourg and Besançon, 1983 (Annales Vuibert, Paris, 1983, pp. 70, 122). The examination for Besançon seems a little harder than average, but serves to indicate the range of competence envisaged.

33.   The motor mechanics test includes, for example, questions on volumes of cylinders and on applications of Pythagoras (CAP *Mécanicien Réparateur*, Opt. A, B, D, Académie de Paris-Créteil-Versailles, 1986).

34.   CAP *Vendeur: Expression Française*, Caen, 1983 (Annales Vuibert, Paris, 1984).

35.   BTEC, *People and Communications*, October 1983.

36. As one French teacher of vocational subjects put it to us: '*un véhicule par lequel on enseigne la culture générale*'.

37. *Not* one full day per week, but just one full day at some point in the whole 'course'!

38. This may simply require referring an aggrieved customer to a superior, if that is the employer's policy.

39. 'Moderation' is educationalist jargon for steps to equalize different examiners' marking. In the present context it has not, to our knowledge, amounted to anything of substance in practice.

40. Quoted from the sheet of Sample Items issued by City and Guilds; there is a curious (unnecessarily cautious?) warning attached to the sheet that they are not 'representative of the entire scope of the examinations in either content or difficulty'; no indication is given of where a more representative selection is to be found.

41. The pass-mark is set at 64 per cent. This is not as high as it may seem since, with four alternative answers to each question, a candidate can achieve 25 per cent simply on the basis of random guessing. As noted above (note 23), almost all entrants pass.

42. More fully: BEP *Commerce: option aux employés des services de vente*.

43. Now revised and known as BEP *Vente: Action marchande*.

44. It would take us too far from our main theme to consider why self-service initially advanced more rapidly in Britain than in France, and why France is now further ahead in the development of hypermarkets; a full study would need to refer, on the lines of the eminent French social historian Braudel, to the residual effects of walled cities in France on town-planning patterns (leading to living in apartment blocks with local shops, rather than the separation of residential and commercial areas required in Britain), and to the strength of associations of shopkeepers in France in restraining permission for the establishment of supermarkets. For a more detailed account of recent trends in retailing (though inadequately emphasizing the changing costs of distribution in relation to manufacturing, as discussed in the first section see N. Alexander, 'Contemporary perspectives in retail development', *Service Industries Journal*, 1988, p. 77.

45. From tables 2 and 5 of *Note d'Information*, Ministère de l'Education nationale, 24 August 1987. That it seems to take a long time for French youngsters to find the right first job was suggested by a survey of 1981, unfortunately not repeated more recently. This compared unemployment amongst those completing CAP and BEP courses a year previously and five years previously. The older cohort showed no more than 'frictional' unemployment rates (5 per cent for men, 10 per cent for women), while the recent cohorts showed very high rates (21 and 45 per cent) partly because it takes time to find the 'right job', and partly because unemployment in general had risen in those five years (P. Marchal and X. Viney, 'Les premières années de vie active des jeunes sorties en 1975 des classes terminales de CAP et BEP', *Formation Emploi*, no. 2, 1983).

46. *Note d'Information*, Ministère de l'Education nationale, 28 May 1985.

47. The greater competition in recent years on the youth labour market, with those of higher qualifications displacing those with lower qualifications, is a repeated theme of a series of articles in *Formation Emploi*, no. 18, April

1987. The notion of *déclassement* (devaluation of qualifications?) has become almost an *idée fixe* with these writers, though neither its economic causes nor educational significance are adequately examined by them. It seems to come to this: education standards have risen throughout the ability range; consequently persons with higher educational standards are today often doing jobs that yesterday were done by those with lower qualifications. On the whole, that should prove an advantage, varying from trade to trade. A summary of the French discussion, translated into English, has been provided by J. F. Germe, 'Employment policies and the entry of young people into the labour market in France', *Brit. J. Ind. Relations*, 1986, p. 29.

48. The definitions are not quite the same (under 20 hours a week in Britain, under 30 in France), but do not affect the substance of the comparison (*Employment Gazette*, October 1987, pp. 12, 17; and *Enquête sur l'Emploi* 1987 Collections de l'INSEE, série D, p. 59). On recent British trends, see I. Brodie, 'Distributive trades', ch. 3 of *Technological Trends and Employment*, vol. 5, *Commercial Service Industries* (ed. A. D. Smith, Gower, 1986), pp. 187–8; a comparison with France has been attempted by A. Gregory, 'The growth of part-time work in grocery in Britain and France', *Retail and Distributive Management*, September 1987, p. 18. Those who take a 'Saturday only' job in Britain are mostly youngsters, such as students, or those on a second job, and account for about a tenth of the total number of names on the payroll (a much smaller proportion, of course, of the full-time equivalent workforce: see Trinder, *op. cit.*, p. 24).

49. Trinder (*op. cit.*, p. 25) draws particular attention to the advantages in taxation and national insurance contributions of employing part-time women for under nine hours a week. The tax advantage is not of course the sole reason, but has made it easier for shops to respond to consumer demand for shopping outside hitherto 'normal' hours.

50. I. Brodie, *op. cit.*, pp. 133, 140; and Distributive Trades EDC, *Technology and Training in the Distributive Trades* (NEDO, 1987), especially the case studies on pp. 84–87, which refer to very short retraining times. Other firms told us of two to three days' retraining for electronic cash registers.

51. A comparison of recruitment into commercial occupations in 1976–78 with a period only four years later, 1980–82, showed a rise in the proportion of recruits with CAP, BEP or higher qualifications (*niveaux II–IV*) from 54 to 76 per cent (M.-H. Gensbittel and X. Viney, 'Formation et accès aux emplois', *Formation Emploi*, April 1987, p. 61).

52. The German approach still supports a course of two to three years' length for adequate skill-training in this trade, and there is considerable debate whether two years are adequate and whether three years are advantageous. The three-year course (for *Einzelhandelskaufmann*) seems to provide more flexibility between trades than the two-year course (for *Verkäufer*). This was confirmed by a survey of those who had acquired these qualifications and subsequently were employed outside those occupations; 56 per cent of those following the longer course had found their training helpful in their present work, but only 24 per cent of those from the shorter course were of this view (*Ausbildung und berufliche Eingliederung*, Haupterhebung 1984–85, table 4.414b, Bundesinstitut für Berufsbildung, Bonn, 1987; and H.

Herg *et al.*, *Berufsaufbildung abgeschlossen – was dann?* BibB, 1987, pp. 119–127). The discussion of these issues in Germany is explicit and helpful: see G. Kutscha and H. Schanz (eds) *Berufsbildung in Einzelhandel*, especially the paper by P. Schenkel (Holland and Josenhans: Stuttgart, 1988), p. 49 *et seq.*, and the series of papers (which appeared after the article on German vocational training in *National Institute Economic Review*, August 1983) for a conference on retail training, *Einzelhandelstag 1982* (Bundesverband der Lehrer an Wirtschaftschulen, Berlin), especially pp. 13, 37.

53. German Federal Ministry of Education, *Berufsbildungsbericht 1987*, p. 191; we have consulted trade unions and employers on the present position.

54. This is not to say that there are no problems of occupational imbalances in training in Germany (the excess numbers trained in baking are well known); but the problems are localized and much smaller than in France.

55. These figures relate to CAPs in all trades in 1983 (N. Coeffic, 'Les jeunes à la sortie de l'école', *Formation Emploi*, April 1987, p. 15). For commercial occupations, the published information is not so recent, but shows the same contrast: of females who had been on CAP courses in Commerce, 38 per cent of those completing an apprenticeship in June 1978 were unemployed nine months later, and 58 per cent of those completing their full-time school courses in June 1980 were unemployed nine months later (these figures do not seem altogether consistent with 55 per cent unemployed amongst those following both routes combined in 1979, as shown in the same source, CEREQ Dossier 22, *op. cit.*, pp. 140, 153, 163). The sampling methods for these surveys are not described in these sources and, *verb. sap.*, they merely refer to *la faiblesse de l'échantillon* (see, for example, Coeffic, *op. cit.*, p. 19); it is not inconceivable that response rates amongst the unemployed were higher.

56. *The Future of Vocational Education and Training* (OECD, Paris, 1983), p. 56.

57. So we were assured by retailing employers in Germany. See also *Einzelhandelstag, op. cit.* A fuller study of French youth unemployment seems to be required, extending beyond retailing, which takes into account the levels of trainee allowances, how they relate to unemployment benefits, and the initial wages of those who have completed their training. Regretably this has not proved possible within the confines of the present research project.

58. Until 1987 most young people having attained their BEP and wishing to take a higher-level qualification would have been required to re-enter the mainstream educational system, joining pupils who are about two years younger, and study for a *Bac Technologique G3 (Techniques Commerciales)*. Since 1987 teenagers having specialized in distribution subjects have had the option of studying for the newly-created *Bac Professionnel: Vente Représentation*, intended primarily for industrial representatives. This vocational *baccalauréat* offers those who have formerly experienced difficulties in the traditional more 'academic' education the chance to gain a *baccalauréat* qualification, and to study with pupils closer to their own age and schooling background.

59. See Gensbittel and Viney, *op. cit.*, p. 48, especially n. 4. The demographic

decline in school-leavers in France in the next five years may also lead to changes in recruitment patterns as expected in Britain.

60. The opinions of large retailing employers in 1986 were that 'it is difficult to use all of the existing first year in some cases' on training, and 'it is not clear that a two-year course on the present basis is a good idea' (Trinder, *op. cit.*, p. 36).

61. CAP, BEP, and *Bac*.

62. It was originally hoped that the NCVQ would complete its work on retailing by April 1987 (Distributive Trades EDC, *op. cit.*, 1986, p. 32); on the industry's lack of clarity as to its needs, see also the HMI report, *Education and Training at Sainsbury's* (DES, 1987, especially p. 10).

63. City and Guilds (Certificate no. 6760), *The Retail Certificate: Levels I and II, Assessment Document* (City and Guilds, 1989).

64. *The Training Information Base for the Industry Agreed Training Provision*, MSC, National Association of Colleges for Distributive Education and Training, and National Retail Training Council, December 1986; and *Financial Times*, 11 April 1988. The Royal Society of Arts new vocational certificates are organized on the same principles.

65. Most young people ought to complete the 'competences' for the award of the proposed retailing NVQ Level 1 in less than three months – so we were assured by retailing experts in Britain and France.

66. *Training for Skills: Qualifications in YTS* (MSC, 1987).

67. The Secretary of State for Education, Mr Kenneth Baker, very recently called for agreed 'core skills' – written and oral communications, numeracy, etc. – to become an essential part of all vocational qualifications (in his speech on Further Education, 15 February 1989, para. 42); but, in contrast to what we have seen of the French system, he does not want them as separate courses ('bolt-on extras', is his phrase!). Thus the difference from the Continental system is likely to remain, supported by the highest political authority in the land.

Acknowledgements

Our thanks are due to the many retailers in Britain and France who cooperated in this inquiry. In addition we should like to thank the following members of educational institutions and related organizations:

In Britain, A. Ayling, Rowan High School, Merton; A. Bellamy, National Council for Vocational Qualifications; J.-F. Boca, Commercial Department, French Chamber of Commerce, London; G. Brown, G. Banfield, M. Lewis and D. Thorne, College for the Distributive Trades; T. Darlington, National Institute of Hardware; R. Hutton, Drapers' Chamber of Trade; P. Johnson, HMI, Department of Education and Science; D. McCrorie, National Association of Retail Furnishers; P. Morely, National Retail Training Council; J. Phillips CBE, former chair, Distributive Industries Training Board; I. Strachan, Cassio College; C. Thorne, Union of Shop, Distributive and Allied Workers; C. Walker, Further Education Unit, Department of Education and Science.

In France, F. Amat, Christine Beduwé, Marie-Christine Combes, Centre d'Etudes et de Recherches sur les Qualifications; B. Bogaert, LP 'Jeanette Verdier', Montargis; P. le Borgne, LP de l'Ecole Nationale Normale à l'Apprentissage, Antony; B. de Clercy, Observatoire des entrées dans la vie active; J. du Closel, Fédération nationale des Entreprises à Commerces Multiples; R. Espenel, Relations internationales, Ministère de l'Education nationale; M.-F. van der Gucht and J. Rouchon, LP 'Pierre et Marie Curie', Sens; J. B. Jeffreys, International Association of Department Stores, Paris; M. Léonelli, LP Duperré, Paris; J. Martinez, Lycée Commercial Mixte, Paris; J. G. Meilhac, Centre de Formation Technologique, Osny; W. Mettoudi, Collège et CFA Rabelais, Vitry; A. Roumengous, Secrétariat des Commissions Professionnelles Consultatives, Ministère de l'Education nationale; P. Saint-Léger, Syndicat national des Maisons d'Alimentation à Succursales, Supermarchés; D. Siwek, Bureau Etudes et Recherches, Ministère de l'Economie; M. Sponem and J. Taupin, Lycée Professionel 'Albert Camus', Clamart; G. Veil, Direction des Lycées sur l'Enseignement de la Vente en France, Ministère de l'Education nationale.

Financial support for this inquiry was provided by the Nuffield Foundation and by the Manpower Services Commission (now Training Agency of the Department of Employment) together with the Department of Employment and the Department of Education and Science; we are grateful to officials from the Government Departments mentioned for much helpful comment (but they are not responsible in any way for the views expressed in this paper).

Our colleagues at the National Institute, Hilary Steedman and Karin Wagner, have kindly saved us from many pitfalls, large and small. The authors are responsible for any remaining defects of fact and judgement.

Index